SEX AND THE OFFICE

JULIE BEREBITSKY

Sex and the Office

A HISTORY OF GENDER, POWER, AND DESIRE

Yale UNIVERSITY PRESS

NEW HAVEN AND LONDON

Society and the Sexes in the Modern World
Christine Stansell, Series Editor

Published with assistance from the foundation established in memory of Philip
Hamilton McMillan of the class of 1894, Yale College.

Parts of Chapter 6 first published as "The Joy of Work: Helen Gurley Brown, Gender,
and Sexuality in the White-Collar Office," in *Journal of the History of Sexuality* 15, no. 1,
pp. 89–127. Copyright © 2006 by the University of Texas Press. All rights reserved.

Yale University Press books may be purchased in quantity for educational, business, or
promotional use. For information, please e-mail sales.press@yale.edu (U.S. office) or
sales@yaleup.co.uk (U.K. office).

Designed by Sonia Shannon
Set in Fontshop Scala and Scala Sans type by IDS Infotech Ltd., Chandigarh, India.
Printed in the United States of America by

Berebitsky, Julie.
    Sex and the office: a history of gender, power, and desire/Julie Berebitsky.
      p.   cm.—(Society and the sexes in the modern world)
    Includes bibliographical references and index.
    ISBN 978-0-300-11899-5 (cloth: alk. paper)

    1. Women—Employment—United States—History—20th century. 2. Women
employees—United States—History. 3. Sex role—United States—History—20th century.
I. Title.
HD6053.B47 2012
331.40973—dc23

                                                                              2011026337

A catalogue record for this book is available from the British Library.

This paper meets the requirements of ANSI/NISO Z39.48–1992 (Permanence of
Paper).

10 9 8 7 6 5 4 3 2 1

For Woody

CONTENTS

ACKNOWLEDGMENTS

This book and I owe many debts. A John B. Stephenson Fellowship from the Appalachian College Association, for which Cindy Aron graciously agreed to serve as mentor, provided important financial support. A Margaret Storrs Grierson grant from the Sophia Smith Collection, Smith College, a Jessie Ball duPont Grant for Student/Faculty Research, and numerous Faculty Research Grants from Sewanee: The University of the South funded crucial research trips. Sewanee's dedicated librarians, especially Kevin Reynolds and ILL staff, Andrew Moser, Sue Armentrout, Heidi Syler, and Cari Reynolds, tracked down every research request, regardless of how obscure, while students Skye Fost, Abby Futrelle, and Ron Allen proved able assistants in libraries and archives. At Yale University Press, Laura Davulis and Christina Tucker promptly and professionally responded to countless emails, which made the final stages of this book much easier, and Dan Heaton edited the manuscript with a sharp eye and keen intelligence.

Colleagues and friends—Kevin Murphy, Donna Murdock, Katherine Parkin, Trish Maloney, Sherri Bergman, Andrea Mansker, Paige Schneider, and Betsy Sandlin—who read all or parts of the manuscript were generous with their time and kind with their comments. Christine Stansell's commitment to the project was especially significant: her encouragement and careful editing during the final revisions made a daunting task doable.

Most especially, this book and I owe a debt of gratitude to an extraordinarily understanding and supportive group of friends and family. Katherine Parkin and Donna Murdock offered crucial insight and advice on the manuscript, but they also eagerly and patiently listened when I needed to vent about the latest setback in a book that didn't want to get done. Sherri Bergman, Scott Wilson, Houston Roberson, John and Elizabeth Grammer, Chris DeRosa, Margaret Marsh, Rodney Hessinger, Martha Hodes, and Bruce Dorsey provided me with all manner of needed distractions and encouragement. Lisa Hill, Pauline Robert, and my parents patiently understood when I postponed visits because the book was "almost done," while Sophie Register never showed even a bit of embarrassment over my work attire—even when her friends were on their way over. Finally, Woody Register read the manuscript, read it again, and then read it some more. His suggestions improved this book, but more important, his love and devotion have made my life infinitely better.

SEX AND THE OFFICE

Introduction

IN 1891 A MEMBER OF THE FIRST GENERATION of white-collar office women published her "Memories" in the *New York Sun*. This typewriter—the term referred to the machine *and* to its operator—had recently retired from office work to take her place as a wife in a cozy suburban home. The new setting and circumstances had not erased from her memory either the many hours she had spent taking dictation or the "risks, and temptations and trials" she frequently had faced as a typewriter who possessed "beauty of face and form." She recalled the time an older man had chased her around a table. Although "he had a look in his eyes," it turned out he was "too dignified to do anything violent." On another occasion a young man had subjected her to the "indignity" of deliberately pinching her cheek. In these early days of her office career, the typewriter had been deeply insulted by the uninvited and unwelcome advances, but she knew her only options were to quit the job she needed or to grin and stay a step ahead of the men chasing her. She chose the latter. In retrospect, she expressed no regrets. From the safety of her married life, she recounted the episodes with a laugh and blamed the men's actions on the novel situation in which the first generation of women clerical workers had found themselves.[1]

Women had initially taken office jobs during the Civil War; by 1870 there were still fewer than two thousand women so employed. As businesses grew and office jobs became more numerous, so did the number of women hired to type, collate, and file the growing piles of paperwork. In 1891, when the typewriter told her story, seventy-five thousand women labored in such jobs and accounted for almost 20 percent of all clerical workers. By that time, she maintained, women had become such ordinary features of office life that men had calmed down; they no longer suspected typewriters of having shady characters or felt the need to test the office woman's virtue. In the last years of her employment, she said, "not a ripple of masculine misbehavior" had disturbed her, aside from the occasional "nuisance" of a man asking to see her socially.[2]

The typewriter was correct in noting the rapidly growing population of women working in offices, but she was quite mistaken in thinking that the ordinariness and prevalence of women in office work would signal the end either of such "misbehavior" or of the suspicions about what women really were after when they entered white-collar occupations. Consider that in 1991, a century after the publication of the typewriter's memories, more than seventeen million women occupied clerical and administrative support positions in the United States. Another six-plus million worked in offices as lawyers, executives, administrators, and managers. And yet in that same year, the very questions that surrounded the young typewriter in the decades after the Civil War—Were workingwomen fair game for sexual advances? Were they trustworthy employees or disreputable schemers?—were directed at the young attorney Anita Hill when she appeared before the Senate Judiciary Committee to testify about her former employer and U.S. Supreme Court nominee Clarence Thomas. A reluctant witness, Hill said that when she had worked for Thomas in the early 1980s, he had pestered her for dates and used work situations to speak graphically about pornographic films and his own "sexual prowess." On one occasion, she said, Thomas picked up a can from his desk and asked her, "Who has put pubic hair on my Coke?" This baffling comment was forever imprinted on the minds of the millions who watched Hill's testimony on television. Hill was not a typewriter but an attorney working at a federal agency on projects of importance to her, and she was reluctant to quit. She stated that when Thomas began to show displeasure with her continued rejections, she started to look for another position.[3]

There is a tendency today to imagine that sexual harassment, as we understand the term, is a timeless phenomenon, that workingwomen have always been vulnerable to the sexual aggression of their male coworkers and superiors. This brief comparison of two historical moments a century apart supports this supposition. Both illustrate work-ingwomen's susceptibility to unwanted sexual attentions and the dangers such advances posed to their ability to earn their livelihood. Yet as similar as these cases are, there are notable differences, especially in the ways in which the women could understand and respond to the behaviors they described.

A quick explication of each makes the distinctions clear. In the late nineteenth century, the typewriter interpreted the men's overtures first and foremost as an "insult." Their actions implied she was not truly a "lady" and called into question her virtue, her standing as a member of the middle class, and her ultimate suitability as a wife. Had one of the men pressed her, she would have had no recourse but to quit, and her concern for her reputation probably would have kept her quiet about why she did so. She recounted her "adventures" only anonymously and after she was married (to a man she had met through her work) and her social position was beyond dispute.

At the end of the twentieth century, Anita Hill had more options and different concerns. She could have said Thomas's unwelcome and persis-tent remarks injured her health and made her job unbearable and filed a legal complaint against him for "sexual harassment." Before feminists coined that term in 1975, the unwanted sexual suggestions, jokes, and physical contact or sexual coercion that could be a part of women's employment experience were commonly acknowledged, but no word or phrase existed to describe these behaviors. Women's rights activists argued that such actions were assertions of male power, a type of "economic rape" that presented a serious barrier to gender equality, and they fought against them. The law was still unsettled when Hill worked for Thomas, and, like many women, she chose to suffer in silence rather than endanger her career prospects. In 1986 the Supreme Court ruled that these "unwelcome" actions constituted a form of sex discrimination in violation of Title VII of the Civil Rights Act of 1964. The Court's deci-sion, however, did nothing to dispel gender and racial stereotypes, and Thomas's supporters used myths about women's veracity and black women's sexual voracity to discredit Hill. Many Americans did not believe her (according to public opinion polls during the hearings, Americans believed that Hill's charges were probably untrue by a margin of more than two to one), but the public telling of her story did inspire countless numbers of women to speak out: in the three months after the hearings, the number of charges filed with the Equal Employment Opportunity Commission (EEOC) increased by 70 percent.[4]

As these more detailed descriptions show, sexual harassment has a varied history. Some workingwomen have always been subject to sexual exploitation, but changing historical conditions as well as individual circumstances affected the way Americans thought about unwelcome and coercive sexual behaviors and about why and how women reacted to them. Before 1975 women office workers certainly were subjected to unwanted and exploitative sexual aggression, but they were not sexually harassed. That concept, and the way it envisioned men's and women's natures and motivations for entering the workforce, did not yet exist. A typewriter in the 1890s could be chased around the desk and have her boss's caresses forced on her, but she could not think about her experience in the same way Hill thought about hers in the 1980s.

Sex and the Office, then, is not a history of sexual harassment. Its primary goal, rather, is to historicize Americans' understanding of unwelcome sexual behaviors in the office, including those that the courts and the public now label sexual harassment. However, in the following pages I examine a wide spectrum of sexual interactions because, historically, Americans have seen coercive and unwanted sexual encounters as merely one dimension of the larger sexual culture of the office. For instance, while some women suffered when men used their position to extort sexual favors, others prospered when men exercised their authority to pamper their favorites. And, as the typewriter's story illustrates, not all overtures were unwanted. She herself found romance in the office; and, according to Anita Hill, Clarence Thomas, initially, had hoped to as well. Moreover, the typewriter's and Hill's experiences clearly show that concerns about the sexual dangers women faced always were paired with fears that women would turn men's desires against them. Even in the late nineteenth century, many businessmen made it a rule never to be alone with a typewriter because she might be an "adventuress" with "evil designs." A century later, many people thought Hill's accusations against Thomas were nothing more than a politically motivated attempt to derail his nomination. In 1991 as in 1891, many Americans believed women were every bit as capable of exploitation and deception as men—if not more so. As a result, the story this book tells is as much about continuity as about change.[5]

In the one hundred years between the typewriter's and Hill's stories, Americans talked about unwanted, coercive, and consensual sexual relationships in the white-collar business or government office in a number of dynamic ways. Analyzing these discourses exposes a long history of troubles over and worries about workplace sexuality—a history that prompted and enabled the feminist revision of such behavior in 1975. Understanding this prehistory also helps explain Hill's decision not to pursue her legal options and instead to look for another job—for more than one hundred years, this had been a woman's standard response when her situation became unbearable. Feminists could change the law, but they could not easily change long-standing social beliefs regarding gender, power, and desire in the workplace.

WHY THE OFFICE?

Women have been at risk of—and an unknowable number of them have experienced—sexual exploitation and hostility whenever and wherever their economic needs or social positions placed them under men's authority. Since Mary Bularzik published the first article on the history of sexual harassment more than thirty years ago, we have known that women who left the safety of their domestic "place" had been fair game for a form of abuse that illustrated their marginality in the workforce—that mistreatment often came when they entered someone else's domestic space as maids, servants, or slaves. Since Bularzik, historians have examined women's experiences of sexual exploitation in a number of work settings—from sweatshops, restaurants, and factories to plantations, military bases, and department store selling floors. These studies have shown that harassment differed from occupation to occupation, from one era to the next, in its form, purpose, and intensity, and in terms of the degree to which it was accepted and how it was explained or justified.[6]

The white-collar office also has a unique history. The business (or government) office was unusual in ways that warrant a focus on the actual experiences of white-collar women and men and on how Americans imagined those experiences. Such a focus allows us, first, to examine how expectations about gender, class, and race interacted to affect sexual expression. Second, attention to office work reveals how institutional philosophies impacted sexual behaviors and their range of meanings. The erotic connotations that Americans attached to the rapidly expanding number of female clerks and secretaries emerged in tandem with the bureaucratic ideal of the late-nineteenth-century corporation. Such organizations celebrated (and still do) rationality, instrumentality, and calculability and considered emotions and personal entanglements as dangerous disruptions to the real purposes of business. Management's task—indeed its purpose—was to design organizational structures that eliminated those human elements that lowered productivity. As the sociologist Max Weber noted a century ago, this rationality was considered the "special virtue" of bureaucracy, and it was assumed that institutions would flourish "the more perfectly the more bureaucracy is 'de-humanized,' the more completely it succeeds in eliminating from official business love, hatred, and all purely personal, irrational, and emotional elements which escape calculation."[7]

This passionless ideal became real as it was translated into prescriptions and, often, achieved as denial; sex should not be in the office, and therefore many people either refused to acknowledge that it was or minimized its presence. This perspective hid the ways in which sexuality, gender, and feeling were crucial to the functioning of businesses and corporations (and which organizational sociologists have spent the last thirty years trying to expose). It also put the lion's share of blame on women. Their presence and "feminine" qualities threatened organizations, a point Sigmund Freud reinforced in 1930 when he argued against women's involvement in public life by noting that men had achieved great success in government and commerce by embracing rationality and sublimating their sexual desires—in other words, by keeping out behaviors associated with women and the private sphere. Since women were the newcomers who had stepped onto male terrain and littered it with sexual and emotional landmines, and since they were both the least legitimate and the most expendable employees, they would be the ones responsible for ensuring that the bombs did not explode. They would be advised on what to wear and how to act to avoid a detonation, and they would be the ones to leave in the event of a blow-up.[8]

Throughout the period of this study, Americans have held constant to competing views of white-collar women's sexual experiences. Women were either victims or flirts, vamps, and gold diggers; over time, as society increasingly acknowledged women's sexual desires and their sexual agency, the balance of opinion shifted toward the latter designations. Concern about women's vulnerability diminished, though it never completely vanished in the period before the renewed feminist movement exploded in the late 1960s. This transition suggests that sexual freedom had its costs. Women gained a small measure of autonomy, but they lost the limited degree of protection that had existed when a large segment of the population believed they were inherently innocent; the array of individual, social, and legal responses to sexual mistreatment narrowed.

As popular ideas regarding women's sexuality changed during the course of the nineteenth and twentieth centuries, the dominant understanding of men's desires remained the same. In this view, nature had given men an active and ever-present sexual drive, which, in many people's minds, made sexual overtures in the workplace inevitable, if undesirable. The pretty typewriter who recounted her experiences in 1891, for example, applied this biological view in her explanation of why the usually dignified older man chased her around his desk, noting that he replaced her with a "very old-maidish" assistant "whose natural expression . . . would sour a pail of milk." The belief in men's essentially sexual character made it easier for generations of Americans to excuse men's unwanted overtures as a courtship misunderstanding or an unavoidable miscommunication between the sexes. On occasion, this principle held even when men's actions crossed the boundary of persuasion into coercion. It also meant that public discussions and popular representations of sex and romance in the office, both wanted and unwelcome, focused almost exclusively on "pretty typewriters" and their latter-day counterparts. Journalists, advice givers, and authors of fiction and screenplays all assumed that women who were not conventionally attractive were safe from men's advances.[9]

The new sexual model that had developed for middle-class and elite white women in the early 1800s also held (and to some degree still holds) that women's desires were less insistent than men's, which gave women the responsibility to establish and patrol the office's sexual borders. But whereas men's nature provided them with a built-in explanation for their sexual transgressions, understandings of women's social role could lead to suspicion of those who entered the office workforce and received unwanted attentions. Even if a woman had not consciously (or unconsciously) provoked such behaviors, she had failed to defend herself effectively, which at the very least meant that she had failed at her duty of keeping men's baser instincts in check. The majority of female office workers, it must be noted, agreed that this responsibility was theirs (and, evidence suggests, some still do), which could lead to feelings of guilt and prevent them from coming to the aid of a woman who received unwanted attentions.[10]

Debates over whether women were aggressive predators or vulnerable prey could get quite heated, but such deliberations burned no brighter in the constellation of anxieties over workplace sexuality than other worries. Some Americans feared that unmarried women working with married men represented a threat to individual marriages and the institution as a whole. Others fretted about the possibility that an executive's sexual adventures with his office help would tarnish a business's reputation or damage its bottom line. These concerns highlight the intertwined histories of sexuality, women's employment, and business. Likewise, the white-collar office was a place where sexual norms, ideals, and meanings were created, altered, and solidified—often in direct response to the rules, customs, and physical landscape of that space. Workers could fit themselves into these parameters or push against them, but as more and more people labored in offices, the sexual attitudes that originated or found expression there took on greater significance in the larger culture.

The number of white-collar workers rose dramatically over the course of the twentieth century, and white-collar work became ever more prominent in the construction of American identity. As corporate capitalism displaced small-scale businesses, the percentage of self-employed middle-class men dropped from 67 percent in 1870 to 37 percent in 1910. The number of salaried workers multiplied eightfold during this same period, with 20 percent of the total male workforce holding white-collar jobs by 1910. Of that number, approximately one in five would spend their day in a business or law office. In 1951 the famed sociologist C. Wright Mills declared that the white-collar type was "becoming more typically 'American' than the frontier character probably ever was." The white-collar world, he continued, contained "much that is characteristic of twentieth-century existence." By the end of the twentieth century, more than seventeen million men, or 25 percent of the male labor force, toiled for most of their day in an office.[11]

And so did millions of women. Already by 1900, about 185,000 women made their living doing office work, and by 1920 more than half a million worked as stenographers and typists, filling more than 90 percent of these positions. By 1930 only domestic service employed more women than the clerical sector, and by 1950 secretaries, stenographers, and typists made up the largest group of workingwomen. The number of women employed in those occupations, combined with the number of women employed in the office in other clerical jobs, totaled 5.25 million, almost a third of all workingwomen and more than 60 percent of all office workers. Thirty-six percent of all employed white women in 1970 worked in clerical jobs, filling three-quarters of these positions.[12]

By the time feminists named sexual harassment, office work had been the leading occupation of women for twenty-five years, a fact reflected in early periodical and newspaper articles that informed readers about the new movement against unwanted sexual attentions in the workplace. Most set their stories in an office, even though white-collar women (who were assumed to be middle class) were by no means the only ones to experience harassment or to be active on the issue. The assumption that a workingwoman labored in an office can be seen, too, in the public comments of Congresswoman Patricia Schroeder, one of the leaders of congressional efforts to create workplace protections for women in the late 1970s. Explaining why it was time for the government to address sexual harassment, Schroeder stated, "We've talked openly about battered wives and battered children. The next thing is battered office workers."[13]

THE SEXUALIZED OFFICE IN AMERICANS' SHARED IMAGINATION
Schroeder used the generic term "office workers," and her comment highlights how the office figured in Americans' social imagination as a homogeneous and familiar space despite differences in size, location, or type of business. Americans thought they knew what happened in an office, even if they had never toiled in one. The press, fiction and film, and even prescriptive literature made this shared understanding possible by generally portraying the office in nonspecific terms. For example, such sources assumed a level of independence on workers' parts, which

facilitated freedom of movement and personal interactions and marked office work as different from factory labor. Only rarely did such sources consider how the configuration of an office or the degree to which clerical work was mechanized affected a worker's autonomy or opportunity for social exchanges. Although each individual office and each industry had its own sexual culture, its own rules about what was acceptable that would depend on any number of factors, part of what Americans knew about the office was that it was, for good or ill, a space of sexual possibility.

This knowledge was gained through a wide variety of visual and print media, which appeared simultaneously with women's entrance into the office. These workers captured the public's imagination, leading to an outpouring of representations of the sexual and romantic possibilities of this new occupation. Titillating humor, racy postcards, and later, silent films all offered a view of the office, especially the boss-secretary relationship, and there was no cessation of these creations even as the newness wore off. Fiction (ranging from popular and serious short stories and novels to pornography), film, television, and newer media still feature seemingly endless variations of the office romance theme. Such commercial representations were directed at a large cross section of (at least before the 1960s) white Americans, including those who never had worked or would work in an office. The steamy encounters of white-collar executives, for example, were standard fare in erotic pulp fiction written for a primarily working-class male audience in the 1950s and 1960s, while middle-class men in this period could find the same messages conveyed in the pictorials and cartoons of the new *Playboy* magazine. Women, for their part, could read about less carnal, but more emotionally charged, office love affairs in inexpensive pulp magazines and mainstream periodicals like the *Saturday Evening Post*. The ever-growing number of female clerical workers over the course of the twentieth century also meant an abundance of prescriptive literature that tackled the thorny problems of "love among the typewriters." And finally, experts in management and industrial psychology offered their takes on the sexual side of human relations in the office.

These representations might not have corresponded to reality, but they did portray the office in a consistently sexualized way—and one that changed little over time. This consistency is especially apparent in film;

the layout of the office (and hence its sexual possibilities) looks virtually the same in *The Office Wife* (1930), *The Best of Everything* (1959), and *9 to 5* (1980)—and is not so different from today's TV series *The Office*. The fact that this view appeared in a variety of sources consumed by a variety of social groups and remained constant over an extended period of time made it easy for Americans to *imagine* a sexualized office into existence, creating a widely shared understanding that seemed real because it was so pervasive.[14]

These sources provide the opportunity to chart changing and continuing popular attitudes toward office romances and acceptable relationships between bosses and their female workers, as well as between coworkers. They also make clear that sexual expression in the office, whether such behaviors were unwanted and coercive or welcome and encouraged, was not shrouded in silence before the women's movement. Though the voices of women who actually had experienced a sexual demand appeared infrequently, women's perspectives were part of this public discourse, especially in such cultural documents as women's fiction and employment advice. In 1961, for example, the National Secretaries Association published *Secretaries on the Spot*, a guide that discussed common secretarial problems and practical solutions. "Discouraging the Office Wolf" appeared at the end, after tips on developing a working filing system and convincing the boss to buy a Dictaphone. Such works acknowledged the vulnerability of women but also gave them the responsibility for solving the problem.[15]

Although there was not public silence regarding unwanted and coercive behaviors in the office, there was an incomplete and historically changing vocabulary in which to talk about these matters, which limited what women could say and how, when, and where they could say it. The historical moment also determined what could be heard—and how clearly. For example, since discussions of men's coercion were so often coupled with deliberations on women's sexual treachery, women's public comments on the subject often denied that they experienced sexual pressure. On the one hand, these dismissals of workplace danger symbolized women's relative powerlessness and ensured the continuation of their employment opportunities. On the other hand, women's denials contributed to what we might think of as Americans' "learned ignorance" or faulty knowledge regarding the existence of sexual demands.[16]

If actual women sometimes downplayed unwanted behaviors, popular representations of the office emphasized their romantic wishes and sexualized their work roles. Silent films took this everyday space and turned it into a "place of display of women's bodies or some unexpected sexual intimacy." These images transformed the office into something more than a mere location for routine business transactions and similarly changed women from workers into sexual objects. These connotations have had a remarkable staying power. The sociologist Rosemary Pringle noted in the 1980s that although "no one seriously believes that secretaries spend much time on the bosses' knee . . . the sexual possibilities colour the way in which the relationship is seen. Outside of the sex industry itself it is the most sexualized of all workplace relationships." The boss-secretary relationship might represent the apex, but historically all unmarried female clerical workers labored under a social presumption that they were in the office primarily to catch a husband, and this expectation contributed to the romantic and sexual aura of the office. Certainly many women were, but popular culture fortified this belief at every turn. At the very least, then, the public's imagination vigorously associated the office with women's desire for romance.[17]

This perspective could color participants' and observers' assessments of whether a woman wanted a man's attentions or not, while at the same time these popular narratives offered real women a language with which to describe their experiences. Although the evidence is limited, it suggests that cultural representations broadly affected the way women responded to unwanted attentions. Some, for example, recounted their experience of unwanted or coercive attentions in the language of the formulaic romances that filled women's magazines; without a feminist discussion of power, oppression, or sexual violence, this was the dominant discourse at hand. Romance, then, provided women with the linguistic means to tell their stories, but it also mediated what they could say and how they could say it, as well as how listeners would understand it. Once sexual harassment had been named, the legal system also noted the significance of these representations. In 1978, for example, a Colorado court noted that "stereotypes of the sexually-accommodating secretary . . . well documented in popular novels, magazine cartoons and the theatre" contributed to harassment of women workers as a class, which meant the behavior qualified as sex discrimination and not just an individual woman's private problem.[18]

In addition to the abundance of fictional representations of workplace sex and romance, the press has regularly covered sex scandals that originated in the office or involved a prominent businessman or bureaucrat ever since the government first hired female clerks in the early 1860s. Sensational stories have always been a part of the news, but in the late nineteenth century they became a standard feature of even respectable papers, and wire services dramatically extended a local scandal's reach. These outbursts of public outrage did more than reaffirm sexual norms and remind readers of the cost of a moral lapse. They served as an opportunity to reflect on larger social issues. In the instances examined here, scandals allowed for widespread discussions of far-reaching concerns that transcended the specific and narrow effects of an illicit affair or immoral transgression. These incidents allowed for reflection on the place of sexuality within marriage, appropriate gender roles and evolving gender ideals, and the ethics of big business.[19]

Scandals exposed the centrality of sex both to the organization of a business and to the practice of doing business, and thereby raised questions about the very nature of business. What, for example, did it say about the character and rationality of American business and businessmen when a prominent executive impulsively divorced his wife and abandoned his children for his pretty secretary? And if a reporter's exposé of the use of prostitutes to close business deals was true, had big business abandoned all notions of decency and fair competition in the face of greed? Did talent or an affair with the boss explain one beautiful blonde's rapid rise through the ranks, and was her forced resignation evidence of gender discrimination or of the threat sex posed to meritocratic ideals? Every time they opened their newspapers, it seemed, Americans—whether they lived in a fast-paced metropolis or a sleepy village—spotted sex and business (or sex and bureaucrats) together in a sordid coupling.

OFFICE SPACE AND THE CONSTRUCTION OF GENDER, SEXUALITY, CLASS, AND RACE

Until quite recently, the sex they saw was decidedly heterosexual, though expressions of sexuality in the gender-integrated workplace were as significant in structuring relations between men and between women as between men and women. For example, when men approvingly commented to one another about a new filing clerk's feminine physique, each "proved" his heterosexuality, and they bonded together as men. Such comments also enhanced men's authority, making the woman into an object they had the power to appraise and ensuring that she would not be seen as their equal. Women could also be used to establish a hierarchy among men, with the top man getting the girl. In other words, the sexualized woman was often more a means to an end—definitively proving a man's masculinity—than the end itself.[20]

The male relationships that developed around the heterosexual objectification of women also provided the opportunity for the expression of homosocial desire. For the vast majority of the period examined here, there was virtually no public discussion of homosexuality in the workplace, yet work-related heterosexual experiences, such as a salesman getting his client a girl to help close a deal, could create tremendous intimacy between men. This intimacy was ostensibly nonsexual, but such situations could also have concealed potentially erotic desires, blurring the line between homosocial and homosexual experience. In sum, we need to be aware of the role such settings and undercurrents could play in getting, keeping, and transferring power among men.[21]

Workplace sexuality created competition among women for a man (or men), but sex at the office especially provoked disagreements among women (and in the larger society) about ideal womanhood. The classic love triangle depicted in fiction and newspaper accounts of scandals, for example, involved a man, his wife, and a woman from his office. The real question, though, was not which woman would get the man but which woman was better for him and, by extension, for society. In setting the wife-mother against the business girl or "office wife," public discussions pitted maternity and domesticity against sexuality and worldliness, caring compassion against a competent companion. In the office itself, sexual attention signified a woman's worth, but this assessment simultaneously diminished the value of experience and maturity that could come with age, which could create hostility between women. A man might feel jealous or resentful of another man's liaisons, but for women, division and disagreement, envy and antagonism seemed to be the certain outcome whenever sex entered the office. Women might bond together against a woman they perceived to be using sex in an unfair way, but this sisterhood was in opposition to a woman, not in support of one, and it reflected women's lowly and vulnerable position. Although the historical record is limited, evidence suggests that women banded together against a woman as commonly as they joined in solidarity to aid a woman who received unwanted attentions or to warn new workers about sexual aggressors.[22]

The physical structure of the office often facilitated these interactions. Open-plan offices, for example, transformed the workplace into a site of visual surveillance that could turn the hierarchy on its head: the (male) supervisor kept an eye on the workers, but a (female) worker could also catch the supervisor's eye in a sexual sense, disrupting the efficient, impersonal ideal and complicating the balance of power. This surveillance could work in the opposite way, too, giving men free rein to gaze on women against their will, while also allowing the men to waste time. Whether one found pleasure or pain in watching or being watched, the spatial dynamics of the office organized personal as well as professional relationships and often infused them with a sexual element.[23]

There were still other ways of evaluating the effects of sex in the office. If the office's geography encouraged sexual observation, the bureaucratic prohibition of desire also made erotic expression the most obvious way to rebel against business's impersonal tendencies, illustrating what the philosopher Michel Foucault describes as the inextricable links between "perpetual spirals of power and pleasure." In other words, the forbidden quality of clandestine liaisons or obvious displays of ardor might have made them all the more tantalizing. It is also possible that sexuality did not work against business, as theory would have it, but actually helped it along. In the mid-1960s, for example, the philosopher-sociologist Herbert Marcuse speculated that sexually attractive workers added an element of erotic tension to dull jobs, but in such a carefully managed environment, passion did not damage productivity. Those employees who found enjoyment and possibility in this sexualized atmosphere, Marcuse believed, would more easily submit to the monotony of their workplace.[24]

The paradox of workplace sexuality is nowhere more evident than in the erotic possibilities of that most exalted symbol of male public success: the "private office." These spaces were the subject of much speculation. Dirty jokes found their punch lines, pornographic stories centered their plot lines, and titillating photos and drawings positioned their figures behind these "closed doors." In real life, these same closed doors could lead to gossip that distracted workers from the day's business and compromised men's and women's reputations for fidelity—to employer or spouse. These moments in which the private appeared in public—whether it was the customary flirtation between the receptionist and the men who walked through the office door, the secret affair that suddenly became the talk of the office, or a public denunciation of a businessman's personal life—exposed the falsity of this manufactured division, while at the same time, reifying and confirming it. Sexuality, far from being an unwelcome intruder, was one of the ordinary ways in which power and authority in the office were created, negotiated, expressed, and challenged.

To say that sexuality was built into the office's geography and could be a pathway to resistance is not to suggest that sex in the white-collar workplace was liberated from traditional constraints; middle-class standards of sexual propriety inhibited office workers' lustful yearnings, and women especially found their behavior scrutinized by a judgmental eye. In large part, this was because one of the social benefits of office work was the widespread assumption that putting on a white collar each day served as a sign of middle-class status. Historians have examined the various ways in which this middle-class label clouds more than it illuminates our understanding of office workers' lives, but this designation was important to many workers, who often vigorously monitored their own and others' behavior to ensure that their work culture bore no resemblance to working-class customs. "Middle class" in this context meant more than money or material reality (indeed, at times certain segments of the clerical workforce earned less than industrial workers). It represented a commitment to certain values, a belief in certain principles—for example, that using one's mind was superior to exerting one's muscles (in part because the former suggested progress and civilization), that it was important to aspire to self-improvement and upward mobility, and that adherence to dominant morals and gender ideals said something about a person's social value, his or her respectability, even if the person's economic worth was modest.[25]

Office work was middle class, though, only if the majority of those who filled such positions upheld these values and adopted middle-class manners, which seems for some workers to have contributed to a heightened self-consciousness about the class implications of a variety of behaviors. Already by 1910, for example, secretaries were emphasizing the difference between their varied responsibilities and the mechanized efforts of stenographers. This distinction often existed more in name than fact, but it preserved secretaries' superiority, especially as more women from working-class and immigrant families sought to enter the clerical field. In a related vein, labor activists found office workers notoriously hard to organize because they associated unions with industrial workers and dirt, a connection that was especially problematic for female clerks who had already jeopardized their social standing by leaving the home to work for wages.[26]

Office workers' anxiety and defensiveness about their status also can be seen in their fascination with symbols. By the end of World War I, manufacturing firms that had cafeterias usually had separate dining areas for office workers and factory hands. In the 1950s a middle-aged secretary made her class-based expectations clear when she loudly complained to her boss about a young stenographer who one day wore her hair in curlers because she had a date after work—"Does she think she's working in a factory?" During the same period, the social critic Vance Packard documented white-collar executives' obsession with even the smallest markers of success; this was a world in which water decanters and pen holders said something about a man's rank.[27]

Sexual behaviors—in and out of the office—especially indicated one's standing. During World War II, for example, some government workers wrote to officials complaining about the sexually charged interactions between male supervisors and young female clerks. On one hand, these letters suggest that some workers actively took steps to guarantee that their coworkers abided by middle-class standards of propriety. On the other, they show that disgruntled employees could use the language of gender, class, and sexuality to voice their grievances. Miss B, for example, charged her supervisor with incompetence, and the evidence she offered centered almost exclusively on his contact with his female employees. She had seen him "twirling [his secretary's] hair around his hand, another time he was pinching her arms and again she was sewing on buttons on his coat"; the secretary had received a raise after only three months. Miss B also noted that a coworker once stated that she had "never worked in an office before with such a common set of girls," who received raises because "they let themselves get felt." In this case, a man's sexual behavior was offered as proof that he was unfit to lead, proof that relied on class-based assumptions of what personal behaviors were appropriate in an office. Class values also informed the assessment by Miss B's coworker of the other office girls. They were "common," although it is unclear whether the coworker made this appraisal before or after the boss's touches. For the historian, it raises the question: Had the boss touched them because they were common, or was it the boss's touch that made them so? Either way, the experience marked these women as interlopers into middle-class space and, possibly, precluded observers from considering whether the boss's wandering hands were unwanted.[28]

Working in an office no less significantly (even if less overtly acknowledged) signaled workers' race. The skyscraper held to the color line. In 1900 in New York City, for example, of the more than 15,000 African American women who earned wages, only 46 had clerical jobs. Meanwhile, almost one-quarter of the 109,000 employed white women worked in the clerical sector. The ratios were about the same for men. Those African Americans who performed clerical work almost certainly did so in the few businesses that were owned by African Americans and served the black community. Nationally, conditions were the same and remained that way until the 1940s, when the number of African Americans employed in clerical jobs or corporate management began very slowly to increase, and some offices began to desegregate. A more rapid change occurred between 1962 and 1974, and African Americans' share of clerical positions became almost proportionate to their numbers in the total labor force.[29]

This history of sex in the white-collar office, then, concerns itself mainly with white workers. These men and women rarely acknowledged how race factored into their understanding of their sexual conduct in the office, but, just as their actions were designed to signal their social class, so their behavior reflected and confirmed the distinction between them and their imagined racial inferiors. A few examples make this connection clear. Already by the early twentieth century some middle-class businessmen were using sexual conquests—including of the "ladies" with whom they worked—as a marker of masculine success. At the same moment, however, whites in the South were using African American men's alleged passions for pure, white womanhood as a justification for segregation and violence. According to cultural notions of race, class, and gender, the "primitive" black man could not control his passions, while the "civilized" white businessman would.[30]

Concerns about black men's desires were again on display in the 1970s and 1980s, when African American men began to occupy management positions in large corporations. Some black executives worried that white men opposed their advancement in part because it made them competitors for the white women with whom they all worked. One African American secretary recalled the reaction of the white men in her office when a black manager hired a pretty blonde as his secretary. "Every time he came out of his office to speak to her some of them would stop what they were doing and listen, and God! You could see them squirming when she went into his office and closed the door." Their discomfort turned to confrontation, and the men tried everything to make the secretary quit, including making jokes to her that made the situation seem "ugly." "Pretty soon," the African American woman recalled, "the girl did quit and the black guy got transferred." As sexual harassment became an issue in the early 1980s, some black managers, reflecting on America's past and the violent ends that befell black men who had been intimately involved with white women, feared they would be especially vulnerable to false allegations.[31]

African American women, by contrast, were prominent in the first efforts in the early 1970s to use the law to challenge sexual exploitation in the workplace. In explaining why this was so, scholars have speculated that these women's experience of racism heightened their consciousness, making them see their supervisor's propositions as reflecting something more than personal attraction. As the legal theorist Kimberlé Crenshaw notes, "Racism may well provide the clarity to see that sexual harassment is neither a flattering gesture nor a misguided social overture but an act of intentional discrimination that is insulting, threatening, and debilitating." African American women's race also shaped their experience of harassment, as one woman's experience makes clear: her harasser "wished slavery days would return so that he could sexually train her and she would be his bitch."[32]

We know the details of this woman's experience because it was documented in the transcript of her sexual harassment case, but the particulars of earlier women's encounters are difficult to find, given that until recently these behaviors had no name. This means it is impossible to determine how many women experienced coercive or unwanted sexual attentions. Yet even if sources were more plentiful, it would still be necessary to place these stories into a larger context. As Sharon Block has argued in her study of rape in early America, "Normative practices of consensual sex are understood only when we know where the category of consensual sex ended and that of rape began." This point is particularly relevant when discussing unwelcome and coercive behavior in the context of employment, especially when the workspace under study is widely considered a place of romantic and sexual possibility. In this project, then, I aim to connect the stories of actual women and men in a variety of sexual relations in the office to the dominant cultural narratives of their time, paying close attention to how shifting ideologies colored their experiences. I examine my subject in chronologically ordered chapters, the first adressing the earliest era of women's employment in offices and the last exploring the recent past, the period when the definition of "sexual harassment" was integranted into employment law and personnel practices. My hope is that such an approach will allow us a glimpse into the sexual and romantic experiences of office workers in the past, including relationships entered willingly and those occurring under duress, as well as providing a greater understanding of how cultural sources reflected and affected those experiences.[33]

CHAPTER ONE

Dangers, Desires, and Self-Determination

COMPETING NARRATIVES OF THE SEXUAL CULTURE OF THE NEW, GENDER-INTEGRATED OFFICE

"HAS LEFT HIS WIFE—Picard Loved Miss Berry," read the front-page headline of the July 29, 1904, *Boston Daily Globe*. According to his wife, Alfred L. Picard, fifty, had sold his prosperous electrical contracting business to start a new life out west with his typewriter, Ella Berry, because he "could not live without her." Destitute, Mrs. Picard was now working as a stenographer and had not heard from her husband since he left in early June. Their marital trouble had started two years before, when Picard had hired Berry, thirty, at seven dollars a week. Within a month, Mrs. Picard asserted, Berry was making twenty dollars a week and "running the office, hiring and discharging the men," her husband now "merely the office boy." Here, it seemed, was proof of a pretty typewriter's ability to wreak havoc on a man's lifetime of hard work and domestic order.[1]

At the end of the account, a much shorter story appeared in which Ella's mother confidently denied Mrs. Picard's accusations and described her daughter as a quiet girl who did not even attend dances. In other words, Ella Berry was not a pleasure-seeking seductress who would engage in an affair with her employer but a victim of slurs designed to injure her reputation. And, to be sure, she appeared at the *Globe's* office the very next day to refute Mrs. Picard's charges and "to be at hand to prevent any new attacks on her good name." She was only nineteen (and, in the *Globe's* assessment, modest and refined), she had earned just twelve dollars a week, and her relations with Picard were strictly those of employer and employee. Berry had not heard from him in weeks and had no idea where he was. She was sure, however, that he was a gentleman who would return to defend her honor.[2]

Picard did return, though not until about a year later, and his arrival in Boston did nothing to help Berry's reputation. After checking in to a hotel, he sent a note to his estranged wife, asking her to meet with him. After a short, tense conversation, he returned to his room and shot himself in the head with a revolver. The suicide made him front-page news again. Though the *Globe* did not mention Berry by name, its report recounted the earlier scandal without noting that she had publicly denounced the affront to her honor. Three months later, she shot herself in a New York City hotel room. Her father tearfully told reporters that even after the *Globe* published her side of the story, everywhere she went "somebody was ready to point to her as a girl who had been mixed up in a disgraceful affair." Seeking work outside of Boston did not help. Within a short time, the scandal would reach her employer and she would be told that she could not remain. Picard's suicide made matters worse, and she grew still more despondent. As she wrote in her suicide note, "I cannot bear this false stain upon my character. . . . I would not do this thing if it were not that I am nearly out of my mind with grief and horror at the awful story which everybody seems to think is true."[3]

The violent ends that befell the young stenographer and her employer were unusual, but the narrative formulas the *Globe* used to recount their lives were conventional and predictable, resembling similar sensational accounts of the sexual goings-on in the white-collar office that were routine features in the nation's newspapers in the late nineteenth and early twentieth centuries—variations of which continue to this day. The *Globe*'s coverage was unusual only because it contained elements of all three of the dominant stories Americans told about the moral character of the office and of the people who worked there. One plotline cast Berry as the unfeeling vamp who made a fool out of a man and mincemeat of his marriage; another revealed her to be the vulnerable victim of either a lecherous man or his vindictive wife, who blamed her marital troubles on her husband's office help. Still one more portrayed her as a new kind of woman, a moral and strong-minded individual capable of protecting (or at least standing up for) herself, even in public. These competing understandings of womanhood were coupled with oppositional conceptions of men, in which Picard was alternately the victim of his base desires, a sexual predator willing to exploit his position of authority, or a gentleman who had failed in his role as protector of female innocence.

These narratives spoke directly to the experiences of urban middle-class Americans who witnessed firsthand the explosive growth of the office workplace in the post–Civil War economy and with it, a new and rapidly expanding workforce of women. But they were also part of a national conversation about sex, marriage, and family life in a rapidly modernizing world. Most especially these tales of intrigue reflected disagreement about the place of women—their role, rights, and safety—in the public sphere. At the heart of debates about the sexual culture of the office lay the question of women's sexual nature and their individual agency. Those who saw women as emotional naïfs wondered whether workingwomen would be able to resist seduction or coercion, while others believed that at least a few willingly engaged in illicit affairs just as they had chosen to enter into a labor contract. For their part, some women office workers asserted their personal integrity and capability, claiming ownership of their virtue and responsibility for their lives.

Such assertions were necessary at a time when Americans were in a panic over the possible links between women's employment and immorality—even prostitution. Concern focused mostly on the young, working-class women who labored in factories and department stores and spent their leisure hours at dance halls and amusements parks. Unable to afford these entertainments on their meager wages, they allowed men to "treat" them, exchanging sexual favors for a night of fun. White-collar women did not completely escape the reformers' gaze: stories in magazines and newspapers regularly told of the dangerous propositions attractive women received during job interviews. An extended series on urban workingwomen in *Harper's Bazar* in 1908 began with a letter from a young stenographer who was ill for two weeks after the men at her first two interviews made sexually suggestive comments. A similar series in the *New York Times* in 1909 concluded with an independently minded young woman running home to her mother and loyal boyfriend after receiving an offer to be a "private secretary." The interviewer's comments on her beauty and his "soft, purring tone" made her "instinctively draw away."[4]

Female office workers and their advocates, however, were able to utilize the intersecting ideologies of gender, class, and sexuality to diminish anxieties about the myriad dangers—to themselves, to men, to families, to society—posed by office employment. By laying claim to the moral authority grounded in the middle-class ideology of female passionlessness, they were able to affirm their superiority to working-class women even when they, too, were workingwomen—and even as many working-class women occupied low-level clerical jobs by the century's end. Everywhere the office workers looked, though, they saw signs that the celebrated belief in female virtue and middle-class respectability was outweighed by deep-seated convictions regarding women's capacity for sexual deceit and men's corresponding defenselessness. No matter how pure her actions, how modest her bearing, for example, Berry's reputation never recovered from the moment of first suspicion; even to be thought to have aroused desire could lead to ruin. Picard fared no better; he was prima facie evidence that a man could become, as his wife described him, a mere office boy in the hands of a scheming stenographer.[5]

Picard and Berry were not the only boss and stenographer to find details of their relationship splashed across a newspaper's front page, and other sources also contemplated this new workplace relationship—one that, in many ways, mirrored the dynamic between a husband and wife. Employment guides, reformers and religious leaders, and even juries offered up opinions. In other words, Americans had countless opportunities to think about women's nature and appropriate place.

OFFICE WOMEN, PLEASURE-ORIENTED MEN, AND THE RECONSIDERATION OF MARRIAGE

Popular accounts of workplace entanglements often focused on the typewriter's irresistible allure, and especially on the threat she posed to men's self-control, a stable society, and marriages. Women and men working together raised the specter of an array of untold immoral possibilities, and, perhaps more troubling, the typewriter seemed to offer greater pleasures than the wife at home. In part, then, these stories spoke to the question of marital sexuality. Typewriters responded that they were not "love pirates" and offered public reassurances that a businessman's wife had nothing to fear. Despite their denials, newspapers regularly portrayed the office girl as a siren who ruined good men and solid marriages.[6]

As the citizens of Buffalo learned in 1893, it did not take long for such destruction to occur. Alice Brand, twenty-six, needed only two weeks to turn Alex Fortier, forty-eight, a respected veteran and chief clerk of the city's Health Department, away from his upright life and his wife of twenty-three years. This was not completely surprising, the Buffalo paper noted, for those who "should know whereof they speak say that when it comes to a fast life a pretty blonde stenographer can do much more execution than wine and cards in destroying a man's standing in a community." When Mrs. Fortier filed for divorce, the city learned of the alliance, which included nights spent at the office on the pretense of conducting business.[7]

Fortier had abandoned his wife financially and physically. In a six-month period, he showered Brand with "clothing, shoes, bon-bons, bouquets and luxuries of many kinds." He also had taken her to the theater, to restaurants, and to an art gallery, where he "got her to sit for her picture half nude and exposed," which he then wore under his watch and showed to his friends and acquaintances. While Fortier showered Brand with gifts, he gave his wife, who suffered from an incurable eye disease, so little money that she could no longer hire household help—a marker of a precipitous decline for a middle-class woman. The Health Department quickly suspended Fortier and demanded Brand's resignation.[8]

Fortier was soon back at work in his office. He confessed to visiting Brand at her home after work and to being "indiscreet at times," but he vigorously denied any improper relations and declared himself the victim of malicious gossip. Mrs. Fortier admitted that she had no concrete proof of his affair and agreed to drop the divorce proceedings. The Health Department chief reinstated Fortier, but Brand was not rehired. She had not denied the allegations, and the chief stated that he would no longer hire women, taking care to note that he was "not slurring 'noble woman-hood,'" for which he had the highest esteem. With Fortier in and Brand gone, the story seemed over. Within a few weeks, however, Fortier had disappeared, leaving a trail of unpaid loans borrowed from friends and concern that he had embezzled from the Naval Veterans Association. A few months later, he was still missing. The papers made no comment on Brand's whereabouts.[9]

Newspaper coverage in this case never focused on the "other woman," or the effect of the scandal on her life; this narrative was about the social calamity that ensued when men succumbed to temptation. Brand "worked hard" and "was pleasant . . . rather than bold," but even if she was something less than a vamp, she was still dangerous. She tested Fortier's self-control and he failed, giving in to his physical desires—and, just as problematically, to the temptations of an expanding consumer economy. Fortier had spent wildly on his lover: clothes, candy, even a bicycle—perhaps a tribute to her New Woman status. But nineteenth-century middle-class men were supposed to focus on work and delay gratification; uninhibited consumption was the provenance of women. They bought things, while men made them—or the money to buy them. Succumbing to the delights of things, then, was no less a threat to a man—indeed, the same type of threat—as yielding to a seductive temptress. In Fortier's surrender to pleasure, everything—the funds of the Naval Veterans Association, the money for his ill wife's medicine, the savings of friends, and the reputation of a once respected man—was consumed.[10]

Why were men like this so vulnerable to the charms of their "pretty typewriters?" Were they, as one critic argued, honest husbands before these women lured them from their homes? Or had these men's wives done something to drive their husbands away? These stories can be read as part of a larger reevaluation of the relationship between a husband and wife and the importance of sexuality in marriage, a reevaluation prompted in part by the rising divorce rate. By the end of the nineteenth century, one of every fifteen marriages ended this way, and middle-class Americans talked about a divorce crisis. The ideal of wifeliness that emerged from commentaries about "pretty typewriters" was domestic, but also sensual. Her primary purpose was still to serve as helpmate, but the new white-collar breadwinner needed a partner in pleasure, too.[11]

In some ways, this reconsideration of the erotic in marriage was linked to the rise of a bureaucratic workforce. With more and more men becoming salaried corporate employees rather than striving for entrepreneurial independence, leisure time increased and took on greater significance. At the same time, the mature industrial economy churned out more and more consumer goods promising to make life more pleasurable and fun. Marriage—and the home and family more broadly—began to be seen as a means to fulfill an individual's need for happiness. While spouses still needed to fulfill their old gendered duties, such as breadwinning and nurturing, they also had to bring excitement to the marriage. But as the rising number of divorces showed, blending the old and the new was often not so easy. Men wanted wives who were domestic and sensuous, virtuous and thrilling. Women wanted husbands who provided, but for much more than the household basics. The emphasis on sexual pleasure within marriage, which increasingly became the guiding principle after 1900, also proved a source of discontent and confusion for some couples.[12]

The case of a wandering industrialist illustrates how the uncertainty surrounding marital sexuality and the modern middle-class wife's role found expression in heated discussions of the sexual temptations of the new heterosocial workplace. In 1908 Mrs. Benedetto Allegretti, the wife of a wealthy Chicago candy manufacturer, sued her husband for divorce because of his involvement with his eighteen-year-old typewriter. Allegretti denounced all typewriters as "love pirates" who menaced happy marriages. Office girls consciously exerted "an influence for evil" on men, who compared their neat gowns and picture hats with the work dresses of the busy homemaking wife. The social reserve that usually guided men's and women's interaction was also gone. According to Allegretti, men knew their typewriters better than the girls' mothers did, and typewriters certainly understood their bosses better than did their wives. And there was always the "sex element to be reckoned with."[13]

When Allegretti's charges made the newspapers in many American cities, typists and their supporters countered her attack, blaming men or their wives for adulterous relationships. A girl who entered such a relationship did so not because she was a business girl, one typewriter maintained, "but because she is that kind of a girl and would do that thing in whatever position she was placed." On the relatively few occasions when improper advances occurred, men made them, and they were "a source of great annoyance to the girls." The "average business woman" was "too level-headed to waste her time on a married man."[14]

Some defenders of female workers noted that office romances often developed between unmarried men and women, a defense that challenged representations of the office as professional, asexual space— although no one addressed the inconsistency. Instead, typewriters used the fact of love matches begun at work to praise the qualities of office women and to criticize businessmen's wives. "It strikes me that

What every Woman Knows

That this Girl is the right sort for Hubby's Office

In its assumption that men proposition only attractive women, this early-twentieth-century postcard reflected the dominant understanding of male sexuality. When talking about sex in the office, then, the discourse focused on "pretty typewriters" and tempted husbands. Author's collection.

Mrs. Allegretti lost her husband because she thought it no longer necessary to appear attractive and dainty before him," one proclaimed. "It is a wife's fault if she allows her husband to stray from her, for by observing the habits of the business woman she can hold him always." Another picked up the thread. If a typewriter married, she would know how to keep her husband interested and amused. Her home would not be a tomb of "gray respectability" but would be filled with pleasure to "lighten the recollection of his heavy hours of routine." Business experience made women more stylish, less selfish and narrowly focused, and more understanding and sympathetic; it was too bad that all women could not work some before marriage.[15]

Some discussions hinted, too, that the time spent at work with men gave women a greater understanding of erotic pleasures. While fiction published in stenography journals in the late nineteenth and early twentieth centuries often showed women finding love with their employers and coworkers as the reward for dedicated service, desire began to appear in other venues. In 1910, for example, the *Atlanta Constitution* emphasized the importance of sexual attraction in its coverage of an office romance that quickly led to marriage: when a pretty stenographer goes to work for a bachelor, there is "apt to be more than an interchange of mere business formalities." Other representations of romantic and sexual interaction in the office were more complicated. While portraying sex as a source of rejuvenation and fulfillment for men, these accounts also suggested its danger and expressed—at best—ambivalence about the character of women who aroused desire.[16]

WOMEN'S POWER, MEN'S VULNERABILITY

Although some accounts scolded men for their lack of self-control, other narratives proved more sympathetic to the man whose desires got the best of him. In these stories, we see what will be a recurring theme in this book: a pervasive fear of women's seemingly limitless power when they put their sexuality to use. Within this anxiety, of course, lay fears about men's vulnerability, not only in tangible terms, such as the loss of money or family, but in the more visceral pain of being played for a fool. Although women's power was often described in terms of behavior—a flirtatious smile, a general sexual willingness—the threat of female sexuality was far more elemental. Women were the embodiment of temptation, with the power to destroy or disrupt individual men, male power structures, and the business of getting work done. Men's sexual desire gave women a weapon by which they could humiliate and "unman" men; if women were to remain in the white-collar world, they would need to be disarmed.

Tales of office temptresses were everywhere. A Texas legislator argued against a bill that would raise the age of consent above fourteen because

Women office workers were controversial, and, as this cartoon suggests, some Americans believed that they would distract men more than they would help get work done. Illustration courtesy of General Research Division, The New York Public Library, Astor, Lenox and Tilden Foundations.

working girls, especially typewriters, would blackmail their employers, urged on by their avaricious mothers. In 1908 newspapers reported the story of Miss E. Bennett, a stenographer who was paid fifteen dollars a week just to look pretty. According to a critic of women's employment, female office workers were "generally quite willing to kiss and be kissed" in order to extract favors from their employers, and "one kiss, properly stage-managed, [was] enough to transform a Democrat into a Republican." The public heard the details of such a transformation in 1909, when Mrs. Alfred Goslin filed an "alienation of affection" suit against Annie Magher, her husband's former stenographer. Mrs. Goslin alleged that Magher used every feminine trick and the promise of untold pleasures to lure him away. As one observer noted, "what man could withstand such a siege?" Even the most successful men were vulnerable. In 1906 the *Washington Post* mocked a multimillionaire whose stenographer rejected his marriage proposal. "Go 'way. Please go 'way," the man beseeched reporters who dubbed him "the first millionaire to have his marriage proposal rejected by a typewriter."[17]

This anxiety over women's sexual power was grossly out of proportion to their actual influence in a period that placed severe limits on women's occupational advancement and strict controls on their behavior. At most, a woman gained a husband, an easier workload, or a more generous salary; in a few cases, cold, hard cash might have been exchanged for a secret well kept. Yet women represented a threat to male authority and individual manliness. Women, consequently, had a difficult argument to make in justifying their place in the white-collar labor force. They simultaneously had to demonstrate that their sex did not unfit them for business and that office work did not endanger traditional gender roles, but was an extension and even an enhancement of femininity. The latter was important in establishing that women would not take men's jobs away or fight for advancement—in other words, that they did not represent a challenge to male power. Yet they also had to illustrate that their presence would not introduce a disruptive element of sexuality. This was not just about reconciling a gender-integrated workplace with existing standards of middle-class morality—the usual explanation. It was a way of showing that women would not jeopardize men's status by arousing their potentially humiliating sexual desire.[18]

We need, then, to read the multitude of discourses on the romantic and sexual culture of the office for what they can tell us about how the dangers of desire found expression and resolution. Such concerns are evident in "For the Sake of the Office," a short story that appeared in 1902 in *Typewriter and Phonographic World,* one of many professional periodicals that provided information about the latest business methods and office machines to the growing number of male and especially female clerical workers. In addition to offering practical employment advice, these journals regularly reported on real-life love matches begun in the office and featured workplace romances in fictional pieces. "For the Sake of the Office," while acknowledging male vulnerability, also turns it into a positive good. The narrative is standard romance, with the classic misunderstanding that must be resolved before the protagonists can be together. It begins with a description of the anger of Mr. Grantly, the office manager, toward Miss Middleton, his stylish, though not pretty, clerk. She has disregarded his warnings about her "friendship" with Mr. McAllister, who works in the office directly opposite theirs. When Grantly confronts her for the "honor and dignity" of the office—for "of course" the "matter was nothing to him, personally," she claims the "right" of selecting her own friends. He responds that he has the right to demand that his employees do not discredit his office. He has spied on her, noting that she meets McAllister every day after work, and has seen her "throw kisses at him." McAllister is married, Grantly hisses, and his warnings were for her safety. When she replies that she already knows McAllister's marital status, Grantly thinks the worst and fires her. But Middleton is no shrinking violet. When Grantly refuses to hear an explanation, she declares him "dictatorial, hasty and unjust" and puts her hand on the doorknob to leave. At that moment, Grantly loses what little self-control he has left and takes a step toward her. She retreats, but his arms were "holding her tightly. She struggled, but to no avail against his great strength. She wondered frantically if he would kill her." But instead, he kisses her and declares his love. He cannot let her go. His jealousy has tortured him, and he has wanted to kill McAllister and himself. After his confession, she blushingly and lovingly confesses, too. McAllister is her brother-in-law, and she was throwing kisses to her baby nephew. Readers know a marriage will soon ensue.

In this happy ending, a number of the tensions associated with women's presence in the office are resolved. First, a man's desire for a woman—which has come close to destroying him—leads to an affirmation of traditional manhood (he will soon be a husband) and the removal and domestication of the temptation (she will soon be a wife at home). Grantly's fascination has made him ineffective at business—"flinging his papers about," spending his time fretting over and watching a lowly employee, and contemplating violence. His anger, jealousy, and irrationality are at odds with the reason and self-control needed in business; in fact, they seem almost feminine. But the ending reestablishes his manliness and justifies women's place in the office. Women are virtuous. They arouse men's passions, but also tame them, providing men with an appropriate expression for their strong feelings: protecting and working for their loved ones.[19]

While romance stories such as this ensured that a man's desire did not lead to his demise, others warned women against mercenary tactics in matters of the heart. *Soul Sonnets of a Stenographer*, a lengthy poem originally serialized in the *Saturday Evening Post* in 1903, describes a woman who awakens desire, but in this case intentionally and for purely selfish ends. Though her heart belongs to Teddy, a handsome clerk who loves her but has no financial prospects, she sets her sights on her wealthy boss, whose wife seems on the verge of death. In the end, she finds herself out of work and all alone. The boss's wife has learned of her flirtations, and her employer fires her. Meanwhile, Teddy has tired of waiting and found another girl. "Oh, what a fool was I to think of giving up my soul for gold," the stenographer laments.[20]

In this clever poem in a popular magazine, readers encountered a variation on a recurring theme: men beware. And women again heard the message not to use their attraction for gain. Stay focused on your work, *Soul Sonnets* warned, and know your place, which meant confining your interest to unmarried young clerks. This poem also showed how a woman's presence could influence the tone of the office. Her daydreams lead to inefficiency, and her flirtations distract both men. If women were to contribute to business, they would need to monitor their behavior to ensure that the environment was morally proper and without desire. In the imagined and actual office, many women not only accepted but eagerly claimed this role.

VIRTUE UNDER SIEGE: OFFICE WORK AND CHALLENGES TO WOMEN'S HONOR

Representations of vamps who destroyed men and marriages and of vixens who reduced powerful men to quivering supplicants coexisted with those that portrayed office women as victims, innocents in need of protection from would-be seducers and despoilers of female virtue. For those who noted the moral dangers of the office, businessmen were not gentlemen. A variety of Americans—reformers, clergy, legislators, social commentators, members of women's clubs—believed that some men would take advantage of their authority over or proximity to an unprotected woman. In 1890, for example, an advocate for women's office employment acknowledged that there were men who claimed to be honorable but "would rather encourage than discourage a possible tendency to weak ways on the part of girls." Though it was the exception, some men would "not scruple to use the little power they may have to serve their own base ends." Yet in this article, as in so many, the real subject was not men but whether a girl would be able to work "without subjecting herself to . . . insult or . . . misconception." At the heart of this debate was a simple question of class and character: could a middle-class woman work and retain her womanly honor, or was life in a business office with relative strangers incompatible with notions of feminine virtue?[21]

In writing about predatory men, commentators entered into a growing and contentious debate about women's sexual nature and their sexual agency. Divided between those who saw women as willing sexual subjects, who could take advantage of a man's sexual vulnerability, and those who believed in women's inherent purity, Americans wrestled with the question: Did a woman have the right—or even ability—to make decisions about her body? Or, looking at the question from another angle, was it even fair to view sexual situations in such black-and-white terms? Was it possible for a woman to give her consent in any meaningful way in situations in which men and women had such differing degrees of power?

Back in the 1840s and 1850s, members of the Female Moral Reform Society thought not. They succeeded in making a man's seduction of a woman by means of a promise of marriage a criminal offense in a number of states. Seduction was a crime because it stole a woman's physical virginity and her personal character. Just as significantly, it was an act of violence against society's values. These reformers made no distinction between a woman's voluntary and involuntary loss of chastity, believing that it was impossible for a chaste woman to consent to sexual intercourse before marriage. By the end of the century, however, such trials occurred less often as social commentators and legal experts began to focus more attention on women's sexual agency, even vengefulness, which troubled seduction's legal theory that a pure woman was incapable of making a sexual choice.[22]

These differing perspectives came into view again in the effort to raise the age of consent. In 1885 the Women's Christian Temperance Union and other social purity reformers, who held to the older view of women's sexual agency, lobbied to make sex with teenage girls a crime. This effort reflected the growing concern about the dangers facing young working-class women who spent the better part of their day working for wages under the authority of a possibly unscrupulous man. On the whole this campaign was successful, but in actual statutory rape cases judges attributed to young women a greater degree of volition than had the reformers. Even though a girl's age was the only relevant factor with regard to consent, judges routinely allowed defense attorneys to question the girl about her role in the seduction, even sometimes to paint her as the aggressor.[23]

These same uncertainties about women's sexual nature and individual initiative infused commentaries on white-collar men's ungentlemanly behavior. When boiled down to their essence, these discussions generally characterized men's actions as the inevitable result of being men. They were dishonorable in their inability to control their desires, but it was in their nature to be ruled by passion. A woman's sexual purity, by contrast, was *the* defining marker of her worth. As such, the lion's share of attention needed to focus on her behavior; *her response* to a man's immoral proposition mattered as much as, if not more than, the proposition itself.[24]

As to the actual propositions, our understanding is clouded by Victorian modesty. Men sometimes took "liberties" with their stenographers or "trifle[d]" with their "self respect." Commentators wrote about women who had suffered "indignities," "gross insults," and "undue familiarity." One man laid an "affectionate hand" on his assistant's shoulder, but at the distance of a century there is no way to determine whether she interpreted this gesture as merely an unwelcome proposition or as a sexual demand linked to her continued employment. We can, however, make two reliable observations about such "impertinences." First, a woman's virtue was possibly imperiled; second, the man had challenged her honor. Her reply, her ability to resist sexual temptation or intimidation, determined what type of woman she was, one of character (that is to say, one who could lay claim to an identity as a pure middle-class lady) or of something else.[25]

The way these beliefs played out in discussions of the office can be seen in a letter a self-described "pretty girl" from San Francisco wrote to a stenography journal in 1895. She acknowledged that her good looks had repeatedly brought unwanted flatteries. Through "force of character" she had learned to ignore such remarks and thereby earned men's respect. But even though she acknowledged that men pestered women with unsolicited "annoyances," she still held women accountable for any sexual transgression. She concluded that a woman was "somewhat to blame" if her employer invited her to dinner since "a gentleman certainly would not ask such a thing were he not encouraged in some way by the girl herself." Men were not responsible, "as it is a well-known fact that it is a man's permission to ask, and woman's to refuse. You can take a horse to the water, the old saying is, but you cannot make him drink."[26]

"Frisco," as she signed her letter, assumed that the majority of men were gentlemen who respected women, but at the same time she accepted that men would pursue and test women, and that this was their role if not their right. These views might seem inconsistent if it were not for her corresponding belief that it was women's responsibility to regulate all sexual interaction and that the strength of a virtuous woman's character was ultimately enough to gain men's respect and protect her from insulting advances. In this regard, Frisco was not alone.

Authors of turn-of-the-century advice guides for office women repeatedly emphasized (and in later years would continue to emphasize) the importance of a woman's behavior in establishing her character, which, in turn, guaranteed her moral safety at work. A commentator in 1894, for example, stated that a business woman's "treatment by her employer depends entirely on the way in which she carries herself before him. . . . This is an invariable rule." A book from 1900 made the point slightly differently in response to the question of whether girls in business were "subjected to a variety of temptations and . . . peculiarly unprotected." The girl who was "pre-occupied with her work, is so impersonal in its exercise that she repels those who would offer insult." Only the woman "who flirts . . . jests openly . . . or apes . . . masculine manners, invites the unprincipled to forget her womanhood."[27]

The consensus was that women needed to be vigilant. Appearance and manners, for example, sent innumerable messages about a woman's social class, which was explicitly tied to conceptions of her respectability.

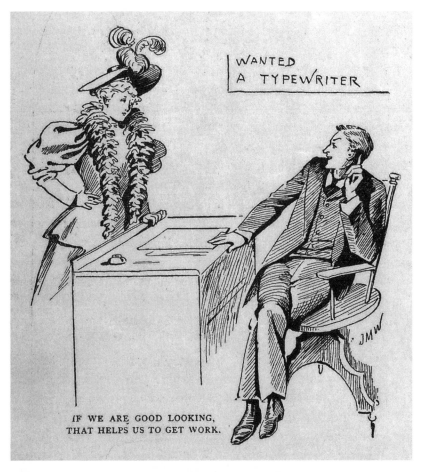

This illustration accompanied an 1895 article in a stenography journal. According to the author, attractive women would have to fend off their employers' dinner invitations, while "ugly" women would have a difficult time landing a position or securing a promotion. Illustration courtesy of General Research Division, The New York Public Library, Astor, Lenox and Tilden Foundations.

Therefore advice on such issues occupied an abundance of space in articles and books geared to office women. The irony, of course, was that such extensive discussion of clothing and social behavior belied the idea of middle-class women's natural modesty. It also contradicted—or at least complicated—the image of office work as middle-class labor and office women as a cut above other working girls. The detailed advice suggests the fragility of this superior status. Caroline Huling's 1906 *Letters of a Business Woman to Her Niece* warned that wearing an "inappropriate" garment was a "sign of low breeding" and could cost a woman her position, as it did one who wore a "décolleté evening dress" to work in the office of a modest attorney. Clothing that seemed to cost more than your salary also caused problems, opening up a woman "to unpleasant suspicion"; an office girl with a sealskin coat would have to defend her character constantly.[28]

Business interactions, too, were fraught with danger. How could a woman determine the difference between "courtesies" and dangerous "impertinences"? According to Huling, a woman could not be hypersensitive, but her entire reputation depended on her ability to distinguish between the two. Some men, she cautioned, might even dictate vulgar material just to test a woman's character. The best strategy, then, was to maintain an impersonal demeanor at all times, avoiding any conversation that hinted at familiarity. Huling believed a "natural instinct" guarded most women and warned them of impending danger. Though women were hesitant "to think evil of one who appears to be a gentleman," they needed to follow their instinct. Men would thank them in the end, secretly grateful that women's modesty prevented them from doing something foolish. Women also would do well to remember that however much a man was amused by a flirt, he would "inwardly despise her."[29]

Advice guides and advocates acknowledged women's vulnerability but asserted that the virtuous woman was ultimately safe; her virtue itself was her protection. But they also noted that women would need to be on guard, scrutinizing their actions lest they give a man the wrong idea. If women wanted to work in an office, they would have to bear the burden of keeping men's bad behaviors in check; in other words, if something went wrong, they would bear much of the blame. Here was a shift. The conviction that pure women were incapable of sexual consent—that is, of making decisions about their bodies—had animated midcentury efforts to criminalize seduction. A variation of this belief informed later efforts to raise the age of consent; a mitigating factor, age, could render a woman's consent meaningless. Those giving advice to office women, however, turned this view on its head. Reputation and purity were still paramount, but women themselves would need to be responsible for protecting them.

Why did advice givers assign to office women the task of patrolling their bodies' borders? To make sense of their perspective, which was infused with considerations of social class, it needs to be placed in the context of Progressive Era reform, especially the full-scale effort to eradicate prostitution during the first two decades of the twentieth century. Though efforts to stop the "Social Evil" had been around for a century, the problem took on catastrophic proportions after 1900: commentators declared prostitution to be a curse more deadly than a plague, an invading enemy set on destroying all that was good and pure. It is unclear whether or by how much rates of prostitution had increased, but by the twentieth century it was a visible, thriving enterprise, with owners, managers, and any number of middlemen. Brothels, for example, operated with impunity in red-light districts by bribing politicians and the police. Embedded into the political and economic life of American cities, prostitution also seemed connected to other dramatic and, to many Americans, disturbing changes—urbanization, new immigration, industrialization—rendering it an issue of national significance. Ultimately, though, antiprostitution activists (especially the white, male leaders) were most worried about women's changing behavior and their abandonment of traditional gender roles. Married middle-class women were filing for divorce and having fewer babies. They spent their days away from home at club meetings, while their unmarried daughters entered the labor force, joining the millions of working-class women already there, albeit mostly in different occupations.[30]

Concerns about the connection between wage labor and prostitution led to efforts to protect workingwomen. Reports assessed the merits of a given occupation or industry based on whether or not it was conducive to morality, examining wages and work conditions, including whether men and women worked "indiscriminately" together, a sure sign of danger. Labor laws, which differed dramatically from state to state, were meant mostly to regulate industry, providing workers of both sexes with safe workplaces. Some laws, however, focused exclusively on women and reflected prevailing beliefs about their proper role: if women had to work, they had to be in jobs that preserved their bodies, minds, and morals for motherhood and domesticity. This meant that some positions were off limits. Worries that a drunk might make a lewd proposition and destroy a woman's innocence, for example, led some states to prohibit women from selling liquor. In 1908 the Supreme Court gave the green light to more legislation of this type when it upheld Oregon's law limiting women's labor to ten hours a day based on their childbearing and -rearing responsibilities. Women were physically weaker than men and apparently morally weaker, too: a limited day would keep a woman's "moral fibre" strong. The Court further justified the legislation by noting the need to protect women "from the greed as well as the passion of man."[31]

Although mostly motivated out of sincere concern, this legislation nevertheless limited women's economic choices and hindered their ability to earn a living; it took control over their employment out of their hands, raising the perpetually vexed question of whether women were competent decision makers. And in terms of what it said about women's virtue, much of the discussion surrounding these laws and similar efforts to protect women from being kidnapped into "white slavery" seemed to be of two minds. Had women fallen into immorality because of their environment, their long hours and low wages grinding them down to the point where they could no longer distinguish right from wrong? Or did some inner depravity, maybe a desire for a life of luxury, explain their life of sin?[32]

This was the cultural backdrop for office women's labor, and it led some reformers to argue that office women needed to be protected from workplace dangers. For example, an Ohio women's group, the Anti-Women Stenographers' Society, devoted its efforts to persuading parents not to let their daughters enter the profession. Gathering evidence from courts around the country, they determined that, in a ten-year span, wives had filed 6,263 divorce petitions naming their husbands' stenographers as co-respondents. In the same period, stenographers had filed almost eight hundred "breach of promise" suits against their employers, many testifying in open court that before their "disgrace" the men had promised marriage. While the Society seemed undecided as to whether office women were vamps or victims, they were clear that stenography was a morally dangerous occupation.[33]

Advice givers who deemed office women responsible for caring for themselves were responding to and countering such pronouncements: if women controlled men's behavior, then there was no need to restrict their employment. Some women office workers similarly asserted their independence in the face of comments about their moral jeopardy. They were neither victims nor vamps, both of which roles suggested something less than a fully developed human being, one in her vulnerability, the other in her depravity. These women's spirited replies sent the message that they were in their rightful place. In vocally denouncing reformers' efforts to help, they also distanced themselves from the working-class women who were the primary focus of reform efforts. Silence in the face of an unwanted or coercive overture protected an individual woman's reputation, but when an office worker made a public declaration that she had not been the target of insults, it enhanced the reputation of female office workers as a group, suggesting that they needed no legislation to shield them from harm.[34]

Before we turn to these rejoinders, it is useful to consider these women's claim. Was the white-collar office largely free of sexual peril, and were women easily able to handle what danger there was? It is impossible to answer this question with any certainty, but we can use the existing scraps of evidence at least to outline an answer. As we have seen, even advocates for female office clerks acknowledged that women sometimes found themselves with a boss who just wouldn't take no for an answer, suggesting these situations were not uncommon. We know, too, that the middle-class ideal of passionlessness, still lingering in the early twentieth century and making the discussion of sexual issues taboo, kept at least some women from talking about harassing and exploitative behaviors. In the late 1910s, for example, a stenographer in St. Louis quit her new job on the very first day because her employer kissed her and said "very insulting things." She confided her story to an employment counselor, who promised to keep it a secret because the stenographer's mother did not want their name linked to something so sordid. In addition, the repercussions of admitting that something happened could be just as bad as the event itself. A study of working girls from 1913 included the account of an office worker who was fired when she refused to have dinner with her boss. Her friend warned her not to mention the incident at her job interviews since it would bring on "suspicion" and only get her "credit for having tried to lead a perfectly good gentleman astray."[35]

Yet it is possible that office workers did receive fewer insults than, say, immigrant factory workers or black domestics whose place on the bottom of the economic and social hierarchy increased their vulnerability. Historians have found much evidence of unwelcome suggestions and coercive demands directed at these groups (though, in the case of factory girls, this might merely reflect middle-class reformers' concern with this population). Nevertheless, some female clerical workers might have had more economic options, perhaps a larger pool of family and friends from whom they could seek assistance when faced with an untenable situation. And perhaps class-based expectations served as a check on many men's behavior. Maybe most businessmen really were "gentlemen" who, though they might test a woman, would never use their position of power to force her, unlike the "coarse" working-class men who supervised factory girls. This was certainly the cultural assumption, and it might have led honorable men to keep an eye on their less principled brethren.[36]

This supposition at least partially explains why some social reformers believed office workers faced fewer temptations than workers in other occupations. A 1905 reform-minded, semiautobiographical novel of working life presented an office job as the pinnacle of female employment. Factories, workshops, and even stores were "recruiting-grounds for . . . 'red-light' districts," but offices were not. A study from 1913 noted that white-collar work required at least some high school education, wages were often higher, and the office itself was "a refined environment." And although some office men were "a little too human," they were "not so intentionally unscrupulous" as in the case of many retail establishments. Writing about the risk of prostitution to working-class girls, Jane Addams named the department store as the place "more than anywhere else that every possible weakness in a girl is detected and traded upon." Every purchaser was welcome if he had money to spend, and the beautiful trinkets for sale created desires that could not be fulfilled on a salesgirls' salary. Office girls, she noted, faced their own perils, especially when they enjoyed an almost social relationship with their employer and coworkers. In general, however, a "careful code of conduct" was developing among competent businesswomen, who held their female coworkers to the same high standard.[37]

In this distinction between office women and other laboring women we see a primary reason why white-collar women might have denied or downplayed the existence of moral danger. Office work was middle-class work fit for white "ladies." To acknowledge that white-collar men often failed to behave as "gentlemen" would diminish the job's status. It would call into question a woman's virtue and her social standing. This is what happened to department store girls in 1913, when the Illinois Senate Vice Commission examined the connection between low wages and their alleged immorality. Newspapers around the country covered the hearings, but these reports had the unintended effect of casting doubt on the morals of *all* shopgirls, which led unscrupulous men to seek them out.[38]

A few years earlier, the International Ladies' Garment Workers Union and the Women's Trade Union League had publicized immoral conditions in garment factories in their efforts to improve working conditions. The labor activist Clara Lemlich, for example, derided shop bosses, who were "hardly what you would call educated men," for the ugly names they hurled at women. During the Cleveland strike in 1911, such publicity generated public support for the strikers; no foreman should be permitted to compel a woman "to sacrifice her womanhood in order to secure an advance in wages," one newspaper declared. Women strikers across the country called for an end to abusive and insulting language and to preferential treatment in return for sexual favors. In making these demands, Jewish and Italian immigrant factory workers consciously claimed an identity as "ladies." As the historian Nan Enstad notes, "Women did not coin a term for the offensive behaviors they fought against; rather, they created terms for themselves that indicated how they demanded to be treated." With interest focused on all workingwomen's morality, and with working-class, immigrant women dressing like "ladies" and asserting they were such, middle-class office women might have felt especially compelled to assert the difference between their work environments and those of other women.[39]

REJECTING VICTIMHOOD: MIDDLE-CLASS WOMEN AND SEXUAL SELFHOOD

Two incidents around the turn of the twentieth century allow us to examine how some office women responded to claims that their workspaces were morally suspect. The first occurred in 1900, when Len G. Broughton, the evangelical pastor of Atlanta's Tabernacle Baptist Church, traveled to Brooklyn for a series of revivals. While speaking to a male-only audience at the YMCA, Broughton declared, "Nine-tenths of the stenographers' diplomas are but so many licenses to a life of lewdness. I'd rather put a through passport to hell direct in a young woman's hands than that certificate which admits her to the upper office of her employer, behind closed doors." He personally knew many Atlanta businessmen who could not hire women because of their bad reputations. He knew others, ranked among Atlanta's leaders, whose stenographers had quit because of "improper and ungentlemanly advances." Every "thinking man and woman," Broughton argued, knew that there were "scoundrels . . . whose business it is to wreck purity." Although Broughton maintained that his statement was an indictment of disreputable businessmen and not an assault on the honor of office women as a class, female office workers and their supporters saw his words as an "undisguised and outrageous attack" upon office women's character.[40]

Within days, they had launched a vigorous defense of female clerks' virtue. In New York commentators used Broughton's outsider status to dismiss his views. He "seems to forget he is not dealing with the colored race of the South," one noted; women who worked in offices were of "a higher type of intellectual development." The *New York Times* mocked Broughton by suggesting a plan under which all private offices would have peepholes through which inspectors wearing noiseless footgear could observe the goings-on. In Atlanta debate was even more intense because Broughton had based his comments on his experience there. Miss Ware, an attractive stenographer with a "refined, sensible face," contacted the *Atlanta Constitution* to voice her indignation, even though she disliked such attention. In her eyes, Broughton's remarks painted all stenographers as "vicious and impure," their unholy destination marked out with "no escape, no turning back." In her opinion, such a reputation could turn the stenographer who lacked a good home, a mother, friends, and knowledge of Christ away from the path of virtue. Such a woman's "pride of character" had probably kept her pure up to this point, but with Broughton's proclamation that all stenographers were "vile and unpure," what would be the use of making the effort? In suggesting that a discouraged and lonely woman could give in to temptation, Ware acknowledged a crack in women's virtue that others were loath to concede. But Ware was also quite specific about the type of woman who was vulnerable: one who was desperately poor, completely alone, and without religion to guard her.

By contrast, the "ninety and nine" who were pure were also "intelligent, refined, cultivated, sensible in [their] views of everything."[41]

In responding to Broughton and in other discussions of women as victims, we see many stenographers vigorously reject the implication of victimhood: that women were weak. Truly virtuous women were virtuous, they argued, regardless of the temptation; to suggest that a woman was in danger was to question her virtue. To the mind of these protesters, a man like Broughton who said he was trying to help women was just as bad as the man who insulted them. In describing office women who were not at risk, these office workers created an ideal of the office woman, one who, not surprisingly, had the qualities associated with a middle-class upbringing that protected her in any environment. Such was the position of "Miss H," who agreed with Broughton's description of lustful businessmen but did not believe the office was dangerous. Whether or not such men would succeed in their seduction depended upon the woman. No woman should enter the stenographic profession unless she was "strong morally, mentally, and physically; unless she has a power higher than herself to depend upon; unless she has firmly instilled into her heart, mind and soul a clear and distinct line between right and wrong . . . unless she has about her that modesty, reserve and dignity essential to a 'womanly woman.' And unless she has practical common sense and a good English education." This woman could be "trusted in any office in the universe, and leave it as pure at heart as when she entered." By contrast, the only woman Miss H knew of who had "fallen" was "weak in every way, with an unhappy home, and no Christian training or influence to help her." This background was decidedly not that of the majority of the stenographers she knew; they were from "the best families in the state."[42]

In 1907 stenographers again asserted their autonomy when the Reverend Geer of St. Paul's Church in downtown Manhattan announced his plan to open an inexpensive lunchroom to save "girls of refinement" from eating lunch at their office, which was an "environment . . . deleterious to their moral welfare." With a lunch club of their own, women could avoid the temptations and flirtations that occurred in an idle business office. Geer also planned to hire lawyers to defend and protect women whose employers were overly familiar or "lacking in courtesy." In such a case, the man would be approached and "possibly brought to the bar of justice." Despite these lamentations, Geer took pains not to overstate his case. Many of the young women were "like kittens—playful and naturally affectionate," and he was sympathetic toward the man who had recently told him, "You don't know what temptations we business men are subjected to."[43]

As in Atlanta, Geer's pessimism about the morals of white-collar men and women aroused indignation. Some stenographers denied they needed to be rescued or reformed. They also disputed the perspective of two "victims" who had written letters to Geer endorsing his plan. The first came from a woman with five years of office experience who had come to expect "improper proposals . . . as a matter of course." The second asserted, "Not one business man in five is a fit character for a young girl ignorant of the ways of the world to associate with." In response, an office worker with eight years of experience replied that she and her friends had never been insulted. She found it "humiliating" to be told that she held her job "more or less . . . at the cost of self-respect"; office women did "not need protection from the wiles and snares of employers and men clerks." The problem, she agreed, was the "kittenish" girl, who had no business in an office and probably imagined the "discourtesy" or brought it upon herself. According to another stenographer, the "average . . . sensible" woman who acted in a businesslike way was as safe in the office as in her own drawing room. A true woman could command respect anywhere, whether in a mining camp or in a business office.[44]

Soon after Geer announced his plan, the *New York Times* interviewed businessmen and heads of employment agencies to get their perspective. Though some acknowledged a few "black sheep in the fold," many denied any danger or declared that there were fewer in offices than elsewhere. There were "men who are not unwilling to take advantage of their long hours together to make an impression," a businessman interested in social problems stated, but few "would be mean enough to make any use of their position as employers or would care for favors gained on such a score." If there was any immoral behavior, he continued, it was the girl's fault, though he did not like to have to say so. "A sensible man," he continued, "keeps his business and his social recreations separated." An employment agency manager agreed: "If there is anything wrong, the girls themselves are to blame." The *Times*, in this article and in an editorial the next day, confirmed this view. "It all depends a whole lot on the woman. We do not like to dwell on that fact, but fact it is."[45]

Given this tendency to paint women as the problem, it is easy to understand those stenographers who denied or downplayed unwanted advances as protecting and asserting their honor. They and their friends received no insulting proposals because their businesslike and womanly behavior generated the respect of the men with whom they worked. Geer himself wavered on women's culpability, and the *New York Times* and the many men interviewed for its article held women accountable for any unwanted attention they received. Such comments suggest that at least for middle-class women who worked in offices for wages, the popular veneration of female passionlessness and superior morality had not surpassed an older distrust of female sexuality. In this context, issuing a strong denial was the only feasible strategy to maintain your reputation. And in rejecting offers of protection and insisting that "sensible" women could "cope with any man," some office women also carved out for themselves a place of independence and self-definition. The women who maintained that they had not encountered any challenges to their virtue denied the legitimacy of labels such as vamp, victim, or vixen that continually swirled around their occupation and around workingwomen more generally. They could protect themselves and did not need the help of reformers, ministers, or men. Such assertions declared women's autonomy and moral integrity while protecting their class status and their place in the workforce.

This is not to say that this strategy was completely effective or empowering. *Declaring* that a "womanly woman" would not be insulted and could easily handle the rare man who trespassed did not necessarily stop insults or trespasses. Embracing a gender ideology stipulating that gentlemen respected ladies could only go so far in controlling men's behavior, given the corresponding belief in men's carnal essence. Furthermore, these women framed unwanted or coercive sexual attentions as a problem involving individuals—more specifically, a problem involving an individual woman's character—and not an issue that was connected to the structural inequalities and vulnerabilities facing workingwomen as a whole. These women did not acknowledge the possibility that mitigating factors, such as a woman's financial need to keep her job, could play into a woman's "consent," rendering it more complicated than a genuinely free choice.[46]

Emphasizing women's ability both to make their own moral decisions and to see them through meant that women were both on their own and limited in their response when they did encounter improper proposals or behavior. In the 1910s a St. Louis real estate agent forcibly kissed his seventeen-year-old stenographer and then placed his hand between her legs, stopping only when someone entered the office. He fired her later that day. When she told her mother what had happened, the mother went to the district attorney, only to be given the runaround. Her daughter's word, she soon realized, was not enough for anyone to take the charge seriously, and she dropped the matter. In this example, we see how constructing the problem as one between individuals—as opposed to a social problem affecting office women as a group—put women at a disadvantage: the word of a young girl was no match for a businessman's. Women's public denials of unwelcome and harassing behaviors also might have increased the likelihood that a woman who experienced unwanted attentions would feel ashamed because of the perception that it was in some way her fault. One woman was still mortified many years after an older coworker had repeatedly hugged her. Even after he no longer worked at her office, she worried that people considered her immoral. Finally, the independence women claimed came at the price of carefully monitoring—even denying—their sexuality.[47]

But if speaking out too loudly was as likely to cast aspersions on the woman's character as on the man's, the gains of denial probably outweighed these numerous drawbacks. Such a perspective is supported by the efforts of women garment workers to draw attention to immoral behavior in factories. Although exposing these behaviors sometimes garnered public support for strikers, at other times such disclosure actually worked against the women. In the small city of Kalamazoo, Michigan, citizens perceived union organizers who discussed such issues "as being hysterical and lacking in refinement and tact." Highlighting difference or portraying women as victims could further relegate women to a lesser public role than men enjoyed.[48]

STANDING UP TO MEN: TOWARD A PERFECT FUTURE

Concerns about sexual interactions in the office were connected to a host of turn-of-the-century anxieties, most especially those having to do with women's changing behaviors. But while reformers were working to pass laws to protect women from moral danger in the here and now, at least one woman, Ella Wheeler Wilcox, was thinking about the issue in spiritual terms and contemplating how women's responses to "unsolicited" advances could change men for the future. Wilcox was a popular poet and journalist who rose to fame in the late 1880s. Although she never received any critical acclaim, Wilcox's writings enjoyed a large audience through the mid-1910s. In the late nineteenth century, in both her prose collections on relations between the sexes and a syndicated newspaper column, she addressed the situation of workingwomen, applying the principles of New Thought, a spiritual movement that explored the boundaries between mind and matter and was popular from around 1880 to World War I. Wilcox's ideas were an important counter to the dominant discourse, both urging female action and offering an incipient critique of masculinity.[49]

Over and over, Wilcox stated that virtually all men repeatedly subjected their female employees to uninvited attentions, and she also rejected the widespread conviction that "no girl is ever insulted . . . unless she first commits some indiscretion of deportment, dress, or speech." According to Wilcox, that view was perpetuated by the rare woman who had never been approached, because there is "nothing in life the average woman so much resents as having other women offered temptations which she has never known." Wilcox was adamant that a woman should never give in to men's enticements, regardless of how desperately she needed a job. She also reminded her readers that men's overtures were never a tribute to their beauty or charm, but happened to "thousands of girls all over the civilized world." As to the men, they were not especially immoral, but they were "self-indulgent" because society—and women—allowed them to be.[50]

Wilcox's explanation of men's behavior fit into the century-old debate over what qualities—male desire, competitiveness, and rationality, or female virtue, altruism, and spirituality—would lead to social progress. This question was most evident in women's turn-of-the-century efforts for reform and political rights; many suffragists, for example, argued that the introduction of women voters would purify politics, replacing greedy self-interest with humane consideration and thereby restoring order to the Republic. Shadows of this debate were also apparent in arguments made in support of female office workers, which suggested that their presence would serve as a check on men's less civilized behaviors and thereby benefit the workplace and the public sphere as a whole.[51]

Examining the relative merits of male desire and female virtue was also a focus of those involved in New Thought. The movement attracted individuals, especially women, who believed in the power of unseen spirit and concentrated thought to change their lives and the world. A number of women's rights activists were involved, finding in New Thought's principles validation for their life choices: if a woman felt in her soul that her life and body were hers to control, then her activist efforts were appropriate even if they challenged gender roles and the social order. Most New Thought participants saw men's lustful, competitive desires as a destructive force, leading to unethical business practices in the public world and disharmony in the private sphere. Their answer was for both sexes to aspire to the ideal of sexual purity and compassionate reason that characterized middle-class womanhood. The majority also embraced evolution as evidence that humanity could advance, that the future could be one of harmony and cooperation, not conflict and competition.[52]

Wilcox's analysis of unwanted and hostile sexual behaviors in the office reflected this faith in the superiority of the female perspective, as did her advice on how women should respond. She laid out her theory in reply to the letter of a self-supporting teenager, who had approached several Wall Street businessmen about clerical work. Each offered her a job at a good salary but took back the offer when he learned that she would not "answer [his] requirements outside of the business line." Finally she took a position with a man who saw that she was a good, honest girl, but he nevertheless soon caused her downfall. After two months, he fired her because he wanted a new face in his office. "Pity the working girl who is cursed with beauty and a fine form," the girl concluded.

Wilcox acknowledged that the girl's experience was unjust, but she believed that these situations provided women with a unique opportunity to help advance the cause of humanity. Men were now more civilized than they had been centuries before when they used "to kidnap and carry off to castles or dungeons a young woman who resisted their blandishments," but they still had a long way to go. A woman's carefully reasoned rejection of an offer of worldly progress in return for a sexual favor could be a chance to take a step forward. It would do no good for a woman to get mad or launch into a sermon, Wilcox reasoned. However, if the woman thought of herself as a sort of "kindergarten teacher," she could give the man a "lesson in the beauty of self-control," and he would most likely stop insulting women. If he did, this newfound respect for women could be passed on to his children, at least according to the then dominant theory of Lamarckian evolution, which believed in the heritability of acquired characteristics. A woman should not, then, "become bitter or pessimistic as a 'man hater' because of these experiences," but rather see them as her contribution toward a more enlightened future.[53]

New Thought offered an optimistic way to view the world, but many critics charged that it was escapist, allowing for a cheerful denial of very real injustices. Someone who focused only on thinking positive thoughts might not see a need to work for social change. In fact, some women's rights activists leveled this complaint at Wilcox. While seeing her as an inspiring role model, they lamented that she would not fight for suffrage or use her popularity to speak out directly for women's rights. Certainly this critique applies to Wilcox's advice on how to respond to unwanted and exploitative sexual attentions. She presented these behaviors as simply one stage in evolution's long journey and characterized progress in the present moment in terms of the direct interaction between one man and one woman. Insults and unsolicited propositions would someday disappear, but a woman would see little difference in her life-time. In the meantime, the sufferings women endured further purified their souls.[54]

Despite these limitations, Wilcox brought attention to the very real problems white-collar women faced. Quite possibly her writings made some readers more sympathetic to workingwomen, especially those who had given in to their employer's demands. Perhaps her numerous articles provided solace to women who had been insulted. And, although Wilcox did not call for organized reform, her analysis did blame men for their actions and, in a gender critique that suggests the future, saw masculinity itself as a negative force, problematic for women and society. The significance of this broader critique can be understood best by comparing it to other arguments in this period made against "trifling" with pretty type-writers, which often made narrow and self-interested appeals. Noting that many female office workers were young, middle-class ladies compelled to labor after the loss of a male breadwinner, authors called on an employer to imagine his typewriter as his "own dear child." Life was uncertain. Could a man be sure that his "sins" against his office girl would be forgiven, or might "revenge" one day be visited on his own innocent daughter forced to earn her own bread? Wilcox, by contrast, held men to a higher standard—to the standard of female virtue—and urged individual women to confront those men who fell short. Wilcox's writings on this topic seem to have stopped shortly after the new century began, and New Thought shifted focus as well, becoming a sort of gospel of success, an emphasis less connected to women's workplace worries.[55]

INDIVIDUAL RESPONSES TO HARASSMENT AND BETRAYAL

Some women, not content with making the future a better place, refused to let men's actions determine their lives. Some of the women we will meet in this section encountered unwelcome behaviors, and their varied reactions remind us that experience is subjective. Their stories also highlight women's limited options when faced with unwanted attentions. Other women were involved in consensual relationships that went wrong, and they used the law to achieve justice when employers exploited their affections.

One woman's experience from 1889 tells us both about the types of insulting behaviors women received when they transgressed their "appropriate" sphere and how some women created new behavioral standards fitting for their new ambitions. An article in a professional stenography journal profiled an unnamed woman who started her own typewriting business and through gumption and hard work became successful in a very short time. In order to build up a clientele, she went around to law offices and introduced herself, sometimes with a letter of introduction and sometimes without. Such assertive behavior clearly violated gender roles. It showed masculine initiative and ignored the social rule that a lady should not speak to a man to whom she had not been properly introduced. Her actions, then, left her open to insults. An older, distinguished-looking man took the opportunity to test her moral boundaries, peppering their conversation with personal questions and inappropriate comments. Finally, he threw her a kiss and suggestively told her he would come to her office very soon. These actions clearly suggested that he questioned her character, and they deserved a scornful, "Sir, how dare you!" But rather than getting angry or offended, she politely smiled and returned the conversation to business. She was determined to succeed, and, though she found his behavior annoying, his attempts to be familiar posed no real danger. By locating the fine line between denouncing and permitting these improper attentions, she was able to flatter him and gain his account, while making him understand, both then and afterward, that she meant business.[56]

This woman made a conscious choice to tolerate challenges to her honor in exchange for a chance to achieve her goals. But her gutsy story also challenged the views of the journal in which it appeared. In 1890 the publication warned that women's wage earning had brought "a perversion of freedom and an independence and boldness not becoming her sex." The typewriter also rejected the wisdom offered by advice givers. While they cautioned women not to be overly sensitive to a man's accidental and temporary "trespass," they nevertheless urged women to "resent instantly" any "disrespectful conduct" and to seek another position immediately once it was clear that a job was "unfit for any woman with an atom of self-respect"—even if it meant lower wages. It seems likely that advice givers would have counseled this typewriter to cease all contact with the overly friendly older man. In rejecting their advice, she defined her own standard of female honor and took personal responsibility for defending it.[57]

Historical evidence is scant and inconclusive for women's recourse to the law, but a few cases give a glimpse into the range of options available to women for redress. In Brooklyn in 1893, Frances Viola James, twenty-three, filed a misdemeanor charge against her former employer, William Tyrer, thirty-eight, for sending a postcard "of a nature tending to annoy and persecute her." James had worked as Tyrer's typewriter for three and half years. During that time, she stated, his attentions were "quite obnoxious," and she repeatedly had told him to stop. Undeterred, "he fell on his knees . . . and said that something very terrible would happen if she did not marry him." Shortly after, she quit and began to work elsewhere. Tyrer allegedly sent many postcards to her new work address "threatening her." These cards, she maintained, endangered her new position, though it is unclear exactly how. It is likely that they were numerous enough to call attention to her, and certainly the subject matter was potentially scandalous, casting a shadow on her reputation and making her far from an ideal employee for a respectable business. No doubt they also distracted her. For his part, Tyrer declared the charges "ridiculous" and noted that he would "not marry her if she had a million dollars." There is no record of how this case was resolved.[58]

It was unusual enough, though, to elicit comment from the local newspaper, which published an editorial about the case, "Independence of Women," describing the young woman's charges as a response to a failed courtship. James was evidence of a new kind of woman, one whose employment had emancipated her from the domestic imperative. With the ability to support themselves, typewriters could choose when and whether to get married and no longer had to listen to the "nonsense which wooers have poured into their ears." This case, the newspaper argued, should set to rest the myth that men married their typewriters "because of the arts which the latter have employed to entrap them into matrimony."[59]

There are a number of assumptions about gender embedded in this editorial. First, it assumes that Tyrer is a gentleman, if a persistently annoying one. There is no suggestion that he made any dishonorable or coercive request and no mention of the unspecified threats. Second, though the editorial seems relatively positive about women's new place in the white-collar labor force, it stops short of a full recognition of women's right (or need) to work. The piece focuses on changes in courtship brought on by women's employment and increased economic independence. Yet there is no comment on how Tyrer's actions endangered James's ability to earn a living. We can imagine that her job was, at the very least, unpleasant as she warded off his advances. And ultimately she felt compelled to leave. To take the unusual step of bringing charges against him, James must have thought her economic livelihood was at risk, or perhaps her safety or reputation.

James's case exposes the limits of the existing legal statutes to help women when faced with unwanted and persistent behaviors. Though Tyrer allegedly bombarded James with annoying letters, her case addressed only the particulars of one letter sent through the mail. The extant evidence does not provide us with details on the specifics of the charge (only that, if convicted, he could have received up to a year in prison) or allow us to make any definitive statement about why charges were based on this letter and not others. Possibly this threat was more explicit, violating postal regulations by intimating physical harm. There is no mention of Tyrer physically following James, though even if he was, there would have been nothing she could do: antistalking laws would not appear for another hundred years.[60]

By 1909 women had worked in offices long enough that relationships between men and women in at least some involved obvious flirtations and provocative conversations. Not all women liked this informality, however, as the story of Mary Fisher, a onetime Radcliffe student, makes clear. When she made her displeasure known, she aroused her male coworkers' wrath. Fisher had been hired as a stenographer in the office of Boston's health department, but was suspended after eight months. She believed her suspension was unjust, the result of her refusal to submit to her male colleagues' excessive familiarity or to listen to their racy remarks. She decided to turn her diary over to the mayor, and newspapers eagerly reprinted its salacious details.[61]

One male clerk exposed her "by innuendo and suggestion" to the "foulest insults," talked of "personal matters of the most objectionable character," and threatened to subject her to the "indignity of being embraced by him." When she "strenuously objected," he felt insulted. It is clear that Fisher did not want or in any way solicit this clerk's attentions. Yet to look at it from his perspective, no harm had been done, since, as Fisher noted (disdainfully) in her diary, "hugging bees" were common and other women enjoyed them. The clerk might have been just playing around, or he might have been playfully expressing his attraction. In either case, it is easy to imagine that he was both embarrassed and angered by Fisher's visible distaste. He also might have thought she was playing hard to get. Much of the conversation Fisher found offensive was about courtship and assumed that all unmarried office women were looking for a husband—a common and largely accurate assumption. In fact, even Fisher might have had a beau: she seemed not to mind one man's frequent visits to her desk. What she did mind was when a few of her male coworkers came up and teased her about it in his presence. When she later asked one of them not to make such remarks again, he replied that the man was a "splendid catch." When she retorted that her private life was none of his business, he, too, felt insulted.

Fisher was offended by her male and female coworkers' personal comments and scandalous discussions, but it seems that at least initially such attentions were made in a friendly way, an overture to the new girl. The sections of her diary published in the newspaper were not dated. Assuming that they appeared in the order in which they were written, it is possible to perceive a shift, a progression from inclusion to persecution, as she rejected her coworkers' overtures and made known her outrage at their lack of "propriety." From making a teasing remark about a man she might like, the men in her office advanced to forcing her to look at pictures of women provocatively dressed in nightgowns. Fisher had incurred their ire, and some seemed determined to make her pay for refusing, in her words, to be brought "down to their level." "Their level" also might have referred to their social class. Boston's clerical sector included large numbers of working-class men and women who might have found the Radcliffe girl's obvious disgust as infuriating—and as worthy of retaliation—as she found their behavior. Class as well as gender politics were likely at play in making the health department an unhealthful environment.[62]

Unwanted and hostile sexual or romantic overtures were a part of office life, but consensual relationships also developed and led to happy lifelong unions—or not. In situations in which a woman felt romantically and/or sexually betrayed by her employer, "heart balm" tort laws, especially those addressing the breach of promise to marry, offered a remedy. These torts, which also included seduction and alienation of affection, originated in English common law and evolved over time to reflect the democratic understanding of marriage that developed after the American Revolution. Seduction and breach of promise, in particular, were premised on the notion that virtuous women needed protection from duplicitous men in the open market of courtship. A breach of promise lawsuit allowed a person to sue for damages when another person failed to fulfill an agreement to marry. For women, the damages sought were generally not for direct losses, such as the expense of a wedding dress, but for more intangible costs, such as the humiliation associated with being jilted. In validating such damage claims, courts acknowledged women's economic vulnerability. Women had limited means to support themselves, and a soiled reputation jeopardized a woman's marital chances.[63]

A lawsuit from 1911 appears to describe a straightforward instance of a man misleading a woman as to his intentions. A jury in a small town in Oklahoma awarded a stenographer thirty thousand dollars, half of the worth of her former employer, a prominent attorney. Breach of promise was about marriage, but the newspaper focused instead on the woman's claim that when she was first hired, her boss "enjoyed no prestige," and that it was "through her efforts that he became successful and accumulated a fortune." The jury was out just long enough to write the verdict in her favor. This newspaper account is quite brief—virtually no details of the relationship are included, and there is no way to assess whether the stenographer's claims were true—but its brevity makes its message all the more clear: this woman, in the eyes of the jury and the newspaper, had been betrayed.[64]

In New Jersey that same year, Emma Milani, another stenographer who worked in a small office with an attorney, brought a breach of promise suit against her former employer William Delorenzo. Delorenzo admitted that he loved Milani, but he denied that he had proposed to her. How could he have? he argued. He had also been in love with another woman, whom he had married. Milani produced a packet of poems filled with "words of warm love" to support her claim, and the jury awarded her the sizeable sum of five thousand dollars. The newspapers' "he said, she said" coverage limits our ability to ferret out what really happened, though the *Washington Post*'s placement of the story above an article entitled "Police Crusade on Mashers" might suggest that the paper saw it as a case of male exploitation.[65]

Tort law also offered a few options for women who experienced unwanted sexual advances, though it is not clear that white-collar women utilized these options. A woman had no legal recourse when an employer or coworker propositioned her—though she might have been insulted, in the eyes of the law, there was "no harm in asking." When someone verbally impugned a woman's chastity to or in front of others, however, the law offered a remedy: sexual slander. Only a woman could bring this suit, which assumed a chaste reputation was a woman's prize possession; if it was impugned, a woman could suffer tangible losses. Judges proved sympathetic to plaintiffs most of the time, and at the turn of the century, teachers, in particular, used this remedy; rumors of immorality could especially damage the professional opportunities of a woman who worked with children. By this time, too, women in some states were able to recover damages for indecent assault and seduction on their own behalf (as opposed to the compensation, as was historically the case, of a father for damage to his property, such as when an unmarried daughter became pregnant). In the case of assault, a woman needed substantial evidence of her physical resistance. In the case of seduction, there were some cases in a few jurisdictions in which the courts accepted that an employer's economic threats had compelled the woman's consent, and she received compensation. Such victories, which acknowledged inequalities of power and included an interpretation of coercion that went beyond physical force, were short-lived; within a few decades, legislatures were working to repeal heart-balm torts.[66]

As the actions of heart-balm plaintiffs and the Radcliffe graduate Mary Fisher make clear, some women refused to remain silent when they felt betrayed, or to take the blame when men insulted them. The office historically had been male space, but these women would not cede control of it to men. Yet even as these women made their female perspective known, sex in the office was destined to become more visible as middle-class, white-collar men began to rely increasingly on sexual exploits as a marker of manliness. Although a variety of printed sources portrayed humiliation or destruction at the hands of a pretty typewriter as a real threat, it is worth remembering that taming that same woman could make a man appear more masterful. For men, we will see, acting on desire entailed risks, but also gains.

Moreover, women who held to Fisher's Victorian standards of morality would increasingly find themselves mocked as old-fashioned. In 1915 efforts to protect office women again made the papers when the Boston clubwoman Charlotte Smith demanded a law requiring that any man who had a stenographer in his office must have a wire cage surrounding her. As in the past, female clerical workers rejected this plan to protect them, but their dismissals were strikingly glib: "Don't Make a Monkey of Me," one joked. Another offered her thoughts on the sexual dangers of the workplace: "There is more noise than anything else to a lot of this kind of talk. . . . To my mind, it is an individual problem and one that could be helped by no uplift movement. The girl usually is to blame. Let her work out her own problem." Even a member of Smith's club rejected the idea: If wives gave "their husbands a little more affection no wire cages would be needed."[67]

By 1915 most of the controversy over women's presence in the office had died away, and more young, middle-class women were relaxing their sexual boundaries; the response to caging stenographers seemed to reflect these changes. But if the earlier focus on women's virtue pushed discussions of male power into the background, where they could only faintly be heard, there was in the controversy over the cage virtually no acknowledgement of the occasional "black sheep." Rather, the lecherous boss was simply an "amusing movie myth." During business hours, one stenographer maintained, men wanted only to make money. Gone, too, was the former emphasis on men's and women's character. Women's responsibility for managing sexual interaction continued, but there was no corresponding assumption that a "gentleman" would naturally "respect" a virtuous woman. The idea that the office workplace was morally dangerous for women was quickly vanishing, even as women (as workers or wives) increasingly bore the blame for men's sexual transgressions, and, as individual women on their own, handled unwanted or coercive attentions.[68]

CHAPTER TWO

White-Collar Casanovas

GENDER, CLASS, AND (HETERO)SEXUALITY IN THE OFFICE, 1861 TO WORLD WAR II

IN 1889 J. EDGAR ENGLE, A SUPERVISOR in the U.S. government's Pension Bureau, turned to William T. Ford, another supervisor, and, drawing his attention to one of the women clerks, declared his eagerness to "have a piece of that." According to Ford, Engle ultimately succeeded in seducing the virtuous girl and then bragged about it. Ford, an attractive man of fifty-five, told this story to a congressional committee, which was investigating accusations of immorality in the bureau, and it is possible that this story was untrue, an effort to get Engle in trouble. Ford, meanwhile, had troubles of his own. A clerk had accused him of suggestively asking her to be his "friend" and of demoting her when she refused. He denied the charge, accusing her of misunderstanding an innocent remark and his enemies of using this conversation to get him fired. Testimony also elicited that Ford and another man had "quite a rivalry . . . for the admiration of the ladies" in the office.[1]

By the late nineteenth century, women were an important part of the white-collar world as workers and, as this testimony makes clear, as objects that could be used in various ways to further men's ends. A sexual comment became a moment of male camaraderie, a chance for men to assert their difference from women even as more female clerks entered their workspace. A competition for women's attentions also offered an opportunity to distinguish oneself from other men.

And finally, an allegation of immorality could derail an enemy's ambitions.

In particular, women's presence facilitated a new understanding of white-collar masculinity, one that was firmly in place by the end of the 1930s and encouraged expressions of (hetero)sexuality in the workplace. As social and economic changes, such as the rise of corporate capitalism and the Great Depression, made it hard for white-collar men to attain established badges of importance, some men used sexual behaviors to claim a type of manly success when more conventional markers of achievement were beyond their reach. For men whose professional accomplishments needed no bolstering, sex could be used to set oneself apart further, one's erotic exploits signaling a level of autonomy such that ordinary moral and social restrictions need not be followed. For men on the bottom of the ladder of success, the opposite was true. Their limited access to women, represented by both their subordinate position in the office ranks, which placed them next to women but with no power over them, and their inability to earn a wage sufficient to marry and claim a woman as their own, indicated their inadequacy as men. The sexualization of the white-collar workplace blurred long-standing distinctions between public and private spheres, professional and personal behaviors. Sex, in countless new ways, became a part of men's business as usual.[2]

FORGING A NEW MIDDLE-CLASS MANHOOD

Evolving understandings of manhood began to appear in the second half of the nineteenth century, as a quick glance at government employment makes clear. Male clerks were typically apologetic and defensive about their public-sector jobs, which signaled an unmanly dependency and a limited ambition at odds with the competitive opportunity of, say, a business proprietor. These men's labor produced no goods and made no money, and the relatively static nature of a salaried position also seemed incompatible with the relentless drive for mobility that characterized the individualist ideal. In 1889 the *Washington Post* queried male federal clerks about their job satisfaction, and the majority disparaged the work. A government man "never amount[ed] to anything," said one, while another believed that the work was suitable only for those who lacked "the American go-ahead spirit." As the one woman interviewed stated, "I would not like to have my daughters marry men in Government employ."

The system of patronage added another dimension. For some men, political patronage displayed their social and political ties to other men and showed that they mattered. Others, however, resented what they saw as the supplication needed to land a job or to advance, a view shared by civil service reformers who, in their efforts to institute a meritocracy, decried the emasculating effects of the spoils system.[3]

Women's presence in the federal workforce also compromised government workers' manliness, despite differences in the way they were treated. The Treasury Department first hired women in 1861 to clip and count currency. Men had not previously performed this job, which made the hiring of women less controversial: from the beginning, it could be dubbed "women's work." This also made it easier to justify paying them half of what the lowliest male clerk earned. Women were cheap, a fact not lost on officials, and they were soon working in other federal agencies, supervised by and sometimes alongside men. Even when women performed the same tasks as men, however, they were paid less and generally denied promotions. These women were members of the middle class, who, for one reason or another, needed a job.[4]

Only three years after women entered the Treasury Department, a special congressional committee began investigating accusations of fraud and "gross immoralities" there. Male supervisors, witnesses testified, had offered women raises in exchange for sexual favors and had made sexual propositions to others. Miss Weedan accused her boss, Spencer M. Clark, of offering her a bribe of hundreds of dollars for "dishonorable purposes." After she refused, he allegedly told her that he made "a good friend, but a bad enemy." Others, it seemed, consented. In a sworn statement, Jennie Germon maintained that she had spent two nights at Clark's home while his wife was away. Another woman testified that a friend, who also worked for Clark, often came home drunk in the early morning hours after drinking ale in his private office.[5]

The committee's final report disputed the accusation that the Treasury Department had been "converted into a house for orgies and bacchanals" and exonerated Clark. Some of the women had lied, the committee determined, while Weeden's charge boiled down to an unresolvable case of "he said, she said." Not everyone, however, was convinced of Clark's innocence. A minority report alleged that politics had prevented a full investigation into the charges. This faction had evidence that the married, middle-aged Clark had been arrested at a brothel in New York before taking the job in Washington. The majority considered this earlier behavior irrelevant and not subject to investigation, but for the minority, behavior—character—was the only issue. A man who seduced women, an adulterer, a patron of brothels, was not fit for a position of public trust. In this view, the refusal to examine Clark's past suggested that there was no connection between a man's public and private behavior, a position the minority rejected. They chose to believe the women based on evidence of their reputable private lives. Weedan, for example, was now married to a policeman, and her father was a "worthy mechanic."[6]

The minority's position sheds light on the nineteenth century's focus on a man's character (or lack of it), and a man of character behaved the same in both his private and public life. Self-control was central to character, providing the resolve to achieve success, and much of this effort focused on reining in sexual yearnings. For most of the nineteenth century, gentlemen sought to control their carnal desires as a way of distinguishing themselves from the rough working class, which valorized sexual exploits. Parents, doctors, and religious leaders all warned boys to resist their sexual urges if they wanted to become men of character with the strength and drive to succeed. Medical literature argued that the human body had a finite reserve of "nerve energy" and that the reckless or excessive expenditure of semen depleted men's vital force. Giving in to sexual temptation destroyed their will and exhausted the reserves they needed to prosper. Only by defying their sexual drive did men obtain maturity and acquire accolades, but, paradoxically, this defiance confirmed men's essential sexual nature. Indeed, many advice guides from this period talked about the connection between success and self control in highly sexualized language; men needed to manage their "potent spirits" and maintain an "erect character."[7]

Although men were urged to channel their sexual drives into achievement, many "respectable" middle-class men—married and single— rejected the prescriptions for self-control. Brothels, saloons, and gambling dens thrived during this era of character. Prostitution and other forms of commercial sex promoted a sense of male camaraderie that could transcend class differences. Already in the 1830s, some urban bachelors, rich and poor alike, had created a masculine identity around these sexualized leisure pursuits, rejecting the dominant culture's call for a manhood centered on self-restraint, work, and money. Though not banned from polite society, these "sporting men" were nonetheless expected to indulge their baser nature far from middle-class ladies. However, once women entered men's workspace, the possibility emerged that manly sexual expression would no longer need to be confined to the illicit culture of brothels or other sexualized places, but could find a more acceptable outlet in the public world of work. Coercive and consensual encounters certainly became a possibility, but so too did a wide range of sexually charged behaviors that could be infused with new significance.[8]

The experience of Frances Cougle, a federal clerk in Washington from 1882 until her death in 1902, hints at the impact of this virility in the white-collar office. A widow with a young daughter, Cougle had to rely on her own labor—and her family connections—to survive. A descendant of a Revolutionary War hero, Cougle knew many powerful men, whom she enlisted in her effort to secure federal employment. One suggested that her employment could be viewed as the act of "gentlemen" offering a "National tribute to the memory of an old Patriot." But once employed, Cougle found that her supervisor, Mr. Gitt, was no gentleman. According to her, he was "constantly in his shirt sleeves" and told two women that he did not care "whether a woman was a harlot or a virgin if she came and did her work." In fact, Gitt preferred women who were not "ladies." In 1885 Cougle reached her boiling point after "a most deliberate and unprovoked insult was given to every lady" in her office. The insult involved Miss Hamilton, who, after sitting on Gitt's desk one Saturday, left the office early after placing a note on her desk that read, "This lady has gone with my permission. Gitt." Cougle had nothing but "unbounded contempt" for Hamilton and women like her, and promised Gitt that she would contact the influential men she knew if such insults were repeated. She also wrote Gitt's superiors complaining that he showed "gross favouritism, laxity of rules in this connection . . . having women sitting on his desk, and at his feet, detracting from the dignity of his position & the Division." Gitt's supervisors took Cougle's complaint seriously and assigned an investigator to look into her charges. However, after learning of her tendency to name-drop, the investigator determined she was a "crank" and closed the case.[9]

Gitt was a supervisor in a large bureaucracy. He had power over others, but he knew that he was, in turn, under someone else's thumb.

And, of course, any advancement probably required not only doing his job well but also currying someone's favor. In an organization so visibly structured around levels of power, men who supervised women may have used their authority as the base on which to build a new understanding of manhood—especially given that gender limitations ensured that those women would never have power over them. Women's presence in the workplace, a formerly all-male space, performing clerical work that was not appreciably different from men's work, was disturbing: if men treated women as coworkers, it would suggest that they themselves were not so different from the women. When they viewed female workers through the lens of heterosexual desire, though, they could assert their difference. In this respect, Gitt's public and somewhat defiant proclamation that Hamilton was free to go established his authority in two distinct ways: he was in control, and he phrased his control as a favor granted to a pretty woman. Cougle described a man who acted less like a boss evaluating his employees based on the quality of their work than like a man rewarding women according to their feminine qualities. Gitt had transferred the gender relations of the private sphere into the workplace, reaffirming his manliness by replicating the masculine role in social relations.

Other developments also facilitated the development of the white-collar Casanova. By the late nineteenth century, Americans had come to see sexuality as crucial to an individual's sense of self. The increasingly common use of the terms "homosexual" and "heterosexual" in the first quarter of the new century were part of this transition. In the public's mind, homosexuals were "fairies," effeminate men who desired other men, which made heterosexuals manly by default. Given the new importance of sexual identity and the growing visibility of homosexuality, middle-class men's sexual interest in women could serve as the marker of a true man, offsetting countless challenges to their masculinity. Since men increasingly leaned on heterosexuality to prop up their gender, it should be no surprise that expressions of sexual desire for women often appeared in the workplace.[10]

WHITE-COLLAR MASCULINITY AND "SEX AT THE OFFICE" HUMOR

Around 1910 a joke appeared in the *New York Sun*. A businessman in a tall building on Broadway is absentmindedly looking out his office window. His attention is caught when he notices a "remarkably good looking stenographer" bringing in some papers to her boss in an office across the street. Though her boss had been busily working, he stops when she enters, and the observer sees her eagerly sit down on his lap. The observer is outraged and "dying to let them know that some one saw them." He finally notices the name of the business on their window and calls on the telephone. When he sees the boss answer, he shouts, "Take your stenographer off your lap!" But did the boss do it? No, the punch line tells us. Instead, he hung up the phone and pulled down the window shade![11]

The *Sun* was by no means alone in printing jokes about pretty stenographers and passionate employers. Although it would be easy to dismiss these jests as inconsequential, to do so would be to overlook the role sexualized humor played in establishing the dynamic between white-collar men and women. Typewriter girls complained that these flippant remarks were yet another obstacle to overcome in earning their daily bread, the funny stories "slings and arrows" to be endured. For their part, stenography journals urged "thick-headed" humorists to end their jokes "full of coarseness and double *entendre*," which undermined typewriters' reputation. We know much less about how men of this period felt about this humor, though we do know that sexualized representations of office women appeared often enough and in such a variety of media that it is unlikely any white-collar man missed them. Although we cannot know with certainty how such images and jokes factored into these men's daily lives, we can use the scholarship on sexual humor to speculate on how they might have contributed to a white-collar masculinity that included or even required expressions of sexuality in the workplace.[12]

Scholars have identified the basic principles of sexual humor and shown how men in the past and present have used it to create and sustain social bonds *as men*. As Freud first noted, all jokes are aggressive—someone or some group is always the "butt"—and in this quality lies humor's power to create solidarity: shared aggression toward an outsider establishes a sense of unity—even superiority—that can gloss over differences among the insiders by creating a clear "other." Humor's power to form bonds is especially strong because it allows for unbridled aggression; speaking the forbidden is acceptable because it is "just a joke." In "dirty jokes," the pleasure of expressing aggression is paired with the thrill of sexual rule breaking. Yet to be funny, humor must also give expression to and transmit the underlying assumptions of those who read or hear it, which can support (or subvert) the existing social order. The assumptions embedded in "dirty jokes," according to the scholar Gershon Legman, are that women exist solely as outlets for men's desires and every woman is available to any man, despite any protestations to the contrary. Sexual humor set in an office, then, could perpetuate the belief that stenographers and secretaries were there to fulfill men's erotic needs, while binding men together and expanding the distance between the sexes.[13]

While it is easy to imagine how the *telling* of dirty jokes could create a sense of male camaraderie, it is somewhat harder to envision how such gender solidarity could be created when an individual man read a joke in the newspaper. Yet it seems likely that the process worked similarly. Any man, regardless of the color of his collar, could certainly read a joke and feel manly—that is, relate to the male perspective portrayed in it. In so doing, he would have both confirmed his difference from (and possibly superiority to) women and momentarily engaged in their sexual objectification. For white-collar men such jokes might have had more significance.

Returning to the joke that began this section, we see that it takes as its starting point the sexual objectification of women and the assumption that even a woman at work is sexually available. More important, it sends the reader a message about white-collar men's virility. The observer's outrage is reminiscent of Pastor Broughton's words to the Brooklyn YMCA about businessmen's immorality, but this humorous story is no sermon. The morally upright observer is not the hero; he is the butt of the joke. His principles mark him as weak or effeminate; the boss dismisses his objections with nothing more strenuous than drawing a shade. If humor is one of the mechanisms through which gender ideals are created and sustained, then this story can be read as sending a nuanced message about middle-class, white-collar manhood. It is not just that such men were expected to be sexual and to take advantage of any such opportunities. Rather, we see that the man of achievement—the boss—gains access to women as part of his success. In this way, the story provides an opportunity for male bonding while it also establishes a status hierarchy. All male readers can unite around the objectification of the pretty stenographer and the humiliation of the prude, but working-class and low- or midlevel white-collar men were also reminded of the superiority of the man in charge, as evidenced by his privilege of spending time in his office completely alone with an attractive helper. In this joke, the pretty stenographer is merely the symbol of the man's (sexual) success. Her presence is necessary, but she is in no way the subject of this story: this is a conversation among men about manliness.

Humor that addressed men's fear of the sexual power of the pretty typewriter discussed in the previous chapter also provided lessons. Here, laughter potentially neutralized the threat women posed and lessened men's vulnerability by making it into a joke. In this humor, the message was clear: only a fool would fall prey to the scheming seductress or his own desires. Typical was the tale of the beautiful but incompetent employee who flattered the boss to keep her job. In the version that appeared in the *Washington Post* in 1909, the new stenographer assures her employer that her speed will increase once she masters his "literary style." Her previous supervisor had a small and ordinary vocabulary, but his is large and sophisticated. Warmed by her flattery, he stammers that if there is anything she needs, she should just ask. This joke makes no secret that the boss is a fool, unable to recognize a woman's sexual wiles. The pleasure, then, came from the reader's ability to congratulate himself that he would never fall for such ploys. In this way, the joke helped to assuage men's anxieties about their vulnerability, but it also urged men to treat women as objects and enemies. In this joke and many others in which a woman got the best of a man, the woman's voice was actually heard: she was an assertive subject acting in her own interest. If men were to remain in control, if they were to express their manliness through sexuality, women best remain silent objects.[14]

A woman's voice and a man's humiliation were again at issue in an amusing story from 1895, which appeared in the *St. Louis Republican*. The chief clerk of a large corporation was dictating a letter to his stenographer to be signed by his manager. In the middle of the dictation, he decided to pay her a compliment: "What very pretty hair you have, Miss Blank!" Miss Blank smiled, but said nothing. After she finished her transcription, she gave the letter to the manager, who noticed the "pretty hair" sentence in the middle and called her in to explain. "Why, I only put down just what Mr. Brown said," she innocently replied, and soon Mr. Brown became the butt of all manner of jokes among the men in the office. Within a few days it became apparent that Blank or Brown would need to leave, and Miss Blank handed in her resignation.[15]

Here we see a woman get the best of a man; his desires have made him look foolish in front of other men. But it is important to note that Brown was emasculated even before Miss Blank handed the letter to the manager. This joke spoke to the reality of supervision that characterized the modern office and contributed to many men's sense of office work as

Early-twentieth-century postcards featured a seemingly endless array of bosses and their willing female employees in compromising positions. This postcard draws attention to the personal privacy afforded successful men: the man walking by outside the office is unaware of what is really going on "behind closed doors." Author's collection.

unmanly. As a clerk, Brown did not have an autonomous voice. He was a subordinate whose words would always be monitored and judged by a man higher up. Indeed, this fact provided Miss Blank with the opportunity to play him for a fool. She paid for her assertiveness with her job, illustrating women's low place in the office hierarchy. But Brown suffered a significant loss as well: his humiliation was made visible for all to see, which might have hurt his chances for promotion. For the turn-of-the-century reader, this joke would have been all the more meaningful given the numerous romance stories which happily ended with the shy boss dictating a marriage proposal to his dedicated assistant. Those men had the autonomy to speak boldly, while the clerk was not successful enough to declare his feelings.[16]

The sexual privileges of success found visual expression in humorous postcards, which pictured a private office with a secretary on her boss's lap—sometimes with, sometimes without an outraged wife bursting in. These postcards were part of a growing gallery of images that presented sex as an inevitable part of office life. With captions that read "Busy at office" or "Our busy day," many of these postcards mocked businessmen's importance and integrity. Yet their underlying message was still clear: professional achievement secured intimate access to willing women. It also secured freedom from surveillance. Large businesses arranged the office's physical space to maximize workers' output by enabling supervisors to watch their every move. This supervision demanded tremendous self-discipline from employees, a constant vigilance that they always look busy. For men already feeling emasculated by office work, such scrutiny increased their insecurity. The private office, then, was a highly visible symbol of a man's status because it spared him from one of the most demeaning aspects of business life. It meant a man was free from (visual) supervision, his body unleashed from constant self-monitoring—a natural state that when paired with a pretty stenographer seemed to naturally suggest sex. In this way, the trope of the boss with his secretary on his lap was not just a sign of a man's power (or abuse of it) or even of forbidden sexuality; it also symbolized the freedom and autonomy that seemed to elude so many white-collar men.[17]

Gray-haired bosses, pretty typewriters, and angry wives were also standard fare in material produced for a primarily working-class audience. This love-triangle theme appeared in early short comedy films, as did narratives in which female office workers successfully defended themselves against or sought retribution for unwanted or coercive attentions. Historians argue that these portrayals were popular and amusing because of their irreverent challenges to respectability and the way they upended hierarchies of authority and gender. Over time, silent films disappeared and humorous postcards diminished, but Americans' access to far more graphic depictions of sex in the office increased. "Tijuana Bibles," sexually explicit comics anonymously drawn, originated among the working class in the late 1920s and were popular through World War II; by 1950, a thousand or so titles had been cheaply printed and secretly sold in places like barber shops and bowling alleys. The bibles' graphics exposed readers to taboo sexual behaviors engaged in by actual comic-book characters; their images flouted copyright while the narratives brazenly challenged authority.[18]

In bibles set in an office, the boss's dignity is stripped away as the comics expose his sexual inadequacies and sordid perversions, and employees turn his desires to their ends. One modeled on the popular

In the Tijuana Bible "All in a Day's Work," Dagwood Bumstead, the bungling hero of the *Blondie* comic strip, which began in 1930, spends the day engaged in a variety of sexual activities with a number of naked secretaries, the result of his boss's decision to allow his employees to wear "informal office clothes."

comic strip *Smitty the Office Boy*, which began in 1922, begins with the boss bargaining with the new stenographer: "How about it, Miss Titts? Five bucks more a week if you act nice." After taking a look at his "thing," she demands ten, and they seal the deal. Soon, however, the stenographer is turning not to the boss, but to the teen-aged Smitty to fulfill her sexual needs, and when the boss finds out, he fires him. But the stenographer has the last word: "If you want to jazz me," she tells the boss, "he stays!" In bibles like this, the boss has the power to compel a woman into intimacy or the money to make it worth her while, but it is the man—or even boy—far down the ladder who is man enough to satisfy her.[19]

Sexual humor contributed to the framework of a white-collar masculinity that emphasized (hetero)sexuality and defined the office as sexual space. It encouraged men to see the women with whom they worked as sexual objects, not colleagues or competent workers, and in this way it linked men together. It also divided men by associating physical intimacy with these women as an essential element of a man's success. Constructing this manhood, though, was a never-ending project in a permanent state of repair. As numerous scholars have shown, gender identity is not something that an individual "just is," or even that he or she ultimately achieves, but rather, it requires continual verification. In this sense, we can think of the reading or telling of a joke as a small performance of manliness. But if most men could only joke about sex in the office—sometimes in a way that poked fun at the man in charge—real successful men could actually acquire the status symbols that humor helped to establish and infused with cultural meaning.[20]

Ample evidence regarding hiring practices from the beginning of women's clerical employment, for example, suggests that men consciously chose young, attractive, unmarried women whose age, appearance, and marital status reaffirmed both the subordinate and sexual aspect of female office jobs. Women over thirty had extreme difficulty landing jobs, since their age suggested a greater degree of equality with the boss and a maternal instead of sexual relationship. Men regularly called employment agencies asking for a "pretty blonde," and business schools lamented that bosses would rather hire a "dreamy-eyed Venus," than a woman who could do the job. Beautiful women were status symbols, which explained men's opposition to the introduction of

This ad appeared in *Fortune* in 1931. The secretary's brightly illuminated legs suggest
that her dictation skills might be secondary to the clearly distinct value of her physical
charms. Sexualized images such as this confirmed the importance of the man with a
secretary and illustrate that sexuality was built into the rituals and geography of the
workplace.

mechanical recording devices, which would have lessened the need for
stenographers; as one executive in the 1920s explained his resistance, "it
is just human nature for a man to prefer to have a young lady alongside
his desk." In this way, stenographers and secretaries really were sexy

"objects," a possession that reflected positively on the status of its owner. In 1906, one businessman made the connection explicit when explaining why he turned down a qualified candidate, "The fact is simply this: I have a handsome office, newly decorated, and I must have a secretary to match."[21]

THE DOUBLE LIVES OF BUSINESSMEN: SEX AND SUCCESS

What did this view of secretaries as decorative possessions say about businessmen and their character? In 1915 the suicide of a young typewriter exposed the tensions between the old ideal of honor and self-restraint and the new masculine ethic of pleasure, consumption, and sensuality. Lillian Cook, eighteen, worked in the office of the Mayo Radiator Company in New Haven, Connecticut. One day she left the office at noon, taking a revolver from one of the desks. A week later, searchers found her body and discovered that she had shot herself in the heart. In their investigation, police uncovered the double life of her employer, the millionaire Virginius J. Mayo, whose professional reputation seemed wholly irreconcilable with his disgraceful private affairs.

Mayo, who was in his mid-fifties at the time, was an American success story, but he was not a man of character. He had started out as an electrical engineer in the 1880s and now owned a large manufacturing plant and employed more than one hundred workers. He belonged to numerous sporting clubs and was known as a "big-hearted" employer who, when the weather was bad, had his three chauffeurs drive his employees home in some of his fourteen cars. The distinguished businessman was also a ladies' man. In addition to a young wife in New Haven, who had financed his business, Mayo maintained a $20,000 home in Brooklyn, where Lois Waterbury, a woman in her early twenties, who had occupied Cook's position in Mayo's office a few years before, lived with their two children. When his secret life was exposed, Mayo was far from repentant: "I haven't any regard for the conventions and neither has [Waterbury]. I . . . don't care what the people say."[22]

Mayo vigorously denied any romantic involvement with Cook (including a report that he had asked the employment agency from which he hired her to send him "a pretty girl, no matter how inefficient or incapable"), but within a week of the revelation of Mayo's "dual personality," two other women who had "lives" with Mayo surfaced. There was the wife and three children in Scranton, Pennsylvania, whom he had deserted around 1900. Another woman from Mayo's office, Susie Wahler, twenty-four, also appeared. She had taken over Waterbury's job, and Mayo had either seduced or assaulted her, in either case leaving her pregnant with a child who was now two. When she told Mayo she was pregnant, he would not let her quit right away. Instead, he "begged" her to stay "as they were just changing the bookkeeping system, and he wanted to make sure the new methods worked all right." He had offered to set her up in her own house and give her $18 a week to care for the baby, but she refused and was now living with relatives. Prosecutors combed through Mayo's "escapades" to find something with which to charge him, but their hands were tied. The state could indict him for bigamy only if one of his wives filed a complaint, and they were unwilling. His wife in Pennsylvania filed for divorce, which was quickly granted and included an undisclosed cash settlement. Wahler sued Mayo for child support and for damages for assault, and he settled out of court for $5,000. Early in 1916 his Connecticut wife sued him for fraud, and a jury awarded her $100,000.[23]

Mayo's excesses resonated with two related anxieties: how to limit the right of businesses to do as they pleased and how to curb the Social Evil. The rapid industrialization and intense competition of the last three decades of the nineteenth century had led to the development of business methods and legal structures, like the trust, to eliminate rivals and gain a monopoly. This process had created corporate giants like Standard Oil and colossal fortunes for a few men, but brutally low wages, dangerous work conditions, and insecure employment for many laborers. The depression and labor unrest of the 1890s convinced many Americans that neither existing law nor workers' plight was enough to turn corporations away from their greedy pursuit of profit. In the early twentieth century, these concerns led politicians, journalists, and social reformers to look for ways to control big business, leading to the passage of antitrust laws and the creation of regulatory agencies like the Food and Drug Administration.[24]

The latter embodied a fundamental Progressive Era belief: public and private spheres of activity were inextricably linked. A packinghouse that passed off rotting meat to unsuspecting shoppers could sicken an entire family at its evening meal. And, of course, this connection was at the heart of investigations into the relationship between workingwomen's low wages and their low moral standards. Progressives also saw similarities between commercialized vice and corporate capitalism. Prostitution rings were no fly-by-night operations but highly organized structures of unknown proportions, and they seemed to have borrowed the strategies of monopoly capitalism to increase business and to insulate leaders from responsibility for their misdeeds.[25]

Critics of big business often pinned the blame on business leaders' lack of character, and the absence of personal integrity was implicated in prostitution as well. Teddy Roosevelt believed the problem came from men overdoing the American ideal of "independence in initiative and action," and the solution was to train men "in conscience and character" until they grew to abhor "greed and tyranny." Religious leaders offered a similar explanation; corporate leaders had failed to recognize their personal responsibility to their employees and the public. Moreover, many of the newly rich lacked the "character" to use their wealth appropriately and suffered from "moral anemia" in their private lives. A scholar investigating the problem of prostitution also focused on a new outlook: "The old-fashioned notion that life is for the discipline of character and that indulgence in pleasure not well earned is an evidence of weakness, now sounds almost quaint in its austerity."[26]

Why all the nostalgia for the days of manly character? By the onset of World War I, this older ideal was competing with new constructions of manliness—and not just in terms of sexual attitudes. As white-collar work increasingly became the standard path to success for middle-class men, personality seemed to be as important as character in distinguishing oneself from the man at the next desk. As late as 1910 success manuals pitched to men of modest means asserted that character counted most and condemned the greed and intemperance of the new corporate order. Nevertheless, already by the 1870s a new literature made it clear that character alone would not be enough. The novels of the prolific Horatio Alger, for example, showed basically honest, self-reliant young men making their way toward respectability. But these men's success can be attributed to their qualities as con men; in addition to being ambitious, Alger's heroes were manipulators, men of great personal magnetism who compelled people to follow and obey them.[27]

In the adventures of Virginius Mayo, the press had a perfect foil for exploring the tensions between the old emphasis on character and a new focus on personality and appearance. On the one hand, Mayo, with his fine reputation for honesty and quality work, represented the nineteenth-century middle-class entrepreneurial spirit. On the other, in his dealings with women he was completely without honor. Mayo was a respected businessman, but in his personal life his idea of duty was to set up his mistress and their illegitimate children in an expensive home. When his other mistress refused to have an abortion, he offered her money. His pleasing personality was just the kind a man would need to get noticed in the corporate bureaucracy or to succeed as a salesman or ad man who persuaded people to buy what they did not need. But in the newspapers' view, the women who found his pitch persuasive would have been better off without the "goods" he offered. Men might need to be a bit manipulative to succeed, but there could be severe social consequences if this duplicity spilled over into their private lives. These concerns were apparent in the many stories describing how women had fallen for Mayo. As the wife in Scranton said, "He witched me with the romance of his personality, and I eloped with him." Wahler, who had been present when Mayo's wife stormed into the office and denounced her husband and Waterbury for having an affair, observed, "There was something about Mayo—I can't describe it. He was so good and kind—it seemed. He made everyone do just what he wanted by being good to them." She was "not a bad girl," but "fell under his influence."[28]

Mayo seems to have used whoever occupied the position as his stenographer to meet his intimate as well as business needs, and events in his office confounded any easy distinction between personal and workplace activities (Wahler, for example, had never spent time alone with Mayo outside of the office). He introduced romance into his relationships with the women in his office with the courtshiplike practices of giving jewelry at Christmas and treating some girls to an outing to the New York auto show each year. His wife's outburst, which made public his affair with Waterbury, also made everyone present a party to his romantic life. What disapproving readers likely found especially troubling, though, was how his female office staff responded to these incidents. A woman concerned with her virtue should have run after witnessing the scene in the office, but Wahler seems to have jumped into Mayo's arms as much as she fell under his influence. Instead of making his infidelity a mark against his character, it seemed to make him all the more intriguing. And here, in the newspapers' narrative, lay the danger. The lure of consumer pleasures and the growing emphasis on personality made it easier for Mayo to achieve his immoral ends.[29]

In 1919 the state had its chance to weigh in on Mayo's character when his wife in Connecticut filed bigamy charges because he had failed to pay her the $100,000 the jury awarded her for fraud. He was found guilty. At the sentencing hearing, the prosecutor described the sixty-two-year-old as "a vicious and criminal Don Juan" guilty of "no mere soft or innocent philandering," and asked for a sentence "at least enough to deter others from similar practices and inclinations." Mayo received one to three years in jail.[30]

Prosecutors were apparently willing to turn a blind eye to the occasional extramarital tryst, but Mayo had gone too far. He had used his success to facilitate and fund an immoral life, and this mattered more to him than the respect accorded an honorable businessman. He lived solely for the spoils of his success, such as a stable of willing women, and had abandoned conventional sexual morality without so much as a backward glance. Those white-collar men who found it impossible to find a masculine identity in their work and looked to women to fill the void would need to do much the same. Mayo was far richer and more accomplished than the average businessman, but his behavior was not as far outside the norm as one might think.

The midwestern fiction writer Sherwood Anderson was also troubled by what he saw as the hypocrisy of American businessmen, a failing that, for him, was represented most vividly in their attitude toward women and sex. Anderson began his career in advertising in Chicago in 1900, and in his memoir he recalled these men's obsession with sex. He had first noticed this "always, all day long, talk of women" when he worked in a factory as a very young man, and he believed that this preoccupation was easily explained: mass production had robbed men of the opportunity to define themselves through their work. When Anderson entered the white-collar world, he found the same thing. Men told off-color stories at work and then went out for a night on the town away from their wives. After drinking too much, one would suggest, "What about some women?" After a few phone calls, they would end up at an apartment that was really nothing more than a brothel—although the discreet exchange of money allowed the men to think the women really liked them because they were important.[31]

Most of the "bright young businessmen" Anderson knew were unfaithful to their wives, but prominent older men, too, wanted women. A man of importance who belonged to Chicago's posh Union League Club, a gathering place for bankers and manufacturers, asked Anderson to find him a woman while his wife was away in Europe. He had heard that Anderson was a writer and hoped that he knew some artistic, bohemian types. This man had a city apartment for such trysts, but was tired of paying women for sex. For men who depended on customers or clients for their livelihood, whether in insurance, publishing, or advertising, a "stud book"—a list of places that provided women and drinks and were safe from the police—was an important part of closing deals.[32]

Anderson was much less troubled by the immorality of these behaviors than by what they said about American manhood: that modern business was a form of prostitution and businessmen were "whores" who sold their manly selves for a salary. Finding your manliness through sex, though, was no answer for him. For one thing, businessmen's sexual exploits marked them as hypocrites, publicly honest and respectable one minute, privately sordid the next. Their actions also led to unmanly self-delusion. The businessman who maintained that he was faithful to his wife because he had not kissed his mistress was no man. Nor was the company president, a church deacon, who told Anderson to take clients out to "entertain" them, but then sermonized that he would not want company money "spent for anything evil." This man, in Anderson's view, was a fraud.[33]

Anderson wrote his memoirs years after he left business, and both his antipathy toward advertising and his romanticization of the preindustrial past probably colored his views. Nevertheless, the recollections do suggest the large role sex had come to play in the world of business, and they highlight the overlap between men's professional and personal lives. There was also a misogynistic strain, as the historian T. J. Jackson Lears observes. "Customers have to be taken care of," Anderson repeatedly noted in his critique of business, and he clearly saw taking care of others as women's work. He described the men who wrote ad copy with him as "girls" whose chewing-gum jingles sullied the craft of writing. Most especially, Anderson disliked how industrialization had created a materialist world, with everyone focused on possessions and status; this was a "matriarchy," he believed, a female civilization in which men felt out of place.

Since there was no real work to be done, this society also forced men to find self-expression through sex. Women gave men their manhood, but Anderson resented the power this gave women.[34]

SEX-CESS: AN ALTERNATIVE ROUTE TO MIDDLE-CLASS MANHOOD

The memoirs of W. Ward Smith, a New Yorker involved in a number of political and business ventures beginning in the late 1910s, provide us with another vivid portrait: this time of a man who defined himself almost exclusively through his heterosexuality, a definition facilitated by his social class. Smith used sexual exploits both to claim a type of manliness and to excuse his business failures. Wealth eluded him, but women were everywhere, and they easily succumbed to his charms. While other men made it big, he made it with women—on occasion even with the wives or daughters of those successful men.[35]

Smith was born in 1893 into a middle-class, professional home that seems to have experienced a decline in fortune from previous generations. The family, which included distinguished Puritan ancestors, clung to the edges of New York society, and Ward attended a private school with sons of the elite. He enjoyed prominence in New York's Republican Party in the early 1920s and moved from career to career: lumber, insurance, banking, land speculation, and magazine publishing. In every enterprise, he failed. He declared bankruptcy twice and spent most of his adult life dodging creditors and living beyond his means. He married three times and had affairs with innumerable women.[36]

Smith documented these trysts and his business adventures in a chronological "letter" to his son, Page, and this evidence of paternal virility was Page's primary patrimony. In other words, Ward's sexual triumphs were not incidental; they gave both purpose to his life and something to bequeath to future generations. Ward wrote the letter over a period of more than thirty years, and ultimately it totaled over ten thousand pages. Page Smith, who had heard his father refer to this narrative on various occasions, received it and a trunk of supporting documents upon his father's death in 1968. A respected historian, Smith decided to publish an edited version.[37]

Ward Smith's descriptions of his sexual encounters read like entries in a catalogue, providing a basic account of who, where, when, and what sexual acts—the latter graphically recalled. In some cases, more detail is given, but this letter was basically a record of his conquests. What is striking is how many of these women were secretaries and stenographers whom he met in his business dealings. Most of the affairs occurred in the 1920s, when he was in his late twenties and early thirties, although this period was by no means singular. In 1937, for example, the forty-four-year-old Smith proudly listed thirty-nine women with whom he was sexually intimate. One of the few to merit more than a sentence or two was his secretary Sylvia, whom Smith had hired to help him in his (ultimately abandoned) attempt to become a city council member. "Young, luscious, and not averse to being fondled," Sylvia masturbated and fellated Smith in the office, keeping him in "white heat." Smith's earliest sexual experiences, too, had been with office women: his father's secretaries. He began to work with his father, a gas company executive, after graduation from high school. Whenever his father was out of the office, he and one of the secretaries made love, and she was the first woman he ever "completely undressed." When his father caught him lying on top of another secretary in the mailroom, he fired the woman.[38]

Smith did not need to depend on his father to gain access to women. As he describes it, New York's crowded subways provided the opportunity for " 'feeling parties,' " and women never objected. Once he arrived at work, there was more sex. In the late 1910s Smith and his secretary would slip into the large closet in his office after completing the day's work. In the early 1920s, while out of town on business, Smith and a male coworker both had sex with the woman who was doing their mimeograph work on her desk; as he noted, "It was a nice way to top off a busy day." Other men also were sexually involved with their office help. One man was careless about where he left his used condoms, much to the embarrassment of the other employees who would find them, and Smith took advantage of an affair between a boss and his secretary by using the man's time away from home to seduce his wife.[39]

Reading this document can induce a state of disbelief: could one man really have had so many casual sexual contacts? Page Smith, having seen how women responded to his father, did not question the veracity of the letter. He also argued that his father's "obsession" was a response to the anonymity and sexual mystique of the city, and certainly there is much to this analysis of the early-twentieth-century city as a sexually suggestive space. The subway system compelled astonishing but fleeting physical intimacy with strangers, and we know that women were constantly approached with sexual propositions as they walked the city streets, especially if they were alone. Historians also have documented a highly visible gay male world in New York City in this period that included multiple public locations that were used for sexual assignations; young heterosexuals also frequented these places. And the passage of Prohibition in 1919 created a thriving underworld of speakeasies and nightclubs where sexual interaction between men and women was part of the appeal. But what about sex at work? Did the sensations of the city spill over into the office from nine to five? Page Smith argues that the women "gave" themselves to his father with such abandon because of his sexual magnetism and in a rebellion against sexual repression. But the office women might also have had motives suppressed by Ward Smith's reminiscences of his own prowess. (As he admitted, it was easy to remember what others did to him, but not what he did or said to others.)⁴⁰

In other words, can we venture anything about the women from this record of male bravado? How did Beatrice, a sexually inexperienced secretary who fellated Smith in the stockroom and worried about pregnancy because she swallowed his semen, understand their encounters? Ward provides us with no information about how their interludes began, but he does write that sometime after he left his father's employ, Beatrice sought to speak with him. She was getting married soon and feared their interactions had taken her virginity and might have affected her ability to bear children. As we shall see in the next chapter, she was by no means the only office woman to know virtually nothing about sex or reproduction. Even if Beatrice was eager to explore her sexual desires, her inexperience and ignorance limited her ability to give Ward her *informed* consent.⁴¹

Certainly not all office women were so naïve. Florence, a beautiful legal stenographer and single mother, engaged in sex partly for financial reasons. She had many "boyfriends" who gave her money, including Smith, and by mixing "business with pleasure," she added ninety to three hundred dollars to her monthly salary. Her affair with Smith was passionate for several months, though her work interfered, and her sexual enthusiasm waned as more stenographic opportunities presented themselves. Her business, Ward moaned, "really came between us."⁴²

Florence was not the only office woman to use sex to supplement low wages. Sherwood Anderson recalled that the "safe places" businessmen

went were often filled with women who needed extra money for silk stockings and fur coats; if a girl was young and attractive, she could earn in a
few hours with an older man what she made in a week. Florence and
these women were simply partaking in the sexual economy of the city that
historians have established as a relatively common part of the experience
of workingwomen in the early twentieth century. In previous decades,
reformers were much concerned over these exchanges of affection for
money, excitement, or things, but by the 1920s, when Smith met Florence
and Sherwood Anderson began his memoirs, such activities appeared
almost ordinary. Florence's ardor cooled, though, once economic independence was in sight; perhaps she looked forward to separating sex from
money.[43]

In fact, the complicated interplay of women's economic need and
men's desire appears often in Smith's recollections. In the spring of 1930,
at the beginning of the Great Depression, Smith managed a travel magazine, and the Depression seems to have furthered his adventures.
Freelance female authors offered "free ass" as an inducement to purchase
their manuscripts, and Smith joked that he and the other men would base
their decisions on who had the "better tail" rather than the "better tale."
He also hired "luscious" stenographers who "loved to screw." But Smith's
picture of a happy harem rests uncomfortably with his recollection of the
women's response to a "playful" prank. Another executive placed a
condom in the desk drawer of every stenographer. At least one or two
were "indignant," but even they, Smith notes, did not leave or send for the
police. He interpreted this inaction as a sign that the women enjoyed the
sexualized atmosphere of the office; he was unable or unwilling to see a
connection between the crumbling economy and the women's toleration
of the practical joke.[44]

Economic considerations and sexual expression could be linked in
other ways, and on at least one occasion, a woman tried to make the
pairing work to her benefit. In 1931 Smith was arrested for the attempted
rape of Hannah Rentzer, who had come to his apartment in response to
an ad that his wife had placed for a stenographer. Smith maintained that
the woman's complaint was a "frameup for a shakedown," and a few
weeks later the judge came to the same conclusion and dismissed the
case. In the interim, the tabloid press presented the story as a
Depression-era tale of rich versus poor. "It isn't always so pleasant to work

for a wealthy society man as the movies so often suggest," commented the *New York Daily News*, despite the fact that Smith was flat broke at the time. Rentzer had been impressed by his "aristocratic manner and thought he would be a fine boss," but as she was taking a transcription test, she said, he began to tear and rip at her dress. She managed to fight the "beast" off and decided to file a complaint "for the sake of other girls who might fall into similar traps." Smith feared that he would not be acquitted and described this period as one of "continuous day and night nightmares of the most hideous and terrifying type."[45]

What is so shocking, then, is that a few years later Smith placed a want ad as a way to gain sexual access to women. He was in Los Angeles and had learned that some men rented a room in a nice hotel and then took out an ad for a photographic model. If the man was a big spender, the hotels would "let him have his fun," and beautiful women desperate for jobs showed up in droves. With his secretary around for a cover, Smith took each woman into a room where she would demonstrate her modeling poses. Soon he would ask her to disrobe so that he could take her measurements. Before the day was over, nine "measuring jobs" had led to sexual interaction. He did not even have to "urge" the women, he excitedly noted, "the slightest suggestion was readily understood and they would roll over on their backs before you could get your pants unbuttoned. It was . . . perfect bliss."[46]

What could Smith have been thinking in seeking out sexual opportunities that could possibly lead to an accusation of rape like that which had so frightened him just a few years before? One reason for his sense of impunity might be that he concocted this plan with a friend, who backed out at the last minute because he feared his girlfriend would find out. One of the points Ward's letter makes clear is that the seduction of women served as a form of manly entertainment and camaraderie. As we have already seen in the tryst with the mimeograph girl and the magazine executives' boyish play, men often bonded through sexual interactions with women. It is possible, too, that exploiting the "casting couch" was such a long-standing tradition that a legal complaint was unlikely.[47]

Of more significance is Smith's attitude toward women who worked for a living. Despite his lack of traditional masculine success, Smith seems to have felt entitled as a member of the "silver spoon" set. He had been brought up to believe that he was a "superior sort" because of his genealogy, and in the office Smith encountered women whose pedigree in no way matched his own. By the 1920s growing numbers of women whose parents were immigrants and women of ethnic descent were entering the white-collar world as the demand for clerical help grew, and these women, such as the mimeograph girl and file clerks discussed above, along with waitresses and other service providers, seem to have received the lion's share of his attention. Smith clearly saw these women as beneath him. For example, although he proclaimed a measure of love and an abundance of desire for many of the Jewish women he bedded, his memoirs are filled with anti-Semitic statements. Smith certainly did not limit his sexual adventures to women who were socially "beneath" him, but relations with these women did provide him with the opportunity to feel powerful. He assumed they would be willing, and their "willingness" in turn confirmed his superiority and manhood. His belief that all women "say 'no,' even when they most want it" only added to his sense of sexual privilege. Most businessmen did not have Ward's blue blood, but it is possible that they, too, were aware of or assumed a social distance between themselves and some of the women they encountered at work. Here, again, gender *and* class politics probably determined sexual expression in the office, especially since some middle-class men were anxious in sexual situations with women who were their social equals.[48]

Even at its upper-class best, though, sexual masculinity was an insecure masculinity. Smith used his "preponderant sex urges and uncontrollable cravings" to justify his business problems, but it was a difficult rationalization to make. Many successful men he knew also chased women to excess, so what spark of brilliance did he lack? And basing his masculine identity almost exclusively on his sexual exploits also carried the risk of failure. Smith always felt he was "bluffing" his way through life, and he always suspected that he was an "inadequate lover," despite women's protestations to the contrary. Although he liked the flattery, when a woman told him how wonderful he was, he always felt she really wanted it "harder or bigger or a fur coat." And despite his reputation for having "a way with women," he believed that other men—especially successful men—were having more sex than he was; they were just more discreet.[49]

Despite the increased public visibility of sex and the lessening reticence to talk about it, claiming a masculine identity through heterosexual acts was difficult because sexuality was still largely considered a private act and could not be openly or fully discussed. Although a man could certainly lie about his business triumphs, ultimately his rise up the corporate ladder or tangible indications of his wealth would bear out the truth. In the sexual arena, it was difficult to know with certainty the details of a man's erotic life; a man could hide or exaggerate his conquests and no one would know for certain. And women's testimony could not be trusted since they often had much to gain by lying about a man's performance. For a man like Smith, though, it was still a way to show his manliness and exhibit an expertise—a type of talent—in lieu of business acumen. In many ways, then, Smith was lucky. His numerous failures did not permanently mark him as a loser because he came of age at a time when his pleasure-seeking, womanizing masculinity was increasingly seen as a legitimate mark of manly success; as his son noted, in Ward Smith, "Horatio Alger joined forces with Casanova."[50]

Other men were not so fortunate. When they failed, they could not use their passion for women as a convenient scapegoat, nor could they rely on family connections to secure yet another line of credit or another job—and another office filled with women to soothe their wounded pride. For male clerks, bookkeepers, accountants, and other men on the lower rungs of the corporate ladder, relations with women were often just another sign of their masculine disappointment. Such men could feel like men when they ogled the attractive receptionist or shared a dirty joke, but ultimately virile manhood operated the same way as any ideology that bestows identity and value: it was not just about who or what the man was, it was also about what he was not. In this case, manliness was conferred by a sexual access to women that other men lacked.

LADDERS AND UNIONS: "REAL" MEN CLIMB, CONFRONT, AND GET THE GIRL

At any given moment a number of masculine ideals exist, at least one of which is culturally dominant and generally corresponds with the qualities associated with men with some type of institutional power. Low-level white-collar men, however, found themselves in a no-man's land, unable to achieve the standards of masculinity of middle-class white-collar men, working-class men, or even men who defined themselves primarily through their heterosexuality. These men's frustration, apparent already in the early years of the twentieth century, reached a new level of public acknowledgment in the popular culture of the 1920s and in the efforts to organize the white-collar sector during the Depression.[51]

Corporations were aware of men's frustration and used the metaphor of the "ladder" to give men a sense of hopefulness that could counter the feelings of emasculation engendered by their lack of autonomy and the similarity between their work and that of women clerks. Despite significant differences in status, authority, and salary, the ladder's rungs linked men at the very bottom with those at the top of the hierarchy and showed a clear path to success. Some companies, for example, published stories of men who had risen through the ranks in their in-house magazines to convince workers that advancement was possible and to suggest that manly individualism was not at odds with one's status as a company man. By the 1910s Americans had come to see climbing the ladder as a sound strategy in a complicated and rapidly changing economy.[52]

Even so, by the 1920s many Americans seemed sympathetic to low-level men's plight, as the verdict in a nationally publicized murder case showed. Both in their early twenties, Shirley McIntyre, an attractive stenographer, and Walter Mayer, an accounting clerk, met in 1923 at New York City's Chase National Bank. He fell for her and asked her to marry him. She said yes, only to change her mind when, as he saw it, her head was turned by a "few fools" who gave her a "taste of high life" that his modest income could not afford. What was worse, McIntyre not only rebuffed his pleas and scoffed at his threats of suicide, she also called him "inferior" and insinuated that he was not good enough for her. As he explained to a friend, the woman he loved had "openly and laughingly insulted" him. Mayer went to McIntyre's apartment, where he shot her twice before turning the gun on himself. He survived his wounds, and a year later was well enough to be tried for murder. The prosecutor requested the death penalty, but jurors "beamed sympathetically" as Mayer explained that his fiancée had chosen "things" over love. Even McIntyre's mother testified on his behalf. The jury convicted Mayer on a lesser charge with a plea for leniency.[53]

Such a verdict would have been incomprehensible at the time of McIntyre's death. In the year between her murder and his trial, public sympathy shifted to him; he was now the true victim. In their coverage of both the murder and the trial, newspapers agreed that this tragedy spoke to the problems young, white-collar men faced as they tried to marry and start a family on a clerk's salary. At the time of the murder, however, news stories portrayed Mayer as a jealous stalker (a view supported by the existence of three letters which indicated he had planned to murder McIntyre) and, most especially, a failed man. With McIntyre earning sixty dollars a week and Mayer only fifty, this was an "ultra-modern tragedy of the pay envelope," one easily explained by existing gender roles. As the feminist Doris Stevens explained to a newspaper reporter, when McIntyre called him inferior, he realized that he was—to her! Bested by a woman in "man's own field," Mayer knew he "was a failure in both love and the struggle for existence." Stevens saw McIntyre's business success as a sign of progress and looked forward to the day when men could accept women as their economic equals. By the time of the trial, this egalitarian view was gone.[54]

Now coverage lamented women's economic autonomy and material desires, both of which added to the masculine burdens of young, white-collar men. Had they met in the nineteenth century, one reporter observed, they might well have settled into marriage. But in the "new age," girls had jobs that made them "independent—even of men." In Mayer's eyes, his situation had been hopeless. "There are big jobs for a few men but oars in the galley for all the rest of the slaves," he had told a friend. Chained to an adding machine, he was going nowhere, as the woman he loved and worked with could plainly see. Her doubts about his prospects, he said, "affected his efficiency" and further "rendered him incapable of progress."[55]

The widely publicized explorations of Mayer's romantic and career frustrations, the theater of the trial, and the jury's slap on his hand shed light on how men's *and* women's occupational prospects affected romantic and sexual relationships in the white-collar office in the first decades of the twentieth century. When he blamed his crime on the materialistic woman he loved, he inserted himself into the worried discussion surrounding workingwomen's financial self-sufficiency, relaxed sexual morals, and provocative presence in public spaces in the late 1910s and 1920s, which we will examine in the next chapter. Yet when Mayer additionally tied his frustrations to the plight of the white-collar man trapped on the lowest rungs of the office ladder, he connected his tragic office romance to the unease many middle-class men felt about their place in the corporate economy. Mayer was a good man, the jury decided, honorable in love, ambitious in his career dreams. The difficulties of achieving manly success in corporate America and the desires enflamed by a consumer society were really to blame for McIntyre's death.

Around the time of McIntyre's murder, a survey of office workers indicated that men on the lowest rungs were increasingly pessimistic about their ability to overcome these difficulties, and their misgivings were confirmed by the popular culture of this period, which more and more made a distinction between representations of men at the top and the bottom of the corporate hierarchy. Successful men appeared as strong-willed and powerful, while clerks and bookkeepers completely lacked self-determination. White-collar workers in popular novels in the 1920s expressed the same frustrations as Walter Mayer. In a novel published in 1927, for example, the low-level man trapped by the corporate system compared himself and his coworkers to "poor fish . . . miserable galley slaves . . . mice in a trap." This critical view of white-collar work was visually expressed in the 1928 film *The Crowd*, in which the hero, Johnny Sims, faces a life of endless toil as anonymous clerk number 137 in a large insurance company. In many of these narratives, the white-collar worker's failure to achieve the masculine ideal was represented most vividly through his relationships with women. Johnny's wife continually nags him about getting a promotion and becomes cold when he does not. In a film from 1923, a clerk pretends to be a manager when his fiancée seems horrified by his low position. A true story in *Sunset* magazine that year told of a man whose wife of twenty-three years left him because she felt ashamed of his position as a clerk.[56]

In 1935 and early 1936, the Bookkeepers, Stenographers and Accountants Union emphasized in their recruitment efforts the connection between a man's limited opportunities and an unhappy private life. A fictional story in their newsletter recounted the thoughts of Frank Robbins, biller number 37, in the Accounts Department of Consolidated Electric, as he listened to the sounds of the May Day parade floating in through his window. Frank had worked for the company for twelve years, but advancement had been slow to come. Day after day spent adding number after number had numbed his mind, and his work had also hurt his marriage. Pay was so low he had to live far outside the city, where rents were cheap, but the long commute meant he was exhausted at night and

In the 1930s white-collar unions issued a challenge to male office workers: were they manly enough to stand up to their employers and demand better treatment? Image courtesy of Tamiment Library and Robert F. Wagner Labor Archives, New York University.

"Well! Well! So our bookkeeper is getting married! And it seems only yeasterday that you came here. Let's see, it was 1918, wasn't it? From now on, my boy, you're getting $25 a week!"

In this union cartoon from 1935, the bookkeeper makes barely enough to marry, while the boss has plenty of contact with women, as symbolized by the drawing of a naked one on his office wall, which might have implied a connection between the exploitation of workers and the sexual exploitation of women. Image courtesy of Tamiment Library and Robert F. Wagner Labor Archives, New York University.

in a hurry in the morning. There was no time to love his wife "properly," and she now turned away from his caresses. In this state of mind, Frank begins to consider the workers' parade. Wondering whether "pen pushers," who produced nothing tangible, could go on strike, he quickly realizes that pen pushers matter most, since they keep track of how much money people owe. Momentarily inspired, he thinks about joining the parade, but quickly changes his mind. There might be riots, the workingmen might be rough, and he was just a white-collar adder.[57]

This attack on the manliness of low-level, white-collar men appeared alongside the union's class-based arguments. The union chastised white-collar workers for caring more about feeling "genteel" and "socially above" the industrial worker than they did about decent wages. The BSAU aimed a special message at men, suggesting that they were not manly enough to stand up to the boss. "Do they have white blood as well as white collars? Are their livers lily colored?" one article asked. Illustrations especially made this point by contrasting the timid, stoop-shouldered clerk with the corpulent, cigar-smoking boss or the brawny and bold laborer. Some drawings ridiculed corporate attempts to portray their businesses as a happy family led by caring patriarchs by showing the indolent boss reaping the rewards of his children's labor; these representations reduced the male clerk to the status of an adolescent son, not the head of a family.[58]

We do not know whether this masculine shaming worked, whether white-collar men took the bait and joined the union to show that they were every bit the men as the "horny-handed" factory workers. We do know, however, that this masculine collar-color competition worked both ways. In 1934 Industrial Workers of the World organizers told factory workers at Cleveland's American Stove Company a story about a white-collar cuckold:

> A docile male office wage slave developed a yen to have the
> afternoon off. He had noticed others getting time off by saying
> they were fairly well caught up with their work and wanted to go
> to the ball game. He made the same pitch, and it worked.
> However, he was not interested in ball games and soon went
> home. He opened the front door quietly and saw his boss making
> love to his wife. . . . Quickly he closed the door and went to the
> ball game, feeling lucky his boss had not caught him in a lie.

According to the folklorist Archie Green, by targeting blue-collar workers' sense of masculine pride, organizers hoped that this story would lead them to join the union and take on their employers—unlike the emasculated office worker who was so timid that he escaped to the ball-game rather than reclaiming his wife. Labor leaders' use of masculine ideals as an organizing tool for both white- and blue-collar men shows just how powerful cultural standards of manhood were and how much they could affect a man's sense of self. In these ideals issues of power and struggle were directly connected to women and to sex. We see again the boss's access to women and the notion that his life was filled with plea-sure, not labor. We see, too, how low-wage, subordinate men, regardless of where they worked, understood their workplace exploitation as inter-twined with disappointments and indignities in the most private moments in their private lives. Masculine identity included both sex and work because they were inextricably linked. Virginius Mayo's success afforded him two wives and at the very least one mistress. Ward Smith's prominent background provided him with innumerable business oppor-tunities and untold women. Meanwhile, the inferior Walter Mayer's low wages and dead-end job placed the comforts of a wife and home out of reach, and the docile office slave could not even keep his wife's affections for himself. Advantages in the workplace led to advantages in the sexual, romantic, and/or domestic realm.[59]

By the 1930s workplace or work-related sexual expression had become an important component of many men's sense of themselves as white-collar men, and women in the office had become symbols as well as workers. Men could use women to establish their place in the pecking order and as a marker of success. Even for men on the lower rungs, heterosexuality could be a large part of masculine identity, as men participated in after work "entertainment" that might be part of their job. Others sought plea-sure with sexually willing office women or took advantage of economi-cally vulnerable ones.

Women workers had to cope with the repercussions of their symbolic role whether they wanted to or not. Scholars have argued that changes in dominant understandings of masculinity work to guarantee men's continued supremacy in light of changing circumstances, and certainly the white-collar Casanova helped to extinguish the threat women workers posed to male authority by ensuring women would be viewed primarily in terms of their sexual desirability. Popular culture encouraged and supported this understanding of middle-class manhood, and it further sexualized the female office worker, thereby calling into question her status as a competent worker. Yet as the stories told here show, women were not simply victims but rather individuals who responded differently depending on their circumstances and desires. Women were economically vulnerable, but this did not necessarily mean that they were without agency, and as Ward Smith learned, a few attempted to turn men's desires against them. In the next chapter, we will focus on the 1920s and 1930s from women's perspective, examining in detail their experiences of and responses to the increasingly sexualized office.[60]

CHAPTER THREE

Betwixt and Between

NEW FREEDOMS AND NEW RISKS IN THE SEXUALLY AND PSYCHOLOGICALLY MODERN OFFICE

IN 1926 HELEN WOODWARD, a successful advertising copywriter, published her memoirs, liberally spiced with the amorous adventures of her coworkers. Everyone, it seemed—from the plainest typewriter girl to the loftiest executive—had a turn at office hanky-panky, and, in Woodward's eyes, such adventures were just the amusing asides of an ordinary day at the office. They certainly did not merit any hand-wringing or any effort to protect pure womanhood: "So much nonsense has been written of the dangers and temptations to young girls in business offices," she chided. "Girls find temptations when and where they are ready for them, in offices or out of them."[1]

Woodward's laissez-faire narration of the office's secret life reflected a number of post–World War I changes, including the by-now ordinariness of female office workers, a new consensus on female sexuality, and an inclination to view life through a psychological lens. In the 1910s alone, the number of women employed in clerical jobs grew 140 percent, totaling over 1.4 million in 1920. With this many women working in the public sphere, the old discussions of the moral peril of gender-integrated offices no longer made sense. Questions about the role of sexuality in the workplace, however, did not cease with the acceptance of women; indeed, sex was now even more a topic of interest.[2]

In the early twentieth century, Victorian morality and especially the idea of female passionlessness were under attack. While some working-class women's practice of "treating" was hardly news, by the 1920s it was apparent that young middle-class women, too, had rejected nineteenth-century sexual ideals. Sexuality had undergone a cultural reassessment. Now a variety of experts (and many Americans) agreed that sexual expression was vital to men's *and* women's mental and physical health. In terms of relationships in the office, though, not a lot had changed. Certainly there was no denying that sexual intrigue and the skyscraper were on familiar terms. Nevertheless, there was still widespread agreement that the ideal office was one in which the sexual and personal were absent—or, at the very least, strictly contained. Commentators still assigned women the task of ensuring that desire did not erupt, and this responsibility was now understood to be a part both of their job description and of being a modern—sexual—woman.

Establishing and policing sexual boundaries was always difficult, but post–World War I changes made the task more complicated. In the new climate, men increasingly used sexual exploits to prove their masculinity; any vestige of the old Victorian view of male desire as a weakness and impediment to business success was gone. Rather, writers reversed the terms, arguing that a strong sex drive was a source of strength and power. Meanwhile, respectable women's newfound libido meant that those in public no longer needed protection from men's coarser natures. The passionless woman had embodied a moral authority that commanded men's respect, but the new feminine ideal told women to make themselves alluring and to solicit male attention, thereby lessening restraints on the expression of male desire. At the same time, the revolution in manners and morals never came close to ending the sexual double standard: a woman's reputation still mattered in the marriage market.[3]

Psychology, which employment experts and advice givers began to use in the 1920s to explain sexual conflicts in the workplace, added another level of difficulty. Woodward applied this perspective when she chirpily recounted a story in which the "repressions" and "suppressions" of a generally sexless man erupted one night while he and a woman in his office were working late. After the woman politely turned down his sudden and unexpected proposition that they have some "fun" together, he locked them in her office. When she threatened to scream, he calmly noted that such a scandal would be worse for her than him. Falling to his knees, he continued to make his case: since he doubted she had any "moral scruples" anyway, what was the harm? When this argument failed, he began to plead—at which point she calmly laughed: "You look awfully funny crawling around on your knees." Ashamed, he silently left, never to speak of the incident again, though they continued to work together for many years.[4]

Woodward's appraisal of what probably was a frightening ordeal appropriated psychological concepts and reflected the larger cultural transition toward understanding problems as the result of personal circumstances, not structural inequalities. Woodward's and others' faith in the modern workingwoman's ability to thwart such advances denied women's economic vulnerability and downplayed their subordinate status. It also overestimated their sexual savvy; some women were ill prepared for the personal interactions they encountered at work. Such women, however, would no longer summon the responses of the past—social reformers holding hearings about the sexual exploitation of working girls or sympathetic preachers raising money for their protection. These impulses had faded by the time of World War I, and with them, the incipient social critique of women's inequality and men's power. In their place, workingwomen found explanations that emphasized individual neuroses and called for individual solutions. As a consequence, women heard the same advice they had always heard when faced with unwanted or coercive advances: find another job.

PSYCHOLOGY AND THE GENDERED LIFE OF THE OFFICE

The female office worker was not at a loss for advice during the 1920s and 1930s, with newspaper columns, magazine articles, and employment guides devoted to her experience. These authors wrote for middle-class women (or working-class women with high school diplomas and high aspirations) and presented the office as a refined place in which the position of private secretary was the pinnacle of achievement. Such a position brought better wages and increased authority, but, most significant, this glamorous job lifted its possessor above the masses of clerical workers from humbler origins, who were well represented among the nearly two million women—about 40 percent of all employed women—who labored in an office in 1930. The mechanization and rationalization of clerical tasks in the largest companies had facilitated this change and created a greater variety of jobs, especially low-paying clerking and bookkeeping positions that often resembled factory assembly lines. For this routine labor, employers often preferred working-class teenagers who had not completed high school. These young women were happy to escape the dirt of the factory and enter a higher-status (though not always higher-paying) world, and their families, especially immigrants, saw clerical work as a small move up the class ladder. These changes also created a more precisely defined occupational hierarchy, with the middle-class "office wife" at the apex, the working-class stenographer a rung below, and filing clerks and machine operators farther down the ladder, where there were few opportunities to climb.[5]

The office was more diverse, and it was also a site of sexual tension, about which advice givers spoke quite openly. Elizabeth Gregg MacGibbon's *Manners in Business*, which merited a lengthy review in *Time* magazine in 1936 and was reprinted fourteen times in the next decade, was one of the most explicit. In her view, only the most obtuse employer would deny the presence of sex, though she quickly qualified this position. In most businesses, "any outward manifestation of attraction between the sexes is frowned upon by the management, and the dynamite is kept in the cellar, so to speak. . . . For the most part men and women learn to work side by side in business, sublimating their primary urges and becoming almost unconscious of each other's sex."[6]

As MacGibbon's Freudian vocabulary of sublimation makes clear, her assessment involved a familiarity with psychological principles. In the 1920s a new psychology developed, centered on questions of human motivation. A multitude of printed sources informed the literate public about neurosis, repression, maladjustment, and personality types. In particular, popularizers emphasized the importance of sex drives, arguing that those unconscious desires affected decisions and behaviors in areas—like work—that seemed to have nothing to do with sex. Though historians identify the period after World War II as the time when the United States fully became a psychological society, already in 1924 a social critic declared that the country had experienced "an outbreak of psychology." Even the Sears, Roebuck catalogue, which found its way to some of the most remote areas in the country, made Freudian ideas available in titles such as *Sex Problems Solved*. By the end of the decade, applied psychologists believed they could apply their knowledge to business—for example, finding the right person for the right job or helping an individual "adjust" to the workplace. In speaking so openly of sexual instincts, then, MacGibbon showed herself to be current with modern psychological thought, as were most advice givers. Some, like MacGibbon and Frances Maule, who wrote nine employment guides between 1934 and 1943, began to write after working for many years in advertising, the first profession to apply psychological insights to business.[7]

Psychologists emphasized that "womankind is emotion kind," and employment guide authors used this assessment as evidence that women found it more difficult than men to become "unconscious" of their coworkers' sex. This idea was not new, of course, but it seemed to have diminished by the 1910s, contradicted by the success of thousands of women in the very jobs they supposedly sabotaged with their excessive feelings. Developments in psychology in the 1920s and 1930s, however, renewed the discussion. Psychologists set out to prove that masculinity and femininity were real (not culturally created) and matched to biological sex; empirical studies would show indisputably that men and women had dramatically different psychological temperaments. The influential Terman-Miles personality test, for example, gave masculinity points to those who said they did not enjoy listening to other people's troubles; femininity marks went to everyone who disliked playing with snakes. The results? The masculine psyche was adventurous, aggressive, and self-assertive; the feminine was domestic, timid, and emotional. Scores were also linked to psychological well-being: a man with high masculinity numbers was mentally healthy, while a woman with such points was psychologically unstable.[8]

Theories of difference also shaped the companionate marriage ideal, which was firmly in place by the 1920s and called for deep emotional connection and intense sexual passion. The mutuality, however, did not challenge men's authority at home, since the husband would need to educate his wife about the erotic. Indeed, sex itself upheld gender roles. Experts defined pleasure through vaginal penetration as feminine and denigrated the allegedly masculine clitoral orgasm. In 1928 the marital adviser Theodoor Van de Velde warned against the woman-astride position in intercourse because of its psychological risks: the "complete passivity of the man and the exclusive activity of his partner . . . is directly contrary to the natural relationship of the sexes and must bring unfavorable consequences if it becomes habitual." Limits on appropriate

expressions of female desire increased in the 1930s, as high unemployment threatened men's dominant role as breadwinner; in this moment
of gender anxiety, a woman who expressed too much interest in sexual
pleasure, even within marriage, seemed unnatural.[9]

One way of thinking about the renewed emphasis on gender difference is to see it as an anxious response to the dramatic changes in roles
that had been and were still occurring. Terman and Miles, for example,
did more than describe gender differences and "prove" that they were
real; they prescribed gendered standards for individuals' mental health.
These poles seemed to provide a certainty—gender is natural—in uncertain times. Women were passionate now, but healthy ones still possessed
to a greater or lesser degree the feminine traits associated with the ideal
Victorian lady.[10]

Commentary on women's employment adopted these same views.
Even before the stock market crashed, Ernest Groves, a prominent
sociologist, argued that a woman who was "coarsened or hard-boiled" by
business would "repel men." Profitable employment, he believed, would
lower the marriage rate as women became overly choosy and rejected
their suitors. In this climate, any woman who expressed dissatisfaction
with women's place in society was dismissed as someone who had failed
to make a proper sexual adjustment. At the very moment that employment opportunities offered women the chance to forgo marriage and
choose economic self-sufficiency—or at least to weigh their options—the
new understanding of womanhood ratcheted up the stakes in marriage,
now deemed the protector of female normalcy. As the historian Nancy
Cott notes, psychologists established that healthy female "adjustment"
consisted of "serving men's needs and pleasures."[11]

Doubts about ambitious women twisted into outright hostility as
Americans watched the unemployment rate rise, peaking at close to
25 percent in 1933. Women had made strides in business during the
1920s, with some women advancing from clerical positions to office
managers or even executives, but these gains disappeared in the
Depression, during which women with college degrees fought for positions as clerks, and stenographers and typists turned to domestic work.
Advice givers encouraged women with some education and marketable
skills to look for positions in feminized occupations like interior deco-
rating, retail sales, and, of course, clerical work. But to land office

jobs—and to keep them—women would need to be impeccably feminine in attitude and appearance. According to one vocational counselor, by the mid-1930s, a pretty smile, youthful grace, and an eagerness to please mattered much more than ability—though to be sure, some commentators had been saying this for years. Historians have understood this advice as a response to the circumscribed opportunities of the Depression and as a way to circumvent the antagonism directed at women workers, but a close reading of employment literature makes clear that psychological understandings of gender difference also influenced authors; at the very least, psychology naturalized advice that developed from the exigencies of the time.[12]

Gender roles were front and center in a 1935 article in *Fortune* on women in business. The modern office necessitated a "daily, intimate, and continuing relation," which was much easier between a man and a number of women than between a man and a number of men. This was a "relation based upon sex," but this did not mean the relationship was sexual. The "blond stenographer with the slick sleazy stockings and the redundant breasts" was not the symbol of the office; the dedicated "daytime wife" who would experience her employer's death as a "painful widowhood" was. Women's difference from men—"their conscious or subconscious intention some day to marry, and their conscious or subconscious willingness to be directed by men"—rendered them "amenable and obedient" and without ambition, making them perfect secretaries and subordinates.[13]

Though the daytime wife's devotion was ideal, it needed to stop short of the desire that was the rightful province of a man's legal spouse. To this end, advice givers sermonized on the sin of behaving unprofessionally. According to Emily Post, guardian of American manners, women's inability to be impersonal was their "chief flaw," especially when it manifested itself in a "crush" on their employer (although an industrial psychologist did note that crushes could be an asset when "expressed in a doglike devotion and loyalty to [a boss's] every wish"). Another writer pinpointed the problem: women had learned their chief job was to attract, "to arouse a personal response." Unfortunately, this instruction caused them to "make love affairs of their jobs." They responded to criticism as though their boss had broken their engagement, and if he smiled at another woman, he aroused as much jealousy as if he were their best beau. Advice givers also warned women not to use sex appeal to advance their careers—that "dangerous and thankless game" was likely to back-fire. And if a woman disregarded the wisdom of leaving love affairs outside of the office, writers all agreed that her choice of men must keep strictly to her own office rank.[14]

As for men, according to advice givers, they were all business—this despite the goings-on we saw up close through Sherwood Anderson and Ward Smith. However "inflammable" a woman's charms made men outside the workplace, they proved "invincibly" cool to even the most attractive girl inside the office. As Maule told her readers, an employer wanted to be able to take his female employees for granted "very much as he does his office machines." Certainly he wanted them to look attractive, but only because he "naturally prefers to have about him persons who are pleasing to the eye." "Sex appeal" would probably irritate him, though, especially if it distracted male employees. According to advice authors, men rarely played a role in instigating romantic and sexual intrigue. Their behavior fell under the category of innocent flirting and "quite harmless masculine admiration . . . that is not intended to be taken seriously." An attractive woman could expect a lot of this attention, but to take it literally was "not quite fair—not playing the game according to the rules." Edith Johnson, writing for the *Oklahoman*, was unusual in recognizing that men made the "love moves" in business, but she believed it was merely "masculine privilege . . . a habit . . . a tradition." Women needed to under-stand that such behavior really did not signify much, that men thought "nothing of it." A guide published in 1940 picked up the same thread. A woman should never take a pass in the office as a compliment, since some men were "always eager to test their batting averages." But if a modern girl should not take such attentions seriously, she also could not be "prissy." Men did not like women who construed their innocent remarks as propositions; a woman who expressed concern about being insulted would be mocked as engaging in "wishful thinking."[15]

PSYCHOLOGY AND UNWANTED ATTENTIONS

Although advice givers insisted that men's attentions were meaningless, some did acknowledge that a woman might encounter unrelenting, inap-propriate, or unwanted romantic or sexual overtures—and they made clear that it was her responsibility to control these situations. However, their assessment of why men acted this way and their advice on how to respond relied on a completely different paradigm than the one used in the late nineteenth and early twentieth centuries. No one lashed out at such men for their lack of character, instead attributing their actions to some (likely temporary) personality disorder. Writers also no longer employed the language of ladies demanding gentlemen's respect, nor did anyone claim that a good family background and strong Christian morals would keep women safe. Now "business training" taught the modern working girl how to "handle situations of this kind."[16]

One hopes she paid attention in class that day, since guidebooks unanimously agreed that if a woman could not personally handle a man's "strictly dishonorable" intentions, she would have to quit. One wonders, though, about the effectiveness of their advice. A book from 1939 recounted that one woman stopped a man's unwanted invitations by going out with him dressed in oversized, frumpish clothing. According to another, a woman needed to "manage" such a man by ignoring him: "She must learn not to see that his glance is too fervid, not to feel that hand that rests on hers or the arm that slips around the back of the chair." This maneuver had to be accomplished with "tact and politeness, for it is not the rebuff that counts so much as the way in which it is done." Frances Maule warned women never to carry their troubles "higher up." Men were the valued employees, and "rarely" would management admonish one of them. Most likely someone would suggest "that a girl usually brings these things upon herself."[17]

How are we to make sense of this advice? On the eve of World War II, advice givers offered women no more options (maybe fewer) than they had forty years earlier, when female workers were new and controversial. Yet there are other ways to read these texts. Although they did not challenge male prerogatives and accepted without question the powerlessness of women's lowly place, they did offer protective strategies—avoid, ignore, run. And the advice to keep the sexual and romantic out of the workplace shifted the focus from femininity onto a woman's identity as a competent worker. It also made sense for the time: why get involved in a situation that could get you fired or force you to quit when jobs were tough to come by? The books' recommendations also were in line with the advice offered in the pop-psychology "how-to-succeed" manuals that flooded the market in the 1930s. Dale Carnegie's best-seller, *How to Win Friends and Influence*

People, was typical of this literature. Failure, in his opinion, was the result of personal shortcomings, not external factors such as the Depression, and the key to success was to transform your personality to become more pleasing to others. This involved learning how to handle people, but criticism would only wound a man's pride and arouse his resentment. The trick, then, was to "change people without giving offense." In this regard, employment guides were very much artifacts of their time, reflecting the dominant view that made the individual responsible for his or her fate and linked success at work to adapting to one's role and getting along with others.[18]

But even when responding to behaviors they classified as merely annoyances, women were at a loss as to how not to offend, suggesting that women had gained sexual knowledge and regained desire at the expense of a certain type of power and ideological protection. MacGibbon included a letter from a woman who wanted advice on how to deal with the "business girl's pet peeve," the inevitable man who was "given to hand holding and occasional kisses." These men were not serious threats, but the letter writer believed that this behavior made her appear undignified and affected how her employers thought of her. As a "modern girl in a modern office," though, she could not "rise up and proclaim herself insulted." Given these restrictions, what could she do? As it turned out, MacGibbon, too, was unable to devise a solution that would stop the degrading behavior and not seem old-fashioned. She offered the letter writer the standard counsel: the man meant nothing by these attentions, and she should ignore and avoid him. If he persisted, she would at least have the "consolation that angels could have done no more."[19]

MacGibbon's psychological explanation of this man's behavior further left women to find their own way out of their troubles. She described such men as being at "the dangerous age." Approaching forty and grieving their lost youth, such men could not resist the presence of a pretty girl. This assessment mirrored that offered by Margaret Quayle, who in the early 1930s applied the most recent findings of modern psychology to business girls' "personality problems." Quayle, too, noted that men who acted like adolescents presented a problem to women, but these untoward attentions had nothing to do with them personally. Such men were "suffering from some form of arrested emotional development" and needed an able psychologist. In other words, psychology reconfigured women's sexual vulnerability in the workplace from a social problem requiring some type of general reform to one of individual men in need of psychological treatment. Psychology explained this behavior as a temporary condition that would ultimately be resolved. In this way, though, a man's maladjustment became a woman's malady. And of course, experts believed women suffered from their own personality disorders. According to Quayle, the woman who was "unhappy unless she is adored by men and who will go to almost any extreme to get their attention [was] frequently met in business offices." If a woman often found herself on the receiving end of sexual overtures, she probably possessed "an unconscious need which [she] is seeking to satisfy in a very neurotic way." Frustrated single women also spent too much time daydreaming about marrying their wealthy boss, which could distort the relationship between a woman and her employer.[20]

In this psychological model, men's and women's personality disorders could lead to sexual behaviors in the office that disrupted business. Yet even though guidebooks acknowledged the contemptible "Felix the Feeler," authors often hinted that even the blameless woman was somehow at fault. Maule described a woman, Jocelyn, whose boss pursued her so relentlessly that she had to choose between her job and her virtue. Jocelyn appealed to the personnel manager, who, unbeknownst to her, owed his job to the miscreant boss. The manager therefore told her that she was vain and had "mistaken mere fatherly kindness for evil intent." After this conversation, she had no choice but to quit. Maule recognized the injustice, but her sympathy extended to Jocelyn's boss. Who, she asked, could resist a girl who was "just too beautiful, too lavishly endowed with the life force, to be allowed around a business office!" This perspective, however, forestalled any critique of men's rationality and presumed right to lead. The boss's susceptibility to a pretty girl qualified him as a man even as it did not disqualify him as a businessman. His emotions—construed here as manly sexual desire—did not unfit him (as a woman's did her) for a position of power in the public world. These stories also called into question the suitability of women in the workforce by reviving a long-standing view of the woman as temptress, even when, like Jocelyn, she couldn't help it.[21]

Maule's perspective on masculinity reflected the latest psychological theories. *Why Men Fail*, a series of articles commissioned by the American

Psychiatric Association and the American Medical Association, contained an essay describing women workers as the dynamite that could blow up a man's career or "fatally disrupt" an office full of men. For some men, sexism hurt their career. This prejudice injured women who found their professional opportunities severely curtailed, but it also harmed men who were too biased even to listen to a woman's business idea, which might cost them a profitable suggestion. For others, "sex allure" was "no less deadly." The authors warned men to be on their guard against the female worker who sought out amatory adventures and distracted every man from his work. Some men even refused to hire a beautiful secretary because they feared their wives' displeasure, their own weakness, or what their business associates might think. On occasion, an especially attractive assistant could elicit such jealousy or rivalry in a man's colleagues that collegiality and profits declined. Sometimes a woman was just too pretty to work in an office, the authors mused. Such a woman should try to find a sales job, where her beauty would be an asset rather than a liability.[22]

According to this essay, women threatened men's success in two different ways, emerging from two distinct psychological sources. Sexism originated in men's "desire to dominate" and was always born of the unconscious fear that a woman might take away some of their power. The problems associated with "sex allure," however, came from men's instinct for "race continuance," which was naturally aroused by a beautiful woman. A quest for control animated men's prejudice against women, and the authors condemned this bias as irrational and unjust. But men who pestered their eye-catching employees were simply being men. When the women had to quit, they were just casualties of nature. Since psychology also argued for the naturalness of gender differences, and since it was men's role to provide and protect, it was again natural that women would be the ones who needed to find other employment. In this way, psychology further contributed to the belief that the office was men's legitimate space, not women's. Psychologists understood the desire for power and how it contributed to gender-based discrimination. However, they did not apply this analysis to behavior that today probably would be regarded as discrimination, described as sexual harassment, and understood as a way in which men use their authority to intimidate and control women workers.[23]

Maule's compassion for Jocelyn's boss reveals a fatal flaw in her and other writers' guidance. On one hand, they portrayed men as all business, but, on the other, they expressed a degree of understanding when men's instincts got the best of them. Where did this leave women? Advice givers cast beautiful women as inevitably disruptive, but they also ordered women to be attractive and feminine, placing them in a double bind ensuring that they would bear the blame for or the consequences of unwanted sexual expression. Advisers devoted countless pages to instructing readers to make the most—but not too much—of their physical attributes. Employers did not like women who dressed mannishly, but guides also cautioned against being too feminine, which would destroy the impersonal ideal and cause a man's mind to wander in dangerous ways. More than one writer told women not to flutter their eyelids, but advice could be maddeningly vague. A nationally known employment counselor advised readers to cultivate "glamour," which she defined as "a definite appeal—not the questionable kind where biologics play too large a part—but the kind where charm and imagination, grooming and personality are all involved, each in its proper proportion."[24]

Advice instructing women to be attractive but not to arouse imposed an impossible and disingenuous standard. Like their counterparts from thirty or forty years before, advice givers encouraged women to control men's behavior through their clothing and manner. This view assumed that men's desire, at least in the workplace, was awakened only by the most obvious display of sex appeal, and it held women responsible if they failed to find the line between attractive and alluring. At least one author, though, tacitly acknowledged women's impossible position in a column titled "There's Luck in Being a Plain Girl." She believed that plain women found jobs hard to land but easier to keep, since they did not usually become emotionally involved with their bosses or the men in their office, which often led to the woman's dismissal.[25]

Guidebooks' discussion of men who would not take no for an answer also deflected attention away from taking the issue seriously by using class-coded language that implied that these men were somehow not genuine members of the white-collar world or were low on its ladder. As one author explained, such men were "coarse-grained, and without sensitiveness or sensibilities, [and] cannot recognize these qualities in others."

These men regarded women as "prey." Edith Johnson was the only author to speak of these behaviors specifically in the context of the Depression and the opportunities for exploitation that a shortage of jobs created. Employers in factories and offices forced female employees to be their "daytime wives," but such men were not those at the top of a company. They were underlings compensating for their "sense of inferiority." In the world of advice givers, success and sexuality were completely distinct; a successful white-collar man would never use his position to extort sexual favors from the women in his office because it was bad business.[26]

Scattered evidence from other sources, however, including women workers, suggests that successful men's minds were not always on business. In the mid-1920s, an organization devoted to expanding women's occupational opportunities surveyed secretaries throughout the United States. A secretary had to "guard against attentions" from the men with whom she worked, one noted, and such situations often led to the woman's resignation. Another commented, "Close contact with employer often requires much common sense, understanding, knowledge of human nature, and tact, to prevent it from becoming *dangerously* personal." In 1937 the annual meeting of the National Office Managers' Association included a report on a study of twelve thousand secretaries who had been fired from sixty-four companies. Two-thirds had lost their jobs because of their or their bosses' "personality and character defects." During the question-and-answer, audience members commented that some women's flaw "probably consisted of an unwillingness to go night-clubbing with the boss." Evidence from alienation-of-affection suits brought by wives against their husbands' secretaries further showed that men could take the lead in office affairs. The courts dismissed at least two such cases because the prosecution could not prove that the secretary had pursued her employer; indeed, all indications suggested that the boss was the aggressor.[27]

THE POWER OF KNOWLEDGE IN WORKPLACE DESIRES

Employment guides imagined office women to be sophisticates who alternately invited and fended off men's advances. But was this portrait accurate? A small study in New York City in the mid-1930s investigating women's psychosexual development suggests that many were sexually and socially naïve in a way that complicates the image of women who knew the score. For at least some, the office provided their first opportunity to interact with men of a different social class, religion, or ethnicity. In the few instances in which romantic and sexual relationships began there, men seemed no less the initiators than the women, and the latter's inexperience gave the more knowledgeable men a decided upper hand. Women brought their desires to the office, but differences of power, status, and experience made it unlikely that they would achieve their dreams.

Fifty-eight of the 108 women surveyed worked in an office. A twenty-four-year-old graduate of a religious college performed general office tasks at a publishing company. A Jewish girl, eighteen, who had completed high school, worked as a receptionist in a law office, and another high school graduate, a twenty-one-year-old second-generation Catholic, clerked at Metropolitan Life Insurance. One Jewish woman approaching thirty worked on a billing machine. A second-generation Jewish girl, not yet twenty and with only two years of high school, put in sixty-hour weeks as a switchboard operator and stenographer at a printing firm, a grueling job, but one that beat unemployment.[28]

The women ranged in age from eighteen to thirty-one; nearly three-quarters were twenty-five or younger (in 1930, more than half of all clerical workers were under the age of twenty-five). Of this young group, only six had lost their virginity, compared with half of the women older than twenty-five. Almost half were Jewish. All had attended some high school and well over half had graduated; nine women had attended college. More than half were first-generation Americans, and four were immigrants. Almost one-third had experienced some type of sexual abuse as a child. The vast majority, it appears, lived at home or with relatives, which was the norm for office workers under twenty-four. Generally speaking, these women were not of the class or from the religious and ethnic groups most employers preferred for the most desirable positions.[29]

The women knew little about sex, suggesting that Ward Smith's secretary who worried that she might have conceived a child through oral sex was not unusual in her confusion. One churchgoer, a Methodist, had received some information in high school biology, but she did not understand it and was too embarrassed to ask for clarification. A graduate of a Catholic college who worked as a secretary at the YWCA had only cleared up her questions about reproduction in the previous year, and a twenty-two-year-old Presbyterian daughter of Scottish-born parents knew even less. Her mother told her about reproduction when she was sixteen, but the facts were presented so sentimentally that the woman entered the interview thinking that a baby was born through its mother's navel. Lack of knowledge could translate into disgust toward sex. A Jewish stenographer, who had a greater understanding than most, had only just abandoned her belief that intercourse was "loathsome and vulgar" (even though she had been dating a young man for two years and had let him fondle her breasts). She did not believe it could be "genuinely pleasant," but she was determined to adjust.[30]

What a woman knew and what she did not know left her ill prepared to comprehend her desires or a man's desire for her; this disadvantage was evident in cases when a woman found herself involved with an older and more worldly man she met at work, as the experience of a twenty-year-old Catholic stenographer makes clear. Her strict Sicilian parents had told her nothing about sex, and her knowledge of other topics was similarly constrained, as she spent her days inside watching the children. After she ran away from home at thirteen, her parents sent her to a convent, where she learned clerical skills. At sixteen, she found employment in an office—and an attractive, well-educated Irish Catholic coworker in his mid-twenties. Their relationship progressed slowly in the course of day-to-day interactions. She was having trouble at home and felt he was her only real friend. She tried to reawaken his interest in religion, but their discussions led her to lose interest in the church. He talked to her about books, music—and sex. Though initially she "didn't believe it," after a year and a half she consented to intercourse. She did not find this pleasant, but she knew it pleased him. Their sexual intimacy continued for six months. Although she felt guilty, she did not stop because she loved him as she loved God and "almost prayed to him." At some point she realized that he did not love her, and at the time of the interview he was living with someone else. She had given up her good job to get away from him and now could not find another. "Kind of lost my mind," she told the interviewer. "Realize now it was all a mistake."[31]

It is not adequate to think of this woman as a victim in the making, a delicate flower unaware that it was about to be picked. As an adolescent she had rebelled against the gender limitations of her culture, determined to claim a larger sphere of life (as many Italian girls did). Yet it is hard not to think of this woman as a casualty of sorts—one whose experience represents a white-collar twist on the usual tale of abandonment and betrayal. Her seduction happened in the office in the context of her employment, which had awakened her desires—not just for successful men or even middle-class things, but especially for knowledge. Her position in this world was tenuous given her ethnicity, her limited education, and, of course, her gender. At the same time, her place in this world had rendered her unfit for the old one. She was searching for office work and, as she told the interviewer, a man who was "sincere . . . Would respect and love me, No one ever loved me in return . . . Well-educated, can't stand ignorant people. Hard working." Meanwhile, she was living at home, a sexually experienced woman in a tradition that cherished chastity, a woman seeking wisdom in a culture that believed ignorance protected innocence.[32]

Women like this wanted more out of life, but their workplace relationships did not always work out as they had hoped. A twenty-seven-year-old secretary, who had left high school after two years, spoke to the interviewer about her uncertainty regarding a six-year affair with her married supervisor, who was in his early fifties. Here again, the relationship had developed gradually; working together led to invitations to the theater and dinner and, ultimately, to sex, though with much initial hesitation on her part. She now realized she was "getting nowhere" with the affair and was unsure about her next step. She did not feel she should demand anything of him, but his concern only with doing the "right thing" by his wife frustrated her: "I feel he ought to do something about me too." Since the man had not shown any "definite intention" of divorcing his wife, this woman's hopes of "enjoying marriage, having a home of my own to express myself in, hav[ing] the companionship of someone I love" were unlikely to be fulfilled. Yet her initial decision to enter into this entanglement was not so surprising.[33]

By the 1920s women of all classes were eager to participate in the new "dating" culture, which was more informal and less supervised than the "courting" it replaced. Dating involved a trade of sorts: he paid, which gave him the advantage, and in return the woman "owed" him something. Although the economics were similar to the older form of "treating," dating involved a more sustained relationship, and scholars have linked it to the rise in premarital intercourse and "petting" among women who came of age in the 1920s and early 1930s. The greatest changes occurred in working-class women's behavior. Their wages left little for pleasure, making them dependent on men to pay for nights out, and the places a successful businessman could take a woman had to make their attentions particularly attractive. Certainly the experience of an "utterly gullible" twenty-four-year-old secretary suggests as much. Her desire to be swept away and to experience Boston "in a very grand style" led to an ill-fated trip to the Ritz Carlton with her new boss. He was arrested for grand larceny shortly after taking her virginity, which led to a breakdown. Two years after the event, the interviewer could still describe her emotional state as "far from indicative of a well balanced stable personality."[34]

According to the survey's interviewers, the new dating system created a type of fear. Women worried that if they did not "allow the boys these privileges," they would "very soon be left out of things." However, they also were anxious that if they permitted such liberties, no one would marry them. It was the double standard, morphing in new circumstances. The former concern seems to explain the behavior of an Irish Catholic freelance stenographer, twenty-seven, who was sexually intimate with three men she encountered through her work. She was "morally conflicted" but unwilling to stop, even though she acknowledged, "With all three men it's been unimportant to me. They all help me in my business, and all they want of me is sex." Despite this last comment, this was not a situation in which a woman bartered sex for occupational success; one of the men had suffered business reverses, so she now did his typing for free, and she had no real interest in marrying him. Unable to say no, incapable of deciding what exactly she wanted, self-employed and sympathetic in a bad economy—this woman seemed sure only that these men's attentions gave her a type of prestige. This was certainly her mother's perspective. Though it seems unfathomable that she knew what really happened on her daughter's evenings out, she was nevertheless "flattered" by her child's popularity. Dating came with a sexual price, but it also confirmed a woman's value by showing her worthy of the money being spent.[35]

Although few of the women in this study had been involved with men from their offices, for some, their contact with businessmen seemed to have altered their conception of the ideal man. A twenty-three-year-old

Protestant secretary dreamed of a future with a man who was not like the men she was dating. She longed for one who was "very thoughtful and kind, not too much of a man of the world, a business executive. About 5 years older than I," a description that seems patterned on the successful men she saw at work. For other women, those men became the objects of sexual desire. A Jewish secretary, twenty-six, who had only one year of high school and a business course, yearned for the chance to improve her education and to kiss her boss. The interviewer described her as sexually well adjusted, and she had recently lost her virginity to her steady boyfriend, a conscious choice based on her wish for the experience and because she found him attractive. She also fantasized about her boss. As she explained: "Sometimes on my job, in taking dictation certain terms I associate with sex and make me blush. . . . Words like 'ball bearing' excite me. My boss sort of interests me, would enjoy his kisses, but he never comes near me. . . . Feel very much at ease and informal with him. I am the aggressor." The erotic, it seems, could infuse everyday routine.[36]

The risks these women faced when entering into relationships with men from their workplace were in many ways no different than the risks they took when they met men in, say, a dance hall. There, too, young women often unwisely took men at their word. Whether on a date to the movies with a man from her neighborhood or in an after-work assignation with a man from the office, a woman was alone in establishing and enforcing her sexual limits. However, a woman in a failed workplace affair might find it harder to forget; a ruined reputation or a broken heart potentially carried emotional *and* economic consequences.[37]

OFFICE GOSSIP: ESTABLISHING THE RULES OF WORKPLACE ROMANCES

Interview records do not say whether anyone in a woman's office knew of her affair. Nor do we know whether the stenographer who found her boss desirable confided her feelings to another girl at work. Employee-produced newsletters from unionized offices in New York City in the 1930s and early 1940s, however, highlight the emotional life of the office—the personal relationships and private conversations that went along with getting work done. Romance was on most workers' minds, and it was quite public.

Women comprised the majority of employees in these offices, and newsletter reporters minced no words in showing that they were on the prowl for men. In 1940 the gossip columnist for the *Do-News* sadly informed her readers that a new male employee was "not eligible, so take back those glances you've been throwing in his direction." When another company needed a new typist, the four women in the typing pool gave the newsletter a set of *their* job specifications: "Applicants must be tall, dark, and handsome. Interviews after 5:30." In 1938 *Our Office Echo* noted for "the benefit of all anxious feminine readers" that the new union organizer was good-looking and single, and his favorite forms of relaxation were "tennis—and attractive women." Men, too, were shown to bring their desires to work. A poem described an apprenticeship in girl-watching, "Teddy eyes the women—Izzy keeps track / Pretty soon he too will catch the knack." And a similar rhyme from another shop suggested the disruptive possibilities of an attractive woman:

> Friend Kay's legs very highly rate
> for all the boys have asked her for a date
> She just says "no" and kills their joys
> I guess she's wise to Credit Clearing boys.

These bits of office "scoop" show that work structured romantic interactions and that workers' sexual and romantic interests organized work.[38]

Historians have noted that companies in the early twentieth century created policies prohibiting romantic relationships between coworkers or designed gender-segregated workspaces in part to lessen the possibility of romantic or sexual encounters. They also have shown that workers routinely disregarded these policies and found ways around enforced separation. Less has been said, however, about workers' creation of their own unofficial rules. These newsletters suggest that employees used gossip and humor to establish and enforce standards of acceptable and unacceptable behavior. One newsletter, for example, contained the observation that "a married woman from our office staff is talking about all the cute fellows from the different stores throughout the city. Wonder if she's taking inventory?" This comment alerted fellow employees to a coworker's marital troubles, but it also seems to carry a critique of her inappropriate interest in other men and a warning to her and other women against becoming too wild. Another gossip column contained the item:

"COOL OFF!!! That's what we told Lou Meltzer. What is there about Lillian that attracts all the new fellows?" Here, a columnist censured a man's pursuit of his female coworker and possibly reproved a woman's behavior: Was Lillian doing something that caused men to transgress appropriate boundaries? These newsletters completely collapsed the public and private; indeed, it seems as though nothing was private in these offices. "Who receives calls from a young man now, the same young man who used to call someone else here?" the "Scoop" reporter asked in April of 1939. Two years later the reporter spotlighted another romance: "What young lady was caught looking at herself in the mirror after leaving a certain office, just to make sure she looked pretty? Won't say any more."[39]

These snippets did more than update readers on their coworkers' latest sexual or romantic intrigues. Scholars have noted that gossip often says as much about the teller as the person being talked about. Comments about an individual's sexual behavior might also be a covert way of addressing workplace tensions that have nothing to do with sex. Rumors and innuendo can establish and enforce sexual boundaries, but they also can be a way of reaffirming hierarchies, asserting status, or solidifying social bonds. Sex was a necessary part of these offices in more ways as well. The imagined opposition of sex to work rendered it highly useful to comment upon and resist the most restrictive aspects of employment, and the insertion of the sexual into these workspaces seemed to restore an element of humanity to jobs that sometimes felt dehumanizing.[40]

Female office workers did seek out romances, but advice givers, influenced by psychology's emphasis on gender difference, assumed that men were too interested in making money to think about such things. In their view, men played by the rules. Even the rare man of a "predatory nature" abided by a "code" and annoyed only women over twenty-five. And when a man hit middle age and momentarily lost his head, it was easy for a woman to return his mind to business. These men were almost always married, which gave a business girl the "upper hand" and made men "easy to control." Women were the ones who had to be reminded of workplace conventions. Don't flirt. Don't take things personally. Especially don't bat your eyes. These endless admonitions hint at a distrust of women when it came to matters of the heart or libido.[41]

Gone were the days when working girls needed protection from wily seducers and men who just would not take "no" for an answer. Women had gained new sexual freedoms. These liberties, however, came with the responsibility to be more personally vigilant or to suffer the consequences on their own—and some women seemed inclined to throw caution to the wind. According to her interviewer, the Jewish woman in New York City who got turned on during dictation and fantasized about her boss was "a little annoyed that he hasn't tried [to kiss her], though they frequently have been alone in the office." If in fact she was, one can hardly blame her. She labored in a culture saturated with images of the salacious secretary and innuendos about "confidential dictation." According to advice givers, real offices had virtually nothing in common with the sexualized "reel offices" of fiction and film, but the numerous stories of office relationships thus far recounted suggest otherwise: offices were often hotbeds of sexual and romantic intrigue. Truth, it turns out, was not necessarily stranger than fiction, though certainly real life had fewer happy endings.[42]

CHAPTER FOUR

Gold Diggers, Innocents, and Tempted Wives

The Skyscraper in Fiction and Film

THE FIRST TIME DAVID DWIGHT, the villain of Faith Baldwin's 1931 novel *Skyscraper*, gets Lynn Harding, the beautiful young heroine, alone, he muses about the building in which they spend their days. "A skyscraper is a little city, it is a little world, it is . . . a phallic symbol." When Lynn blushes, the reader knows she is a good girl—and that her workplace is distinctly sexual. In the early 1930s millions of Americans heard this message: Baldwin's novel was initially serialized in *Cosmopolitan*, then reprinted as a pulp paperback, and finally made into a film, *Skyscraper Souls*, in 1932. *Skyscraper* was part of the outpouring of romance stories, novels, and films set in the office in the 1920s and 1930s, all of which left no doubt that this workplace was erotic space. This representation was definitely not the ordered world of the employment guides, which acknowledged desires but maintained that they were best kept under wraps.[1]

Young workingwomen made up a sizable portion of the audiences for these materials. And thanks to scholars of popular culture, we also know that these representations could serve as a "narrative template" onto which consumers plotted their own lives. In other words, fictional depictions of sexual and romantic interaction in the workplace might have shaped actual workers' expectations or reactions. Of course, mass culture's messages are diverse, and the possible individual interpretations are endless. Yet these narratives were so ubiquitous and their consumption by young women so voracious that they deserve consideration. If it is impossible to say with any certainty how these stories affected women, we do know that workplace sexual intrigues occupied a place in many Americans' imaginations.[2]

And if women office workers did use popular culture as a guide, the lesson they took away was not so different from the assessment of sex and romance put forth by advice givers. Fictional office women were also completely on their own to handle the attentions of men, wanted or not. In these mediums, too, playing with desire was risky business, both to a woman's reputation and to her womanly ambitions of landing a suitable mate or maintaining domestic bliss. When a woman found herself in danger, most often she had only herself to blame: she had used her beauty to advance, had felt flattered by a man's attention, or had neglected to quit at the first sign of danger. Men, by contrast, were more purely victims. When they found their lives destroyed by a dictation-taking gold digger, the culpability rested solely in men's sexual nature.

GOLD DIGGERS IN WHITE COLLARS

Gold diggers first appeared in the mid-1910s and by the mid-1920s were common figures in fiction and film, possibly because they were ideally suited for exploration of the changes in gender ideals discussed in the previous chapter. Gold diggers differed from the seductresses discussed in Chapter 1, whose stories focused most on men's foolish behavior. Gold digger plots—though still showing men as powerless to resist temptation—emphasized the financially strapped woman's material desires. These stories no longer represented avarice as leading to an inevitable decline (recall the poem from the first chapter in which a woman who only flirted with her rich married boss lost the man she really loved and her job), but regularly showed women successfully parlaying sex appeal into class advancement.[3]

Throughout the 1920s gold digging was not the usual province of stenographers and secretaries; Cinderella was their story line, and it relied on loyalty and service to one's boss, not the manipulation of men's desires. Although this plot of dutiful secretary rewarded with a ring continued in the 1930s, two of the most controversial gold digger films of the decade, *Red-Headed Woman* (1932) and *Baby Face* (1933), featured white-collar women with decidedly working-class pedigrees. This shift suggests that the changing demographics of the clerical labor force, the new understanding of female sexuality, and economic hard times had contributed to a growing distrust of office women. These films were produced during the so-called pre-Code era, the period between 1930 and mid–1934 during which film studios pledged to uphold the Production Code of 1930 but regularly disregarded its rules. Yet even in this moment of lax enforcement, industry censors demanded changes in *Red-Headed Woman* and *Baby Face:* almost by definition, the theme of a seductive woman capitalizing on her physical charms in the workplace was incompatible with the code's warning that a film should not "lower the moral standards of those who see it."[4]

Hollywood heroines who converted questionable morals into queenly riches enraged reformers, who worried about the message they sent. Young women of every social class made up a sizable part of the filmgoing audience, and they did more than just passively look at the screen. A study from 1929–33, for example, included a comment from one who declared that "love pictures" made her "kiss and pet much more" than she otherwise would. Young female viewers also devoured movie magazines, which encouraged them to identify with celebrities and gave those stars the power to shape or influence moral standards. By the early 1930s social scientists were querying reform school inmates to see whether films gave them the idea of making "easy money" by, among other things, "gold digging men."[5]

In *Red-Headed Woman*, the ability to take dictation is what allows Lil Andrews to move from the wrong side of the tracks into close enough contact with the upright businessman Bill Legendre to employ her feminine wiles. Gold digger films played on the notion of men's animal nature, a notion that gives sexually knowing women like Lil unparalleled power; as "Red" sneeringly replies whenever someone questions her ability to persuade, "He's a man, ain't he?" In this case, though, Red's class makes matters even worse. When Bill's wife learns about the affair, she is most upset that Lil is so common, "a girl like that." But as Bill shamefully responds, "That's just it. Sometimes it is a girl like that, that . . ." Although he cannot bear to finish the sentence, it is clear what he is thinking: that arouses desires a red-blooded man cannot deny.[6]

Some scholars have argued that Depression-era audiences saw gold digger films as a parody of the ridiculous belief in men's sexual vulnerability, but it seems just as likely that some female viewers saw these stories as suggesting a path they could follow. Certainly this was a worry of industry censors. While the film was still in production, they expressed reservations about the "glamour" that surrounded the "common little creature," and it is not too far-fetched to think the setting of *Red-Headed Woman* played a part in their concern. Lil in the office was not the same as ex-showgirls in a swanky apartment looking for sugar daddies, the setting of one popular film that featured rapacious women. Lil was a stenographer, and this ordinary job gave her the chance to put her true skills to work. As she confidently tells Bill, it is useless to resist. She knows he wants her because he looks her "all over" whenever she takes his dictation. Bill is soon divorced and remarried to Red, and they live in the biggest house on the right side of town. However, when the right sort of people refuse to accept her, Lil turns her charms on other, wealthier men, ultimately securing a very happy ending with a Frenchman as old as he is rich.[7]

In 1933 Warner Brothers, trying to replicate *Red-Headed Woman*'s success, released *Baby Face*, which is almost exclusively about power and gender exploitation. Lily Powers's father owns a mill-town speakeasy and pimps her to a politician in return for protection for his business. When the still explodes, killing her father, Lily moves to the city, where she uses her sexual power over men for *her* material gain, setting her sights on the men who run the Gotham Trust Company.[8]

Censors told the producers that the audience had to leave the theater having clearly learned that immorality did not pay, which led to a number of changes in the original story line. The writers had initially emphasized women's victimization in a male-dominated world and presented female sexuality as a weapon to even the odds, thereby rendering Lily's actions understandable, even sympathetic; as an old friend tells her, she can either use men or be used by them. In the released version, this friend warns Lily against using her beauty for gain, and the new ending punishes her for disregarding this advice. She begins her journey by sleeping her way into an entry-level clerk position and uses her looks to ascend from there, ultimately landing a position as bank president Courtland Trenholm's wife. But when he needs her to return the jewels he has given her in order to save the bank, she refuses; by the time she realizes that she loves him more than money, he has shot himself. The film concludes with a scene of the bank's board of directors discussing the Trenholms, who have given their every cent to save Gotham Trust. Courtland, who has recovered from his self-inflicted wound, is now laboring in the mill in Lily's hometown. This ending condemns immorality, but it especially puts gender and class relations back in their expected places. Lily's sexual power has been domesticated and returned to the private sphere, where it no longer represents a threat to business or businessmen. She is now a devoted wife who chose to exchange her earthly riches for love. Her husband is again in control of their relationship, but he has paid plenty for letting a woman and his desires get the best of him, as has almost every man Lily touched.

Yet even with this sanctimonious ending, the film still presents life as a battle between the sexes. Lily makes one move up the ladder by provocatively leaning over a manager, Mr. Brody, as she shows him a letter. Brody, who had just said there were no openings in his division, suddenly reconsiders. The next scene finds them in the office's restroom after work, where they are discovered by Ned Stevens, Brody's supervisor. "Brody, this is an outrage," Stevens sternly reprimands, "—a man in your position. Get your check at once." As Brody leaves in disgrace, Stevens turns his attention to Lily: "Young woman, there's no place here for a girl of your sort," to which Lily quickly replies, "It wasn't my fault. What could I do? He's my boss and I have to earn my living." Stevens is unmoved by this explanation, so Lily turns on the tears. "I'm so ashamed!" she sobs. "It's the first time anything like that has ever happened to me." This injured innocent approach meets with a more approving response, and Stevens offers the insulted girl a job as his secretary, a significant promotion.

In this scene, we see gender, power, and desire at work. There was an unspoken agreement between Lily and Brody; she knew her promotion came with a price. But when they are discovered, he has no way to justify his actions and so loses his job. Lily, however, can use sentiment to keep hers. She received no sympathy when she spoke straightforwardly (if, in her case, dishonestly) about the connection between power and sexual exploitation; Stevens was unmoved. After all, as the advice guides made clear, the correct response to such a situation was to look for another position. The only chance to keep her job, then, was to play the victim and hope for rescue, a strategy that worked. Indeed, it is Lily's talent at playing the part of the virtuous maiden abused by unprincipled men that most contributes to her rise. Lily advances by appealing to men's desire to be more honorable than other men as well as to their sexual desires; in other words, she exploits masculinity itself. Taken as a whole, the film's view of mutual and constant exploitation presages the polarized opinions of sexual harassment today, one emphasizing men's abuse and the other focusing on women's deception. In the end, *Baby Face*'s sympathy seems to rest with the victimized men. Their abuse injures Lily, and, through her, larger moral standards. But her decision to play on men's vulnerabilities is truly dangerous. Marriages and morals are at risk, as are big business, a system of meritocracy, and a clear class and gender structure. Such a woman *in the office* represents social disorder of the highest magnitude.

Gold diggers did not exist only in Hollywood's imagination: in the mid-1930s, a movement to stop living, breathing gold diggers took off in an effort to repeal "heart balm" torts. Even in the early twentieth century, when a few office workers sued their bosses for breach of promise, critics were criticizing these lawsuits as nothing more than legal blackmail perpetuated by sexually shrewd women and out of sync with emerging ideas of women's equality. These discussions often focused on leggy chorus girls and seductive shop clerks, women and whose social class or choice of occupation already marked them as morally suspect. As the opposition gained momentum, the white-collar mercenary was sometimes used as evidence of just how deceptive women could be: as early as 1915 a joke warned men to read carefully the letters their stenographers handed them to sign, lest one end up as Exhibit A in a breach of promise suit. By 1940, ten state legislatures, in all parts of the country, had abolished or severely limited these actions, and fifteen other states had considered, but not passed, similar bills. That so many states considered reform suggests that many Americans believed women no longer needed protection from sexual predators and could not be trusted when it came to matters of love and money.[9]

The reform movement took off in 1935, when Roberta West Nicholson, the only female in Indiana's state legislature, introduced a bill to repeal the state's heart balm laws, making an argument based on gender equality that other reformers echoed. "Women do not demand rights," Nicholson urged; "they earn them, and they ask no such privileges as these." Others believed the laws were irreconcilable with egalitarian principles because they implied women's continued economic dependence on men and challenged the new companionate marital ideal in which a woman chose a husband based on her feelings, not his finances. Reformers also adopted the perspective of legal scholars who had long argued that the law of contracts should not govern love; business relationships necessarily involved a degree of suspicion, but affection was not a commodity, and romantic relationships should be based on trust. (Ironically, this argument gained traction even as the dating system was further transforming sexual and romantic relationships into commodities. In both situations, men were advantageously positioned to set the exchange rate.) This view upheld the distinction many Americans made between public and private behaviors. Reformers even used suits featuring the irrational love notes of rational businessmen to show the unreasonableness of heart balm laws—a position that overlooked the reality of romance and sexuality in the workplace.[10]

Many reformers, however, seemed motivated more by an intense distrust of women than by a sense of fairness, leading to a curious alliance of those who believed that they were helping women with those who wanted to ensure that women could not harm men. One jurist described the laws as nothing more than a means to "inflict some public hurt upon a man by a disappointed woman," and even the equality-minded Nicholson believed that "many an itching palm has masqueraded as a broken heart." A discernable class prejudice also ran through anti–heart balm efforts. The cases had become so associated with scandal and deceit, many argued, that no woman of "modesty and good breeding" would bring a charge; a "sensitive and refined" woman would never "parade in public her wounds of the heart." Here, then, was another double bind: if a proper woman would never think of bringing a suit, then to do so was de facto evidence that the woman was improper and thus had probably fabricated the charge.[11]

But of course any plaintiff can lie, and the potential for blackmail applies to any tort. Furthermore, the notion that money is poor compensation for lost love could be applied to many losses that make their way into the courthouse. Historians have found nothing to substantiate the claim that heart balm cases were especially disposed to extortion or invention, and legal records show a diversity of plaintiffs. Substantiation is also lacking for reformers' assertion that juries handed down excessive awards to pretty plaintiffs playing innocent. The anti–heart balm movement, we are left to conclude, harbored a deep, abiding suspicion of women. In this way, though, it simply mirrored the perspective that legal experts offered in other situations in this period. In common-law marriage cases, evidence that a woman had *acted* like a man's wife was no longer enough to establish a marital relationship. And though jurists had long argued that most rape charges were fabricated, distrust continued to grow: in 1931 a physician asserted, "Probably ninety-nine out of one hundred would be nearer the truth." According to the historian Angus McLaren, heart balm reforms also reflected anxiety about male authority in the face of women's growing social and economic power. In his view, reformers were most concerned with protecting men, and in states that repealed the laws, the effect was to uphold men's sexual prerogatives while removing any fear of financial consequences. Reformers also might have been interested in protecting men's dignity. Plaintiffs could use love letters as evidence of a relationship, and one early critic remarked that even the "hardest headed business men have often made themselves in their letters to appear to be the most glorious fools."[12]

The themes of equality and distrust flavor the story Senator John McNaboe used to generate support for New York's reform bill, and it involved a secretary and her employer. In this case a young midwestern woman maintained that from 1928 to the end of 1934 her boss promised to marry her, but then changed his mind. As a consequence, she was suing him for $100,000 for breach of promise. To McNaboe, the suit was clearly a scam, since "any girl intelligent and self-respecting enough to make her own way in the world might have been expected to smell a rat long before the boss broke the bad news." This woman had admitted to having "played along" with her boss for almost six years, and, thus, in McNaboe's mind, she had exhibited an economic and sexual autonomy tantamount to renouncing any right to sue for damages. At the very least, her innocence was inexcusable for a woman in her position, and therefore she was to blame. In the opinion of a recent legal scholar, McNaboe's decision to recount the story of a secretary was not accidental. In doing so, he indicated that the woman who was willing to barter her honor for riches was no longer a woman beyond the pale. She was now to be found in ordinary offices, where she represented an ever-present danger. In the heart balm controversy, we see again the popular belief in—though, as we saw in the last chapter, not necessarily the reality of—the modern workingwoman's sexual savvy, and a concomitant assumption that she could take care of herself. We see, too, that white-collar workers were no longer portrayed as more moral or refined than other workingwomen; modern sexual ideals applied to all women now, and the office included women of all social classes.[13]

Sensational trials involving wealthy men and women seeking hundreds of thousands of dollars fueled reform efforts, and in a handful, the plaintiff was the woman who had typed the man's letters, though these women never received more than a tiny fraction of what they sought. Avarice might have motivated these women, but in more prosaic cases—those involving everyday clerical workers and asking for much smaller damages—unchecked greed does not seem to apply. Moreover, the modern, post–World War I office worker seems no better equipped to take care of herself than had the earlier generation of stenographers who had used breach of promise suits to achieve a degree of justice when their employers jilted them. In a case from 1913, for example, a stenographer sued her former employer after he broke their engagement when she became ill. Her female lawyer showed to the jury's satisfaction that he had pursued her, taking her to dinners and the theater and finally proposing. Witnesses confirmed this point, testifying that he had referred to her as his future bride. His rejection had "subjected her to a great deal of ridicule," but she was also now sick, single, *and* out of a job. A similar case from 1927 followed the same pattern: a woman sued her fiancé after he broke their engagement. She had worked as his secretary for many months without compensation and also had lent him money. She was lonely now and also low on funds. The jury awarded her $10,000.[14]

Supporters of women's political and economic rights were right that tremendous movement toward equality and liberation from rigid gender roles took place in the first decades of the twentieth century. But some women, because of their class and ethnicity, their religious upbringing, their age—in other words, the sum of their individual circumstances— were farther from that goal than others. Ideologically speaking, breach of promise suits did hurt (or certainly did not help) women. Such cases presented women in a negative, lesser light; women either needed protection or society needed protection from them. For *a* woman, though, these laws could represent her best chance at achieving justice—not just for having lost at love, but for real financial losses. This might have been especially true in cases involving white-collar women whose emotional and economic lives intertwined. As the legal scholar Mary Coombs argues, filing a suit was not a mark against a plaintiff's character, but a sign of her character: she refused to accept her victimization without a fight.[15]

The tension between what was good for women writ large and what helped an individual woman was also apparent in the counsel offered in employment guides. Their advice was seemingly directed to the individual woman who read their books, yet, as we have seen, their guidance to keep things impersonal, to handle problems of unwanted attentions on one's own, did not help the actual woman who encountered a flesh-and-blood man who would not take no for an answer. In the abstract, such advice could not be faulted; it was a useful approach to avoid conflict. In lived reality, both the suggestions in prescriptive literature and the abolishment of heart balm torts in some states left women to take care of themselves, which some were better able to do than others. Women had achieved a variety of new freedoms, but these liberties also increased individual responsibility without commensurate gains in power, making romance and sexuality areas in which women were even more on their own to protect themselves against unwanted or intimidating attentions.[16]

EXPLOITATION AT THE MOVIES

In the early 1930s Hollywood tackled the issue of the woman who was forced to choose between unemployment or undressing for her employer. The Production Code sought to protect not only dominant moral values but capitalism as well. To that end, films that portrayed financial hardship as endangering a woman's virtue always muted any economic critique. And since the films were also meant to entertain, what gender or social analysis there was had to fit the requirements of formula or genre.[17]

One of the few exploitation films set in an office ultimately spoke more to broader social concerns about women's character and the institution of marriage than to the specific issue of sexual extortion. In the comedy *Big Business Girl*, beautiful Claire "Mac" McIntyre is an ambitious college graduate who has secretly married her college sweetheart. She is determined to land a good job, but a stenographer position in an advertising agency is the best she can do. She quickly gets promoted to copywriter because, as she overhears her boss comment to a friend, "A girl with a chassis like that can be a half-wit and get by." Mac is angry, but she decides to use her attractiveness to her advantage and engages in a flirtation with her boss. This, of course, leads to danger, and Mac finds herself with an employer who won't take "no" for an answer. At the moment of truth, Mac's husband appears to save her, but misunderstanding ensues, and the story quickly transforms into a classic love triangle in which the lecherous boss becomes a legitimate (if devious) beau who imperils the wholesome couple's marriage. Domesticity is restored by the film's end, and what had begun as a tale poised to examine the connections between power, employment, and sexuality becomes another example of the "familiar story of coy secretaries, leering male employers and sedulously locked office doors" that approached satire.[18]

According to Hollywood, men were not the only ones to leer. The role-reversal comedy Female, released in 1933, also made light of an employer's power and an employee's sexual vulnerability, confirming traditional gender ideals in the process. Allison Drake capably and confidently presides over a large automobile company, which she has inherited. When not focused on the bottom line, she fixes her gaze on the attractive young men she employs. When she finds one she likes, she invites her unsuspecting prey home to "discuss business." At the office the next day, she is again the steely-eyed executive, leaving the man humiliated and heartbroken, but with a hefty bonus added to his next paycheck. Allison quickly dispenses any man who declares his love to a branch office far away, and one such scene leads Allison to declare, "From now on I'll have nothing but women secretaries." Of course, the real problem is that she has only met "yes" men, whom she rightfully tosses aside.

A real man comes in the person of Jim Thorne, a new employee whose invention is crucial to the company's success. When Allison commands him to her home, he goes, but he refuses her advances. You may be the company president, he tells her, "but I was engaged as an engineer, not a gigolo. And I'm not holding my job by humoring any little whims of yours." This dominant male's "no" awakens the domestic "yes" slumbering in Allison's soul. She soon tearfully declares to her board of directors that business is "no place for a woman," and convinces Jim that she loves him more than work. He will make cars, and she will make babies.[19]

Here again, genre and formula combine to present exploitation as something unreal, an inconsequential joke. The seduced secretary whom Allison puts in his place after he presumptuously sends flowers can hardly command the audience's sympathy; after all, he got a bonus and a night of lovemaking. And Jim, the only man who refuses, ends up with the ultimate promotion. Meanwhile, Allison really just wants love. In other words, the role reversal in the film is illusory. In particular, the film misrepresents an employee's ability to resist his or her employer's demands. Jim has something the company needs. He expresses no concern that he will find a pink slip in his box in the morning. Rather, he matter-of-factly tells Allison that the next time she wants to talk business, she needs to do so at work. Female employees, as a rule, were without such a bargaining chip, especially during the Depression when the skills most women possessed were in large supply.

FAITH BALDWIN AND LOVE AT THE OFFICE, MIDDLE-CLASS STYLE

The crises of the Depression also led to the return of the idea of the workplace as a danger to women, but now the office threatened a woman's feminine role as much as her moral virtue. When women first entered the office in the late nineteenth century, some commentators worried that women's ability to support themselves would lead a few to think twice about giving up a good job for a poor husband. Arguments that clerical work was actually the perfect training ground for future wives lessened this concern, though its echoes were sometimes heard, as in Walter Mayer's murder trial in 1926, when the defense hinted that the victim, Shirley McIntyre, was too independent. As the economy crumbled, this anxiety returned; women's wage earning created unnecessary materialistic desires, and exposure to successful older men soured an unmarried woman's impression of men just starting out. Popular culture also introduced a new threat to marriages involving the relationship between a working wife and a successful businessman; the controversy over married women's employment during the Depression might have included fears that working wives encountered too many sexual temptations.[20]

These concerns were apparent in Faith Baldwin's fiction. Baldwin was one of the most popular writers in the twentieth century, reaching the height of her success in the 1930s. Many of her novels were serialized in magazines like the *Saturday Evening Post* that self-described "business girls" read, and many featured white-collar heroines. Baldwin's perspective was solidly middle class and mainstream, and in many ways her views about workplace relationships paralleled those offered by advice givers like Frances Maule. Baldwin made clear, for example, that women should not try to parlay their personal charms into professional gain, and she, too, assigned women the task of controlling men's—and their own—desires. But Baldwin was, of course, writing romances; her stories assumed that love and lust would find expression in the office and that these passions would test the heroine's moral fortitude.[21]

In *Skyscraper*, Baldwin focused on the issue of young women who judged their male peers by the standard of men who had already made it. The novel's heroine, Lynn, finds herself in Manhattan after her physician father encounters hard times. With family connections, she lands a research position at a bank, earning a salary of nineteen hundred dollars a year (almost double the wage of an entry-level typist). Lynn is ambitious, and she is also confused about her choice of a mate. She loves young Tom Shepard, whom she meets in her building, but his future is far from secure and initially, his attitude toward a working wife is far from progressive. By contrast, the forty-eight-year-old attorney David Dwight, whom Lynn meets through her work connections, has "everything—position, money, brilliance, and the most enormous acquaintance and experience." When he offers to divorce his wife, everything is within Lynn's reach.[22]

But Baldwin makes clear through David that the things older men offer represent a danger to beautiful young women's values and to their appropriate place in life. Early in the story, when Lynn has already fallen in love with Tom and just met David, the former laments his low income for the sole reason that it makes marriage impossible, and he knows Lynn will meet "undesirable people" at work—that is to say, "*attractive men with money.*" Here, Baldwin shows that the desire beautiful women naturally arouse in the workplace is dangerous to them and especially to the young men who are their rightful suitors. David, as it turns out, can offer Lynn things, but nothing of real value. He is a Casanova, always seeking to prove his "own potence" and always unwilling to acknowledge his role in his many seductions. He is also in the midst of a midlife crisis and sees Lynn as a way to reclaim his youth. This emotional dishonesty merely reflects the deceitfulness of his character. He secretly uses information Lynn has naïvely given him to play the stock market, replenishing his fortune and imperiling her bank and Tom's reputation. For an audience that had seen the stock market crash less than two years before and now watched the unemployment rate rise, Baldwin's linkage of financial and sexual predation makes it obvious that David is no prince and the skyscraper no palace ball.[23]

Baldwin also focused on the sexual temptations facing a working wife. Depression-era magazine fiction, scholars note, celebrated the independent and adventurous woman as long as she was single, but castigated the career-oriented wife. Baldwin's stories stopped well short of rebuking the ambitious wife, though making it clear that a young wife's success might endanger her husband's self-respect, which was already under siege from the constant threat of unemployment. But a husband's emasculation was about more than economics. Baldwin's heroines were sexually desirable and desiring: would they be able to resist the successful men they encountered if they respected them *and* found them sexually arousing, especially if their husbands fell short of traditional markers of masculine achievement?[24]

In tackling these issues in 1932's *Week-End Marriage*, Baldwin stepped into the raging controversy over married women's employment. In the 1920s feminists and others began to advocate for the working wife, arguing that employment provided economic independence and personal rewards and was in line with the new egalitarian marital ideal. Critics saw this behavior as a reflection of an excessively individualistic society and as dangerous to families and to men, who did not need more competition. Despite this censure, the number of working wives increased by 40 percent during the 1920s, primarily in the white-collar sector. During the Depression, however, the hostility against working wives dramatically increased. Lawmakers limited married women's opportunities in government positions, and married female office workers, especially in the banking and insurance industries, found themselves out of a job or unable to find one. The domestic chaos of a dependent husband and a breadwinning female, one author warned in 1933, was a problem "vastly more terrifying than the economic wolves howling at the apartment door." By the mid-1930s, as the attack on working wives grew, defenders abandoned the rationales of the 1920s and presented wives' wage labor as self-sacrifice, arguing that women would rather be at home.[25]

Public discussions about women's selfish individualism or unfair competition with men did not include any explicit discussion of sexuality, though alienation of affection cases in which a husband sued his wife's employer for breaking up his marriage provided evidence of its presence. As early as 1894 a stenographer's angry husband brought suit against his wife's wealthy, married employer for luring her away. By the late 1920s a few men tried to hold employers responsible for the theft of the affection of women who met their adulterous love interests through work. An aggrieved husband blamed his wife's boss for leaving her unchaperoned on a business trip; within a month, she had left her husband for the other executive who had traveled with them. These cases, as rare as they were, highlighted the sexual threat married women's employment posed to their families and raised the question of employers' legal responsibilities when employees' personal and professional relationships became intertwined—issues that would be of major concern by century's end.[26]

Baldwin's *Week-End Marriage* does not involve any litigation, but it does show the connection between financial independence and sexual autonomy. It begins with the wedding of two young white-collar workers whose decision to marry involves much economic negotiation. Traditional Ken wants a wife at home whom he can work *for*, while ambitious Lola wants to keep her job. She prevails, and all is well until Ken, through no fault of his own, gets demoted on the same day Lola gets a promotion to private secretary. He takes his bruised ego out drinking each night with his buddies, where they flirt with girls. She is rightfully resentful and finds an opportunity for payback when Peter Acton, a successful older man, walks into her boss's office on business and asks her to lunch.

Lola, like all of Baldwin's heroines, is a woman of character, so the reader knows she would never engage in an adulterous act. Yet Acton is nevertheless a "temptation." Representing the possibility of a life of luxury, he exacerbates Lola's discontent and adds another problem to her already troubled marriage. When she tells Ken she lunched with Acton, he tells her Acton is interested only in sex. Though he is right, Lola will not admit it. When he forbids her to see Acton again, she mutinies. She is the breadwinner, and she will lunch with Acton as often as she likes. This rebellion (and her pleasure at catching the eye of an attractive, wealthy man) leads to danger. Acton seems unwilling to take "no" for an answer, and Lola worries about the consequences of offending a friend of her boss. This hazard is averted when Acton falls in love with Lola and proposes, which creates an even greater peril to her marriage. His passionate embrace makes Lola realize how much she loves Ken, and the novel ends with Lola abandoning her career to support him in his new position as the owner of a gas station. Removed from the public sphere, Lola is safe from temptation. However, Baldwin assures readers that Lola will not be spending all her time in the kitchen; she will do the book-keeping, and it will be *their* business.

In *Wife Versus Secretary*, a novella from 1935, Baldwin again portrays the office as erotic space, though this time it is the boss's marriage that is in danger. Yet according to Baldwin, the stay-at-home wife has little to worry about if her relationship is sexually sound. Sexual feelings will naturally develop between a man and his secretary, but these desires do not necessarily threaten a man's marriage, especially since most secre-taries, like Helen Walsh, are professionals who will not endanger their position by giving in to passion.

Helen is Van Sanford's private secretary. A stunning blonde, she endures countless propositions from men who come to see Sanford, though she has mastered the art of friendly discouragement to ensure she makes no enemies for her boss. Van, however, is less moved by Helen's sex appeal: "Damned efficient and, as an afterthought, damned good-looking." His amatory affections belong exclusively to his wife, Linda, who has given no thought to her husband's secretary until her friends, including one whose husband had an affair and now has a male secretary, see Helen and note her attractiveness. Her jealousy aroused, Linda begins to make comments to Van about Helen, which insult him—and give him ideas. On a business trip, Van and Helen find themselves in each other's arms, but after a sizzling kiss, they stop. Van is interested in escalating this intimacy, but Helen refuses, even though her ardor is aroused. "We have a pretty fine relationship, you and I. We won't jeopardize it," she states, and he agrees, though this did not mean he would never again think about her sexually since no man, not even one who deeply loved his wife, was "wholly immune."[27]

In this story Baldwin spoke to a broad change in the understanding of the adulterous white-collar male. As we saw in Chapter 1, the idea that office women were "love pirates" out to hijack husbands developed in the late nineteenth century, along with women's employment, and reflected the fear of female sexual power and especially the emerging discussion about the place of sex in marriage. By the 1920s this debate had been absolutely settled in sex's favor, and talk about wives, bosses, and secretaries focused as much on whether the former was living up to the new marital ideal of companion and lover as on the latter's seductive ways. In this accounting, if a wife was not and her husband left her for his office help, she had no one but herself to blame. In portraying Linda as an ideal wife and warning wives not to look for trouble where there wasn't any, Baldwin picked up on a favorite topic of female newspaper columnists. These advice givers consistently told wives to worry less about pretty stenographers and to think more about their own behavior. A wife who spent too much money and failed to take an interest in her husband's hopes and worries made the loyal secretary seem appealing by contrast. And wives who wore sloppy clothes and a surly attitude also made attractive and agreeable office wives look mighty good.[28]

Most of these criticisms were not excessively cruel. One advice giver, for example, told a wife to "pretty herself up, love her man devotedly, and believe in him" as a way to thwart the "sleek, wily, manicured creatures" her husband encountered at work. Yet the din of this disapproval must have left a ringing in wives' ears since their marriages were at risk if *they* failed. Here, as with employment guides' advice to female office workers to be impersonal lest they arouse some man's sexual instinct, women—wives or secretaries, but not men—are to blame for the eruption of illicit desire in the skyscraper. And, as even Baldwin shows with Van and Helen, once the explosion occurred, it was up to the woman to put out the flames.[29]

Businessmen, these sources suggest, might have a slow fuse, but once lit, it burned fast. Yet when Baldwin joined the chorus of advice givers who argued that a happily married man noticed his employee only when his wife put the idea in his head, her tone was off. Helen, after all, has to fight off virtually every man who comes to see her boss—were so many men saddled with sexless wives? And, of course, Baldwin's other office romances included plenty of men on the make. Linda, the heroine of *White Collar Girl*, published in 1933, is a young, unmarried securities broker who encounters an amorous businessman on a sales call. She spends a "frantic five minutes dodging around desks" before she finally slaps him and leaves. Her initial anger, though, quickly turns to amusement: "Such things . . . were bound to happen. . . . Men." In this brief passage, the sole purpose of which is to describe Linda's job and her determination, Baldwin presents such behaviors as natural.[30]

Baldwin's portrait of the sexualized office was tame in comparison with Hollywood's adaptations of her stories. While she occasionally showed a woman attempting to use her attractiveness for gain, such characters always served as a warning to readers, and she never presented secretaries as so much marital poison. Although Baldwin's *The Office Wife* ended with the secretary marrying her boss after his amicable divorce, the novel warned readers against falling in love with their employers and delineated the new companionate marriage ideal. The 1930 film adaptation, however, documented a designing secretary's stratagems, such as arranging the office chairs to provide a view of her legs during dictation and practicing ways to hike up her dress accidentally. The film's conclusion was the predictable outcome of a "seductive secretary" and a

WIFE: *And I think I'll give your typist some silk underthings—
what size does she wear?*

This cartoon accompanied *Life* magazine's 1930 review of the film adaptation of Faith Baldwin's *The Office Wife*. The film was entertaining, but, according to the reviewer, it did not answer the fundamental question: "Does a husband kept at the office mean that his secretary is kept?"

successful man who comes to think of her as a "reward for concentration on his toil." This and other films clearly contradicted Baldwin's and newspaper columnists' assertions that a modern wife had nothing to fear from her husband's female employees. Film adaptations also went further in portraying men as distinctly sexual creatures. Tom gets fresh with Lynn (and gets a slap in return) the first time he meets her in the skyscraper's lobby, and he is all hands and kisses after that as they court in her office. When not in the boardroom, David Dwight is with his secretary in the bedroom of his apartment, which is conveniently located on the building's top floor. When Linda tells Van's mother that she thinks he has cheated with Helen, her in-law offers a justifying consolation: "It's horrible but you mustn't be too hard on him. . . . You wouldn't blame a little boy for stealing a piece of candy if left in a room with a whole boxful."[31]

CINDERELLA OR CINDERS? THE BOSS AS HERO OR HEEL

With the exception of *The Office Wife*, Baldwin avoided a rags-to-riches ending, though other authors more explicitly addressed the issue of social class in romantic relationships between bosses and their female employees. Confession magazines and even labor activists penned their own stories about workplace encounters. Not surprisingly, their perspectives differed, and the heights of happiness found in the endings of true-confession dramas corresponded with the depths of despair that concluded labor's tales. These stories make clear that negotiating gender was only one part of the sexual politics of the office; expressions of desire also were intimately linked to issues of class.

Confession magazines like *True Story* and *True Romance* paired a vivid portrayal of sexual or ethical dangers with the possibility of romantic reward. Confessions, which got their start in 1919, specifically targeted working-class women, some of whom by the 1920s were filling the new low-skilled, often mechanized clerical positions. Confession readers wanted to learn how women like themselves solved problems that they, too, might face; this, then, was not escapist reading but rather instructional material on how to achieve happiness, defined as a strong marriage and solid family life.[32]

In "Not the Marrying Kind," published in 1934, Delight Torrance faced the challenge of staying sweet in the face of her wealthy employer's "insinuating little remarks" and offers to "be nice" to her. Delight had secretly loved Melvin Blake from the moment he hired her, but he believed she was just another "pretty girl, come to New York like a little gold digger, hunting for some one to pay her rent." For three years he hounded her "in the worst way a man can hound a girl," learning that she was "decent" only after she cared for his ailing mother while he was out of town. "I ought to get down on my knees and apologize to you," he declares. "Tell me, Delight, did you ever think you might care a little for me? That is, if I weren't such an awful beast to you?"[33]

True Story presented Blake's relentless attack on Delight's virtue as a courtship misunderstanding, while underscoring many long-standing views regarding women's moral safety in the workplace. In portraying a boss repeatedly making sexual propositions to a self-respecting woman, even though she continually rebukes him, this romance contradicted those who, like the employment advice givers, maintained that a man would quickly cease pestering a woman who responded coolly to such advances. However, it also reaffirmed the view that women were somehow in control. A man might be unremitting in his pursuit, but efforts to persuade always stopped short of coercion or an ultimatum. As a result, a "decent" girl was always safe. This is not to say that such a woman might not be tempted. Delight endures a dreary existence, and she often dreams of the luxury she could have as Blake's mistress. When he does not fire her for refusing his offers, she more than once considers quitting, as the moral peril increases each day. In the end, her fortitude leads to a wedding ring, the focus squarely on the woman's respectable choices, not the man's despicable behavior (which, after all, was merely an effort to protect himself from scheming women).

Delight is a good girl who must endure the sin of being thought a bad one. In accordance with the confession formula, she does not rail against this injustice or reflect on how women's economic needs give their employers the power to insult them. Instead, the story accepts this injustice as nothing more nor less than real life, and certainly nothing Delight can change. The only issue is whether she will give in to Blake's tempting offer or retain her virtue. In other words, it is not just that confession stories put the responsibility on an individual woman to control workplace sexual expression as guidebooks and other fictional tales did. Rather, the formula's refusal to blame others or outside forces for a woman's problems excluded any other response. This was decidedly not fiction that prompted social change or critical analysis of gender or class relations.

In another version of office romance, Katinka Vroom's personal dilemma arises when her wealthy boss, Courtney Bell, asks her to dinner after they have been working late. Tinky, the sole support of an invalid mother, is a hardworking secretary who wants nice things, like stockings that are "silk to the top." Silk stockings also symbolize a moral purity, a "standard to live up to," and she diligently avoids "flaws and runs" in her personal life. She agrees to dinner, and a personal relationship slowly develops, though a former boyfriend warns her that such a man would only want her as a "playmate" and accuses her of being a gold digger. The situation comes to a head when Bell asks Tinky to take dictation at his apartment for an important meeting. The possibility exists that this assignment is just a ruse, but a refusal means possible unemployment. Trusting her instinct that Courtney is "silk to the top," as well as her ability to defend herself in case he is not, Tinky goes, and after successfully completing her work gains a marriage proposal.[34]

According to this story, facing the possibility of sexual danger at work is simply part of an office woman's job. Employment guides, of course, sent readers the same message. However, Tinky needs her job; she would be unable to follow the example of the women who quit in similar circumstances in the "true" stories the guides recounted. Confessions more straightforwardly acknowledged that women's economic vulnerability made them susceptible to sexual exploitation, though this acknowledgement was not paired with any more practical advice than the guidebooks gave. Delight endures, Tinky follows her pure moral code, and both continue to be dedicated secretaries, rewarded for their devoted service with a happily-ever-after ending. Confessional magazines presented marriage as the means to true happiness for women, but this meant that stories resolved dangerous situations with nothing more than romantic hopes.

Other stories provided other lessons on the dangers of office life, but what was at risk was always the same: the woman's chance at marriage and happiness. One young secretary finds her married boss so intriguing that even his most ordinary dictation "sent an odd thrill through her," echoing the excitement described by the *real* secretary we encountered in Chapter 3. Even though this fictional worker knows better, she nonetheless feels "a queer tingling flame" when he declares his desire, and she allows his kisses—a choice she deeply regrets when the young man she truly loves finds out. In another story, a secretary who has determined to marry wealth has strayed so far from what matters most in a woman's life—love—that she cannot tell whether she cares for her boss or just his money. By the time she realizes her true feelings, she has almost lost him. These stories end happily, as romances do. But here again the confession formula has drawn attention to a woman's mistakes while leaving her employer's actions unexamined. An older female office worker who serves as the moral voice in the first story declares the married boss to be "one of the finest men the lord ever made," while the young secretary has been a "silly little fool." The materialistic secretary is completely to blame for her romantic woes; her boss is a man of sincerity and good intentions throughout. Confession stories added their voice to the chorus of those who charged women with policing sexual boundaries at work, though, unlike the employment guides, they did not discourage office romance and most certainly did not portray the successful boss as off-limits. Confession magazines kept the Cinderella dream alive, presenting office work as a route to class mobility.[35]

Labor union publications abhorred these fairy tales, which they believed undermined class consciousness and made organizing women office workers more difficult. Already before the Depression, clerical jobs in some cities were hard to come by, but beginning in 1932 clerical unemployment began to rise sharply; at the same time, more job seekers flooded the market as manufacturing jobs disappeared. The time seemed ripe for unions, but white-collar workers refused to believe that they were part of the working class because, labor organizers complained, popular culture functioned as a "pleasant hypodermic," rendering the "patient immune to almost anything," including long hours and low wages. Movies always seemed to end "with the boss pleadingly proposing to some rapturously divine stenographer," and given women's vanity, all stenographers fancied themselves "pretty enough to merit a proposal from their employer." Labor activists also chided the advice giver Elizabeth Gregg MacGibbon for her emphasis on appearance. Office women already knew that looks mattered; what they needed was higher wages to pay for better clothing and grooming.[36]

In 1936 a story in a New York local's newsletter made the point that a woman was better off pinning her hopes on a union than on her employer.

Sedelle Hirshorn has a New Year's Eve invitation from a very eligible accountant in the office where she works, but she is not interested. She has gone without a winter coat so she can spend New Year's weekend at a swanky resort, where she hopes to find a wealthy husband. As she dines on caviar for breakfast, she spots her boss, Matthew Silverman, and realizes that opportunity has knocked. Silverman's eyes gleam every time he sees her, and he repeatedly comments on how wonderful she looks, though she casually dismisses his compliments on the clothes she has borrowed with an, "[Oh, it's] just a rag I found in Bergdorf-Goodman's." When he asks her to come to his office when they return to the city, Sedelle thinks that she has finally found her prince and takes out a loan to buy a new dress. But, no, Silverman has called her in not to declare his love but to cut her salary. Business is always slow after Christmas, and he is sure she will be able to afford it more than the other girls.[37]

Confession magazines and advocates of organized labor offered different perspectives on white-collar bosses. Union supporters warned women not to be seduced by the seeming intimacy of the office. When they forgot that they were employees, they contributed to their own economic—and possibly sexual—exploitation. A boss's glass slipper might fit his stenographer's foot, but the reality of social class ensured that he would never give her a ring. Confession magazines saw things the other way. Bosses were really princes, true love could bridge differences of wealth and culture, and the fear that a boss would take sexual advantage of his female employee proved to be the fable. Of course, only this last plotline found a paying audience: the commercial appeal of happy endings easily beat that of dire warnings.

In the late 1920s, one female journalist explained women's fascination with romances set in the office as a way of "making some sense" of their tedious labor. Theories put forth by scholars of more recent popular romance novels make a similar point, emphasizing that these narratives provide women with a way to reenvision, symbolically, real work-related problems—their boss, just like the fictional ones, really cares about them. These stories might have made some women temporarily feel better about their jobs, but they also sent other messages beyond the basic point that women had love on their minds. Women closed their magazine or left the theater having been shown the hazards of carelessly arousing desire and having been warned to think twice about careless flirtations or letting material things turn their heads. Men, they also learned, were usually not the villains the heroine had feared. But if men's questionable behavior was all just a misunderstanding, there was no mistaking a gold digger's intentions. Women in these films lacked institutional power, but men's vulnerability to a pretty face gave women a way to even the odds. In the imaginary skyscraper, it was men, not women, who needed protection from shameless seducers.[38]

CHAPTER FIVE

Morals and Morale

MANAGING SEX IN BUSINESS, WORLD WAR II TO THE EARLY 1960s

IN JUNE 1959 *MODERN OFFICE PROCEDURES* PUBLISHED "Love-in-the-Office," urging companies to develop policies to tackle this "explosive" personnel problem. And problem it was. In the late 1950s individual corporations and American big business as a whole saw their reputations soiled by sordid scandals and began to realize they could no longer ignore love's "cost." An affair between two married coworkers could demoralize other workers and hurt efficiency. An irate spouse's outburst in the lobby—"Your company is wrecking my home!"—could lead to gossip or make clients think twice about how well a business was run. The stakes were too high to trust that individuals would behave in a professional manner. Instead, businesses needed to "face up to the facts of life."[1]

From the beginning of World War II through the early 1960s, a variety of concerns—from winning the war to ensuring profits—focused attention on sexual expression in the white-collar world. Already during the war, the expansion of the "Human Relations" movement in management philosophy drew attention to how the work environment affected employee morale. After the war, with one in five privately employed Americans working for one of the top two hundred corporations, the independence of the nation's men seemed at risk. Commentators often worried about these men becoming "soft"—in body as well as mind—as they idled their days away, lost in the hierarchy and conformity of an "organization." Impotence or perversion among businessmen implied something unsavory about capitalism and thus took on national significance in the Cold War effort to prove American values superior to those of communism. And, of course, after the beating the Depression gave the reputation of free enterprise, American corporations did not need any more bad press. By 1949, four thousand companies had their own public relations departments, and big business could not afford to be seen as subverting mainstream American values.[2]

Although war—both hot and cold—provided new contexts, the issues were mostly the same as they had always been. Could a man who engaged in illicit activities in his private life be trustworthy and honorable in his public one? And regardless of the answer, psychology virtually always came into play. Even the "Love-in-the-Office" article applied its insights in its suggestions of how supervisors could cut the "office Romeo" down to size. If public ridicule, restricted access to the secretarial pool, and a "serious warning" did not work, he would have to be let go—and fast, if any of the women complained. The new focus on employees' feelings and work-group dynamics sometimes led to the censure of men whose actions created what would now be called a "hostile work environment." However, the psychological perspective still promoted the long-standing tendency to blame women—whiny wives or stunning secretaries—for men's transgressions.[3]

WORLD WAR II AND THE DEMORALIZING EFFECTS OF OFFICE FAVORITES AND VULGAR SUPERVISORS

Already in 1939 the federal workforce had begun to swell when Congress appropriated more money for defense. Agencies expanded rapidly after Pearl Harbor; within a few months, Congress received complaints about the waste of public funds in agencies concerned with the war effort. In October 1942 the House responded by authorizing the Committee on the Civil Service, headed by Robert Ramspeck, a powerful Georgia Democrat, to investigate the employment of civilians. In addition to holding public hearings in Washington, Ramspeck gave radio and newspaper interviews in which he urged federal employees to report examples of superfluous positions, "personal patronage," and discrimination in appointments and promotions. Hundreds wrote in, detailing a wide variety of job-related grievances.[4]

A small subset of the letters—about fifty—contain evidence of sexual and romantic relationships in the workplace, both consensual and unwanted. They constitute a rare cache of evidence about sex in the office under the pressure of war exigencies. It is impossible to know whether the accounts were true, but they can be used to examine what federal employees thought about sexual and romantic relations in the workplace and how managers responded to complaints that sexual behaviors were disruptive. Efforts to keep up morale on the home front and to ensure efficiency at work had the unintended (and possibly unprecedented) effect of allowing government workers—especially women—to voice their thoughts about the sexual culture of the office and to speak out against unwanted sexual overtures. Some people believed that a man's "immoral" behaviors should disqualify him from a position of authority, and government agencies did, on occasion, take seriously charges that a supervisor's sexual or romantic actions hurt morale. But in terms of productivity and esprit de corps, it was not only men's behaviors that were problematic.

For every woman who wrote to the committee complaining about unwelcome sexual attentions, a dozen others, mostly women over the age of thirty, objected that young women used their sexual attractiveness to gain favors. In their view, this violation of the system of meritocracy undermined the war effort and the principles of equality and democracy for which the war was being fought. These letters exposed older female workers' fears of losing their jobs to younger women and in many ways mirrored the long-standing tensions between secretaries and wives. Although letters sometimes portrayed supervisors as unwitting fools and women employees as naïve innocents (or vulnerable breadwinners), the picture of sex in the office was mostly one of different but equal powers in which men and women made conscious and uncoerced decisions that each deemed individually beneficial. Men, letter writers believed, could grant favors, but it was a woman's beauty—and her willingness to capitalize on it—that set partiality in motion. Correspondents were not surprised that men surrounded themselves with attractive women whenever they had the chance, but it was still women's role to set a high moral standard in order to keep men's baser natures in check—a time-honored view, as we have seen.[5]

Already in the late nineteenth century employees had complained that bosses handed out favors to attractive workers; they protested that preferential treatment was immoral, unjust, and inappropriate, and a sign that the boss and his pet lacked refinement—they were not "ladies" or "gentlemen." Letters written during World War II contained similar charges, laced with class tensions. Mrs. M, a widow with a college degree and more than twenty years of civil service experience, described an office in the War Department in which attractive, uneducated young women, including one "very ill bred girl from Kansas," had been put in charge of the older "decent, respectable ladies" and declared a number to be "surplus." These young women were cheating on their soldier husbands and had gained their power by playing around with the boss, who was "nothing but an I.B.M. salesman from St. Louis." Investigators took this accusation seriously—they had received similar complaints about this office, and this writer's educational credentials and decades of experience distinguished her from some other correspondents—and called for a full-scale investigation. Investigations, however, were far from guaranteed. Accusations of favoritism involving a beautiful young woman were common, and committee investigators dismissed any letter they felt was motivated by personal animosity."[6]

With so many of the allegations coming from older women, such letters may represent an attempt to resist or speak out against the usual sexual politics of office work. Men had long expressed a strong preference for young and attractive secretaries and stenographers, and there is no evidence that their attitude changed during the war. It was certainly still apparent after the war, as seen in a 1951 article advising business girls on how to get along with their bosses. It began with an executive's pronounce-ment, "If I have to be surrounded by women eight hours a day . . . they've got to be attractive. I can't stand women without sex appeal!" Even if most men would not so openly admit it, the author noted, this was what "most businessmen think." As a study of "older" office women in the early 1950s confirmed, age restrictions were particularly prevalent in office work, which had the highest proportion of young women of any occupation, especially of women under twenty-five; the shortage of clerical workers during the war and after diminished this prejudice, though not the prefer-ence for younger women. Given this reality, personnel experts might have missed the mark when they asserted that women's emotional psychology made them especially sensitive to any show of favoritism. Older women knew that their skills and experience did not make up for the fact that their "waist lines [were] not thin enough."[7]

Older women's feelings of vulnerability were certainly understandable, and their assessments of young women, especially those in Washington, also might have been affected by media coverage of young "government girls" who flocked to the capital to aid the war effort. The number of women working in Washington rose dramatically, from 53,038 in 1940 to 153,844 in 1945, and press coverage focused on those who were young and single. Journalists covered the housing shortage and the alleged shortage of men. "Girl workers," articles proclaimed, needed "pleasant and continuous association with young men" to be productive and committed to their jobs. In 1944 the issue of young workers' morality made the news across the country when Dorothy Berrum, a seventeen-year-old War Department clerk from Wisconsin, was raped and murdered by a Marine she had just met on a Washington street. According to a witness, when the marine took Dorothy's arm, "she laughingly accompanied him," unaware or uncaring of the danger. Commentators questioned whether the government had done enough to protect these women, but also wondered whether some were psychologically unbalanced, prone to "sexually amoral" behavior. In this assessment, female victims, not the male perpetrators, were the problem. (In 2004 a former "government girl" recalled Berrum's murder in an interview. She blamed Berrum, describing her as "a little promiscuous" and having "led a marine too far.")[8]

Stories such as Berrum's fed into general concerns about immorality in wartime and the disruption to family life and traditional gender roles caused by men's absence and women's increased public presence, which created new possibilities for sexual adventure. In many Americans' view, single women's "promiscuity" threatened the war effort and the country's moral fiber; a military victory would mean nothing if servicemen returned home to girls who had surrendered to sin. Little was said about the values of the men with whom these women were intimate. Authorities targeted prostitutes, but attention also focused on good girls gone bad in a fit of "uniform hysteria." The "government girl" was not singled out, but as a young, unchaperoned woman, she was suspect.[9]

In some offices, sex and romance were said to permeate (or poison) the atmosphere. An employee of the Treasury Department called the Ramspeck Committee's office to let them know that two supervisors had stopped work at 1:00 P.M. on Christmas Eve and had a party for their

"He says as long as he's going to be tied to a desk for the rest of the war, he may as well relax and enjoy it."

By the time this ad appeared during World War II, images of a boss with a secretary in his lap had been a staple of humor for at least four decades. Courtesy of Shore Antique Center, Allenhurst, New Jersey.

employees. One man asked his secretary to act as hostess "instead of his wife," and liquor was served—against Treasury rules. Invitations, the caller continued, went only to stenographers "who were fast and 'the party type'"—the same women who had received promotions over the "better stenographers," who were not invited. The subject of office parties and their effect on productivity and morale seems to have first surfaced during the war. Businesses had long used leisure events, like picnic days for employees and their families, to solidify workers' loyalty by explicitly linking their work and personal lives. The get-togethers that raised eyebrows during the war, however, were not family affairs. These parties created animosity between office women, and they exposed tensions between those women and their supervisors' wives. As this discussion played out in newspaper advice columns, it was—as it had been in the past—a conversation among women, in which one or the other—the wife who welcomed her husband home with her "face smeared with cold cream" or the "brazen hussy" at work—was to blame for men's behavior. The man who stepped out on his wife and strung the naïve office girl along was chastised, but commentators continued to downplay such behavior as the natural "masculine viewpoint." As one wife matter-of-factly stated, a young secretary "always intrigues" a middle-aged man who was in the "rather exciting position of giving her orders and having her wait on him."[10]

The "office party" attracted the attention of Mary Haworth, the *Washington Post*'s popular advice columnist, in early 1943. Haworth published a letter from Pat, a wife who suspected her husband, forty-four, was involved in a flirtation with his twenty-one-year-old secretary, a "nondescript" girl new to town and in her first job. Pat believed that the intimacy had begun at his division's Christmas party at a downtown hotel, which involved dancing and drinking but no wives. How, she asked, could she stop things before they progressed into a full-blown affair? Haworth urged the wife to confront her husband, confident that, once exposed, this "intrigue" would be robbed of its "mysterious, phantasy-world, 'just-between-thee-and-me' glamour (or sex) appeal." Pat's husband would realize how his career could be hurt by his involvement with such an "underbred" girl, who was bound to talk.[11]

Pat's letter struck a nerve, and readers responded with stories and concerns that mirrored those recounted to the Ramspeck Committee. Such parties and the boss-secretary relationship in particular, one wife anxiously wrote, represented a profound threat to family life on which "civilization" rested. She suggested that women "return to the home." Haworth reassured her that "with a few sordid exceptions" women did not hold their jobs through "glamour appeal to erotically vulnerable bosses"—but readers set her straight. Men now demanded "glamour" girls, a female government worker with twenty years' experience stated, and a young secretary described coworkers who thought nothing of dating married men as long as it stopped short of an "affair." These women laughed when the boss lied to his wife about working late and showed off the candy and stockings their "dates" gave them. Haworth minced no words condemning these "hard boiled" types who viewed every man as a "sucker." The "racketeer-flirt" should not be emulated.[12]

The *Post* had hired Haworth in the 1930s to disseminate the insights of psychology and psychiatry, and she actively sought the advice of mental health experts when responding to readers' problems. She also published contact information for relevant social agencies and during the war referred federal employees to the government's counseling services. Haworth encouraged a nineteen-year-old government girl, for example, who after only three months in Washington had been "betrayed" by an older, important coworker and was now pregnant, to seek out a counselor in the War Department. These counselors, Haworth further editorialized, should take action to "safeguard" other "equally gullible" workers "from potentially ruinous association" with this man, who had so "callously and deliberately victimized" one. If he continued to refuse to take responsibility for the pregnancy, she unequivocally stated, he should be fired as a "precautionary investment in office morale."[13]

The emphasis on morale marked an important historic development. It signaled the new attention that students of personnel management directed to cultivating the "relations" among employees and between workers and supervisors. "Human relations" established a new context in which to understand and respond to complaints about both sexual relations between supervisors and their employees and unwanted sexual advances at work. This social-psychological approach, which gained a foothold in the federal government during the war, emphasized the role individual psychological needs and group interaction played in productivity. Haworth's columns often discussed workplace morale, tinged with human relations theories. In the pieces on office parties, she called those that excluded wives "extremely vulgar" and maintained that they seemed to be the invention of government personnel with no counterpart in private business. Such parties "could not possibly contribute to department efficiency over the long haul; but would, rather, have an insidious effect to the contrary," especially when they led to an illicit affair. That the men in question were often part of military agencies might have made this issue all the more vexed. Wartime domestic propaganda emphasized not the fight against totalitarianism but the struggle for keeping hearth and home safe. Yet here were officers who had avoided the front lines engaging in behavior that threatened the sanctity of their families. They were safe, but their wives and children faced a threat as ominous as Hitler—the predatory office wife![14]

Letters to the Ramspeck Committee support Haworth's contention that sexual and romantic relationships hurt office morale. The committee received more than twenty-five complaints about one particular office of the Internal Revenue Service, which employed a few hundred people. Most grumbled that the man in charge handed out plum jobs to his friends, but a few specifically described sexual relationships that had demoralized workers. These letters provide a glimpse into how workers understood a supervisor's unwelcome attentions and efforts to use his authority to gain sexual access to women. The majority despised such a man, but their perception of the women involved was more nuanced. A woman could be the object of sympathy, but only if she clearly resisted; if, however, a woman benefited from her supervisor's advances, she seemed to lose the support of her coworkers even if she had not initiated the inter-action. The boss had the power to fire and hire, but letter writers believed that women still had a degree of agency and judged them according to their response. Their relative lack of power did not justify a reaction that chose gain over suffering.[15]

Two letters clearly show the double standard at work in complaints to the Civil Service. Mrs. H, for example, was the kind of victim whose plight elicited sympathy. An anonymous letter described an office Christmas party five years before, when Mr. D, a married supervisor, had given Mrs. H a ride home. Although the letter did not describe the details, it asserted that if Mrs. H "wanted to make trouble for him (as someone else did, but it was hushed up and the girl was discharged for nothing else but exposing him) I doubt that he would be here." Unfortunately, Mrs. H "needs her position very badly and is afraid to talk." The women in the office "know the story of what he tried to do to her while under the influence of liquor and how she had to run into her home for protection." Mrs. H "doesn't speak to him to this day and neither does [sic] a few others whom he tried the same tactics on." Given Mrs. H's economic vulnerability and evidence that Mr. D was capable of retribution, the letter expressed nothing but compassion.[16]

However, the suspicion of women even in situations in which they were at a disadvantage can be seen in another anonymous letter regarding this office, this one alerting the committee to a Miss J, who had received a big raise. "Would it be on account," the letter-writer queried, "of Mr. S getting drunk at an office party . . . and her letting him kiss her on the dance floor in view of all the employees present. It is one way to get ahead." What were the possible scenarios here? The letter might be no more than a personal grudge expressed in a sordid fiction. If taken at face value, though, it shows hostility toward a woman who profited—or, more accurately, who did not profoundly suffer—from a powerful man's sexual actions. Maybe Miss J took advantage of a drunk and orchestrated the kiss with extortion or opportunity in mind: Mr. S might have given her a raise to ensure that she did not make a stink, or possibly the kiss signaled that Miss J was willing to exchange sexual favors for favorable treatment, leading to a larger paycheck. But it is just as plausible that the kiss was unwanted, and she was unsure how to respond. Did she feel afraid, embarrassed, or humiliated? All we know is that she was not fired, nor did she quit. In other words, she was not visibly injured and therefore not a candidate for sympathy. Instead, she was exposed to gossip and innuendo that she had traded on sex. Women, it seems, were still virgins *or* whores.[17]

Coworkers might have assessed women in light of these ancient moral categories, but authorities were interested in other issues. Supervisors were more likely to *hear* those complaints indicating that a man was hurting employee retention or office morale. We can see this in the way the Ramspeck Committee listened to a woman who spoke out against the supervisor of a records facility in the South. She wrote that the boss was "continually having affairs with the young women in the Branch; that the girls who try to work and who offer suggestions for betterment are often cussed by [him] for their interference; that [he] allows his 'girl friends' to come into the office at all hours, and that on a few occasions, girls have come to work in the mid forenoon highly intoxicated." The investigators took these charges seriously because they dealt with productivity and passed the complaint on to the Pentagon. Pentagon officials had already investigated and determined that the office was run efficiently. They found, though, that the supervisor's "speech and actions on various occasions were offensive to the female employees of his office and out of keeping with his position." He was transferred to a less responsible position.[18]

In similar cases, efforts to revive dispirited female workers were at odds with protecting individual men and/or a department's reputation. Ramspeck investigators expressed "serious interest" in a complaint about a branch office of the General Accounting Office. The committee had received a lengthy letter from Mrs. R about her married supervisor, Mr. T. Mrs. R described an office where coworkers enjoyably spent their leisure time together—except when Mr. T behaved inappropriately. On the day of Mrs. R's wedding, a drunken Mr. T repeatedly called her home and said insulting things to her young daughter. He got even more drunk at the reception, and "his actions were beyond the decency of anyone present." Conditions at the office returned to normal on the following Monday, but a few days later Mrs. Q brought charges against Mr. T that threw the whole office into turmoil. They had been having an affair for many months, which, according to Mrs. R, had broken up Mrs. Q's marriage. Mrs. R was not involved in Mr. T's affair, but he blamed her for his troubles because she had talked about them with others. He began to humiliate her publicly, and, when she asked him to stop, he refused.

After a few months of this treatment, Mrs. R's nerves were shot, and she requested a transfer, which she received. At this point she also filed a complaint. Pulling together the languages of class, gender, and professionalism, she stated, "The embarrassment suffered at the treatment of this person makes it absolutely necessary that I prefer charges against one so completely immune, in the first place from gentlemanly traits and lacking in the second place, the first knowledge of how to treat an employee." Mrs. R also included a copy of a statement made by a former coworker who was waiting to hear back regarding a complaint she had filed against Mr. T. After just two months of working under him, this woman had asked to be transferred because she "had endured the insulting remarks and attitude of Mr. T . . . to a point beyond which I could not endure. His remarks were in this style, 'Why are you taking your jacket off?' 'Am I giving you hot flashes?' or 'Who are you on the make for this morning?'" Her impression was that he "should definitely be removed from a position which required contact with people, particularly women, as we do not, we cannot respect him and *I do not stand alone in my impressions.*"

Mr. T's behavior was disruptive enough that he was ultimately transferred and demoted two pay grades, but punishment for the perpetrator did not necessarily mean justice for the woman most affected. During the investigation Mrs. R was continually harassed. As she stated in a sworn deposition, the top two men in the office brought her in and demanded that she drop the charges. One pounded his desk and screamed, "Don't you see the light these charges put this office in, in Washington?" She refused but was so upset she resigned. She asked the Ramspeck investigator to assist with her reinstatement, but the last correspondence in the file was not hopeful. The investigator believed Mr. T's punishment was "very lenient" and wanted to help, but GAO's personnel office seemed unwilling. Mrs. R's charges had been sustained, but the investigator feared she would be a "scape goat," losing her job and her civil service benefits for "embarrassing" powerful men. The committee's interest in this case reflected its concern with investigating complaints that suggested an entire division was mismanaged, particularly if workers had been distracted from their jobs. Though the evidence is scant, the new emphasis on the connection between morale and productivity might have led to more concern about men who created a generally inhospitable environment for women workers.[19]

But it seems that this additional care did not extend to situations involving just one man and one woman and not the office workforce as a whole. Two cases involving women who worked as secretaries in defense agencies suggest that a woman who complained about a supervisor's unwelcome advances would not easily find relief if she was the only target of his unwelcome or insulting behavior. Mrs. C wrote the Ramspeck Committee to protest her low efficiency rating. She had been assigned to the chief clerk at a training center, who told her she would be his "personal secretary." He repeatedly told her that she was the "best stenographer in the office," but, she stated, "his attempted over friendliness was not welcome." In retaliation, he shifted her around from place to place. When his "persecution" became "almost unbearable," she requested a transfer to another office, but he refused. She then appealed to the chief of staff for relief from the chief clerk's "insulting talk and attitude," but he ignored her side of the story after conferring privately with her boss. Mrs. C tried to take her complaint farther up the chain of command but was repeatedly turned away. Finally, in desperation, she went to the commandant's home, after which she received a transfer. Her low rating, however, endangered her chance of a promotion or continued employment; the file did not say whether her appeal was successful.[20]

Sex was a human relations problem if an entire office was involved, but it was just failed seduction—and therefore just a woman's personal problem—otherwise. The case of a stenographer in a navy office, Mrs. P, whose complaints about a supervisor's unwelcome advances landed on deaf ears, reveals another instance of this logic. Her specific complaints were not so different from others that provoked official action. What seemed decisive in her case was that she was the only target of this man's aggression and harassing behavior. Mrs. P went to work for Commander E in early 1942, and all was well until July, when he dictated a legal opinion that included explicit references to sexual acts. When Mrs. P arrived at work the next day, she went in to the commander's office to dust his desk, which she did daily. According to her description of what happened next, he then

> engaged me in conversation with the flattering remarks that it was a pleasure to have me in the office and immediately thereafter he aggressively moved forward and slipped his arm around my waist and said, "You are so lovely, so desirable, I must have you." We struggled and as I pulled myself away I felt the hot breath and sensuous lips of the Commander's touching my cheek. On this occasion there was no one else in the office but the Commander and myself. My normal self-respect surged forward and I expressed in understandable words my feeling of resentment by slapping his left cheek and said, "Let me alone, let me along, let go of me. If you ever touch me again I will knock your head off." Thereupon he stopped his action. I brushed back my hair and rearranged my clothing and about this time the other members of the staff began to arrive.

Mrs. P told no one of this exchange, but from that moment on the commander's attitude toward her changed. He began to criticize her work in front of others, and for the next four months he assigned her nothing but form letters to type. She appealed to her coworkers, but no one was in a position to speak on her behalf. After taking her complaint to the next level, which did little to change the commander's behavior, she decided to file charges, at which point an official investigation was launched according to navy regulations. She was reassigned for its duration. Mrs. P's statement, which described in detail the encounter with the commander and his subsequent hostility, contained an unusual postscript that explained her reasons for filing the charges:

I feel that I can speak with candor and experience, a married woman and a widow. I am no child. I have some knowledge of the virtues and weaknesses of mankind and it is the farthest from my wish to disarrange the process of this office. I have always been willing to overlook this situation and to carry on, if left alone, in the normal way. [As a result of my] refusal to conform to the wishes of the Commander [he] has . . . on every occasion thereafter, gone to extreme measure in his desire to humiliate and punish me. I am not in any measure misled or concerned with my sex appeal. Having attained my age plus my experience in the world I have no illusions on the question of human relations. I recognize . . . my duty to my employer. . . . In return, I feel that I am entitled to receive consideration and courtesy from my employer.

Three weeks later, Mrs. P withdrew her charges, though she made clear that she was not retracting any part of her story. She had been moved from the commander's office, and nothing was to be gained by pressing the case. She intended to work hard and anticipated no more difficulties. But trouble returned a few months later when she received a "Fair" efficiency rating after previously receiving "Excellent." She appealed, and, during this process, she described the circumstances under which she had dropped her complaint: Commander W, Commander E's superior, had told her that he would testify against her if she did not. When she replied that she had done nothing wrong, he had said, "That doesn't make any difference—Commander E is of the Navy." She was a mere civilian, and in such a case, "who the guilty person was made no difference." She did not want to resign because she had not told her coworkers of Commander E's attentions and believed a permanent transfer or resignation would mean a stain on her character that she could never live down. Despite her protestations, she was transferred, but Commander W continued to demand that she drop the charges. She appealed to an admiral, but his response is not known, and there is no indication Commander E ever received any punishment or reprimand for his actions.

Mrs. P wrote Senator Ramspeck after she had dropped her charges but before receiving her low efficiency rating, and his office seemed unsure about how to proceed. A female investigator made the notation: "A serious complaint—but one that may be as much her fault as his." Another investigator spoke with Mrs. P, who had been unable to find a new position and was still in the same division, though not the office "where she had the trouble." He was unable to help her, and the final notation merely said that she would contact them if she wanted their further assistance.[21]

The circumstances of Mrs. P's complaint and the language in which she voiced it are highly suggestive, although with only the written record from which to judge, it is difficult to discern why the initial investigator felt that Mrs. P might have shared in the blame. However, by examining this case through the lenses of personnel theories and cultural attitudes toward female sexuality, we can better understand how Mrs. P's charges were both voiced and heard; in these contexts, the investigator's response makes sense. As we saw in Chapter 3, already by the 1930s personnel professionals were using psychological principles to understand work-place behaviors, finding, for example, that female office workers in partic-ular exhibited a neurotic need for male attention. By World War II the federal government employed psychiatrists to evaluate personnel who seemed psychologically troubled and counselors to help with personal problems. Although no one explicitly suggested that Mrs. P was mentally unstable, perhaps those investigating her case brought a psychological perspective to their evaluation—including gendered beliefs about women and romance.[22]

The sexual connotations of the "office wife" may also have prejudiced the investigator against seeing Commander E's kiss as anything more than a clumsy and impetuous attempt at seduction. Mrs. P's daily dusting of his desk suggests a certain domestic intimacy, though government training manuals emphasized that it was a secretary's job to cater to the boss's every whim. Similarly, her description of the encounter, at least by twenty-first-century standards, seems more *True Confessions* than straight-forward reportage. Did investigators read Mrs. P's recollection of the commander's declaration, "You are so lovely, so desirable, I must have you," and think that this was just an innocent misunderstanding inflamed by a woman's romantic imagination? If so, one wonders what other narra-tive strategy Mrs. P could have used. Her story is remarkable for its detail; there is no euphemistic he "attempted over friendliness." But its language also recalls those formulaic stories of office romances that centered on the resolution of a romantic misunderstanding. Such stories permeated the culture, providing an obvious template for recounting her experience. This is not to say that Mrs. P hoped her case would be resolved with a happily-ever-after ending. Rather, romance was the language at hand. She might have made sense of her experience through or fitted it into this ubiquitous plot—there was not yet a feminist discourse of power, oppression, or sexual violence to use. Nevertheless, Mrs. P did not stay silent but rather insisted on defining her own experience. She did not want her boss's attention, and she certainly did not want his retribution. She repeatedly stated that she was "willing to overlook" the commander's moment of weakness and move on, but he would not let the slight go. And this was the point the investigator seems to have missed. Even if the initial encounter was "as much her fault as his," only he had the authority to exact revenge.[23]

Finally, in wondering whether Mrs. P was in some measure to blame, the investigator was simply heeding the words of commentators and employment advice givers who had long held women accountable for unwanted attentions, a view which continued during the war and through the postwar period. In 1944 the advice columnist Mary Haworth roundly criticized a woman who worked as a stenographer for a federal department head and whose husband was overseas. For six weeks she had accepted a ride home from her married boss, and, three days before she wrote the letter, he had refused to let her out of his car. At first she was confused, but "then his actions left no doubt." She slapped him and screamed, and a passer-by came to her rescue. Her boss "acted like nothing had happened" the next day, but she now feared him and "the possibly dangerous situation."

Haworth made clear the woman had nothing to fear. Her boss was "stupid" and had temporarily "lost his head," but he was hardly of "monster caliber." The woman did have something to learn, however: to be "businesslike" and "impersonal" with all the men at work. Her boss had an "elastic code of conduct," but he was acting on the "mis-que" she had provided by accepting the favor of a ride home, which signaled that she was as without principle as he. The ride demonstrated spiritual disloyalty to their marriage vows and violated their civic obligation to conserve gas ("a gallon wasted may wantonly visit death on our fighting men"—a not so subtle reminder of her husband's potential sacrifice). "Is it surprising," Haworth asked, "that he ventured to assume your standards might be equally lax in all respects? Let's be fair to the boob." The only course of action was to quit, and fast, before the "coward" discharged her to save face, "possibly with detrimental allegations about [her] character or efficiency." Haworth concluded her advice by encouraging the woman to talk to an employee counselor whose job was to help workers "in distress." The counselor could "go to bat" for the woman in arranging a transfer for the "sake of office morale."[24]

Since federal agencies often worked with the media to spread the war message and alert those, like single pregnant women, about available services, this column might have reflected a problem with which employee counselors were familiar. Haworth's matter-of-fact suggestion that the woman request a transfer hints that this was counselors' standard policy. If so, her assertion that the "trouble had origin in the girl's attitude" likewise implies that the man would not be held accountable in any way. Indeed, whereas Haworth had strong opinions regarding the treatment of the seducer in her column on the naïve government girl's pregnancy, there was no such outrage here. It was the woman's fault and the boss's "faux pas." Thus the limited cases we know of in which a supervisor forced his attentions on a subordinate suggest that management viewed such incidents as inept efforts at romance and any retribution as the understandable, if cowardly, response to rejection. Since the women had failed in their role as moral gatekeepers, they would be the ones to suffer. However, in cases that endangered office morale, chances increased that supervisors would hold a man accountable since productivity was at risk.[25]

We do not know whether this attention to men's hostile behaviors continued after the war, although we do know that federal agencies were especially interested in the sexual behaviors of some of their employees in the postwar years: suspected homosexuals. The wartime concern with morale and efficiency may have given women a unique opportunity to challenge objectionable behaviors, but with the country's shift in focus, this chance was probably lost. Cold War anxieties led to an all-out effort to purge homosexuals from the ranks of the civil service because these "perverts" threatened the nation's morals and national security. This attention was new. As the historian David Johnson has shown, before and during the war a good number of Washington's federal clerks, male and female, were homosexual. (So were the military's. Officers channeled men they believed to be gay into feminine clerical or stenographic jobs, which allowed them to create their own community. And some lesbians in the Women's Army Corp worked in clerical positions, including as General Eisenhower's secretary.) Homosexual clerks were not necessarily closeted, and some even enjoyed a teasing relationship about their sexuality with coworkers; though government workers could be fired for "immoral behavior," personnel managers seem to have turned a blind eye before 1950. That changed, and given the zeal with which government officials pursued gays and lesbians—for example, special investigative teams watched bars and hangouts and forced those they exposed to "name names"—relationships between coworkers necessarily became secretive. The fear of being thought different or deviant permeated Washington during this time, which also might have kept women silent about a supervisor's unwanted attentions, especially since the tendency to view behavior through a psychological lens intensified after the war.[26]

The persecution of gays and lesbians is just one example of the fading of the never-clear line dividing Americans' public and private worlds in the postwar era. Gays and lesbians took each other to office parties to appear straight and silence any rumors that could cost them their jobs. Others were extraordinarily discreet. One lesbian who worked as an economist in the Treasury Department recalled, "As long as I didn't live my private life, [the government] didn't have anything on me." Heterosexual white-collar workers in the private sector also saw their private lives, including "private" behaviors they exhibited in the office or in the course of business, examined under a spotlight—most especially those men whose illicit actions imperiled a corporation's reputation and profits.[27]

PSYCHIATRY AND THE ADULTEROUS WHITE-COLLAR MAN

The postwar period saw the rise of a new traditionalism, which centered on rigidly defined gender differences and the containment of sexual desires, especially women's. Psychiatrists and social scientists were prominent among the enforcers of this orthodoxy, patrolling against "abnormal" sexual behaviors and "deviant" gender transgressions. Even

as mass culture increased the visibility of all things sexual, experts vigorously argued that erotic expression must be limited to marriage to ensure
social stability. Once children arrived, husbands' and wives' adherence to
standards of masculinity and femininity took on added significance as the
model for future generations. The exhortations to adhere to "normal"
behaviors amounted to more than a preacher's Sunday proddings; such
conformity was necessary to ensure victory in America's ideological battle
with the Soviets and to provide a veneer of stability in an unstable world.
America's national character, its very identity, resided in these intimate
activities.[28]

But everywhere one turned there were signs that Americans were not
behaving as they should. Married women, including those with children,
flocked into the workforce, especially in the growing clerical sector. In
1948 Alfred Kinsey published *Sexual Behavior in the Human Male*, which
made two especially shocking assertions. First, more than a third of
American men had engaged in at least one homosexual encounter, and
second, half would be unfaithful to their wives at some point. Many businessmen refused to participate in Kinsey's study, which he attributed to a
desire to hide extramarital intercourse; even so, 27 percent of his married
subjects who had attended college admitted to infidelity by age fifty. Men
from this educational stratum also were more likely to fantasize about sex
and to view pornography than other groups. Meanwhile, in the view of
many social critics, white middle-class men seemed to be getting soft,
their vigor sapped by suburbia's creature comforts and the necessity of
making themselves blandly ordinary in order to rise in a corporation. The
America of rugged individualism was giving way to a land of people-
pleasing paper-pushers. To put this all differently, the white-collar world
was at the heart of the country's uncertainty: on the one hand, it was a
primary site of unprecedented prosperity and a symbol of American
superiority; on the other, its inhabitants' challenge to gender and sexual
norms seemed to endanger the nation's achievements and its future. In
this context, scholars, the press, and ultimately business management
placed sexual and romantic relationships in the office (and the connection
between sex and business more broadly) under close examination. These
experts and commentators' findings reflected the era's devotion to a
quasi-Victorian gender system (though women were now thoroughly
sexualized) and enthusiasm for psychological explanations.[29]

In the wake of Kinsey's study, psychiatrists probed the psyche of middle-aged, white-collar adulterers, and the evidence, from the case studies of marriage counselors to the distraught letters sent to advice columnists, suggests that a large number of these men strayed with women they met through work. Infidelity, psychiatrists agreed, was a sign of mental illness, though few were as disturbed as the man who believed he deserved a mistress and brought his young "secretary" home from the office to taunt his older wife. Psychotically predatory men who changed secretaries until they found one who was amenable to an affair were also relatively rare. More often, at least in the view of psychological experts, these men's affairs merely reflected the crisis that predictably came with growing older. The respected Freudian psychoanalyst Edmund Bergler compared this calamity to menopause, though in his view the origins of men's troubles were "exclusively psychological." Bergler believed this type of neurosis occurred so frequently that he devoted an entire book to this "revolt." Meanwhile, the popular magazine *Science Digest* reported that age-related depression could cause "a respected businessman and responsible head of a family to suddenly become an irresponsible dissipator." Such behaviors were common as men made a "last desperate attempt" to restore their "sense of adequacy and confidence" by "throwing off the shackles of sexual restraint."[30]

But if this moment of masculine anxiety was unavoidable, middle-aged men often blamed women's behaviors for setting an affair in motion. Such was the case in the story of a prominent advertising man, married for twenty-four years, who had carried on a two-year affair with his younger secretary. As he told Bergler during one of their sessions, his wife could be tender and loving, but most of the time she was suspicious and complaining, which had led to his unfaithfulness.

BERGLER: So you looked around for a gayer, less reproachful person? Did you find her in the girl in your office?

MAN: I understand the allusion to "office." I know, it's bad policy if the boss starts something with an employee, even if she's more than willing.

BERGLER: You're making it sound as if she took the initiative, or even seduced you.

MAN: No, she didn't. Wait, now that I come to think of it, she *did* seduce me. Not sexually, I mean. But with her flattery,

admiration, hanging on to my words as if I were an oracle, she
did the trick. Of course, if she weren't young and attractive, it
wouldn't have gotten her anywhere.[31]

Pushed by his nagging wife, pulled by his secretary's beauty and adula-
tion, and betrayed by his own mortality, this executive seemed destined to
begin an affair, largely because of the women in his life.

In the postwar period, the wife-blaming first voiced in the 1920s
continued to grow, with attention focusing now on the ways she failed to
be supportive. One middle-aged man squarely placed the blame on his
wife. Her crime was harmlessly flirting with a younger man, which to
him was the ultimate act of betrayal, since he had spent his "whole life
earning a good living" for her. He slept with a young woman who worked
in a branch office of his company as an act of sheer revenge. Another
chronicler of infidelity noted that a husband whose wife did "not realize
how much he needs support, particularly when things do not go well,"
was "ripe for affairs." This, every bit as much as "propinquity," was the
reason men cheated with their assistants.[32]

Criticizing wives was not new, but now the importance of a sympathetic "other half" took on new significance as business erased even
the pretense of a line between public and private. As the journalist
William H. Whyte noted, companies often interviewed a junior executive's wife before offering a promotion. They needed to see that she
understood her role—not to nag or push, but to rejuvenate her man for
the "next day's battle." Corporate wives also had to mature and develop
along with their husbands. Business travel exposed the postwar "organization man" to a stylish crowd and sophisticated things. If his wife had
"stayed at home—literally and figuratively," it could lead to "outgrown
wife" syndrome. The irony, of course, was that corporate leaders
bemoaned the growing gulf between a man on the rise and the girl he had
married in his youth (who, if too much of a rube, could endanger his
corporate ascent) at the same moment social critics urged young people
to marry early in an effort to avoid premarital sex. In this regard, the
values of business and society were to some degree at odds, but, in evaluating spouses and offering their view of the ideal corporate marriage,
companies indirectly entered into the sexual and romantic lives of their
employees.[33]

If an unsympathetic wife pushed her husband away, what of the women he was pulled toward? Secretaries "glamorize[d]" their bosses and looked at them as "catches" whether they were married or not. Many also acted seductively, some "deliberately to insure their jobs." Other women were unaware of their seductive ways, and "sometimes a woman who has flirted outrageously with her boss is shocked when he makes a pass at her." The majority, however, were conscious of their alluring ways, and most psychiatrists agreed that the woman who became a married man's lover was as unbalanced as he; as Bergler noted, "neurotics always attract neurotics," and any "halfway stable" woman "automatically and unconsciously avoids the rebel's hopeless troubles." The psychiatrist Frank S. Caprio believed that cheating wives and unmarried women involved in adulterous affairs fell into one of two types: "the passive, predominantly neurotic woman who is the victim of the married man, rather than the hunter," or the "aggressive type who may be an outright psychopath and who will stop at nothing to annex her man." The latter was the female counterpart to the office "wolf" and often sought out young, sexually inexperienced men.[34]

In this view, although some women were predators, even the "victims" bore some degree of blame, a position that might have colored psychiatrists' assessment of nonconsensual relationships. For example, in his discussion of long-term affairs Caprio described a typical "maladjusted" woman who had gotten involved with a married man in her mid-twenties and a decade later found herself living a "spinster's life." She had a good job and nice clothes, but no future and no man other than her married "week-end lover." Such women had "generally poor judgment," a point made clear in Caprio's summary on how such liaisons began: "Sometimes the woman starts the affair out of expediency. She may have given in to an employer, to keep her position or to advance it by bestowing her favors. When this is the case, she has the added burden of shame. She has not even the excuse of honest, if foolish, emotion. She is at the prostitution level."[35]

Caprio's assessment makes no distinction between an encounter resulting from duress and one deliberately planned. Both fell outside the parameters of normal sexual motivations, and both were condemned; context was irrelevant since any break from acceptable sexual practice was a sign of maladjustment. Women had long been told they had no choice but to quit if an employer gave them a sexual ultimatum, but that advice was moral and most especially pragmatic: a soiled reputation and lost chastity could have real-world repercussions worse than the trouble of finding another job. Caprio, however, made the issue one of "basic underlying neurosis" and so declared that "moral prejudices must be held in abeyance." In this view, a woman's decision to submit to her boss's demands was no longer a sign of weakness of character or financial desperation. The psychological diagnosis obscured the difference between a woman who consciously used sex to advance and one who was forced to have sex to keep her job. It also allowed Caprio to see both situations as potentially leading to long-term consensual affairs. Caprio was not the only psychiatrist to trouble the boundaries of consent; some women, others argued, had an "unconscious desire" to be sexually attacked.[36]

THE BUSINESS OF SEX

Although a man's adulterous behavior most often could be traced to a psychological break, some indiscretions originated in the "competitive and hard-paced" aspects of modern business and middle-class materialism. A young man desperate to advance might send his wife into the arms of his superior or convince her that his affair with a wealthy woman could help him make contacts. Sometimes a man traveled on business and found himself "entertained" by the secretary of the man he was in town to see, in which case he might "be tempted beyond his resistance." By the late 1950s publicity of such situations made many Americans think that the "reach of the business spirit into sex or perhaps the reach of the sex drive into business enterprise" had been achieved.[37]

One national occasion for this realization was the CBS radio broadcast, on January 19, 1959, of Edward R. Murrow's "The Business of Sex," in which the famed journalist who had stood up to Senator Joseph McCarthy exposed the practice of a wide range of companies that routinely employed call girls to close deals and wrote off the cost as a business expense. Some companies, Murrow charged, kept prostitutes on their payrolls, listing them as employees in the Public Relations Department; in New York City, as many as thirty thousand women made their living helping to grease the wheels of industry. Anonymous sources for the story included an executive who maintained that in some businesses top executives determined the type of entertainment a prospective client would receive, while in others mid- or low-level men made sure the customer's needs were met. A number of women—educated, attractive, charming—recounted their experiences of being paid fifty or one hundred dollars to "date" businessmen. One had worked in white-collar offices where respectable married men had repeatedly asked her out; she considered her present situation, in which she received cash for such excursions, clearly preferable. Another told of securing a "verbal agreement" for an order before she went to bed with a customer, because at this "psychological moment" a man was in a "very anxious mood."[38]

Murrow's program ended with an assessment of the larger cultural implications of using sex to promote business. The "honorable activity" of supplying the needs of the community for a "legitimate reward," a Catholic priest lamented, had degenerated into a "lustful, uninhibited pursuit of money." It was "scarcely necessary to detail the corrosive effects such a flouting of divine and human law would have not only on the moral character of business men but on the society which bears their stamp." Murrow concluded by highlighting the larger questions the program raised, including whether such business practices indicated a general moral decline or merely reflected what was "happening in other parts of our culture through the phenomena of bigness and organization."[39]

Big businesses immediately dismissed the charges as absurd, and most newspapers denounced them as a "smear" against American business. When reporters queried the public relations men of large corporations, they declared the charges to be "utterly unbelievable," although they issued their denials off the record. The National Association of Manufacturers, the voice of American business, issued a statement labeling the broadcast "mostly a hoax," an effort by the politically liberal Murrow to divert attention from congressional investigations into the nefarious practices of organized labor. The chain of Hearst papers, including the San Francisco *Examiner* and New York *Journal-American*, demanded an apology for the program's "outrageous insult to the great institutions that form the backbone of America's economic strength." Connecting Americans' sexual behavior to the country's national character, critics condemned the program for providing fodder for the "propaganda machine of international communism." People throughout the developing world would soon hear that the United States had "reached such a state of decadence its business could be transacted only with the aid of 'call girls.'" Two months later, the syndicated columnist George Sokolsky was still bemoaning the blot on America's good name: newspapers in Communist China had seized on the story, since anything that "makes materialistic America look mean and selfish and inhuman is given the widest circulation." Some companies had tried to claim these expenses as business deductions, the IRS confirmed, but such charges, when discovered, were disallowed.[40]

Murrow's report touched on more than Cold War nerves; it spoke to the same concerns regarding the state of white-collar manhood that motivated psychiatrists studying adultery. Postwar critics feared that corporate work demanded of men a feminine supplication that sapped their manly self-reliance—and their libido. The novelist Norman Mailer asserted, "When a man can't find any dignity in his work, he loses his virility." William H. Whyte ominously noted that some white-collar men expended so much energy worrying about their jobs that they could not sexually satisfy their wives; one executive's wife, an "attractive gal," had turned to drinking to forget her erotic frustrations and was now "practically an alcoholic." In this respect, then, the sex-in-business scandal at least proved organization men were still *men*. As the *New York Post* asked in response to a *Journal-American*'s editorial, did Americans really want "the Russians to believe that the virility of capitalism thrives only in boardrooms, never in bedrooms? No, a thousand times no." The whole affair, according to the columnist Max Lerner, was simply the most recent incarnation of the intertwining of sex and power. The peccadilloes of modern capitalists had their antecedent in the indulgences of ancient kings, and the corporate expense account was "one of our most interesting rituals."[41]

The questions the broadcast raised struck at the heart of postwar concerns about gender, sexuality, mass culture, and the potentially harmful effects of uninhibited consumption on the individual's and the nation's character. The producer defended the story, arguing that it "was not about sex." It was "really about the social ethic of our society. It was about the way we value each other, the way we use each other, our capacity to treat each other merely as commodities." For the *Nation*, the program merely highlighted the socially corrosive effects of consumer capitalism. Since it was no secret that businesses offered potential clients "bribes" to gain their signature on the dotted line—fur coats, electric shavers—why would anyone think they would draw the line at sex?[42]

Why not? One reason was that relying on sex to close deals suggested a decline in American manhood not just morally but in the even more fundamental qualities of individual initiative, independence, and authority. Decades before, Sherwood Anderson had decried business-men's sexual practices and the enfeebled ideal of manliness they engen-dered. Now a chorus of pundits took up the theme, and the problem seemed bigger than the questionable decisions of individual men. This was about a new American character—or at least the work of sociologist David Riesman implied that possibility. In his 1950 best-seller *The Lonely Crowd*, Riesman described the new "other-directed" man who was so motivated by a desire to please and drive to consume that he had aban-doned all personal integrity.[43]

Even before Murrow's exposé, many Americans had the chance to contemplate white-collar masculinity during the 1957 trial of Nella Bogart, a green-eyed Polish refugee charged with violating the federal Mann Act, which prohibited the transportation of women across state lines for immoral purposes. Bogart had allegedly provided prostitutes for General Electric's sales convention in Atlantic City and entertained clients in her Manhattan apartment. The proceedings did not provoke the national reaction of Murrow's report, but major news sources took note. According to *Time*, for example, G.E. had taken the concept of "being nice to big customers" too far. Bogart's attorney did not deny that she was a prosti-tute, but he did ask the jury to consider whether the G.E. executives who testified to hiring Bogart were "any better than the women they used." By framing the defense in this way, Bogart's attorney implicitly put American manhood on trial. Like Riesman's prototype, G.E. men seemed so moti-vated by keeping their jobs and getting ahead that they had abandoned their inner moral compasses. Jury members might not have made this connection, but they did vote to acquit, since it was not "fair" to punish Bogart and let all the men go scot free.[44]

There was also nothing in the trial to reassure those who worried about American men's softness: Nella's testimony suggested that she was in charge. Much was made of the night she convinced two customers to purchase seven carloads of appliances. The next day, however, one of the men called G.E. and canceled half the order. When the salesman called

Nella to tell her the bad news, he also told her not to see the customer if he contacted her, which he did within a few days. "You can't come to see me unless you take the order you originally took," she snapped, and it was quickly reinstated. A few years before the trial, the anthropologist Margaret Mead had argued that modern men had to "re-earn" their masculinity each day, and that "beating women in every game both sexes play[ed]" was an important element in their daily reclamation. If Mead was correct, one wonders how the G.E. customer or salesman felt.[45]

Even if a woman occasionally got the better of a man, the Murrow broadcast showed how important women were in creating links between men. Here was the historic exchange of women updated to meet the specific needs of corporate capitalism. The gift of a woman gave a business a competitive advantage. It united two men, and its illicit nature ensured—demanded—that the relationship be one of trust. According to the president of a large international company, there was

> absolutely no doubt that prostitution per se does help business. This is the fastest way that I know of to have an intimate relationship established with a buyer. It's an experience which has been shared, whether it's together or not makes no difference. The point is, that I know the buyer has spent the night with a prostitute that I have provided. In the second place, in most cases the buyers are married, with families. It sort of gives me a slight edge; well, we will not call it exactly blackmail, but it is a subconscious edge over the buyer. It is a weapon that I hold. . . . There's no doubt about it—it is a good weapon to have.[46]

The vice president of another company focused on the building of genuine friendships, not opportunities for extortion, and his comments also suggest a possible paradox: in a homophobic time, these high-octane performances of heterosexuality might have facilitated, for some men, the expression of homoerotic desire—even if in a masked or covert way. He and another executive had rented a boat to take two of their best customers on a weekend fishing trip, bringing along four attractive and intelligent women for fun. He described the effect of the adventure:

When you reach the point where they're ready to go away with you for a weekend; Where you're going to bring girls along or for a night . . . you have created a very, very close personal relationship which cannot be replaced. Everything else you do with them, nothing is illegal or immoral. This is a stage of a relationship when you have reached this point with a person that, you sleep together in effect, and have girls together, you couldn't get any closer to them personally . . . and he will do everything within his power to be able to help you.[47]

According to Murrow's report, out-of-town clients expected such treatment, and a study in the early 1960s of the sexual behaviors of successful Americans described the practice of providing sex for traveling businessmen as "somewhat standardized, understood, almost institutionalized." Here was another difference from the 1920s that Sherwood Anderson had described. Then, a salesman's "stud book" was one of the tricks of the trade. Now this trick appeared to be standard operating procedure in companies' PR departments. If this was in fact the case, it would have been hard for a man to resist if he wanted to be considered a real man. Obligatory *public* acts of heterosexuality became an even greater part of white-collar masculinity.[48]

But if such adventures were good for business, they were not beneficial to marriages, especially those of the men whose job it was to ensure that clients were amused. Shortly after Murrow's report, the advice columnist Ann Landers published a letter from a wife whose husband worked in public relations and was regularly out until the wee hours of the morning entertaining customers. This was no job for a married man, Landers responded, and the wife needed to tell her husband as much. A sociologist studying this phenomenon was more sympathetic. A white-collar man, even one with a college education, might have no marketable skills other than charm and a face people trusted. Working in a firm's "sex for sales" department was such an employee's only way to make a decent living. There is no evidence that Murrow's broadcast endangered these men's livelihood, and G.E. survived its prostitution scandal unscathed—though it did begin to invite wives to *one* yearly sales convention. But the sex-and-business imbroglios certainly did not help corporate America's image. Shortly after Murrow's report, another scandal—this one involving an Eli Lilly executive—raised questions about the leaders of American enterprise.[49]

MANAGING SEX: CORPORATE REPUTATIONS AND THE BOTTOM LINE

The affair between Connie Nicholas and Forrest Teel began as the stereotypical tale of an unhappily married executive and a woman from his office. They first met when Connie went to work at the Indianapolis pharmaceutical company Eli Lilly in 1941. At the time, he was in his late thirties, an ambitious salesman on his way up, and she, an unmarried clerk in her late twenties. When Forrest happened into the file room one day, he instantly took a liking to Connie, and from then on he made frequent visits. Knowing that he was married, she turned down his repeated invitations. In 1942 she married a soldier, but Forrest continued his pursuit, despite her continued refusals. Then, inexplicably, about a year into her marriage and two years after meeting Forrest, Connie had a change of heart. When she bumped into Forrest downtown one sunny day, she accepted his invitation to have a drink.[50]

Soon the affair was going strong. In an effort to save her marriage, Connie quit her job in 1946, but she could not give up Forrest, and she divorced in 1947. During the next few years, Forrest and Connie went on romantic trips and saw each other at least two nights a week, his status as a prominent businessman affording multiple excuses for his absence from home. But he would not divorce his wife. Around 1951 Connie began to date other men, ultimately marrying a General Motors salesman in 1952. Connie had stopped seeing Forrest, but just a few weeks into her marriage he started to call, and within a few months she had resumed the affair, taking advantage of her husband's business travel to see Forrest. Divorced a second time in 1958, Connie was again free, and Forrest's son was soon to graduate from high school, setting the stage for Forrest to divorce his wife. It seems, however, that he did not like Connie's pressure, and their relationship began to cool.

But Connie persisted. She called him at work, and he hung up. She began to drive around town, looking for his hard-to-miss white Cadillac, though he sped off when she found him. She tracked him down, and he admitted that he was seeing someone else: that someone, she soon figured out, was a young secretary at Lilly. In July, Connie left a suicide note at her home and went to the secretary's apartment. Forrest's car was there, and she climbed in and waited. When he finally left around 1 A.M., he found Connie. They argued, and she shot him three times. She returned to her car and drove to a local lover's lane, where she drank a thermos of barbiturate-laced juice. When the police found her the next day, she was barely alive. After many months in the hospital, Connie went on trial for first-degree murder, a premeditated crime punishable by death in the electric chair. Her defense argued that she had not meant to shoot Forrest; the gun had gone off during a struggle after he struck her. Twelve married men decided Connie's fate, while the entire world watched and listened. The judge allowed film and radio crews to cover the trial, and CBS News and Movietone sent reporters, as did *Life* magazine and newspapers from as far away as Australia. The jury convicted her of voluntary manslaughter. She was sentenced to two to twenty-one years and was paroled after two.

Scholars who study scandal—an event that attracts attention as something deserving of moral opprobrium—note that although they are distinct from social problems, scandals often come to symbolize a problem for the public and thus can influence the response to the problem. Scandals also must be situated within an institutional structure, such as business, politics, or religion, because they represent a violation of the public's trust in that institution. In the prosecution's view, the "double divorcee" represented the dangers of sexually uncontained women to men and the institution of marriage. "She accepted monetary and other gifts from him. She accepted all he could offer her under the circumstances," the prosecutor noted in his opening statement. "In return she fired three death-laden bullets into his body and gave him a bed on a cold, hard slab in the city morgue." Forrest, however, was a gentleman who protected his mistress to the bitter end; as headlines reporting on the first day of the trial screamed: "DYING TEEL WOULDN'T TELL!" Connie, the prosecution tried to show in its cross-examination, cared nothing for moral laws. Did she give any thought to Forrest's wife or son? Did she really think it was proper that Forrest sometimes brought his son to their liaisons? And what about her husbands? Connie would admit only that she knew adultery was wrong. Finally the prosecutor pressed her on the number of men she had dated between her marriages: was it between ten and fifteen? Connie testily responded that she could not remember, but the questioning left a clear impression of the damage and destruction a sexual woman left in her wake.[51]

But there were other ways to make sense of Connie's life, and *True Story* cast it as a morality tale of the inevitable end of illicit love and especially the temptations facing working wives. Connie was no femme fatale but a romantic, feminine woman who loved to cook and loved Forrest too much. Neither Connie, whose parents had died when she was a child, nor her soldier husband stood a chance against the wealthy, suntanned "big shot." In such an uneven contest, it was hardly surprising that Forrest "tired of Connie when her looks began to fade." The magazine sympathetically asked its readers to imagine "how old—and used, and betrayed—Connie must have felt" when she found out about Forrest's new love. Connie had learned what millions of mistresses already knew: adulterers were selfish, and when they moved on, their mistresses had no legal or moral recourse. The article concluded with the author's thoughts on Connie's life. One of Connie's friends had told the author, "Connie always wanted what she couldn't get—but in a way she was always lucky. Men have always been attracted to her." "Lucky?" the author reflected. "The really lucky women are the ones who find their happiness in marriage, in caring for a good husband, rearing children. These women don't want what they can't have. They're content to fulfill their quiet destinies."[52]

In framing Connie's life this way, *True Story* reaffirmed the postwar domestic ideal and offered its thoughts on the growing number of married women who worked outside the home, whose numbers had increased from 12.5 percent in 1940 to almost 30 percent in 1960. As we saw in the previous chapter, already during the Depression authors noted the sexual dangers lurking for the married woman in the skyscraper, and with their numbers expanding and the culture obsessed with normative sex, comments continued. Although she did not directly reference Connie, within six weeks of the trial's conclusion the advice giver Mary Haworth published two columns warning married women against workplace entanglements. Even a flirtation was playing with fire, and working married women needed to grow up.[53]

And what about the man dead in the morgue? What example could be taken from his life? After its opening statement, the prosecution said little about Forrest. For its part, the defense subtly suggested that he had gotten what he deserved. "It takes two to tango," Connie's attorney reminded the jury, but he also did not want them to think too much about morality, which could hurt her cause. Yet there was an undercurrent of class politics at play here. The prosecution asked prospective jurors whether they could set aside their moral judgment, but it also queried, "If evidence shows that Mr. Teel occupied a position of great importance in the business world, that wouldn't prejudice you one way or the other, would it?" Jury members had to be free of this bias, but the letters the judge received suggest that some Americans viewed the case through this lens. They were split between those who thought Connie was a "gold digger" or a "sex-crazed you-know-what" and others who expressed sympathy. Those focused on Forrest saw his behavior as connected to his position. "Money won't clean his soul or make things right for the life he led that poor woman," one commented. "Too many men are getting by with just such doings." Another observed, "Evidently Forrest Teel used these working girls as his 'PUPPETS.'" Both parties were "equally a discredit to decent society," according to a writer from North Carolina, and Ann Landers seems to have shared this view. In the middle of the trial, she published a letter from a married father who had an affair with a girl in his office; she "threw herself" at him and was now pregnant. "I don't have to tell you that sometimes the flesh can be weak," he confessed to Landers, but she was unsympathetic. Rejecting his assessment of the woman as a "dangerous troublemaker," she noted, "No girl can make this kind of trouble by herself."[54]

Social concerns about corporate excess and white-collar workers' preoccupation with their social standing also help explain Americans' fascination with Connie's trial. By the time of his death, Forrest was second in command at one of the largest pharmaceutical companies in the world, and he lived a life that showed his success. He owned a plane and resided in the city's most exclusive area. And then there was his Cadillac, *the* symbol of achievement in the 1950s. At Lilly, as at other corporations, visible markers made the pecking order clear, with top executives gaining access to private dining and washrooms and receiving Cadillacs—all painted white. Though Forrest never recorded his thoughts on how a beautiful secretary contributed to a man's reputation, executives elsewhere saw "an attractively turned-out" assistant as a potent symbol; as a 1957 employment guide for secretaries noted, "In the same way that men take great pride in owning sleek new cars, they feel that a Cadillac-caliber secretary also adds to their prestige." In such an environment, it was logical to believe that Forrest traded Connie in for a younger model.[55]

The trial seems to have made the chairman of Eli Lilly's board ponder the connection between status seeking and questionable values. Started in 1876 in a tiny lab in Indianapolis, Lilly was a family-owned and -run company until the early 1950s and had resisted creating its own PR department until the mid-1950s. It was the city's largest employer, and the family was known for its charitable generosity, not extravagant living. But within hours of Teel's murder, the Lilly name was linked to his in sordid press accounts, first for a few weeks after his death and then during the lengthy trial. The company did not release a formal statement about Forrest's murder. Off the record, the family member who served as chairman of the board got the word out to top executives that behavior such as Forrest's was unacceptable. He also told them to get rid of the white Cadillacs. Some traded them in for other status symbols, while others painted them—possibly on Lilly's tab.[56]

A few months after Connie's trial, a much smaller scandal erupted, but it, too, highlighted the temptations working wives encountered. John Morgan sued Chicago and North Western Railway for half a million dollars for failing to stop—indeed, encouraging—the affair between his wife, a secretary, and her boss. The company had required Mrs. Morgan to accompany her boss on overnight business trips and forced her to work in "long and continual proximate personal contact" with him, thus alienating her affections from her husband. "If the employer cracks down and does what he can to prevent these affairs, that's one thing," Morgan's attorney argued. "If the employer does nothing, knowing the facts, that's something else again." A judge ultimately dismissed the charges when a jury failed to side with Morgan in his individual alienation suit against his wife's boss.[57]

This case attracted notice because it introduced a new legal principle—holding an employer liable for the acts of an employee outside the scope of employment—but even before the case made the newswire services, some executives were beginning to think more about the company's role in managing employees' personal interactions. During World War II, government personnel managers had begun to discipline supervisors whose unprofessional behaviors damaged morale. As the human relations approach took off after the war, more emphasis was placed on ensuring harmonious personal relations in the workplace, which might have drawn more attention to (and possibly censure of) male behaviors women found objectionable. For example, a 1958 guide for executives advised men to avoid "personal" references when working with a woman. Jokes about "flat-chested" women or stories about "parts of the female anatomy" were definitely unacceptable.[58]

Others also spoke to the question of appropriate workplace behaviors, but in a way that focused on the workplace atmosphere as a whole and not just the effects on those individuals involved. Mary Haworth used her column to chastise a boss and secretary in a small office whose morning ritual of drinking coffee and doing the crossword before closing the boss's door (presumably for dictation) had distracted the other workers, who suspected an affair. One of the other secretaries had written to Haworth, who declared the "vaguely honeymoon" behaviors demoralizing, in part because they "vulgarize[d]" the other workers' "sensibilities." This was an unacceptable work environment, and Haworth urged the letter writer to seek other employment. Here was a resurrection, slightly modified, of the advice female workers received when they first entered the office—some workplaces were morally toxic or personally degrading and should not be tolerated. Haworth's assessment of the situation was simultaneously regressive and progressive. On one hand, it smacked of the Victorian mandate to protect one's innocence. On the other, it anticipated future feminist arguments that some situations were too hostile to endure.[59]

Prescriptive literature also urged companies to take greater responsibility in policing the romantic and sexual lives of their employees when those lives intruded into the workplace (though evidence from the 1970s would suggest that few heeded this advice). Mary Haworth continued her crusade against office parties, and others joined the fight. Citizens in Pittsburgh called on the mayor to oppose such festivities, since "drinking at these parties encourages excessive liberties between employees, often superiors and their subordinates, which has a disastrous effect not only upon the character and reputation of each, but upon the future morals and effectiveness of the entire staff." An article warning unmarried women against affairs with their bosses told of an emotionally unstable woman who slept with her married supervisor at an office party and ended up a prostitute. Others told similar stories of illicit liaisons whose origins could be traced to workplace celebrations.[60]

In 1958 and 1959 *Modern Office Procedures* advised its readers to take control of office affairs. There was no need to outlaw the annual Christmas party, but one night of revelry must not lead to months of employee regret and recrimination. In one company, things had gotten so bad that managers had to "station guards in the elevators." Such situations could be avoided by prohibiting alcohol and establishing a "watch-dog committee" to patrol against too friendly conversations between a married man and a secretary or someone else's wife. The journal also surveyed companies on how they responded to "honorable or illicit" workplace relationships. All expressed an unwillingness to pass moral judgment on an employee's personal life, but all agreed that maintaining efficiency and the company's good name were paramount. Though the specific responses varied, none prohibited dating between unmarried employees. But when these employees' efficiency suffered, the majority took action, issuing warnings, transferring the individuals to other departments, or even terminating their employment. In the case of illicit affairs, especially those involving top executives, management generally acted quickly in reply to a basic equation: the higher the executive, the more his lapses could lower the company's worth. As one respondent noted, "A company spending thousands of public relations dollars to build a good corporate image can't afford to see this image destroyed by a single illicit romance." The article concluded by urging companies to adopt the policy of the only firm surveyed that had definite rules. That company told all employees at the time of their hiring that romances should not be conducted during business hours and then outlined the process for employees caught violating the regulations, which could result in termination. This hard line was softened by a step in which management encouraged the employee to see a family counselor; human relations theory humanized the bottom line.[61]

Sometime during the 1950s a marketing expert, in a speech at Harvard's Graduate School of Business titled "The Dangers of Social Responsibility," declared, "The businessman exists for only one purpose, to create and deliver value satisfactions at a profit to himself. He isn't and shouldn't be a theologian, a philosopher, an Emily Post of Commerce. . . . If what is offered can be sold at a profit," he continued, "then it's legitimate. The cultural, spiritual, social, moral, etc., consequences of his actions are none of his personal concern." By 1960 this lecture might have seemed naïve. A good businessman had to be concerned with the moral and social consequences of his and his employees' actions because they could hurt his earnings and/or those of the corporation for which he worked. By this point, though Americans still talked about private behaviors and the public sphere as if they were completely separate, the imaginary line dividing the two was hard to find. Corporations "interviewed" wives to make sure they were executive quality. And personnel journals urged companies to chastise the office Don Juan if his flirtations annoyed female clerks and to patrol the water cooler to forestall adulterous affairs that could lead to gossip, scandal, or even a lawsuit. Passion was a problem to be managed like any other threat to the bottom line. In 1962 Helen Gurley Brown would offer another view, one that celebrated the workplace's sexual energy and attempted to turn it to women's advantage. Brown believed that expressions of sexuality in the office were inevitable and not necessarily a bad thing. "Managements who think romances lower the work output are right out of their skulls," Brown told readers of her 1962 best-seller, *Sex and the Single Girl*. "A girl in love with her boss will knock herself out seven days a week and wish there were more days. Tough on her but fabulous for business!"[62]

CHAPTER SIX

The White-Collar Revolution

HELEN GURLEY BROWN, SEX, AND A NEW MODEL OF WORKING WOMANHOOD

OFFICES, HELEN GURLEY BROWN ANNOUNCED IN 1964, are "sexier than Turkish harems, fraternity house weekends . . . or the *Playboy* centerfold." Everyone was at his or her best at work—clothes, brains, energy—which led men and women to wonder what the other was like in bed. This observation was not completely new, but that Brown saw nothing wrong with sexy workplace waves—even when they became actual (and possibly adulterous) office affairs—certainly was. This was just the latest in what was already a career of provocative declarations. Brown had burst onto the scene in 1962 with the publication of *Sex and the Single Girl*, in which she proclaimed sex to be one of life's greatest pleasures and, more controversially, urged unmarried women to partake in its delights. Social conservatives responded disapprovingly, while legions of women replied by turning the book into an instant best-seller. Brown spent the next few years capitalizing on her newfound fame, and in 1965 took over as editor of the failing general-interest magazine *Cosmopolitan*, transforming it into a guidebook for a new kind of woman, the "Cosmo Girl," to whom she offered advice for the next three decades.[1]

Brown's views had profound implications for the expression of romantic and sexual desire in the office. By the time *Sex and the Single Girl* was released, almost one of every three employed women worked in a clerical or secretarial job. Brown aimed her advice at the unmarried ones, tying their sexual freedom and sexual opportunities to their place in the workforce. A woman's workplace accomplishments could make new types of romantic and sexual relationships possible, and possible on new terms; a successful workingwoman's sexual "surrender" was different than that of the woman who wanted or needed to be supported economically. In Brown's view, then, sexuality and work were not two distinct spheres but rather two sides of the same coin that she believed offered women a richer existence.[2]

Brown hoped to give women a measure of the power that men derived from being sexual agents in the office, revising much of the advice women had long received. In her office, women were not on constant guard to keep relations impersonal lest they give a man the wrong idea. Nor were they disreputable vamps. They did not have to deny their sexuality to protect their reputation or to stay safe. Instead, Brown advised women to use gender and, to varying degrees, sexuality for personal and professional gain.

In this chapter I explore Brown's ideas regarding sexuality and gender in the workplace and the responses to them in the period before she took over *Cosmopolitan*. A tenacious pragmatist, she wasted no time wondering why things were the way they were, but assessed the situation and came up with a response to help *individual* women make the most of their circumstances. Her redesign of the office's sexual landscape further blurred the already fuzzy line that divided public and private behavior and dismantled the obstructions that constrained women's sexual agency. Because Brown was as much a product of her time as a challenge to it, an extended analysis of her outlook gives us a chance to identify early resistance to the office's sexual status quo, exploring the benefits and limitations of a new discourse and the possibilities for change on the eve of the sexual revolution and the women's movement.

CONTEXT: A WOMAN OF (AND AHEAD OF) HER TIME

Brown's attitudes about sex shocked many Americans, but her views did not materialize out of thin air. Sometimes they involved a reconfiguration of contemporary norms, and on occasion, outright rejection of them. However, they always emerged from and engaged with life as Brown experienced it. To make sense of her perspective, one needs to know something about her background and the representations of workplace sexuality that filled her world.

Brown was born in 1922, the child of Arkansas schoolteachers. The family's prospects improved when her father was elected to the state legislature, but in 1932, when Helen was ten, her father died in an elevator accident. Moving to Los Angeles in 1936, Helen, her mother, and her older sister, Mary, struggled to make ends meet, a situation made much worse when her sister contracted polio and was permanently confined to a wheelchair. While enrolled in business college, Brown embarked on what was to be a lifetime of working in an office. At age twenty-five, after seventeen jobs, she landed a dream boss, Don Belding, a successful and influential advertising executive. Brown worked as Belding's secretary, and eventually he gave her the chance to write ad copy. At thirty-one, she began a steady march toward becoming one of the highest paid female copywriters on the West Coast. In 1959, when she was thirty-seven and an old maid by the standards of the time, she married the movie producer David Brown and became Helen Gurley Brown.[3]

Sex and the Single Girl was actually her husband's idea. When he told her to write about what she knew, Brown took her own experiences and crafted them into a manifesto that exemplified the "new moral code of the modern working girl." Her portrayal of premarital sex, Brown maintained, simply revealed a transformation already in progress, which explained the book's appeal: "Other girls who had been doing the very same thing simply stood up and echoed a rousing YES!" In addition to providing readers with man-hunting tips, Brown offered career advice. Presenting herself as a sort of "every secretary" who had overcome poverty, an average I.Q., and a bad case of acne to build a glamorous career and snag a desirable man, Brown sought to inspire women who lacked any tangible assets; if she had made it with nothing more than pluck and hard work, they could, too. She championed the position of secretary as the way to get one's foot in the door and downplayed the value of a college degree. As for swimming endlessly in the secretarial pool, Brown maintained that the "only people who get stuck in secretarial jobs are happily or willingly stuck."[4]

Brown's employment advice was in many ways similar to that of other guides, except when it came to the topic of sexuality and romance in the office; in this regard, the wisdom offered by other advice givers in the postwar era remained remarkably similar to that of the 1930s, even though more married and older women were entering the workforce. Elizabeth Gregg MacGibbon revised *Manners in Business* in 1954, but the chapter "Sex in Business" remained virtually the same. What little change there was served to intensify her argument against expressions of sexuality in the workplace; for example, she added paragraphs that urged bosses and secretaries to behave in a way that would forestall any office gossip and cautioned further against affairs with married men. While the concern about gossip might have been a nod to human relations theory, MacGibbon did not exhibit increased concern with men's actions that might upset women.

If anything, MacGibbon and others seemed more sympathetic to men and their carnal nature. Some "curvaceous women," she noted, should have a warning sign on their desk. Marylin Burke, Dale Carnegie's secretary, began her 1959 guide by warning women against "low necklines" that might "have a tendency to distract." "Sultry pouts, swinging hips, [and] lingering caresses of well-manicured fingers" were also unfair because they took advantage of "male weakness." Employment guides continued to counsel women that most of the behavior they might find offensive or threatening was probably just innocent flirting and should not be taken too seriously. A 1954 employment guide by Esther Becker told a secretary not to tell her boss about the department head who had acquired a reputation for "making a play" for some of the women working under him. Why? According to Becker, "there are some sirens or *femmes fatales* in every department who misconstrue courtesies." These attentions probably were not "little indecencies" but efforts at "giving a girl a lift."[5]

Advice guides continued to tell women that men's overtures meant nothing, but an abundance of popular sources informed women that virtually all the men with whom they labored were on the make. Racy representations of sex in the office became available after World War II in the form of mass-market paperback novels, inexpensively priced and widely available at drugstores and newsstands. Publishers aimed these wares at working-class, heterosexual men, though evidence suggests a broader audience actually read them. Lesbians, for example, read those that included lesbian characters, who often worked in offices. Lena, the she-wolf protagonist of *All Girl Office*, created the "perfect hunting ground": her own consulting firm where the female employees were "'under her' in more ways than one."[6]

With provocative jacket teasers like this, hedonistic cover illustrations, and wildly suggestive titles, pulps quickly attracted the attention of local and state censors, outraged citizens, and, in 1952, Congress—even though the books' covers often bore little resemblance to the story told inside. The cover of *Office Party*, for example, pictured drunken executives and partially undressed secretaries and teased, "the meek ran wanton and wantons ran berserk." This office party, the inside cover promised, was "the one day of the year when sin became king and men and women abject slaves to its every wanton demand, its ever shameful desire." By the novel's end, however, some partygoers were locked in domestic bliss, and those who had sinned the most were farthest from happiness. The use of such endings, which condemned immorality and punished transgressors, was one of the ways that publishers tried to skirt censors' objections. These narratives, then, closely resembled the Cinderella plots from the 1920s and 1930s. Pulp heroines, however, did not keep their passions in check, though their nonmarital sexual experiences did not disqualify them from a happy ending. Instead, these missteps led to self-discovery, ensuring that the women would ultimately embrace domesticity. Beginning in the late 1950s, courts began to hand down decisions declaring that pulps were not obscene, and in the mid-1960s the novels became increasingly explicit about sex.[7]

These books contained enough detail to be sexually arousing, but they also might have spoken to readers' psychological needs. According to scholars, popular reading has less to do with the actual structure of the text than with the circumstances of its readers, who focus on characters and situations that help them make sense of their lives. It is not too far-fetched, then, to think that men could have read these books and found more than titillation. For example, some of the pulps set in an office featured a desperate husband whose future depended on his wife's ability to seduce his superior, a plot that might have resonated with blue- and white-collar readers. For working-class men, the notion that a man's job was in his wife's (sexual) hands was not improbable; during the Depression, automotive factory workers who wanted to keep their jobs sometimes had to make their wives or daughters sexually available to their foremen. And, as we saw in the last chapter, a wife was not incidental to a man's success, as corporations increasingly interviewed a prospective executive's wife to ensure that she would fit in. This situation was immortalized in the 1954 film *Woman's World*, in which three executives and their wives vie for a promotion, including one wife who is willing to sleep with the boss.[8]

Pulps were not the only male-oriented media to set their fantasies in the office. In 1953 a totally new incarnation of the "office vixen" emerged when *Playboy* magazine told its readers that a playmate might be sitting right outside their office doors. *Playboy*'s masculine philosophy encouraged middle-class men to eschew marriage and mainstream norms and embrace sophisticated consumption—fine liquor, fast cars, and nonmarital heterosexual sex. The rub was finding willing women, and the magazine encouraged readers to look at work. One of the magazine's advertising salesmen, for example, discovered Miss September of 1957—a "sexy secretary"—when he called on her boss to sell ad space. One man's "Girl Friday" thus became *Playboy* readers' "Girl Saturday, Sunday, Monday, Tuesday, Wednesday and Thursday." A multipage cartoon from 1956, "The Perfect Secretary," featured bosses chasing voluptuous women around desks, filing cabinets that opened up into fully made beds for those times when she needed to "work late," and other suggestions that the secretary's real job was to meet the boss's sexual needs. In real life, it seems that secretaries' response to *Playboy*'s message was more mixed; a reader in Corpus Christi wrote that he and his secretary read the magazine together, while another corresponded from Buffalo that his secretary quit after seeing one of the cartoons.[9]

Popular novels and magazine fiction in the 1950s that featured businessmen did not so openly portray the office as a sporting ground, but they did represent it as a space in which the manifestation of desire was an occasionally extraordinary but mostly rather ordinary part of daily life. The readers of one novel were introduced to the protagonist as he sat in his office intensely watching a pretty girl ascend a flight of stairs. In a story in the *Saturday Evening Post*, a young man new to the big city spent a lonely holiday season after the men in charge canceled the office's Christmas and New Year's parties because they were "bad for morale." They came to this determination after assessing the fallout from the previous years' festivities. A vice president, who arrived home at 3 A.M. on Christmas Eve, found that his wife had locked him out of the house, and after one New Year's bash, the entire staff spent days twittering over the news that the sales manager and a billing clerk had spent the night locked up in the supply room. Other stories focused on married businessmen at "that susceptible age," when their young secretaries aroused lustful desires the men mistook for true love.[10]

Mainstream popular fiction aimed at women also showed a sexualized office, though here the narrative often focused on the female protagonist finding a suitable mate. Rona Jaffe's *The Best of Everything*, a best-seller from 1958, followed the lives of three young white-collar women. Getting groped by Mr. Shalimar, the married, fifty-year-old editor at the publishing house where they worked, was simply an inescapable (and ultimately harmless) part of their initiation into office life. After this introduction, the story proceeded to show that love and marriage, not a career, were best for women, though husband hunting was far from easy. Jaffe's characters' "obsession" with getting married, as one reviewer noted, bordered on "monomania," so much so that they willingly "sacrifice pride, professional achievement and, above all, [their] chastity, on the wildest chance that so doing will net [them] a wedding ring." This obsession was also the dominant theme throughout the 1950s in popular magazine fiction that featured a female protagonist. Even more than in earlier decades, this era portrayed the office as an ideal place to find a man.[11]

In 1960 the director Billy Wilder added another perspective in the Academy Award–winning comedy, *The Apartment*, an unflattering portrait of the sexual prerogatives of executives, the emotional and erotic vulnerability of female office workers, and the moral predicaments of lowly organization men. C. C. Baxter, clerk number 861 at a large insurance company, quickly realizes that his night school accounting diploma will not take him very far and begins to lend his apartment key to four married department heads who need a place to take their office mistresses and can put in a good word for him in personnel. Sheldrake, the director of personnel, takes note and offers Baxter a promotion—on the condition that he can join the key club. Baxter readily agrees, especially since Sheldrake hints that Baxter could otherwise lose his position for facilitating such immoral behavior. Baxter is both naïve and an opportunist, and he never considers the ethical implications of his career strategy until he learns that Fran, the elevator girl he loves, is Sheldrake's mistress.

Play-Office Sets for Ages 7-12 Brought Out by Eberhard Faber

Two play-office sets that are expected to amuse adults as much as their 7-to-12-year users were given their dual debut at the Toy Fair by Eberhard Faber Toy and Game Company, Inc., Crestwood, Wilkes-Barre, Pa.

"Junior Executive" is complete even to an "Eater's Club" card, and "Junior Secretary" is true-to-life right down to the makeup kit. Each retails for $5.

"Junior Executive," #5585, gives Junior a replica of everything on Dad's desk, for his pre-executive training. There are the plastic name-plate, lettering for it, a desk-

blotter, pencils, ballpens, pen-holder, perpetual calendar, stapling machine, staples, paperclips, checkbook, petty cash vouchers, letter-opener, magnifying glass, ruler, appointment pad and—of course—the indispensible credit card.

"Junior Secretary," #5586, has most of these items, plus steno book, hairbrush, cosmetics, perfume and cologne.

As pictured here, both sets are being used in conjunction with the "Des-K-Way," children's combination desk-and-chair produced by the Earl Randolph Corporation, of New Bedford, Mass.

By 1960 the boss-and-secretary trope was so common that the toy industry's leading trade journal, *Playthings*, used it for laughs in a story about office sets for boys and girls aged seven to twelve. Courtesy of the Brian Sutton-Smith Library and Archives of Play™ at the Strong™, Rochester, New York.

When, on Christmas Eve, she tries to kill herself in Baxter's apartment after Sheldrake insultingly gives her one hundred dollars as a holiday gift, he begins, slowly, to question the bargain he has made. Baxter's quandary is really no different from that of the low-level, white-collar men discussed in Chapter 2, who found themselves forever chained to an adding machine; indeed, *The Apartment*'s opening scene mirrors that of 1928's

The Crowd, in which the hero first appears as an indistinguishable autom-
aton in a sea of gray steel desks. Baxter, too, sees his ability to attract
women and establish a fulfilling relationship limited by his lack of professional achievement.[12]

Wilder presents a world in which executives lack integrity. Baxter
remains a "yes" man even after his promotion; the men who recommended him to Sheldrake still make demands and remind him, "We
made you, and we can break you." After Fran's suicide attempt, Sheldrake
is sincerely worried about a scandal, but he is incapable of sincere feeling
for another human being. He has seen her a few times a week just for
laughs, just as he had seen his secretary, Miss Olsen, before. Ultimately,
the film suggests that women suffer most in a workplace organized
around men's quest for status and power. From an unwanted grope on
the elevator to an office party that seems destined to lead to a good bit of
regret for many women, men's desires—and the sense of entitlement
that comes with their positions—structure the sexual culture of the office.
Even men on the bottom rungs fare better than their female counterparts.
Baxter willingly allows other men to use him in the hope of getting something in return, while Fran genuinely loves Sheldrake. While Sheldrake
plays with his sons on Christmas morning, she battles for her life, and the
contrast, one review noted, was a sharp critique of the "perfidiousness of
men with families playing around with the office girls." Sheldrake's
treachery is complete when, without any fear of reprisal, he matter-of-
factly fires Miss Olsen after she tells Fran about their affair. Baxter, of
course, ends up with the girl, but the movie does not show its hero an
alternate path that will lead to both honor and solvency. As for Fran and
other women like her, they have merely been warned yet again to be on
guard against office wolves who threaten to devour every bit of their
self-respect.[13]

Throughout the culture, in a wide variety of media aimed at a wide
variety of consumers and encompassing a wide variety of plots, the office
was represented as sexual space. Many narratives reflected ongoing
concerns about men's inability to claim a masculine identity in a bureaucratic and consumer-oriented world, and some portrayed in an unflattering light men who misuse their authority. All, however, pictured
women office workers as available and willing (including, except in mainstream magazines, sexually), whether through unabashed lust, hopeful

romantic desire, or youthful naïveté; male attention was never truly or completely unwanted.

Even interactions that authors initially presented as indisputably harassing or exploitative were soon re-presented—*by the woman herself*—as sincere or at least flattering. This retelling transformed victims into assertive agents or agreeable participants and rendered a man's transgression as benign. In the pulp *Office Tramp*, for example, Amy Preston's employer, Mr. Akton, summons her to his office on her first day on the job. When she arrives, he informs her that he called her not for dictation but for "distraction," and within a few seconds he has locked his door and begun to unbutton her blouse, all against her will. Through sheer cunning, she escapes his clutches. When she returns to the typing pool, she learns that Akton has had his way with most of his office staff under similar circumstances, and she becomes a kind of folk hero; another stenographer tells her, "Nice work, kid. . . . I hope you blacked his eye." By the next morning, though, Amy's imagination has transformed her attacker into her suitor, as she muses, "Maybe he did like me. More than just a girl in the typing pool he could fool around with." By day's end, she and Akton have made passionate love on his office couch, though their affair never leads to marriage as she had dreamed. Other media offered the same message. In the film version of *The Best of Everything*, Mr. Shalimar forcefully kisses a new stenographer during a pause in dictation. She quickly breaks free, and he gives her cab fare home. But in the thirty seconds it takes her to grab her hat and run to the elevator, her mood dramatically changes. Her tears have dried into a pleased smile, and her anger and humiliation have given way to happiness: a successful man in a sophisticated city found her desirable.[14]

These narratives acknowledge the power imbalance between white-collar women and their male superiors, but by always casting the woman as an active seeker of love or pleasure and always finishing with a happy ending (even if not with the man she initially desired), the representations minimize the negative effects of this power differential. Such a portrait overstates these women's agency. The majority of the time female characters are acted upon; they do not initiate the encounters but instead are responding to a man's overtures. More significantly, even when women do act, they are never in a position to achieve their aims without men's assistance or consent. The only things these women want are things that only men have the power to bestow, whether that be a ring, a raise or even validation as a "real" woman who has aroused a man's ardor. Helen Gurley Brown offered her advice in this cultural frame. Sexualized offices and women with relatively little power filled the world of fictional representations. Brown accepted the former as an unchangeable and not undesirable reality, but she rejected the latter. In her writings she attempted to show women how to use the eroticized workplace to change their subordinate position.

A NEW MODEL FOR WORKINGWOMEN: THE SEXY CAREER GIRL

Brown's first piece of advice was to work hard, on yourself *and* at your job. As she makes clear in the first few pages of *Sex and the Single Girl*, it is the single girl's presence in the workforce that makes her attractive. More to the point, it was possible for the sexually active single woman still "to be a lady, to be highly respected and even envied if she is successful in her work." Brown elaborated on the importance of a career, a fulfilling sex life, and the connections between the two in her second book, *Sex and the Office* (1964), which urged young workingwomen to take their jobs seriously.[15]

For Brown, work was rewarding in and of itself, *and* it leveled the romantic and sexual playing field; a successful workingwoman could escape many gender restrictions, such as those that limited women's ability to pursue men. Business travel provided one such opportunity, as the story of Evelyn made clear. With the respectability that came from being a professional and the anonymity and daring that came from being out of town, Evelyn became a sexually adventurous aggressor, seducing the respectable general manager she'd been sent to interview. As she recalled, "I was enjoying myself *utterly* because I was seducing *him* instead of getting mauled by some Adonis who was getting around to me simply because I was a girl—maybe number three thousand seven hundred and two on his list." Brown again celebrated the sexual freedoms of the successful woman while on a speaking tour: "It is one thing to say that a cloistered, protected, fragile, parent-dominated flower of a girl is 'ruined' because she has had an affair with a man—but it is quite another to say a woman who possibly has five employees of her own, one of whom is the man she has had the affair with, may never hold her head up again. Her private life and her business life are two separate areas." Of course,

Brown actually exposed how the two were often intertwined, and she also revealed one of the unspoken perks of achievement: if you are successful or indispensable at work, often others will look the other way with regard to the particulars of your private life, even if they go against dominant business standards or social mores. In these examples, Brown's calculus was clear: if you worked and earned like a man, you, too, were entitled to a degree of sexual autonomy.[16]

In Brown's view, a sexy attitude and the calculated application of femininity could help a woman on the way to professional success. That success, in turn, would facilitate her sexual independence. As she told readers of *Sex and the Office*, brains and talent alone would not get them to the top because many men still thought women belonged at home and therefore limited their workplace responsibilities to chores like making the coffee. The way around this bias was not to be an "unnatural penis-envying wolverine ready to spring at a man's jugular vein." Rather, "flirting and being seductive" would lead men to "give you better breaks." In warning women not to be too masculine, Brown merely echoed advice givers' oft-repeated counsel to be sure to appear feminine; however, Brown took this suggestion to the next step, against which they clearly had warned. But wiggling and beguiling alone, Brown repeatedly declared, would not be enough—a woman also needed to work hard at her job. And though Brown urged women to flirt at the office with impunity, she was far more circumspect about them sleeping their way to the top. "You will undoubtedly make certain initial advances in your career if a particular boss has promised them to you," but "these gains are precarious. If anything happens to him, the next boss may not be so susceptible to your charms and you'll be right back in the file room." Ultimately, each woman would have to make up her own mind about using sex to advance, but Brown believed sex alone would not get a woman very far.[17]

She was also clear that a woman who employed her feminine wiles had to be careful to always act like a "lady," since the office was decidedly middle-class space that brooked no transgressors. To this end, Brown provided careful answers to such questions as "How sexy can you look and still further your career?" that were especially attuned to the subtle markers of class. One of Brown's editors, for instance, warned her to "be careful not to advise on clothes and appearance that is cheap. Must emphasize *lady-like* sexiness in office." In response to Brown's instruction to "stand very close to his shoulder and lean over desk when man reading a paper," the same editor noted, "Should be far more subtle! Beware of cheapness in dress or tricks. Much better *you* should hold paper and let man lean over *you!*"[18]

SEXY OFFICES AND CHALLENGES TO MALE AUTHORITY

Brown's advice on how to perform femininity to maximize one's career and improve one's romantic chances generated a good deal of hostility. From the beginning of her success, she believed that critics pilloried her as often for telling women to behave artificially as for advocating nonmarital sexuality. A writer for the *Los Angeles Times*, for example, detected a thorough contempt for men in Brown's "manipulation" and "blueprint" for a "phony" female. This critique continued when *Sex and the Office* appeared. Reviewers chafed at the cynical and "calculating" behavior Brown advocated.[19]

Yet her tips on fashion and beauty, her relentless hectoring of women to improve themselves physically, had been the standard fare of husband-hunting guides since at least the 1920s. What was new—and disturbing—was her advice to bring these techniques into the office, where they could be pressed into service to catch a man *and* to advance up the corporate ladder. Artifice in pursuit of a husband was socially acceptable because such maneuverings did nothing to disturb existing gender norms or male dominance. In courtship, men did the asking; they were in control. If, however, women used these machinations to land promotions instead of (or in addition to) landing men, men could lose control; their power might decrease.[20]

In the context of the concerns about white-collar men's anemic manliness discussed in the previous chapter, Brown's advice really was a threat. Many Americans already believed that women, in their role as consumers, wives, and mothers, had too much influence, and in 1962 *Business Week* reported that corporate men were beginning to hear "the tap of high heels" on their ladder. Brown confirmed the sound. As she confidently told one reporter while commenting on the growing availability of plastic surgery, "The combination of beauty and brains is almost unbeatable . . . and these days . . . there's little reason for the brainy girl to lack charm." Brown, the reporter noted, "paints a picture that could be frightening for the male."[21]

In March 1965 *Modern Office Procedures* published a lengthy interview with Brown, who refused to comment on whether sex in the office was moral or even a good idea. Her main point was simply that it happened and that the participants were as respectable and reliable as anyone else. In response to the question "How can business and romance mix in an efficient office?" Brown replied, "Man-woman stuff in the office doesn't preclude business getting done as usual. . . . You can get both done very nicely." Moreover, she pointedly noted, "It's silly to say that these things do not go on in offices because they do. . . . It also doesn't mean that business falls by the wayside just because two people in the same office are going to bed together." She responded in a similarly matter-of-fact way to the query "Do you think it is normal and intelligent for a girl to have an affair with a married man who works in the same office?" Well, Brown retorted, "Many normal and intelligent women do." Businesses, in her view, should not do anything to discourage office romances, and they had no right to fire the office Don Juan or a woman who had been intimate with many men at work, as long as they were doing a good job.[22]

Modern Office Procedures asked its readers to respond. Two months later, the magazine published an article that included excerpts from letters received from readers, all of whom disagreed with Brown and believed that her attitude would hurt productivity. According to an office supervisor with fifteen years' experience, affairs inevitably created personal problems for those involved, even when they were unmarried. Affairs also built "barriers within the office—gossip, backbiting, jealousy, and all manner of unpleasantness," which made the office an unhappy place to work. The bulk of the piece focused on disputing the notion that a sexy style helped a girl get ahead. More than 70 percent of the letter writers were secretaries, and the rebuttal piece seems more directed to this audience than to their employers. According to the magazine, most of these workers believed Brown's advice could only lead to trouble. They reiterated the long-standing view that single women should not presume to interact personally with their male superiors and should avoid other men in the office, too. One secretary advised women to "be a perfect lady at all times." According to another, the single woman who left her job rather than have an affair was far more common than one who had an affair with a married man.

The article ended with the cautionary tale of a secretary who had spent the previous fourteen years moving from job to job because of unwanted sexual attentions. To verify her story, the magazine interviewed her and found an attractive, intelligent woman in her mid-thirties, whose natural qualities were those that Brown urged her readers to assume: she was "inordinately friendly, strikingly groomed, and the epitome of sex appeal." These attributes, though, had led to problems. Her male coworkers had "taken her amiability to mean availability," and job after job came to "an 'either or'" proposition, forcing her to quit and start again. This woman, the article assured readers, was innocent of doing anything to bring this tragedy upon herself, which made her story an even more compelling morality tale for the women who might have been entertaining the idea of adopting some of Brown's sexy strategies. Just in case the message was not clear enough, the article concluded with the following proclamation: "The girl who uses tricks and sex appeal to get ahead will never succeed in an efficient office operation. And she'll always be unhappy."[23]

If we tally up the advice *Modern Office Procedures* proffered to women, we would have no choice but to conclude that office women were powerless creatures, vulnerable to unwanted attentions, with only the thinnest protection afforded by the cover of ladylike behavior; the office was indeed a dangerous place. Yet what is striking about this article is that while it highlights women's vulnerability and moralizes about how they should act at work, it offers no judgment on the men whose behaviors endangered women or whose ultimatums forced them to quit. A focus on women's conduct allowed men's sexual behavior to be ignored. Given that their subscribers were male office managers, this omission is not surprising. But in its vigorous efforts to persuade women to police their actions lest they elicit undesired sexual attentions, the article actually undercut the dominant view, which held that the vast majority of men did not bother virtuous women. The concluding, cautionary story emphasized the dangers of sexiness, but it also suggested that men approached attractive women, even those who did not mean to send out sexy signals—a point also made in the 1930s in Frances Maule's story of Jocelyn, discussed in Chapter 3. These stories exposed the cultural belief that men's nature was fundamentally sexual—which was, of course, precisely Brown's view and the foundation on which she based her advice. If men "naturally" approached all attractive office girls, though, women had only two viable choices. They could make themselves as unattractive and unfriendly as possible, which, according to biological logic, would keep them safe. Or, they could adopt Brown's philosophy, making the best out of what apparently was inevitable.

The latter possibility and its impact on office men seem to be the real focus of the article's concern: men were the ones liable to end up "unhappy" if a girl used "tricks" to "get ahead." In warning women away from Brown's advice, the article inadvertently exposed male anxieties about the potential power of women in the office and the prevalence of sex in the office. Even before the article began reciting comments from secretaries, it made the following warning in a paragraph explaining how Brown's views hurt office efficiency: "The susceptible male who falls victim to these tricks or even lets them occur is only asking for trouble."[24]

Some reviewers were more dispassionate than the editors of *Modern Office Procedures*, noting that this chatty book's grains of truth should be taken with an equal proportion of salt, yet many vociferously denied the existence of sex at the office, especially extramarital affairs, even though this was hardly news. (As we saw in the previous chapter, *Modern Office Procedures* had acknowledged as much in 1959, and by the mid-1960s sociologists and other scholars had published studies that confirmed Brown's view. One quoted a prominent businessmen who said, "I don't see how *anyone* can miss the sleeping-around of all kinds that goes on.") Archival evidence suggests that the stories Brown told were true (that is, they had happened to Brown or someone she knew), if somewhat embellished. But even if they weren't, Brown's point, in its least outrageous form, was simply that human beings are sexual creatures, and therefore it is impossible to keep sexuality completely out of the office. Her argument that flirtations, crushes, and even sex do not necessarily hurt efficiency and could actually be good for business was just a positive spin on what she believed was inevitable. But by urging women to insinuate consciously the element of sexuality into the workplace, Brown threatened men's identity and authority.[25]

In encouraging workplace relationships, Brown played down women's vulnerability in the office, especially the fact that low-level female office workers might easily lose their jobs. Yet by emphasizing their agency instead of their disadvantage, she gave to "proper," low-ranking women a limited version of the power of pursuit and desire that had long belonged to high-ranking men. Brown's advice encouraged women to interact with men in a new way, both sexually and professionally. The old warnings to watch out for the office wolf had worked to keep all but gold diggers and nonladies subordinate, afraid of too much interaction of any kind and always monitoring their behavior lest they send out the wrong signals. Brown's urgings, however, destroyed this self-protective version of self-surveillance; now the lady in the office would discipline her actions in order to attract attention and, ideally, opportunity. Of course, a sexy woman's power never came close to approximating the power of an executive. It served primarily as resistance to confining gender roles, a sort of "weapon of the weak." Nevertheless, this power could upset business as usual, through which men ruled the office, set the pace, and initiated all breaks.

Brown's advice also might have changed the dynamic between men in the office. Commentators had long noted the status that accrued to the executive whose colleagues envied his sexual escapades; a desirable mistress just might reinforce his masculine image and help him on the way to the top. This avenue to prestige was predicated on the fact that the man was in control, that he initiated the affair, decided when to end it, and never let his emotions overtake him. Once women became sexual agents (even if their need to remain somewhat "lady-like" circumscribed their assertiveness), office affairs for men had to become more treacherous. What had been purely a male prerogative suddenly became less so, and the sexual arena more crowded, when women could do the asking.[26]

HETEROSEXUALITY AND THE FEMININE CAREER WOMAN

Readers might be perplexed by what seems a paradox: Brown's cheerleading for the pleasures of a successful career and her equally insistent chant that every woman needs a man. (Although Brown focused exclusively on heterosexuality in her published writings, she wanted to include a chapter on lesbians and gay men in *Sex and the Office*. In her view, homosexuals were visible and often critical elements of office life, but her publisher demanded that she remove these sections.) On one hand, Brown's creation of an ambitious man-pleaser worked to deflect criticism from women who, by pursuing employment in general and, for some, full-fledged careers, were challenging traditional gender roles. (By 1960,

35 percent of all adult women worked, the majority of them married.) On the other hand, it provided these same women with a way to claim an identity as a "woman," even as they abandoned the ideal of full-time domesticity. In making sense of Brown's philosophy, we cannot forget that her contemporaries—ranging from Dr. Spock to Hugh Hefner to her own husband—claimed that working masculinized women and that women in the workplace emasculated men. Brown was especially sensitive to this anxiety. Her new ideal of the man-adoring, feminine career woman did not silence the critics, but it did allow women to compete with men without endangering their womanliness. Refocusing womanhood on heterosexuality, instead of motherhood and domesticity, safeguarded gender difference against ambitious women. As she noted, "You can be a bank president and still dig men."[27]

In Brown's world, men made you a woman by affirming your sexual desirability—that is, by appreciating your difference. But many men, contrary to what one might think, did not embrace Brown's endorsement of premarital sex; a sexually assertive woman represented a threat to manliness. A review of *Sex and the Single Girl* in *Saga*, a men's magazine, warned that sex was a man's game. Brown's advice could "earn an unskilled, amateur player her rape or murder." According to another review, Brown's "rapacious, aggressive female" degraded "the male in ways the male has traditionally degraded the woman . . . [and] transfers to him all the passive object-qualities the lustful female finds exciting." These critics found the woman who combined career ambitions with a free sexuality especially dangerous. The social critic Philip Wylie described such women as modern day "Sirens," who "must compete with and, if necessary, cripple manhood and masculinity on earth."[28]

Given this antagonism, if heterosexuality was to bear the full weight of upholding gender difference, gender roles during sexual courtship and in sexual acts would have to be crystal clear and flawlessly performed. As Brown told *Playboy* readers in an interview in 1963, "When a man is making love to you, the United Nations building could fall down and if he's really a man, he won't stop for a minute." Elsewhere, Brown told the story of one successful woman who had developed a "technique" to ensure men's pleasure, yet this, too, involved an exact calibration, participating, but "not to the point of infringing upon the male role." If women acted like "women" and needed "men" in the bedroom, Brown seemed to hope, they just might convince men to let them into the boardroom.[29]

We can see both how Brown intended for heterosexuality to uphold gender difference and the limits of her notion of sexual (and personal) liberation in her response to "The Matinee," a lunchtime-only affair. Once Brown began to write *Sex and the Office*, her publisher's staff offered suggestions. Letty Cottin, a staff publicist in her early twenties—who later became one of the founding editors of *Ms.* magazine—contacted a friend who was having an affair with a married man from her office. She agreed to write down her story, which ultimately appeared anonymously in Brown's book. The affair had been going on for two years, and in that time the couple had seen each other outside of the office only during lunch in the woman's apartment. The informant maintained that the Matinee was not uncommon and was particularly ideal when one of the two participants was married. For a single woman there were a number of reasons to have such a relationship; in particular, her sexual needs could be met on her own terms, since a married lover was not in a position to make demands. Nevertheless, a woman also needed to be honest with herself about what purpose the relationship really served: if she was looking for love, the Matinee was not for her. It also demanded strict personal discipline. A woman could never wear another dress back to the office or even use perfume, lest his wife detect it. The rest of the advice (probably Brown's additions) included quick lunch recipes and a reminder to have your birth control and a pitcher of cocktails ready to go when the man arrived.[30]

When Cottin first heard about this relationship sometime in 1962, it came as a complete shock, but she assumed that Brown knew all about such arrangements. In fact, Brown seemed surprised, even appalled. As she noted in the Matinee chapter's conclusion, this kind of affair never happened to her because she "couldn't give up wearing perfume for anybody . . . or be cordial to a guy who apparently never brings his own liquor." Though she went on to insist that she didn't "want to sound like a prude at *this* late date," she nevertheless maintained that "the whole Matinee relationship leaves me a little cold—and not just because of all the inconvenience." While this approach was certainly savvy, since it removed Brown from any direct connection with a story that many readers would have found stunningly illicit, archival evidence suggests her adoption of this position was sincere. As she noted in a letter to her editor, "As you know I was dead set against the Matinee as a chapter because I considered *it* dirty. That is honestly and truly the truth." She continued, "A relationship with no other sweetness and friendship going for it but *lunch* seemed ickey to me."[31]

Brown may have felt that this woman was being taken advantage of, providing lunch, cocktails, and sex for a man and getting nothing tangible (other than sex) in return. This view makes some sense; the Matinee woman does seem to serve the man, and in a domestic, wifely way. Yet this view assumes an immutable gender inequality and perpetual sexual double standard in which, because sex is always somewhat risky for the woman, she should get something more than just physical pleasure from a sexual encounter. The problem for Brown, then, was that the Matinee woman was acting not like a woman but rather like a man. She was in control. Her job provided the financial means to facilitate *her* sexual plea-sure. Brown believed that all women should work, that employment was the foundation from which women would achieve equality and economic and sexual liberation. She also believed that work should not make women into men and offered up a highly gendered model of heterosexu-ality to ensure that it would not. The matter-of-factness of the Matinee, however, robbed sex of many of its performative qualities that confirmed the participants' gender. With this aspect gone, sex seems to have lost some of its thrill.

UNWANTED ATTENTIONS: INEVITABLE, BUT MANAGEABLE

Brown's sexy office advice was new. She identified the measure of power that could come to women through arousing men's desires and urged them to use it. However, like others before her, Brown accepted that women would receive some sexual approaches that were unwanted, even hostile or harassing. Reading her early writings now, one cannot help but be struck by examples of sexual behavior in the workplace that today would be highly questionable, if not illegal. Brown accepted the long-standing view that if a woman could not find a way to deal with these men and the situation got too bad, she would have to quit.

Yet Brown's advice was also different in significant ways. Women who followed Brown's counsel were sexual agents, not innocents, and their newfound ability to say "yes" might have given their "no" more weight. At the very least, they were not embarrassed about sex or ashamed of having desires of their own, which provided them with a wider range of possible responses before handing in their resignation. Brown also counseled women to trust their instincts in assessing the danger a particular man posed. This approach was more proactive, at least in a psychological sense, than others' advice, which counseled women to ignore unwanted attentions, avoid excessively friendly men, and be sure they had not misunderstood a harmless compliment. Brown, by comparison, acknowledged men's behavior for what it was, and her suggestions might have revised the office's sexual dynamic in a way that could help *individual* women. Her carefully orchestrated responses to uninvited propositions had the potential to disrupt the usual gender roles of sexual conquest and temporarily shift the balance of power.

Brown's awareness of the problems associated with unwanted sexual behaviors in the office can be seen in her advice to young women just entering the workforce, who were still too green to determine whether a man was a wolf. In one case, a neophyte accepted the lunch invitation of a nice typewriter salesman who often visited her firm. Thirty minutes later she found herself in a boarded-up beach house twenty miles away looking for some papers he'd supposedly left there. "This chap," Brown declared, "was a genuine creep to have snared a child," though after a brief tussle, Brown noted, he safely returned the girl to town. This young woman lacked the experience to assess a situation effectively, but after a woman had been in the office for a while, Brown believed, she developed a sixth sense about men's intentions. A "grown-up girl might have enjoyed hunting for mythical papers in a beach house," but only because she knew that something other than lunch was a possibility.[32]

Brown took for granted that office women, especially those in the lower positions of, say, file clerk or steno girl, would receive unwanted propositions. Men were in power, and their needs and desires—sexual and otherwise—would be met. However, women could avoid unsolicited passes by advancing into positions of power. Brown was not alone in this opinion. Responding to an early outline of *Sex and the Office*, one of Brown's editors enthusiastically seconded her assertion that it was "heady" to be a man's equal and "delicious" to be courted away from your current employer by another company. The editor also suggested she mention another benefit that came with professional success: "the higher up you go, the more valuable your brain, the less chance that your boss would jeopardize it (if that's the way you want it, or rather don't want it) by wooing your body. Bodies he can get from the secretarial pool."[33]

For the experienced, savvy office woman who adopted Brown's advice, a sexy office was not a danger but the big chance. If she played the coquette, though, she had to be willing to accept the sour with the sweet. The game was in handling unwanted advances in a charmingly graceful and professional way. For example, in response to a secretary who wondered about the intentions of a boss who had invited her into his train compartment "to rest," Brown advised that it was "considerate, assuming he was interested in your rest." Only the secretary could decipher his meaning, but if he was "interested in anything, else—well, he's human and a man and men will always try." It was up to the secretary, Brown insisted, "to say no if it's no you want—and you'll find your boss won't hold it against you."[34]

Let us stop here for a moment and consider the full implications of this statement. It acknowledges female desire and accepts as legitimate a secretary's interest in a sexual relationship with her boss. However, the woman must know what she wants. This self-knowledge gives her the right to be unmarried, sexual, and still respectable, because with this knowledge comes responsibility for her actions. If the secretary chooses to get involved with her boss—if she pursues him or accepts his offer— she must be willing to accept the consequences. Brown was adamant on this point, expressing little sympathy for the woman who said she had been taken advantage of or had too much to drink. Most women, Brown acknowledged, were "raised puritanically," but to deny their part in a sexual experience was unfair and dishonest. To make the point, further- more, Brown recited a litany of people to whom a single girl often said "no," ranging from her parents to the persistent door-to-door salesman. "When a girl *doesn't* say no to a man," Brown concluded, "it's very likely because she doesn't *want* to."[35]

In Brown's view, without both the ability and willingness to say defin- itively "yes" or "no," a woman did not have true sexual freedom, the power that came to women through sex, or the capacity to voice a refusal that would be heard. Brown's woman might be a sexual tease at times (which, Brown argued, was only fair, given gender inequality), but she is quite conscious of what she is doing. And when it comes to sex itself, she also knows her mind. She is not the woman whose "no" might really mean "yes." She is not the vulnerable innocent abused by the predatory male. She enters the office, at least in this one regard, as close to a man's equal. This is not, to be sure, full equality in the realm of sexuality. However, with the ambiguity about what she really wants largely gone, with her greater degree of sexual agency, Brown suggests that a woman gains authority and a small measure of protection against unwanted or coercive advances. We can see this advantage in her advice on how to handle a man who just won't take a woman's charming demurral for an answer. She responds with "a gentle but feminine belt below the belt. Say, 'You're most attractive. You're really lovely, but do you honestly suppose I can sleep with every man who asks me? The answer for now is no.'" There is a bit of equivocation here; Brown was not one to burn any bridges. But, as she continued, "what you've really told him is, 'I'm not pretending to be a virgin. . . . But since most men want to sleep with an attractive woman, don't imply that you are making me a present. . . . I am very choosy. You have to be good to make the grade.'" In other words, when a man knows you have said "yes" in the past and will do so again but have said "no" to him, the message is much clearer. The difference must have been all the starker coming on the heels of the 1950s. Women had always been the sexual gatekeepers during courtship, but the pressure to utter the good girl's "no" was especially keen given the era's determined efforts to contain sexuality within marriage. With respectable women—at least according to Brown's new standard of respectability—able for the first time to say "yes," "no" could really mean "no." That is, Brown averred, women could be more certain that when they said "no," men would not hear "yes."[36]

It is also possible that women's new license to say "yes" meant that they could feel more comfortable responding assertively to unwanted sexual advances. Brown's women were not afraid of sexual desires, men's or their own. These women sought out men, a quest that might have given them the freedom to talk openly about sexuality in a way that women of an earlier time and women who did not agree with Brown's philosophy could not. In her radio show, Brown told a woman to stand up to her married boss who had taken to noticing her. The boss wanted her to work late so they could have cozy dinners—and get cozy afterward. Since it was obvious to Brown that the woman was uninterested in her boss, she urged her to confront him, since "there's no work future with a boss whose chief interest in you is sex." Give your boss an "ultimatum—no overtime unless it's legitimate and then you'll take supper money instead of a table for two—with him." This was the only time Brown counseled such a direct approach, but it was also one of the direst situations—one of the most obviously hostile and harassing—she addressed. Brown made it clear that she didn't think the woman should submit, so the only option was to stand up to her boss. The problem is that a woman's real trouble probably begins where Brown's advice ends. A woman who confronted her boss risked losing her job; a man would not always accept a woman's "no," regardless of how clearly she said it. Brown neglected to address this possibility, perhaps because it was self-evident or she wished to minimize the risks.[37]

More typical was her response to the secretary whose married boss called her at midnight and asked her out for a drink. In this case Brown advised the woman to tell the boss that her boyfriend was with her, but they would be glad to join him. If the boss called her bluff, mentioning her boyfriend's pathological jealousy should do the trick. Brown concluded by reminding her listeners that "no girl need be forced to work for her boss after hours unless she really wants to." By today's standards the secretary's response sounds like a desperate lie by a desperate woman, in which she has to rely on a (fictional) man to protect herself. In many ways, though, this strategy represented an improvement over the options that preceded it. This woman is no insulted innocent, compelled to hand in her resignation on the morrow, but rather a fully sexual adult. She readily admits that there is a man in her apartment at midnight and clearly sees it as her right. Moreover, that Brown advocated such openness about female nonmarital sexuality represents a sea change in women's attitudes about sex. She did not expect the woman to lose her job for her "immorality" or for this acknowledgement of sexual experience to lead to further advances from the boss. Through her sexual, adult persona, this woman has found a way, at least temporarily, to avoid what in the past probably would have been inevitable: quitting, capitulating, or refusing and getting fired. She is not her boss's girl but an independent woman with a full life outside the office. Here and elsewhere, we see that Brown has a clear—if never directly or fully articulated—awareness of women's vulnerability to sexual harassment. Her flattering rejections—"you're most attractive, but . . ."—are contrived to keep doors open, women employed, and men's egos spared. But they also can be read as strategic calculations to most effectively end unwanted propositions; "sometimes a man will relinquish you with less fight if he thinks you sincerely want him but are taking your time." If you have "left no trace of doubt that you consider him a toad . . . he has to keep on trying to prove that . . . he isn't!" Brown's insight into the male psyche might not be correct, but her advice—and the new discourse occasioned by women's new sexual freedom—consistently aimed to help the individual woman make the best of a bad situation in a way that caused the least disruption to the daily rhythms of her life.[38]

Brown's woman might have had a few more weapons in her arsenal than the sexually proper girl of, say, the 1930s, but there were times when she, too, had no choice but to quit. A friend of Brown's who had made her way past the secretarial barrier found herself working for "a vital-parts scratching, nice-girl-deprecating slob," and decided to resign. Although she was willing to do almost anything to avoid a return to the secretarial pool, she ultimately could not stomach his typical summons to begin the day: "Okay, baby, let's strip to the waist and get to work." Her productivity suffered in this hostile environment, and she feared being fired. According to Brown, if you were working for a real "creep," there was often nothing else you could do. In her opinion, this situation was not so different from any type of unpleasant office politics that would cause someone to resign—maybe even preferable to some. In *Sex and the Office* she offered the perspective of female executive who said, "I'd rather have a man making a good healthy pass at me any time than have him cutting my work to ribbons. One is flattering. The other is venal." In Brown's view, since women generally wanted men's sexual attentions and could use expressions of sexuality to their professional and personal advantage, the benefits of sex in the workplace outweighed the potential problems, such as unwanted or even aggressive attentions.[39]

BROWN, "SCUTTLE," AND THEIR HISTORIC MOMENT

New developments soon challenged Brown's perspective on unwanted behaviors, but it serves us to spend a few more minutes thinking through Brown's position. Were her suggestions valid or viable for that instant in time? What, for instance, can we learn from Brown's thoughts on the game of "Scuttle," which she encountered as an eighteen-year-old in her first office job and recounted in *Sex and the Office* (and which fans of AMC's television series *Mad Men* encountered in a 2007 episode)? As she described them, the rules of the game were simple. Every afternoon all the men who were not busy would select a secretary or file girl, chase her through the building, catch her, and take her panties off. "Nothing wicked," Brown assured her readers, "ever happened. Depantying was the sole object of the game." Indeed, after removing her underwear, the woman could put them back on again, if she wished. And how did the target respond? Although the girl "usually shrieked, screamed, flailed, blushed, threatened and pretended to faint," Brown was confident no scuttler was ever reported to the front office. In fact, "the girls wore their prettiest panties to work." And, as Brown pointed out, the women were not without a response. One afternoon four secretaries ambushed one man and removed his pants. Brown's final assessment of the game: she just regretted they had never scuttled her. She was too pale, too flat-chested, and too young to be bothered with.[40]

Brown described these incidents in her trademark "pippy-poo" way years after the fact, and we have little to go on in determining how she felt at the time. Did she really not see anything wrong with such behavior? Did she already believe that offices should be sexy and that women should take unwanted passes as compliments? One clue appears in her 1982 autobiography, *Having It All*, in which she recounted an experience from 1940. Brown's boss used to ask her to come in on Sundays to finish up "extra work." Once she was there, she recalled, "he would chase me around his beautiful quiet office with all those fabulous antiques and sometimes *catch* me, but only for a few hugs and kisses." She continued her story by asking, "Was that so terrible? No, it shouldn't have been part of the job, but how much trouble was I *in*?" Her final conclusion was that of "the millions of naughty suggestions made by millions of male employers to their 'defenseless' female employees yearly, I'd say half cheered the girls *up*, half brought the girls *down*, but probably nothing bad has come out of *most* of them." Brown's ultimate assessment asserted that women weren't helpless, men were ultimately pretty harmless, and, overall, "naughtiness" was no big deal.

Yet possibly the most important part of this anecdote appeared in the sentences that provided introductory background for the reader. In 1940 jobs "were *not* easy to get" and "you did *not* do anything to rebuff or offend a boss, even a horny one, lest he fire you . . ." In this period, she noted, "a lot of passes were surely made," though she could not "remember anything really heavy or bad coming out of it." Though Brown seems willfully and blissfully ignorant of the "bad" things that may well have occurred, the crucial part of the story is that she was well aware of women's economic vulnerability. She needed a job, as did the other women who experienced one or more of the many passes that were made.[41]

Since that was the case and since her first experiences in the office made clear that women got noticed only if they were sexually attractive, it seems perfectly plausible that Brown determined to use her physical charms to get something more than being chased around the office— especially since she liked and wanted male attention. According to Brown, she learned early in life about the power that came from arousing male desire. By the time she had witnessed Scuttle and another office or two, she also had a clear sense that sex was part of office life—or, rather, that men's sexual perspective permeated all facets of business. (This was hardly a secret; the year before *Sex and the Single Girl* was published, a survey of nineteen hundred businesses showed that in at least a third "sex appeal" was a qualification for some office jobs.) Putting these observations together, Brown fashioned a strategy for turning office reality to women's advantage. They would seek to be noticed, gaining the power that accrued from a visibility that pleased men, using it to advance, find a good man, or both. And in Brown's view, paradoxically, although a woman had used sex appeal (along with hard work) to move up, once she arrived, she would find herself less bound by men's sexual gaze.[42]

In some ways, this strategy is a variation of the positive thinking approaches we have seen in earlier eras. It is similar to the perspective of Ella Wheeler Wilcox, the turn-of-the-century New Thought poet discussed in Chapter 1, who told women that if they could not change office life, they could at least change the way they thought about it, using an uninvited proposition to explain to men the error of their ways, which could lead to a more just future. And it is even possible to understand as a type of positive thinking the advice of 1930s authors who urged women to "pretend not to see" unwelcome attentions. Brown takes this perspective one step further. Earlier advice involved cheery resignation or willful denial, but Brown offered optimism and an affirmative plan of action. All of these approaches can be dismissed as utterly useless to the woman who is facing her boss's sexual demands, but the power of positive thinking has a long American pedigree that continues to this day. The 2006 best-seller *The Secret*, for example, portrays positive thoughts as powerful magnets that attract wealth and happiness.[43]

Brown's attitude might be quintessentially American, but her fervent declaration that she knew that women didn't mind being scuttled must still be explained. Details from an early draft of *Sex and the Office* suggest that the game was more mutual than the impression left in the book. On the occasions when there were no women around to scuttle, the men would grab a nap "to be bright-eyed and bushy-tailed for the girls' next counter attack." The women did not report the men to the front office, in Brown's assessment, because they understood that scuttling was not an act of aggression toward them; they were simply "very healthy young satyrs who adored girls." When we add up all the details, what emerges is a picture of an office filled with many young men, a good number of unmarried women, and a lot of down time.[44]

In other words, this office looked a lot like a coed college. Not many years after Brown encountered Scuttle, the "panty raid" craze swept campuses across the country. Panty raids subverted middle-class values and defied authority, but beyond that their meaning was open to interpretation: were the young men who stormed women's dormitories demanding underwear engaged in a type of flirtation or an act of sexual violence? It seems plausible that the women in Brown's office held similarly mixed views. And for those who were hoping someday to meet a marriageable breadwinner who would put an end to their working days, being scuttled probably was preferable to the anxiety Brown felt when she realized that she lacked the physical charms necessary to be chased.[45]

But Brown's attitude toward Scuttle embodies the limitations of her office advice. She did not overtly challenge the way things were but rather helped women—urged them—to turn that reality into something they could use. In terms of sex in the workplace, Brown acknowledged its existence to an unprecedented degree, challenging those who denied its presence or insisted on labeling it as inconsequential, immoral, or counterproductive. Their perspective had reinforced women's powerlessness by making them solely responsible for controlling sexual expression in the office just as they were expected to regulate sexuality in courtship. Brown accepted that it was women's job to manage desire, but by "outing" workplace sexuality and giving women an active role in it, she also hoped to change office culture in way that benefited women. Within the context of the office as she knew it, Brown stretched the understanding of sex in the workplace as far as it could go in advancing women's interests, though each woman was still on her own, regardless of the situation.[46]

In July 1965 the first issue of Brown's revamped *Cosmopolitan* hit the newsstands, focused more on man catching than work. Within a few months, a dying magazine had become a sensational success. But even as women rushed to buy *Cosmo*, others were beginning to organize to challenge the very ideas about gender, sexuality, and work that underlay Brown's advice. Already by late 1965, Betty Friedan, the mother of liberal feminism, had declared *Cosmo* to be "quite obscene and quite horrible" and criticized Brown for not "urging women to live a broader life." Just a few short years later, young, radical feminists offered a more insightful and sophisticated critique. These women assailed the corporate establishment for denying opportunities to women, and the sexualized, serving-a-man position of secretary came in for a good drubbing as the symbol of all that was wrong in the white-collar world. Feminists' assessment of inequality and sexuality was so grave it led one male commentator to predict in 1973 that "good or bad, one of the first casualties of women's liberation is likely to be sex in the office."[47]

In fact, women's rights activists in 1973 were just getting started. In Ithaca, New York, in 1975, they coined the term "sexual harassment" to describe the unwelcome or coercive sexual behaviors employed women encountered. This new interpretation of sex in the workplace bore virtually no resemblance to the way Brown and earlier advice givers understood sexual and romantic relationships in the office, and under this new envisioning, Brown's views came under attack. That same year, Dierdre Silverman, a contributor to the feminist journal *Quest*, criticized *Cosmo* for counseling "a strategy of passive [sexual] manipulation" and advising women to use sex "for their own advantage," both of which she believed encouraged sexual harassment.[48]

CHAPTER SEVEN

Desire or Discrimination?

OLD NARRATIVES MEET A NEW INTERPRETATION

IN APRIL 1970 *HOW TO MAKE IT IN A MAN'S WORLD* hit the book-stores. Written by Letty Cottin Pogrebin, the publicist who had told Helen Gurley Brown about "The Matinee," it borrowed Brown's formula of snappy prose and provocative anecdotes, though Pogrebin counseled readers against using their sexual attractiveness to advance. Instead, she urged them to make an "unspoken resolution" with their male colleagues: "You'll notice me but I won't make you squirm, I promise." Although the husband-hunting sections that had punctuated Brown's get-ahead books in the early 1960s were missing, Pogrebin's career advice trod roughly the same ground, showing little evidence of the women's movement that was in full swing.[1]

The connections to the past were most apparent in Pogrebin's discussion of how to treat men at work. "Compared to the adjustments you must make and the careful psychology you must use to cope with females, manhandling is a piece of cake." Unlike women, she maintained, most men were professional and straightforward. To keep men on their side, women merely had to be mindful of the fragile male ego. In terms of office affairs, Pogrebin agreed with advice givers from the 1930s who believed bosses were too focused on business to indulge in a workplace liaison, despite what popular culture implied. And in discussing those occasions when a man stepped over the line, Pogrebin's tone and advice were not appreciably different from Brown's: a savvy career woman would use her brains and experience to find a graceful way out of even the most threatening situation. In one story, what began as a near-rape by a client in a hotel room was transformed into a "charming anecdote" when the fast-thinking Pogrebin screamed, "Please . . . I'm a nice Jewish girl!" All a woman needed to keep herself safe, it seemed, was a mind quick enough to devise a perfect reply. Pogrebin also recounted situations in which men had threatened to take away their business if she did not submit to their desires, but here, too, she always managed to devise an exit strategy that preserved her personal standards *and* their professional relationship. In Pogrebin's opinion, it was the woman's responsibility to "set the tone and send the message."[2]

However, in the brief time between finishing the manuscript and its publication, Pogrebin changed her views. She now identified as a feminist, and her subsequent writings no longer presented workplace difficulties as personal problems for a woman to resolve on her own. In 1971 she became a founding editor of *Ms.* magazine. On May 4, 1975, the day the first "speak-out" on the newly named problem of "sexual harassment" was being held in Ithaca, New York, the *New York Times* carried a review of Pogrebin's new book of career advice, *Getting Yours: How to Make the System Work for the Working Woman,* which included a chapter entitled "The Sexual Dimension: Even Virgins Get Screwed by the System." Although she did not use the phrase "sexual harassment," Pogrebin stated definitively, "Some bosses extort sex in return for giving a promotion." She dismissed those who believed that it was only natural for sexual tension to develop when men and women worked together by commenting that the words "only natural" were "a reliable cue that someone is trying to keep women down." In June 1977 Pogrebin's *Ladies' Home Journal* column focused exclusively on sexual harassment, urging women to unite with other women and to take their cases public. "You can try humor, charm, resistance and threats," she noted, "but when your voice is ignored and the 'old-boy network' closes ranks against you, personal solutions count for nothing." Almost overnight, Pogrebin's perspective had dramatically changed. Although the transformation in the way many Americans thought about gender and sex in the office was not as quick or as complete, the period from the late 1960s to 1986 was still remarkable for the evolution of such attitudes.[3]

Both the women office workers' movement and the women's movement against sexual harassment objected to aspects of the office's gender and sexual dynamics. In the early 1970s clerical workers began to protest the domestic and emotional chores that occupied a good part of each day and to express resentment that employers often evaluated them according to their appearance, not their job skills. The effort to combat sexual harassment was also designed to show society how women perceived behaviors that had long been accepted. These attempts to change the workplace to reflect women's perspective, however, ran headlong into popular assumptions about women workers that had been around for a century. If many women saw the office as a hunting ground for husbands, was it really so wrong that men hired women based on their appearance? And was a man who used his position to extort sexual favors really so different from a woman who used her physical charms to extract favorable working conditions or a higher wage? These stereotypes made it difficult for some Americans to see the wifely duties of a secretary as sexist and sexual harassment as sex discrimination; instead, they persisted in seeing such expectations and situations as examples—if extreme and unjust—of traditional gender roles and ordinary sexual interactions. Given this unsettled state of affairs, it is not surprising that in 1980 Pogrebin offered her readers the same advice she had offered in 1970: "Don't sex around in your bread-and-butter bailiwick." Despite the sexual revolution and the women's movement—which historians usually credit with changing many aspects of women's lives—any expression of sexuality or romance in the office, Pogrebin believed, could still hurt a woman's reputation as a competent worker.[4]

FEMINISM AND THE OFFICE WORKERS' MOVEMENT

In 1970 *Business Week* warned its readers: "A top man who needs a private secretary may run smack into the women's liberation movement . . . with its egalitarian psychology." A few years later, a newspaper columnist offered further evidence of feminism's influence when he described the scene of a woman walking into an office building snarling, "don't bother," when a nicely dressed businessman politely held the door for her. This woman, and many like her, wanted to be treated as an individual, not "one of the girls." By the early 1970s clerical workers had united against "no pants, dresses only" rules, and some were organizing into company-based women's caucuses or joining feminist-inspired office worker groups to press for a variety of changes.[5]

Nevertheless, the relationship between feminism and office workers was not an easy one. By 1975 nearly half of all women worked, 70 percent of those in full-time positions, and they made up 40 percent of the workforce. A third of these women worked in the clerical sector, although the number of women in professional office jobs previously occupied by men was quickly growing, thanks to affirmative action efforts and the women's movement. The young, often college-educated women involved with the "women's liberation" branch of the feminist movement regularly offered a scathing critique of the subservient nature of office work and its accompanying disrespect. However, these writings offered no practical advice to the woman who had an office job and needed it to survive. Some feminists, including some who worked or had worked as secretaries, stepped into this breach. They created organizations in cities across the country to tackle directly the issues radical feminists raised, acknowledging that the majority of office workers, especially older women and those with few marketable skills, would never be in a position to advance beyond clerical work. Despite this spirit of sisterhood, even a member of Chicago's clerical organization, Women Employed, seemed reluctant to claim a feminist identity: "Everybody seems to get the idea that Women Employed is a women's lib group. This is not women's liberation! It's for equal rights. If that's women's liberation, that's what we are. But we only want what's ours!"[6]

Women Employed was definitely not a "women's lib" group; radical feminists offered a critique that went well beyond fighting for equal rights—indeed, some socialist-feminists who wrote about clerical work were openly disdainful of that goal. Their assessment focused on the position of secretary, which seemed to capture the problems facing all women, not just office workers. In their view, women had been socialized to see their sole purpose as pleasing men. The secretary in a dead-end job who felt superior to less-skilled women and worried endlessly about her attractiveness was the perfect symbol of sexism in that the position glorified men and encouraged women to derive their sense of identity through them. Some bosses, socialist-feminists argued, cynically hinted they were interested in a personal relationship to ensure a secretary's loyalty. And more than one feminist noted the similarity between a secretary and a prostitute. For others, the occupation vividly showed what was wrong with the existing economic, class, gender, and race system, as the title of one article made clear, "The Secretary: Capitalism's House Nigger."[7]

Feminists often commented on the ways in which the ever-visible hierarchy of office work and its connection to a woman's attractiveness created a sense of distrust and competition among women. The most lucrative secretarial positions went only to those who looked and acted like members of the executive class, while women who talked too loud, weighed too much, or were simply too poor to devote large chunks of their small salaries to acquiring an acceptable wardrobe ended up as back-office "rejects." A woman at the top, however, could not rest on her laurels, lest she get edged out by a sexy, young, female from the steno pool. Women office workers had a reputation for cattiness, but feminists saw this as a natural response to their vulnerability: it was "obvious that the men who run the business world want to display pretty young things in the front office—for ranking purposes and for their own sexual tastes." Intelligence or skills were irrelevant; the visible differences among women mattered most, and this visibility made it difficult for women—literally—to overlook their differences. Women would "continue to hate and fear one another," rather than focusing on their employers and their flawed standards that emphasized beauty over brains.[8]

Abolishing "office wife" chores like making the boss's coffee was one of the primary purposes of office worker groups that sprang up in the early 1970s. Started by feminists of different philosophical persuasions, some liberal and some radical, these groups fought for traditional labor goals, such as better wages and benefits, written job descriptions, and opportunities to advance, but they also sought an end to the demeaning personal services that women, especially secretaries, had to provide for their employers. With slogans like "Raises, Rights, and Respect" or "Raises, Not Roses," these organizations—at least twelve local groups with a combined membership of ten thousand by decade's end—used a variety of legal remedies and publicity tactics to change the nature of clerical work and the relationship between bosses and their female employees.[9]

These were not the first organizations to address the issue of respect or to protest against the feminine services bosses expected. In 1904 Elsie Diehl, a typewriter involved in early efforts to organize New York City's female clerical workers, complained that some men paid high salaries to girls who had "winning faces and charming manners." A union would allow "quiet girls who are not charmers to get as good pay for the same work." She also complained about employers' demands for personal favors, such as sewing buttons on trousers. In 1942 secretaries who wanted more prestige for their occupation created the National Secretaries Association (NSA). The NSA did not challenge the gendered aspects of the job, because gender was embedded into its very definition: "Recognizing the invaluable influence of women's life in all she touches, we resolve to . . . lend grace, charm and sobriety to all our dealings, and to maintain poise and dignity under all circumstances." However, embracing a decidedly feminine role did not mean professional secretaries were willing to have their contributions go unacknowledged. A 1959 article in the NSA's magazine suggests that a lack of respect was already one of secretaries' biggest gripes. "The secretary is a person and expects to be treated like one," the author wrote. "She is neither a maid servant or a piece of furniture. She is trying to be an assistant to her boss, a partner, to some degree or another, in all his efforts." Assistant and partner are not the same thing, of course, and other articles also hinted at the difficulty of accepting one's subordinate status. The secretary's role was to adjust to her boss, not the other way around, but sometimes a boss was not worthy of one's loyalty. In that case, if a secretary could not stay silent, the professional thing to do was to quit.[10]

Although they shared a commitment to being treated with respect, office worker groups of the 1970s differed from the NSA in many ways, most notably in their commitment to improving the position of *all* women clerical workers. The founders of Women Office Workers of New York City (WOW) believed that office workers were not immune to feminist ideas; rather, they needed their own organization. Like others involved in organizing office workers, WOW's leaders thought liberal feminists focused too much on bringing women into management, which was not a viable way to improve the lives of the majority of office workers. Instead of competing with each other to get to the top, women should organize with one another around shared employment demands and let go of their white-collar pretensions.[11]

WOW battled against employers' preference for young and attractive women. This issue was a focus of an open meeting held in 1975, which more than three hundred women attended, and it led to a campaign to force employment agencies to follow existing discrimination laws that applied to women over the age of forty, who made up at least a third of the workforce. In the first stage, a WOW investigator called one hundred agencies and placed a job order for a secretary who was a "young girl . . . between the ages of 20 and 25." All of the agencies accepted the order—even the thirty-two that mentioned that age discrimination was illegal. Investigators followed the phone survey with a field test in which two women armed with equivalent résumés visited eleven agencies seeking work. The fifty-year-old sat for hours in their waiting rooms, while the agencies quickly sent the twenty-five-year-old out on interviews. A WOW staff member commented at the press conference announcing the results of the investigation and WOW's discrimination suits against six of the agencies: their "practices are like the sexual politics of singles bars."[12]

WOW also held theatrical protests with the dual purpose of raising awareness about the clerical movement and shaming companies with poor records toward their female employees. Like other organizations of women office workers, WOW offered a new take on National Secretaries' Week, started by the NSA in 1952. Renaming it Women Office Workers Week to emphasize the shared concerns of all clerical workers, WOW turned a token ritual of praising secretaries for their good work into an opportunity to expose bosses' bad behavior. In 1980, for example, a New Jersey secretary won the "Pettiest Office Procedures Contest" for refusing to photocopy *Playboy* magazine cartoons for a salesman who wanted the copies for his clients. Other occasions also provided the opportunity for protest. On Women's Equality Day in 1981, WOW selected Morgan Bank, a company with a thin affirmative action record, as the recipient of the "broken Clock Award." WOW members dressed as nineteenth-century heroines like Susan B. Anthony pulled up to a branch office in a horse-drawn carriage. The spectacle closed the branch for two hours.[13]

WOW's leaders also spoke out repeatedly against negative representations of secretaries and encouraged their members to do the same by noting the most egregious examples in their newsletter. In 1975 the newsletter recounted WOW's recent action against New York Telephone's daily "Dial-a-Joke" line. WOW had received several calls complaining about comedian Milton Berle's secretary jokes, including the following: "One guy I know has a secretary with measurements of 45-23-45, and she's an

CELEBRATE
WOMEN OFFICE WORKERS' DAY!
WED., APRIL 23

PETTIEST OFFICE PROCEDURE CONTEST

HAVE YOU EVER BEEN ASKED TO PERFORM

TRIVIAL TASKS OR PERSONAL ERRANDS

ON YOUR JOB ? ? ?

The WOW Pettiest Office Procedure
Contest is designed to call
attention to the most ridiculous
policies and to publicize
successful ways of changing them.

Enter the contest as many times
as you wish. All entries will
be kept confidential.

SEND IN YOUR ENTRY TODAY!
USE THE COUPON BELOW.

WOW OPEN HOUSE

* Winners and Awards
* Music, Entertainment
* Guest Speaker

* DAY: Wednesday, April 23rd, 1980
* TIME: 5:30 - 7:30 PM
* PLACE: "The Old Stand"
         893 Third Ave. (54th St.)

Donation of $5 includes hors d'oeuvres and a drink (beer, wine or soda).

WOMEN OFFICE WORKERS (WOW) is a membership organization committed to improving
the status, pay and working conditions of New York City office workers.

Detach and mail to: W.O.W., 680 Lexington Ave., New York, NY 10022 TEL: 688-4160

☐ My pettiest office procedure is: _____

_____

☐ Please send me ____ tickets at $5 each for the Open House. Enclosed is $_____

☐ Please send me more information on WOW's Job Survival Kit.

Name _____ Tel# Work _____ Home _____

Address _____ Zip _____

While rejecting employers' treatment of office workers as sex objects, servants, or machines, the office workers' movement also criticized bosses for their childish, petty tyrannies. Image courtesy of Tamiment Library and Robert F. Wagner Labor Archives, New York University.

expert touch typist. She's got to be. She can't see the keys." WOW members complained and received a written apology and a promise that disparaging jokes would be avoided in the future. The same newsletter included an assessment of a typewriter ad and information on where to send protest letters. The ad featured a sleek typewriter on one side of the

This one handles paper, and is fun to watch, talk to, kid with and tease.

This one just handles paper.

A Centrac®Rotary File isn't exactly a fun thing. But it's fun for your customers. They get the NOW service they want when Centrac®lets paperwork and paper-workers concentrate. It speeds order processing, cuts footwork and chit-chat by making thousands of records in-stantly accessible to workers who stay seated around it. The papers move. The people don't. That's the big idea. Maybe somebody should start that idea moving in your organization. Maybe you.

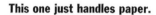

Acme Visible Records, Inc., 1007 Allview Dr., Crozet, Va.
In Canada: Acme Seeley Business Systems, Ltd.

This ad, which appeared in *Fortune* in 1969, makes clear that men liked female office workers for more than their typing or filing skills. Other ads were far less subtle in their portrayal of personal relationships in the office. It did not take much imagination to finish the caption for an ad for steel desks that pictured a boss, a secretary, and a desk with nothing on its top: "Sit on it, stand on it, —."

Secretaries love this file.
It's the strong, silent type.

File drawers opening and closing all day make a lot of noise. Enough to drive a girl to aspirin.

So we designed our file with drawers that just won't slam or screech.

Another nice thing about our file drawers. They pull out all the way. The "zebra" folder is as easy to remove as the one on "aardvark".

There's nothing tinny or weak about our file, either. It's built to take on big loads without getting out of alignment. You know what happens when files lose their alignment. They get stuck.

Our "500" file has a clean, beautiful face. Easy on the eyes. No drawer pulls that stick out like sore thumbs. And you don't need a magnifying glass to read the labels.

In two, three, four and five drawer units. Letter and legal size. In gray, black and beige finishes.

Art Metal furniture looks beautiful and works beautifully—a solid investment for management. We'll be happy to send you a brochure on the "500" files, and tell you where they can be seen. Write today. You'll hear from us, posthaste. **ART METAL INC** JAMESTOWN NEW YORK

© 1967 ART METAL INC., JAMESTOWN, N.Y.

Feminist-inspired organizations criticized sexualized and gender-stereotyped representations of office workers. This advertisement appeared in *Business Week* in 1967.

page and a drawing of an unattractive woman on the other, with the headline "Faster and more efficient than Miss Feldman (and better looking)." WOW's analysis made clear that it was committed to improving women workers' lives both as women and as workers, commenting on the effect of improved technology on employment opportunity and on the continued sexual objectification of office employees. A few years later, the newsletter commented on a new TV show, *Three's a Crowd*, which sought to answer the question: "Which female knows the male boss best—his wife or his secretary?" The host asked the boss such questions as "Did you learn more about sex from your secretary or did she learn more from you?" The secretary would score a point if her answer matched his. WOW repeatedly called attention to derogatory depictions, convinced that such images affected the treatment of real women.[14]

Organizations like WOW had an extensive agenda, but, rather surprisingly, objecting to behaviors that other feminists would soon label "sexual harassment" was not initially an overt part of the movement. Certainly the organization voiced its opposition to the emphasis on workers' attractiveness and sexualized representations of secretaries. But even though its primary goals included gaining more respect for office workers and ridding their jobs of domestic duties, WOW appears not to have *directly* tackled the issue of unwanted or coercive sexual advances until *after* harassment had been identified as a distinct workplace problem facing women in all occupations (and some clerical organizations avoided the issue even then).[15]

If not exactly fighting against these behaviors, feminists of various political orientations nevertheless often described the problem. Some women told of their resistance. Madeline Belkin's 1970 lament, "Drowning in the Steno Pool," urged women to stop accepting "being channeled into deadly, subservient, mindless office jobs." But just because Belkin and others had previously accepted their position in the pecking order did not mean that they had accepted its indignities. Belkin, for example, exacted revenge against one of her bosses, a public relations man she described as "the seducer," by typing his title as "*Pubic* Relations Director" for four months. Other women also found ways to rebel. In 1975 the women in a sales office replaced the "girlie" pinups that made them uncomfortable with photos from *Playgirl:* "It was a marvelous experience to see super-duper macho stud types go all to pieces when confronted with the same thing we have had to face for years—images of ourselves as we could never hope to be."[16]

The socialist-feminist journal *The Women's Page* focused on sexual objectification and unwanted sexual advances as ordinary parts of office jobs about which women could do little given their subordinate position. Men, the author of one article noted, "frequently arrange the desks so that they can look up as many skirts as possible." According to another, secretaries were "invisible" to important men except "when they want to 'take' us to bed, and then they only see our bodies. As we get older they see nothing at all." Even more insidiously, husbands kept their wives in line by telling them "about the beautiful, young, competent woman in their office." An article from another socialist-feminist publication complained that women had "been forced to dress according to some stupid code (and then subjected to fat-assed men leering and slobbering outside our offices as we bend over our files)." The ubiquity of this behavior was made apparent in the comment of a woman with eight years' experience who was excited about a new job because the men seemed different: there wasn't the "usual flirting bullshit with women."[17]

In 1971 *The Woman's Page* published a detailed, firsthand account by a front-office girl who dealt with customers. Around them she was supposed to be a "classy dame," but when the customers were gone, she and the other secretaries were expected to "switch into lively 'sex kittens' " for their managers. One morning, after working at her job for only a couple of weeks, she "felt a pudgy hand . . . plunging into [her] dress from behind" and jerked around to find her employer leering at her. When she responded with disgust, he called her into his private office where he made his expectations clear by criticizing her work while suggestively stroking her arm.

> I stood there. His hostility toward me was so evident that I didn't dare pull my arm away from him. It was my job that was in question now for my impertinence in the outer office. By the time I walked out of his inner-sanctum, I understood that I was not to question his authority nor his right to do and say as he pleased, when he pleased. . . . When he approached me in the future—which he did regularly, stroking me, bending over me at my desk to rub against me, and pushing me against the wall

for a "friendly" kiss—I would extricate myself as fast as possible with coy banter and silly giggles. The rules had been laid down, and I followed them. Not because I thought of myself for one moment as a simpering "sex kitten," but because I would be "punished" with the loss of my job if I didn't.

Other women wrote to feminist magazines and newsletters to vent their anger or urge action against being treated as a sexual commodity. In 1972 a woman in San Francisco wrote to *Ms.* magazine that she was "sick of being fathered, fondled, mind fucked, by frustrated, reactionary men who feel perfectly justified in using me for any role that fits their perverse needs, which are so far removed from 'secretary.'" Her letter focused on her former boss, a racist who alternately propositioned her and berated her for having African American male friends; when he saw her return from lunch with a black man, he fired her. The same year, *Everywoman* published a letter urging readers to resign from Kelly Girl, an agency for temporary clerical workers, because of its sexist ads in the *New York Times*. In one, a blonde smiles seductively below the caption: "Get a free half hour. With Kelly Girl." The ad appeared even as New York's mayor was leading a crusade against prostitution. Yet as the letter writer pointed out, the ad "perpetuated the very ethic that creates the enormous demand and resultant supply for prostitution activity. It is well known that a half-hour is the usual time purchased with a prostitute."[18]

As these examples show, even before "sexual harassment" had a name, both feminist clerical workers and feminists critiquing clerical work had begun to resist the sexualization of offices jobs and unwelcome and coercive behaviors. Feminists interested in improving the position of office workers faced a problem, though: how to object to this treatment without so radically challenging gender relations that women would be turned off the cause. Some feminists were skeptical whether the right balance could be found. In 1973 a clerical worker from California wrote to *Ms.* asking about unions, though she did not think women would join. "From past experiences I have found that most women are so brain-washed by men that they are extremely reluctant to unite and stand up for their rights. They shy away from women's lib with their asinine remarks like 'I don't believe in women's lib. I like men to open doors for me.' Shit, for more money, I'd just as soon open my own damn doors!" This woman's pessimism was not unfounded. Around 1979 a member of the clerical organization Baltimore Working Women said that she did not "totally" like the women's movement because of the way it was changing gender relations in the private realm. She did not want to be treated as her boyfriend's equal if that meant he would not open the door for her when they went out on a date. "He's supposed to be the stronger one, so why not?" In her opinion, women in her organization wanted "to be treated equal as far as our minds are concerned and not as far as man / woman." Changing dominant understandings of "man / woman" interactions was a key part of the women's movement against sexual harassment, but it was a Herculean task. Activists would need to convince Americans that sexual harassment was not about sex and desire.[19]

TRANSFORMING A PRIVATE PROBLEM INTO A SOCIAL ISSUE

If the problem of unwanted and coercive sexual attentions was not exactly invisible, the stories women told did exude a sense that such experiences were inevitable. As one of the founders of the first organization addressing the issue noted, "The images of the boss chasing his secretary around the desk . . . so pervade popular humor and folklore that these advances have been taken for granted." In 1975 that sense of futility ended when Carmita Wood, an administrative assistant in a lab at Cornell University in Ithaca, New York, sought help from the women's section of the university's Human Affairs Program, which was staffed by three feminist activists. Wood's boss had constantly leered at her and made sexual gestures in her presence. At a Christmas party, he pulled up her blouse, exposing her back to everyone there. At another office party, he put his hand on her buttock. Wood complained to her boss's supervisor, but he told her it was her problem to solve. Physically sick from the stress of her employer's unending sexual advances, she quit. When she could not find another job, she filed for unemployment compensation but was turned down. According to the unemployment official, she had quit for a "personal" reason, which did not amount to "good cause."[20]

The feminists in the Human Affairs Program disagreed. When Wood approached them after being denied unemployment benefits, they took her problem seriously and immediately began to investigate how common the problem was and to search for a solution. Within a few weeks, they had put a name to the infinite variety of humiliating,

unwanted, and coercive sexual behaviors that workingwomen had historically experienced. "The phrase *sexual harassment*," one of the women
involved in the naming recalled, was "the first verbal description of
women's feelings about this behavior and it unstintingly conveys a negative perception of male aggression in the workplace." Once sexual harassment had a name, women—as a group—could speak out against it and
document its incidence and forms; what had been an individual woman's
personal, private problem was now a social issue. In this transition, early
activists commented, the "responsibility [was] shifted from the victim to
the aggressor," and a "sense of being able to affect one's own life" replaced
women's "sense of isolation."[21]

The scholar Carrie N. Baker has written a thorough and thoughtful
history of the emergence of sexual harassment as a social movement, so I
will focus here only on those aspects that specifically relate to the white-
collar office and reflect on the long-standing discourses surrounding
sexual expression in that space. That said, office workers were an integral
part of the movement, directly and indirectly. The plaintiffs in the first six
sexual harassment cases labored in offices in the public and private
sectors, working in jobs ranging from office machine operator to secretary to technical writer. The legal theorist Catharine MacKinnon used the
job of secretary (and radical feminist critiques of the position such as
those just discussed) to support her argument that sexual harassment
was a form of sex discrimination. Most women worked "as women" in
jobs in which the sexual element was "pervasively implicit." This made
sexual harassment "systemically inevitable" and not just the brutish
behavior of a bad boss or two. And because the clerical sector employed
more women than any other, media coverage prominently featured office
workers.[22]

In the mid-1970s, white middle-class women with ties to the women's
movement formed two organizations specifically to combat sexual harassment; Working Women United (WWU) and the Alliance Against Sexual
Coercion (AASC) were key players in the initial efforts to raise awareness
of the problem throughout American society. The groups differed in their
analyses of the causes of sexual harassment and in their approaches to
stopping it. They agreed, however, that, though it manifested itself in a
sexual manner, sexual harassment was not primarily about sex. This revision in the established understanding of sexual interactions in the

workplace was both radical and crucial. On those rare occasions in the past when men's sexual behaviors had come under scrutiny, they had almost always been seen as expressions of desire, and concern had centered on the men's character or psychology and the impact of their actions on the bottom line. Almost no one viewed them with an eye to what they said about patriarchy, gender, or power, or saw them as reflections of structural inequalities or cultural stereotypes. As a result, virtually no one considered it unjust to hold women responsible for managing men's conduct. In this view, women were, at the very least, partially to blame. They had invited these attentions through their deportment or dress, or they really enjoyed them, since a firm "no" would discourage any man. As the AASC explained, "Women are often accused of complicity. Even those women who understand their own powerlessness in the situation may worry about their unconscious agreement. Focus on the sexual rather than the power dynamic of this harassment may increase a woman's guilt as society tells her she is responsible for controlling sexual matters." In addition, if sexual harassment was about sex, it was a private affair into which the law or even management should not intrude.[23]

This attitude meant that when a woman did complain, personnel offices would not intervene. Karen Sauvigné of WWU made this point in a presentation, using a secretary's true story. She began by explaining the problem women faced given their secondary status in the labor force: "When the woman encounters a problem on her job, particularly one that is related to her sexuality which is part of, in fact her traditional role . . . it is all . . . considered unimportant, inconsequential, you know boys will be boys." She had seen this in the case of an executive secretary at an airline whose "boss was literally grabbing her in the office daily, holding her breasts and patting her bottom." The secretary protested his behavior, but he would not relent. As a last resort, she went to personnel, where she was told that "the relationship between a boss and a secretary is like a marriage, and personnel will not get involved." Sauvigné called this "one of the major attitudes" that activists had to fight against. As she told the audience, one of their "basic burdens" was in "desexualizing sexual harassments. I mean getting people to see it as a form of harassment and an abusive power, something that has severe economical and psychological effects on women so that it is not seen in the realm of appropriate and to be expected sexual behavior."[24]

In challenging expected workplace behavior, these activists were following in the path of women office worker organizations, and the expansive array of actions early activists included in discussions of sexual harassment meant that the two groups shared a number of concerns. For example, though there were initially many definitions of "sexual harassment," there seemed to be a general sense that at its heart it was "unsolicited, nonreciprocal male behavior that asserts a woman's sex [gender] role over her function as a worker." This, of course, was the same principle office workers had used to critique chores like making coffee or picking up the boss's dry cleaning.[25]

In addition, sexual harassment activists focused on such issues as employers' preferences for physically attractive female employees and the resulting discrimination in hiring against those who did not meet the beauty standard. Susan Madar, twenty-eight, raised this issue at the WWU "speak-out" in 1975. Madar told the audience about her experience with what she described as "the other side of sexual harassment." It was a difficult subject for Madar to broach because, as she noted, "I am admitting something awful about myself," and it "has meant being treated as if I don't exist by the male world. . . . This judgment has affected first my ability to get a job, and second my treatment on the job. I consider this all a part of sexual harassment."

Madar went on to describe her experiences at job interviews and being "harassed sexually in the more obvious ways." In some cases, she did not even apply for a position because for "better paying office work, the want ads clearly said they wanted an 'attractive' girl." At one point when she desperately needed a job to pay her way through school, a man who "had a reputation for hiring mostly beautiful women" interviewed her; she did not get the position. Though her failure to meet the beauty standard kept her from many jobs, it did not protect her from unwanted aggressions. Men had felt her up, kissed her in the elevator, and said, "Let's lie down and do it here, baby." These overtures left her "confused," feeling flattered, insulted, and unsure of how to respond. She wanted to say something, but she worried about offending the men who held her job in their hands, and she also "was always afraid that I was only being made a fool of," in which case saying something would make matters worse.

Madar detailed the insults and violations she had endured, but she focused on the way this less obvious form of sexual harassment divided women, pitting them against one another and keeping them from uniting against their oppression. "Women frequently adopt the male standard, and many treated me with contempt. I would be filled with resentment for the more attractive women, and they were able to put me down." She concluded by noting, "I think we all to some degree experience both sides of this. . . . There's something wrong with us if we are hassled, something wrong with us if we aren't. It's always our fault because we aren't the ones in control, so we can't win."[26]

Others picked up on this topic, bringing out into the open one of the long-standing primary causes of the distrust among workingwomen. An article in the first issue of WWU's newsletter, *Labor Pains*, argued that sexual harassment affected all women, "Many women have said they've never been its victims. We need to understand that sexual harassment is more than repeatedly being touched, propositioned or leered at by a male employer. It is also . . . [women being] measured by their attractiveness, flirtatiousness and availability, not by their job performance and expertise." Older women, pregnant women, and "not traditionally 'attractive' women" were the first to get edged out of the job market by the "sexual harassment system."[27]

To this assessment of men's structural advantage, which allowed them to harass women and discriminate against those who failed to meet their "Desirability Test," AASC added a rich analysis of the contribution of masculinity to harassment. AASC's founders, Freada Klein, Lynn Wehrli, and Elizabeth Cohn-Stuntz, came to the issue through their work in the rape crisis movement, where they encountered women who were experiencing sexual coercion on the job, which engendered unique practical and emotional problems not addressed by antiviolence feminists or workingwomen's organizations. Sexual harassment was an act of violence that reflected and reinforced women's subordinate position. Its root cause, they believed, could not be found in *an individual man's* uncontrollable sex drive, psychological maladjustment, or playful boyish nature, but in *men's* need to dominate. Ultimately, men's sexual control of women was merely a part of the larger system of domination and violence, which infused capitalism and American culture in general.[28]

In AASC's view, sexual harassment was almost "logical," given dominant understandings of masculinity that located a man's power in "economic success and sexual prowess." The majority of men, however, had little chance of making it rich, which made them feel powerless; the most expedient way for a man to regain his sense of power was to assert his superiority over women. As the authors noted, "A man humiliated by his employer . . . has society's permission to beat his wife or have an affair. He can offset the threat to one aspect of his maleness with a 'manly' performance in another." In other words, the harasser was not an aberration but a man following the dictates of his society: "Any man could be a harasser."[29]

AASC interviewed three men to learn how they perceived the difference between harassing and nonharassing situations, and the interviews made clear how gender roles could contribute to harassment, romantic confusion, and the creation of an uncomfortable, even hostile, environment. One of the men, "C," worked in an office that he described as a place where "men and women both do a lot of checking each other out by flirting. They make sexual jokes and listen to the other's response to gauge an attitude." Despite these attempts to assess interest, miscommunication was rampant. According to "C," if a woman was clearly uninterested and he continued his pursuit, that was harassment, but gender roles meant he could never tell for certain: "Like if you flirt with a woman with your eyes, and she consistently avoids your gaze, is that saying no, or is it some coy little playing? I mean isn't that how women flirt?"

"C" accepted this uncertainty as a part of gender roles that prescribed men's aggression and women's passivity, but his remarks also showed how these roles could lead men to dismiss women's concerns. According to "C," men had been taught to notice women sexually and comment, and he believed that most women at work were "flattered" when he told them that they looked "really sexy in that dress." Some, though, found these remarks "very inappropriate" because he was their boss, objections that "C" largely dismissed. This was just the way men were, and nothing anyone said would ever convince him there was "harm done with this aspect of the role. . . . [Just] because I notice her breasts doesn't mean I don't take her work seriously. These two things are independent." "C's" own comments, however, highlighted their interconnection. He had been involved in a brief sexual relationship with a subordinate whose signals he had never been confident of reading correctly. When she abruptly ended the affair, he was angry, and he now gave her all his "shit work because I feel fucked over and no one should get away with doing that stuff." In this situation, "C" no longer found the "ambivalent" aspect of women's gender role "provocative" or "fun," and he used his authority to punish her for rejecting him.[30]

In trying to answer the question of how men distinguished between behaviors that were harassing and those that were not, the AASC asked the men about the larger sexual culture of the workplace, which was the approach adopted in the first large-scale attempt to gauge the prevalence of sexual harassment. In January 1976 the middle-class women's magazine *Redbook* published a questionnaire, "How Do You Handle . . . Sex on the Job," in which readers were asked about their experiences with men's unwelcome or coercive overtures *and* whether they had ever used their sexual attractiveness to catch a supervisor's attention or to obtain other advantages. The varied and complicated ways in which Americans thought about workplace sexuality, which had been around for almost a century, were especially apparent in the choice of answers to the question, "Which one of the following statements best reflects the way you feel?" Possible responses were: "Sexual tensions between men and women who work together are natural. Innocent flirtations make the workday interesting. An attractive woman has to expect sexual advances and learn to handle them. Encouraging the boss's sexual interest is often a way of getting ahead. Women who are bothered by male co-workers are usually asking for it. Unwelcome male attentions on the job are offensive." *Redbook* clearly took the issue of sexual harassment seriously, although its survey suggests that its editors did not see (or at least they thought most Americans did not see) men's ability to extort sexual favors from women as completely distinct from women's ability to exploit men's desires. Both were part of "sex on the job," and one could not be understood without consideration of the other.[31]

The results of *Redbook*'s survey, published as "What Men Do to Women on the Job," showed that sexual harassment was "not epidemic, it is pandemic—an everyday, everywhere occurrence." Nine thousand women responded, the majority of whom were married, in their twenties or early thirties, and working in white-collar jobs. Almost nine out of ten had received one or more of the unwanted attentions *Redbook* asked about, most especially unwelcome sexual remarks. Nearly one in two respondents said that she or a woman she knew had to quit because of harassment. Only 15 percent found men's passes flattering, and most felt sympathetic when they saw sexual advances being made to another woman. Very few said they would suspect that it was the woman's fault. Some felt bitter when they were passed over for women who were less qualified but more cooperative with the boss. Hardly any envied another woman's ability to use her attractiveness to her advantage.[32]

About 30 percent of women had consciously put their attractiveness to work, while others acknowledged that beauty had helped them, though they had not deliberately used it. In addressing these statistics, *Redbook* tackled one of the issues on which those who dismissed sexual harassment would seize and offered up an explanation for these women's behavior, variations of which would regularly appear in the future as activists defended their efforts. The article's author began by straightforwardly stating, "Sex is a versatile force, and it can cut both ways." Women who used their attractiveness were certainly not worthy of admiration or emulation, but, the author continued, "though some of us may not be so innocent as others, women can't be blamed for creating the problem. Both sexes arrive at work lugging the emotional baggage of a lifetime, all the childhood teachings about what's masculine and what's feminine, the cultural myths and social reflexes that make men and women behave as they do toward each other. We've just begun to unpack that baggage." Later articles would more directly blame men by emphasizing men's position of power, but these pieces, too, highlighted the role of gender ideology and the messages society sent women.[33]

In the case of *Redbook*'s "What Men Do" article, focusing on gender roles made it easier for the author to avoid any charges of a man-hating impulse. As we saw in the discussion of the office workers' movement, many women worried about appearing too much like a "women's libber" and resisted feminism because of the ways it could change relationships between men and women. The letters from readers that the magazine received along with the completed surveys suggest that many of these women also were reluctant to criticize men too harshly. In answering the question "Why do men harass?" some attributed it to "a kind of sickness" or "malice," but most felt that men were simply "acting out of habit" or did not "know any other way of talking to a woman."

The author's effort to present sexual harassment in a form palatable for readers who might have been wary of feminism can be seen, too, in the article's repeated reassurances that sexual harassment was not about consensual relationships, only unwanted ones. Early on, the author addressed the comments of a woman who said in her survey letter that the "Women's Movement really had gone too far. Sex is a good thing. . . . There can never been too much of a good thing—even at work." The author wrote: "That's part of the misunderstanding. Most women do not object to evidences of the natural attraction between the sexes, even on the job. They do not complain about sexual interplay between two consenting adults, be it casual flirting or an office affair. But they are rattled and often angry about sex that is one-sided, unwelcome or comes with strings attached." This sex-positive theme continued, possibly reflecting the reality that many Americans' attitude toward sex had changed. On the whole, Americans had become more comfortable with sex, looking much less critically on premarital sex, even for women, and placing much more importance on sexual expression. Along these lines, one reader had come to believe a workplace could both admit attraction and be egalitarian. She had worked in offices with "leering and off-color remarks," but also those in which there was "a kind of cheerful and healthy sexual feeling, where men and women admired each other, dressed up and engaged in a kind of bantering that didn't go over the line of good taste." The article concluded with another confirmation that the movement against sexual harassment was not against sex. "It's easy to be angry. . . . Yet there will always be sex at work, and that's not necessarily bad news. We have to make clear that what we're angry about is not sexuality but the distortion of it. It's the misuse of sex at work . . . that makes it a problem."[34]

HARASSMENT ON CAPITOL HILL: VAMP OR VICTIM REDUX

In the time between the publication of *Redbook*'s questionnaire and the article on its findings, Elizabeth Ray, thirty-three, provided Americans with the opportunity to think about what constituted the misuse of sex at work. In May, Ray told the press that Congressman Wayne Hays had hired her as a clerk at a salary of fourteen thousand dollars a year even though, as she put it, "I can't type, I can't file, I can't even answer the phone." Within a few weeks, other congressmen had become embroiled in a scandal that raised the question of how power and sex operated in the workplace.[35]

It is equally accurate to treat this scandal as the last of the pre–sexual harassment era or as the first of a new age. On the one hand, the preponderance of commentators saw the relationship between Ray and Hays (and those that subsequently surfaced between other congressmen and their employees) as primarily about sexual desire. As a result, commentary focused—as it had back in the nineteenth century in the investigations into immorality in federal agencies discussed in Chapter 2 and in the 1950s prostitution-in-business exposé discussed in Chapter 5—mostly on what the incidents said about the character of the men involved and their fitness to lead. This time, even more than in the past, commentators downplayed men's sexual transgressions; in the wake of Watergate and congressional bribery scandals, a prominent man's adulterous affairs with the women he employed seemed insignificant, even if it involved an abuse of power. Understanding the scandal through the framework of sexuality also meant women's actions would be viewed in light of the sexual revolution, making it especially easy to dismiss them as modern-day gold diggers who sought out these relationships.[36]

On the other hand, a few commentators looked at the scandal through a feminist lens, and one strand was inspired by the women's movement. The second woman to tell her story, Colleen Gardner, a thirty-year-old, divorced mother, did so, according to her attorney, because she was "very much into women's civil rights." Gardner described being forced to have sex with a married congressman to keep her job; she was determined to make Americans see that this was not an isolated incident but a systemic problem. As she told a reporter, "We're not talking about a Congressman's personal sex life. We're not talking about some love affair. We're talking about a sexual program that is part of the job." But the response to Ray's and Gardner's claims highlights how difficult it would be to convince Americans that sexual harassment was a serious social problem. Congressional rules made the situation unique, but commentators' discourse was familiar.[37]

Politicians and the press immediately tagged Ray as a sexual entrepreneur, and she provided them with plenty of ammunition to make their case—after all, her confession coincided with the publication of her tell-all novel. Yet Ray's story was filled with details suggesting that the abuse of power for sexual ends was not limited to Hays's interaction with her. An anonymous tipster, for example, contacted the FBI about another woman who had worked for Hays. The FBI investigated, and the woman told the Bureau that she got on his payroll only after consenting to have sex with him several times a week. When he suggested lunchtime copulation on his desk, she quit. And according to Ray, at least ten other congressmen included sex as part of a job interview and then treated these women "like a date."[38]

Many people were skeptical about Ray, but Gardner's charges were easier to take seriously. She was a "qualified and apparently conscientious office worker," and more significant for her credibility, the press had approached her. The *New York Times* contacted Gardner after learning of a 1973 Justice Department investigation of her allegations that she had resigned her position in Representative John Young's office because of his attempts to pressure her into sex. Gardner was unable to provide any corroborating evidence to support her charges, and the investigation was dropped. She rejoined Young's staff in 1974 and "reluctantly submitted to his advances." When she occasionally resisted, he would become openly critical of her work until she capitulated. In March 1976 she resigned again and later told the *Times*, "it wouldn't have been so bad going to bed with him if he'd at least have let me work, but he wouldn't. . . . He wanted me to be available to him whenever he wanted." She had amassed evidence to substantiate their relationship and Young's sexual encounters with other women on his staff, and she also maintained that some congressmen pressured young male staffers into homosexual acts.[39]

Young denied Gardner's charges, but Hays ultimately acknowledged his affair with Ray, though he insisted that she had not been "hired to be my mistress." And this, of course, was the real issue. Sexual harassment was not yet established law, and the scandal centered on whether the men had used taxpayers' money to feed their sexual hunger, which could lead to criminal charges of fraud. That, it turned out, was impossible to prove. There were no written job descriptions for congressional staff, which meant that there was no way to prove the women were not doing their job or were overpaid; as one of the federal investigators commented regarding Ray, "If she was coming to work every day, it doesn't matter how much shacking up they were doing."[40]

Since it was impossible to prove a crime had been committed, further investigations seemed to have no purpose other than exposing a congressman's immorality, an aim the press, which had been conducting its own investigations, quickly rejected as an unjust invasion of privacy. Less than a week after Gardner's story broke, some journalists were calling for an end to coverage of the scandals. The *Washington Post's* David Broder argued, "Of course it is an affront to decency if the hiring policies of some congressional offices reflect the sexual appetites of the boss rather than the competence of the employees. But . . . these scandals, gamy as they may be, are tangential and trivial compared to the real abuses of power on Capitol Hill." *Newsweek* scolded reporters who "seem to have forgotten that the legitimate object of their pursuit is malfeasance, not misbehavior." None of the numerous editorials mentioned the effect of these men's behavior on the women in their employ. Young was reelected later that year, and Hays resigned late that summer to terminate the House Ethics Committee's investigation.[41]

It was not until the scandals were in full swing that what might be called a feminist perspective appeared, and it offered a different assessment. A *New York Times* op-ed by Caryl Rivers was one of the first, and it rejected the notion that women like Ray were "gold diggers or nymphomaniacs or vultures." Instead, Rivers defended them as ordinary women who lacked the advantages of education or culture and merely wanted a chance at a better life. The piece concluded by describing the author's change of heart on the question of privacy. She had once felt that a man's private life was "private, even if it involves considerable hanky-panky"; now she believed that a "man who uses women like Kleenex" could in no way be "sensitive to the issues . . . raised by the women's movement."[42]

In August, as the scandal was dying down, the *Washington Post* printed a lengthy article on "sexism and sexual attitudes on Capitol Hill." This was the only piece in the coverage of the story to use the term "sexual harassment," and it framed these behaviors within an overall pattern of sex discrimination. The opening account not only showed that sexual harassment humiliated women but also made clear that harassment factored into inequality by prioritizing women's identity as a sexual object over her status as a worker and by contributing to job turnover. In this case, a beautiful, college-educated woman had worked her way into a top position on a congressman's staff. After she was called into a meeting requiring her expertise, her boss "looked her up and down and made a lewd reference to her body" before she could say a word. She gave him the information and left, offering her resignation later that day. Her frustration over receiving a smaller salary than the men in the office came together with this most recent insult, and "something just snapped. I said, 'I don't have to put up with that.' It was really the final blow." The anonymous informant now worried about finding another position, especially because she would need a reference from her former employer. Other women also anonymously told their stories, but whether it was an unwanted touch or an outright demand, what these women shared was a unique work culture that made resistance especially risky. Members of Congress had exempted themselves from the laws that protected employees in the rest of the United States from discrimination and unfair termination.[43]

Congresswoman Pat Schroeder, one of only nineteen female representatives, loathed her colleagues' attitudes toward women and hoped to turn the sex scandals into an opportunity to improve congressional employees' rights. Congressmen, she told the reporter, "feel they have the right to make passes, and they do have that right. They can fire you without reason and with no notice. They can ruin you." Many congressmen believed access to beautiful women was part of their due, and some were even predatory. Alluding to the pioneering whistle-blower Colleen Gardner, Schroeder declared that many women on the Hill had a "Colleen problem." Schroeder had even overheard some of her colleagues talk about a certain type of woman as "prey": one in her twenties, divorced, supporting a child or two, with little education, and without a "whole lot of leverage to say, 'I'm not going to take that any more.'" Schroeder's efforts to establish a voluntary committee to hear employee's grievances garnered few supporters.[44]

Much of the *Post*'s article focused on the way congressmen's desires and demands divided women and kept their attention focused on women's responses, not men's coercive requests—a situation that mirrored the views of federal workers who had complained about sex in the office during World War II. Some women resented the "blanket connotation that all women on the Hill are easily accessible." Others were angry at women in both professional and clerical jobs who were "willing participants in job-related sex, either for the glamour of it all or to further their careers." As one woman commented, it was these women's "fault that the system goes on just as much as [men's]." This lack of gender solidarity especially dismayed Gardner. She had expected other women to come forward after she lifted the veil of secrecy, but none had done so publicly. She thought of herself as different from Elizabeth Ray, but the fact that she had given in to Young's demands blurred the distinction in some people's eyes. As a female lawyer on the Hill commented, "I can sort of understand how she came to that sort of thing but I have trouble with the fact that she would be so complete in doing it," a comment that echoed the century-old belief that any reputable woman would quit. Gardner, however, had "always had the feeling if you proved yourself so skilled and competent, he'd finally leave you alone," a notion Helen Gurley Brown had espoused more than a decade before. The *Post*'s article presented the feminist view of sexual harassment, but it also illustrated many women's unwillingness to place all the blame on men.[45]

Two years after the scandals surfaced, Lin Farley, a founding member of WWU, published *Sexual Shakedown*, the first book on sexual harassment, which included a chapter on the controversy. Gardner's attorney told Farley that he had nothing but respect and admiration for his client, and he was stunned by the reaction of his fellow attorneys. "Are you getting paid in trade?" they would ask. "How's that whore you're representing?" But Farley's focus was on Elizabeth Ray: whose experience she used to explain the larger significance of sexual harassment. Farley began the chapter with a provocative quotation from Ray: "It wasn't something I chose to do. I needed a job." Ray had said this all along, but the press had just laughed. Farley, however, took Ray at her word. Ray did not have a choice because she "did not make the rules. Is there nothing wrong with making sexual demands a condition of work—only in acquiescing to them?"[46]

Farley's main point was to expose how she believed sexual harassment actually worked: it was about institutionalized, not individual male power, and its purpose was to ensure that men would keep that power. "Men," she argued, "control the means of economic survival. This control . . . is also used to coerce workingwomen sexually. Institutionalized male power has thus created its own means of maintaining its superior position—by socially enlisting women's cooperation in their own sexual subservience and accomplishing this by rewarding them when they do and punishing them when they do not." Women who followed the standard advice and quit lost precious time and job experience that might keep them from advancing. Sexual harassment was a means to keep women down in "women's jobs" like office work, to keep them out of male-dominated occupations, and to keep them divided from one another.

In this way, Farley argued, "work, the ostensible equalizer, the location of women's hopes for equality, and the means to her [*sic*] economic independence is subsequently transformed into new enslavement."[47]

THE MEDIA INTERPRET SEXUAL HARASSMENT

Feminists were largely successful in getting media attention, but columnists, newspaper reporters, and magazine writers often included old ideas about male-female workplace relationships in their coverage. Even as most came to accept the basic premise that some men used their power

Cathy
by Cathy Guisewite

In 1979 the syndicated cartoon *Cathy* featured a number of strips in which Cathy's boss, Mr. Pinkley, sexually harasses her. One strip described harassment as a "power play of the worst kind." CATHY © Cathy Guisewite. Reprinted with permission of UNIVERSAL UCLICK. All rights reserved.

over women to extort sex, they took other types of harassing behaviors much less seriously, especially when a coworker was responsible. Those who dismissed sexualized leers, touches, or comments as insignificant often found it hard to reconcile women's difficulty in handling sexuality in the workplace with changes in women's sexual behavior associated with the sexual revolution. That confusion also led to a number of articles about women's harassment of their male subordinates, which suggested that harassment was about individuals and sexual desire, not gender inequality.[48]

A 1978 article in *Good Housekeeping*, a magazine aimed at suburban homemakers, illustrates how quickly the feminist message spread into mainstream culture and how it could be altered in ways that undermined feminists' larger social critique. The piece appeared in the magazine's "My Problem and How I Solved It" series and was written anonymously by a young widow with two children and dozens of bills. Her secretarial skills were rusty, and she was relieved when she found a job working for a balding, married father of three, who treated her in a fatherly way. Within a few weeks, however, paternal solicitude had transformed into intrusive lechery, with comments like, "It's hard for a woman who's used to having a man around . . . nobody to warm your feet at night and all."

Suggestive remarks were soon replaced by demands. After she resisted his kisses, he growled, "Grow up. . . . You either start being friendlier or I'll have to call personnel and tell them you're just not working out." At home, she pondered what to do and experienced a moment of feminist awakening: "I had always considered women's rights as something far removed from me; now I wasn't so smug. I was being treated unfairly because I was a woman." Thinking of the threat to her children's future made her furious, and she confided in a friend, who told her to contact the Equal Employment Opportunity Commission (EEOC), the federal agency charged with investigating violations of Title VII, which prohibited employment discrimination. Knowing that she had some legal options, she asked her boss to lunch, where she told him about her financial difficulties and appealed to him as a husband and father who would not want his wife to be in a similar situation if he were to die suddenly. This approach worked, and he became contrite: "I don't know what to say. . . . None of my girls . . . that is, my secretaries, have ever talked to me like this. It was all in fun. I hope you know that?" She accepted this explanation, and he promised to help her keep her family together. As she described the change, "Suddenly he was no longer an ogre, just a man approaching middle age, searching for something he couldn't find. And he knew that what he'd tried to do wasn't the answer."

This story portrayed a man abusing his power and provided readers with information on where to find help, yet everything else in the article worked against feminists' efforts to reconfigure sexual harassment as a social issue and relied on old understandings to make sense of the situation. Although the article mentions the EEOC, it presents outside intervention as unnecessary because men are moral creatures who honor the sexual boundaries women set. The author is harassed because her employer's other secretaries had abdicated their social responsibility to keep men's passions in check. All it took to return him to the straight and narrow was a gender-infused reminder that his dependents also could be vulnerable if he unexpectedly expired. This was similar to the appeal reformers made to employers in the early twentieth century. Whenever an employer was tempted to seduce his typewriter, reformers urged him to think of what would happen to his daughter in the event of his death. Finally, the boss's behavior was not about sexism. It was about his individual psychological maladjustment, a view that had been around since the 1930s. This *Good Housekeeping* article borrowed as much from the past as it used from the present, and it also set an extremely high bar for what counted as "sexual harassment." Just as an assault by a stranger jumping from the bushes brandishing a weapon had always been seen as "real rape," so this article limited "real" harassment to a situation with an impeccably virtuous victim and a boss issuing the ultimate ultimatum.[49]

The tendency to draw a distinction between either-or demands and offensive or intimidating actions can be seen in a 1977 column in the *New York Daily News*. Writing about a sexual harassment "speak-out," Jimmy Breslin praised feminists for bringing attention to a real problem. Yet, in his opinion, some of the women's experiences were merely "indignities" and did not reflect the "aspects of slavery that the subject indicates." Although we do not know to which stories Breslin was referring, the noncoercive behaviors included an older secretary whose boss pulled down his pants in front of her and, when she objected, replied, "You're from the gutter. Why should this bother you?" In Breslin's and others' view, such behaviors were insulting but not especially serious. Activists, however, disagreed. Such actions marked women as sexual objects, not workers, establishing the workplace as men's—not women's—rightful space. They could also affect a woman's ability to earn a living if, for example, she quit to escape them. These humiliations, like outright demands, reinforced women's subordinate status.[50]

In 1975 the newspaper columnist Jack Mabley used women's altered sexual behavior to dismiss feminists' argument about the prevalence of harassing behaviors. Mabley juxtaposed a *Redbook* survey showing that nine out of ten readers had engaged in premarital sex with WWU's assertion that men regularly subjected workingwomen to unwanted ogles and pinches. "My comments on these two seemingly unrelated stories may arouse wrath among the subjects," Mabley noted, but "there is an excruciatingy simple way for a woman to avert leering and ogling at her body. Conceal it. Wear baggy clothes." In Mabley's view, women brought this behavior on themselves, and in those cases in which they did not, women could easily get men to stop. Mabley acknowledged the existence of employment discrimination, but actions like pinching and leering did not count, given women's new sexual freedom. As we saw in Chapter 3, the abandonment of the ideal of female passionlessness had led by the 1930s to the belief that a modern woman should be able to handle an employer's or coworker's sexual attentions on her own. Rising rates of nonmarital intercourse in the 1960s and 1970s similarly encouraged some Americans to see harassment as more about sex than sexism.[51]

For those who held this perspective, men could be victims of sexual harassment, including when sexually aggressive women pursued uninterested males. A letter to the advice columnist "Dear Abby" expressed this view. "Harassed" was a high-powered executive who had spent his career fending off women's sexual advances. As he told Abby, "I've had female employees lean down and brush my arm with their breasts or sit unnecessarily close while taking dictation. . . . Some have even come right out and said they'd like to go to bed with me!" The problem was in turning such women down, since any man who rejected a woman's favors hurled the "ultimate insult." His experience led him to conclude that if a woman was involved with her boss, "it was *her* idea," and he suggested the creation of an organization to protect men from sexually predatory females.[52]

Abby encouraged "Harassed" to find other interested men, but her opinion on harassment became clearer in her comments on a reader's response to "Harassed." This respondent wrote to clarify what harassment was: "If someone makes a pass and gets rejected and that's the end of it, that is *not* harassment; when the passes continue, despite rejection, that's harassment." It might be uncomfortable for a boss to turn a woman down, the writer acknowledged, but when a woman rejected her boss, she was at risk of losing her job. In her response, Abby objected to this correspondent's focus on women, noting that there were now many women executives with male employees, so it was "not a matter of discrimination against women—it's who outranks whom." Abby, it seems, understood sexual harassment to be primarily about sex. While she acknowledged the role of power, her understanding of its misuse in no way reflected feminists' critique of men's institutional power.[53]

Executive Sweet

*Many office Romeos
are really Juliets*

This illustration accompanied *Time* magazine's first article on sexual harassment, which appeared in 1979. The piece ended with this conclusion: "As more women rise to supervisory positions, it will become harder to tell who is chasing whom around the desk." This light-hearted tone suggested that sexual harassment was not a big problem and was more about romance or passion than power. Courtesy of Kimble Mead.

Abby was not alone in her belief that women with power harassed men in the same manner as men harassed women. In 1979 *Time* published a piece on a study designed to determine the prevalence of sexual harassment. Men and women were asked to self-report, and 31 percent of the men (as compared with 33 percent of the women) said that they had been leered at or touched by a supervisor or coworker of the opposite sex. Though the study's authors emphasized that the experiences were quite different—most of the men had been approached by an attractive coworker and felt flattered, while the women felt demeaned after being targeted by older supervisors who had made similar overtures to other women—the magazine chose to focus on men's experience. The article began with the comment "The woman boss . . . has begun to win a reputation for eyeing the boys in the office" and ended on the same note, thereby blurring the boundary between consensual office romances and coercive and unwanted overtures.[54]

Feminists tried to explain why women's harassment of men was not the same as men's harassment of women, including situations in which a man's subordinate tried to use her sexual desirability to advance her career. Farley understood men's assertions that they, too, were harassed as an avoidance strategy. Some men had described situations in which a woman had tried to use them sexually to gain some advantage, and they asked, "Isn't that corrupt, isn't that immoral and isn't that the same thing?" Farley declared that it was not. When a female attempted to trade sex for employment favors, there was no coercion or force involved. Rather, it was "an attempt to strike a bargain," with no penalties if the man failed to agree. If a man consented, it was a "virtual no-loss situation" for him, and if he felt oppressed by women's overtures, he could strike at the heart of the problem by committing himself to evaluating women solely on skill. Feminists' bottom line, though, was that a female supervisor's harassment of a male subordinate was different because its ultimate purpose was different. A man might be subordinate to a woman, but as a group men were not in secondary roles. Therefore, women could not systematically abuse their power in order to keep men down the way feminists believed men used their authority over women. Feminists were successful in using the media to raise awareness about sexual harassment and to generate support for the idea that the most flagrant abuses of power should not be tolerated. But they were much less successful in gaining mainstream support for the idea that sexual harassment was ultimately not about sex but about keeping economic power in the hands of men.[55]

SEXUAL HARASSMENT AND THE LAW

In the early 1970s, even before activists gave "sexual harassment" its name, individual women had begun to challenge this behavior by filing lawsuits in federal courts under Title VII. Arguing that an employer's demand for sexual favors was a form of sex discrimination was a novel idea, and in all but one of the first six cases, the initial decision went against the plaintiff. Judges viewed these cases as examples of private sexual behavior, motivated by desire, that took place at work but were in no way connected to a woman's employment; their decisions disregarded power dynamics in the workplace.[56]

If the behavior was personal, then an employer should not be liable for it, and if it was solely about desire, then it had nothing to do with sex discrimination. In a case involving an African American woman who worked as an administrative assistant at the Environmental Protection Agency, the defense attorney argued that the demotion she received after repeatedly refusing her supervisor's sexual requests was in no way discriminatory. She had been demoted because of "ill-will based on refusal to engage in sexual intercourse," not because she was a woman. Another case involved a white stenographer and an executive who she said told her, "I can't walk around the office with a hard-on all the time." He gave her the option of losing her job or having an affair and becoming his private secretary. The defendants in this case argued that the court "should not be concerned with the social life of company employees." Judges agreed with these basic lines of defense. Ruling on a case involving an African American data entry clerk who was fired after rejecting her supervisor's sexual demands, a judge argued, "The attraction of males to females and females to males is a natural sex phenomenon and it is probable that this attraction plays at least a subtle part in most personnel decisions." His comments further suggested that sexual behaviors were an ordinary part of work: "If an inebriated approach by a supervisor to a subordinate at the office Christmas party could form the basis of a federal lawsuit . . . if a promotion or a raise is later denied . . . we would need 4,000 federal trial judges instead of 400."[57]

2203

"You were saying at the office today, Miss Dunmore, that in this troubled world, we must learn to live together."

This *Playboy* cartoon appeared in 1970, reflecting the changing racial demographics of the office. Ads for office products, however, did not regularly include African Americans until much later. By the end of the 1980s more black women worked in the clerical sector than in any other job category, as had long been true for white women. Reproduced by Special Permission of *Playboy* magazine. Copyright © 1970 by Playboy.

In 1976 Diane Williams became the first successful plaintiff in such a case. In 1972 she started work as a public information specialist in the Justice Department's Community Relations Service, an office she alleged was a hotbed of sexual intrigue involving affairs between single female employees and their married supervisors. Women who accepted their supervisor's attentions received promotions and interesting assignments, but she repeatedly turned down her married supervisor's requests for dates. Within a few months, he fired her. Press coverage of early cases had been minimal, but Williams's victory led to an explosion of opinion, much of it critical. Editorials mocked this effort to regulate "office hanky-panky." Sexual shenanigans at work were becoming so wrapped in "ridiculous red tape," one lamented, "that they no longer seemed worth the trouble." These writers did not take the problem of sexual harassment seriously, which should come as no surprise, considering that the ruling came down a month before the Elizabeth Ray–Wayne Hays scandal broke.[58]

At the time of the Williams ruling, the EEOC, the agency charged with investigating Title VII complaints, was just beginning to consider sexual harassment. In early 1975 the Commission had issued a brief in support of one of the first plaintiffs, and in 1977 it ruled in favor of a woman who had been fired when she refused to wear a revealing outfit that impeded her ability to perform her duties and encouraged sexual propositions from customers. In this case, the Commission defined sexual harassment as any "conduct which injects sexual stereotypes into the work environment." The EEOC's involvement increased in 1979 in the wake of a number of scandals in Washington, D.C. Many involved harassment and abuse in D.C.'s city government, and an informal survey of employees at the federal Department of Housing and Urban Development showed sexual harassment to be a serious problem. A number of newspapers covered this story, including the *New York Post*, which headlined its story, "Why They Go Beddie-Bye with the Boss: Survey Shows It Helps a Girl Get Ahead." This headline suggests how difficult it was for some Americans to understand the coercive nature of harassment. The survey showed that seven out of ten women refused to bow to their supervisor's demands and, consequently, were denied promotions and raises. This article, however, chose to focus on those women who had capitulated, the majority of whom said it did "wonders" for their careers, thereby perpetuating the notion that women used sex to their advantage. In response to this survey, a House committee charged with investigating the Civil Service called for a number of initiatives, including creating EEOC guidelines on sexual harassment to facilitate the processing of complaints and to provide guidance for private employers.[59]

The EEOC, under Eleanor Holmes Norton, issued its proposed guidelines in April 1980. Adopting the two-prong quid pro quo and hostile environment definition proposed by Catharine MacKinnon in her 1979 book *Sexual Harassment of Working Women*, the guidelines prohibited "unwelcome sexual advances, requests for sexual favors, and other verbal or physical conduct of a sexual nature" when they were a condition of an individual's employment, were tied to employment benefits, or had "the purpose or effect of substantially interfering with an individual's work performance or creating an intimidating, hostile, or offensive working environment." The guidelines also held employers liable for virtually all their employees' actions, even if they did not know of the harassing behavior.[60]

MacKinnon had begun work on a project to show that sexual harassment was sex discrimination in 1975, when she was a law student at Yale. In doing so, she joined women lawyers like Ruth Bader Ginsburg, who had been working on the issue of sex discrimination since 1970 with mixed results. Equal protection law began with the premise that women and men were "similarly situated," and looked for differences in treatment from there. If those differences were arbitrary or unreasonable, the behavior was illegal. MacKinnon rejected this approach: men and women were not similarly situated in the labor force, and the law needed to acknowledge this difference from the start. Courts should focus on the issue of "inequality" and whether an action led to a group's systematic "disadvantagement." If a practice—like sexual harassment—contributed to the maintenance of a group's second-class status, then it would be illegal. Under this theory, an employer's sexual blackmail would be outlawed, but so, too, would those insinuations, gropings, and leers that made work conditions unbearable and often caused a woman to quit.[61]

Making the argument for the latter was a much harder sell, both legally and socially. According to MacKinnon, though, a hostile environment was, in reality, an unspoken quid pro quo. If a woman protested against a man's innuendos, gestures, or touches, it would likely anger him and lead to some type of retaliation. As a result, a woman had to walk a very fine line: playing along, but not to the point where it aroused an explicit "how about it?" that would require a direct rejection. Offering an analysis of contemporary masculinity, MacKinnon argued that some men wanted to know that they could "accidentally" touch a woman at will or "innocently" pepper their conversations with double entendres without her resistance. If she did resist, the quid pro quo that was always implicit became clear. The "tolerate it or leave" in the woman's mind immediately transformed into the boss's "now that you don't tolerate it, you're leaving," and this was why a hostile environment needed to be ruled illegal. MacKinnon, of course, was not the first to make these observations; from the late nineteenth century through the 1930s and all the way to Helen Gurley Brown, advice givers had acknowledged these dynamics. MacKinnon's assertion that such harassing behaviors should be illegal, however, differed significantly from earlier advice to quit, ignore, or coyly demur.[62]

Although criminal or tort law could be applied in many cases of sexual harassment, MacKinnon rejected these approaches because she believed that harassment was both a group and an individual harm. These means of redress also carried other problems. For example, though sexual harassment sometimes involved rape, it would be difficult for a woman to meet the law's standard of force, since her participation had been gained by "coercing her consent, rather than by coercing the act itself." In other words, existing law did not accommodate the reality of rape when it occurred in the context of work. "Because of his power as an employer," MacKinnon argued, "the perpetrator gains legal immunity as a man." Torts had their own ills. Unwanted sexual touching might be actionable as battery or intentional infliction of emotional distress, but MacKinnon—citing the distrust of women seen in efforts to repeal "heart balm" torts in the 1930s as evidence—worried that the widespread belief that women lie about sex would make it difficult to achieve justice. Existing sexual torts also reeked of moldy sentiments about women's purity. Standing up to sexual harassment had nothing to do with upholding morality or protecting women's delicacy and everything to do with ending sexism.[63]

MacKinnon used racial analogies to make this case. No one would any longer publicly use " 'black people's work' as a classification," but the notion of "women's work" raised nary an eyebrow. No court would tolerate an employer who required African Americans—but no one else—to dress a certain way because he liked the way it made them look. But, of course, men regularly hired women whose looks they liked, and looking a certain way was often a part of women's job requirements. Katherine Gibbs's secretarial schools aimed to make their students into a "pretty package" for their employer, but why, MacKinnon asked, has no one acknowledged "that such attitudes would be acted upon, that, to continue the metaphor, packages are meant to be unwrapped by the purchaser?" If these situations were unacceptable with regard to race, MacKinnon wondered, why weren't they when they involved the female sex?[64]

When it issued its guidelines, the EEOC asked for public comments, which led to some minor changes and the addition of a new provision addressing the concerns of a worker who might lose out on an employment opportunity because of a coworker's sexual involvement with the boss. The addition to the final guidelines appeared under the heading "other related practices," and the EEOC noted in its presentation to Congress that it was not "an issue of sexual harassment in the strict sense." This addition read, "Where employment opportunities or benefits are granted because of an individual's submission to the employer's sexual advances or requests for sexual favors, the employer may be held liable for unlawful sex discrimination against other persons who were qualified for but denied that employment opportunity or benefit." This wording presented the employee who benefited as submitting to sexual advances, not instigating them. But as one activist noted at the time, this addition confirmed the stereotype of women sleeping their way to the top. It should not be surprising that citizens raised this concern when contemplating the initial guidelines. After all, fears about women using their sexual wiles to gain some advantage had been around since women first entered the labor force, and workers, historically, had complained about a boss's favoritism, which usually involved (if the complaining party is to be believed) his preference for a beautiful and sexually willing young woman.[65]

Indeed, the issue of women who benefited from sexual relationships at work—whether those relationships resulted from a woman's invitation or her boss's coercion—had been a topic of discussions of sexual harassment from the beginning of the movement. In 1976, for example, the author of one of the first critical articles stated, "Female employees are not always helpless victims. . . . Some of them are entrepreneurs. Ask any woman whom she'd rather work for: a lecherous man, or her boss's idiot mistress. Those who have been in the latter position know about harassment." In commenting on their victory, Diane Williams's attorney said, "What happened to Diane was not unique. . . . Unless you were a good looking woman and submitted to sexual advances you were not promoted. Also a lot of good looking women were promoted who might not have been entitled on the merits."[66]

This discussion continued during consideration of the EEOC's guidelines. A newspaper columnist, for example, pondered whether the qualified men and unattractive women who didn't tickle the boss's fancy were victims of sexual harassment when they were passed over for a woman, qualified or not, who was sleeping with the boss. The columnist took his ruminations one step further, adding a twist to the classic quid pro quo scenario in which a boss offered a woman a promotion in exchange for sexual favors and denied it when she refused. Would this still be sexual harassment, the columnist wondered, if she wasn't qualified to begin with and wouldn't have been in the running anyway? Certainly these comments spoke to a legitimate area of concern—ensuring that the workplace was grounded in a system of merit—but they also reflected the nagging suspicion that had always surrounded discussions of workplace sexuality: the woman was in some way to blame. The genuine victims, then, were employees passed over because they had never caught the boss's eye. Such a view put the focus on women, not on the men in power, whose demands, bargains, or even acceptance of a woman's offer set the inequitable process in motion. And while the EEOC responded to concerns about favoritism and women using their desirability for gain, it took no action on calls to expand the definition of harassment beyond sexual behavior to include nonsexual, gender-based harassment or to acknowledge that sexual harassment intertwined with and exacerbated age and race discrimination.[67]

In 1986 the Supreme Court issued its first ruling on sexual harassment, *Meritor Savings Bank v. Vinson*, confirming that Title VII prohibited both quid pro quo and "hostile environment" harassment. In 1974, nineteen-year-old Mechelle Vinson found a job as a bank teller-trainee after a chance conversation with a branch office manager, Sidney Taylor. In 1978 she charged Taylor with forcing her to engage in sexual intercourse on threat of termination more than forty times over a period of two years, with subjecting her to unwanted fondling at work, and with raping her on several occasions. By the time Vinson filed her case, a Washington district court and the D.C. appellate court had ruled that quid pro quo harassment violated Title VII. Vinson lost her case, but by her appeal hearing in 1982, the D.C. appellate court had upheld the hostile environment claim in the *Bundy v. Jackson* decision, using MacKinnon's argument. All that awaited was a Supreme Court ruling to affirm these positions. As it turned out, Vinson's case would be the one the Court heard.[68]

And it was complicated. Unlike most plaintiffs at this time, Vinson had not refused an ultimatum and been fired; she had given in to keep her job. These circumstances made it easy for the bank to paint the relationship as consensual and Vinson as a bad woman seeking to destroy her former lover. (As MacKinnon, who wrote Vinson's brief and served as cocounsel during the hearing, privately noted to explain this predicament, "If you're fucked, you're fucked.") To add insult to injury, the argument went, a completely innocent party (the bank) would have to pay the price for a woman's vindictiveness. The bank was not alone in this view. The EEOC, now chaired by future Supreme Court Justice Clarence Thomas, sided with the bank against Vinson.[69]

Despite this substantial opposition, the Court issued a unanimous decision for Vinson. The Court's opinion complicated the idea of consent, confirming that a woman could unwillingly participate in sex even without a knife held to her throat. Such a nuanced view had not been heard in the discourse of sex in the office since the early twentieth century, when a few reformers had defined a gray area—"involuntary submission," as one described it—somewhere between coercion and meaningful assent that took a woman's economic circumstances into consideration when evaluating her sexual experiences. But feminist scholars also have noted a number of problems with the decision, focusing especially on the Court's pronouncement that "the gravaman of any sexual harassment complaint is that the sexual advances were unwelcome." This requirement, which appeared in the EEOC guidelines, shifted the focus to the victim and her behavior and raised such questions as "Did she do something to lead him on?" or "Did her 'no' indisputably convey her displeasure?" These questions reflected the centuries-old distrust of women, especially in matters of sex. Once again the law, as it had in the 1930s efforts to abolish "heart balm" torts, entertained the question "Are women victims or vamps?" *Meritor* also stated that the "complainant's sexually provocative speech or dress" was "obviously relevant" in determining whether the behavior was unwelcome, and although subsequent decisions limited this dictum, a discussion of a woman's lifestyle can still be deemed relevant, especially during the discovery phase of a case.[70]

In some scholars' view, the overarching problem with the "unwelcome" requirement is that it shifts a court's focus to the man's perspective; his interpretation of a woman's words or actions can take precedence over the woman's intended meaning. As scholar Louise F. Fitzgerald notes, it also reflects the cultural belief that "sexual advances by any man to any woman are by definition welcome until she proves otherwise." In this way, the decision legitimated gender roles that had been around since the nineteenth century; it was men's right to ask and women's responsibility to protect themselves and social morals by saying "no." The court required a woman to make her displeasure known in unambiguous terms, but it exempted a man from taking any steps to ascertain whether a woman welcomed his attentions. In Fitzgerald's opinion, women's burden is especially onerous given the lingering cultural assumption that a woman's "no" might really mean "yes" or "maybe," and that formal complaints often lead to reprisals. Finally, scholars have pointed out that the notion of "unwelcomeness" makes sexual harassment about sex— attraction, desire, and pursuit—even though "sexist or sexual hostility," such as being called a whore or finding used condoms planted in your workspace, are the most common types of harassment and virtually always accompany unwanted sexual attentions.[71]

The "unwelcomeness" requirement perpetuated the sexual double-standard, but it is easy to understand why the EEOC added this element to its guidelines; some sexual overtures in the workplace were welcome. An EEOC spokeswoman made the agency's position on consensual relationships clear when the draft guidelines were released, saying, "A lot of times, boy meets girl on the job. We don't want to stamp out romance." This comment was probably aimed at those critics who described feminists who worked to end harassment as "militants" who denied the reality of sexual attraction in the workplace. Feminists repeatedly stated they were not opposed to consensual relationships; indeed, as one commented, "One purpose of a campaign against sexual harassment is to make it more possible for women to enjoy sexual freedom—as active participants, not as passive recipients." Nevertheless, commentators repeatedly portrayed feminists as hostile to romance and sexuality. More common were critics who worried that efforts to rid the workplace of harassment would also rid it of joy. One commentator charged the EEOC with "legislating love" and predicted that regulations against harassment would "inhibit" and "intrude upon" romance. To some degree he was right. The EEOC's guidelines and the Supreme Court's ruling did lead management to take a closer look at consensual relationships.[72]

Doralee Rhodes had finally had enough. Her boss, Frank Hart, had insisted that she accompany him to a convention, but when she arrived in San Francisco, she quickly learned there was no meeting. Hart also "accidentally" knocked things off his desk so he could peer at her cleavage as she bent to pick them up. She had politely refused his invitations and overlooked the leering, but when she learned he had been telling the entire office that they were having an affair, she exploded. "So you've been telling everybody I'm sleeping with you, huh? Well that explains it. That's why these people treat me like some dime store floozy. . . . I've put up with all your pinching and staring and chasing me around the desk because I need this job. But this is the last straw. Look, I got a gun out there in my purse. . . . If you ever say another word about me or make another indecent proposal, I'm going to get that gun of mine and I'm going to change you from a rooster to a hen with one shot. Don't think I can't do it." Doralee was mad, Frank was frightened, and audiences were amused as Dolly Parton put Dabney Coleman in his place in the hit comedy from 1980, *9 to 5*.[73]

The film, produced by Jane Fonda and inspired by her friend, Karen Nussbaum, one of the leaders of the women office workers' movement, relentlessly satirized the sexist boss who terrorized his female employees. Hart referred to them as "his girls," freely offered comments on their appearance, and ordered anyone with two x chromosomes to make him a cup of coffee, threatening her job if she refused. He abused Violet Newstead, his office supervisor, offering promotions to men she had trained because they had families to support—even though Violet was a widow with four children. He even refused to allow employees to display personal photos in their cubicles. Yet the comments of some film critics suggest that the film overplayed its hand: was any boss *really* as sexist as Frank Hart? In other words, the film was funny because Hart was so outrageous, which suggested the problems women faced were not in reality so severe.[74]

In making clear that the majority of women worked to support themselves and their families and not to find romance, 9 *to* 5 added a new category in the catalog of representations that cast the sexual politics of the office as a funny joke. Nevertheless, it also perpetuated one longstanding stereotype: the secretary as home wrecker. Fonda's character gets a job because her husband, in the midst of a midlife crisis, has left her for his young assistant. The film, then, represented both an important new perspective and a continuation of old views. On the whole, a similar combination of change and continuity describes the period from the late 1960s to 1986 in terms of attitudes toward unwanted and coercive sexual behaviors in the workplace.

The most dramatic change was that women's concerns about unwelcome attentions were no longer ignored. In 1967 the columnist Mary Haworth brushed off a thirty-year-old secretary, divorced and with a child to support, who wrote for advice on how to handle an overfriendly boss. The secretary had already quit a number of jobs because of flirtatious married employers, and now her current boss was staring at her during dictation and asking her to stay late. Haworth's response was dismissive: "Assuming that you do have the problem stated . . . I would say it signifies that you personally need first-hand analytically oriented counseling help, in coming of age, psychologically and socially." A "grown-up" would have told these men in no uncertain terms that she was uninterested. Haworth's response embodied the age-old position that it was a modern workingwoman's responsibility to handle these overtures, and that a firm "no" easily and effectively dissuaded even the most ardent of men. A decade later, advice givers like Haworth could have responded with a feminist analysis. That approach would have focused on the woman's economic vulnerability: a single mother was in no position to endanger her job. It also would have seen her spotty job history as evidence of the seriousness of sexual harassment and how it ultimately functioned to keep women trapped in low-paying jobs. Two decades later, the secretary might have been told to contact a lawyer. Under *Meritor*, women no longer had to handle these situations on their own.[75]

Feminists succeeded in changing the dominant narrative to consider relations of power and complicate notions of women's choice, but their larger critique of how sexual harassment systematically worked to perpetuate the subordinate status of workingwomen and sustain men's institutional power never achieved widespread public acceptance: many Americans continued to view sexual harassment as primarily a problem involving individuals and sex. The adversarial nature of the legal system— woman against man / employer—contributed to this tendency. By the early 1980s discussions of sexual harassment centered on a limited range of behaviors the government and judiciary had defined as discriminatory, rather than on widespread cultural attitudes regarding women, work, attractiveness, and sexuality, which led to inequality. Worry about a lawsuit might make employers pay attention to the gender dynamics of the office or give an individual man pause, but fear was a qualitatively different motivator from the serious reflection feminists had urged. The judicial system could effectively address the discriminatory conduct of wrongdoers, but it was ill-suited to effect broad changes in the ways Americans *thought* about gender, sex, and power at work.[76]

CHAPTER EIGHT

Two Steps Forward, One Step Back

WANTED AND UNWELCOME ADVANCES AFTER "SEXUAL HARASSMENT"

IN 1979 LORI REDFEARN ASKED A FEMINIST organization to recom-
mend a book on "non-sexist business behavior." Redfearn worked for "truly
an equal opportunity employer," but the idea of equality was still new, and
problems occasionally surfaced. She was to draft an interoffice memo
emphasizing that the company required all employees to "treat each other
with respect. No servile behavior is expected . . . no arrogant behavior will be
tolerated . . . [and] manipulative behavior is a thing of the past." Redfearn
described the three situations she found most troubling. First was the "business of married male executives snuffling after pretty young clerks and
junior secretaries." In 1979 a company could say nothing "about the morality
of this kind of behavior"—just as women in the 1930s felt they couldn't after
the 1920s revolution in sexual mores—but these maneuverings led to
gossip and cost a fortune in lost working hours. Her second concern
centered on the few "hard case male chauvinists" who cracked jokes about
women's anatomy to their young, female coworkers. The women resented
the demeaning remarks but felt they must giggle and be good sports to
protect their jobs. Finally, Redfearn objected to young women who showed
up for work in tight pants and five-inch heels. Suggestive clothing was inappropriate in their industry and, in Redfearn's view, "all of this energy invested
in alluring, sexy attire is baffling because most of the male members of the
staff are married and not worth the effort of enticement."[1]

Redfearn believed that these behaviors undermined equality, but the most striking aspect of her letter is how similar the sexual culture of this office was to those that came before—despite more than a decade of efforts aimed at improving women's standing in the workplace. These continuities are the focus of this chapter. It begins with Mary Cunningham's meteoric rise and spectacular fall at Bendix Corporation and an examination of how female executives in the 1970s and early 1980s, when they were still a novelty, handled the issue of sexuality in the office. On one hand, the specter of the vamp haunted their every move; now that there was actually a "top" to which women could sleep their way, ambitious women had to monitor their actions to defend against a career-destroying accusation. On the other hand, once women began to occupy more professional positions, consensual relationships among relative equals became an exciting possibility, although to achieve this egalitarian ideal would require men to rethink the way workplace conquests contributed to their masculine identity. For managers, the growing number of women in important positions meant they no longer could solve the problem of a soured office affair by firing the female. Developing a workable policy on consensual relations, however, continued to be an almost impossible task that many companies avoided.

After establishing in some detail exactly where the understanding of "wanted" sexual overtures stood at the moment when the U.S. Supreme Court definitively established the illegality of "unwelcome" ones, I devote the rest of the chapter to a quick survey of the office's sexual terrain up to the present. An examination of some of the most noteworthy moments and dominant debates reveals that the myths, narratives, and concerns that have been around for the past century and a half continue to be as accepted and persuasive as they ever were. The comments that Supreme Court nominee Clarence Thomas allegedly made to his employee Anita Hill, for example, were not so different from the "insults" women in the early twentieth century endured. More significant, Republican senators' efforts to discredit Hill by insisting that she would—or should—have quit if Thomas had really said those things rested on age-old understandings of gender, sexuality, work, and morality. Such continuity suggests that Americans' long-standing fascination with sexual expression in the office is about something more than mere sex. Rather, sexuality has been a signifier for all aspects of masculinity and femininity, a way of picturing and maintaining gender difference—and possibly a gender hierarchy—even as women entered into men's world, took up men's jobs, and acquired some of men's power.

AFTER THE REVOLUTIONS: LOVE AND SEX IN THE OFFICE IN THE 1980S

After the EEOC issued its final guidelines in late 1980, companies scrambled to institute policies and training programs that sent a message to employees that sexual harassment would not be tolerated. These efforts were as much about protecting businesses from liability as about ending unwelcome overtures, and management often criticized the new regulations. A 1981 article in the *Wall Street Journal*, for example, noted employers' concerns about situations in which a woman was "partly responsible" because of a "provocative dress or demeanor" and their worries about "unfairly damaging a man's reputation because of what often is essentially an unproved or perhaps unprovable allegation." Men, however, were not the only ones to find their reputations destroyed because of allegations of sexual impropriety. A woman who had scaled the corporate ladder was vulnerable to accusations that she had reached her high position through an intimate relationship with a powerful man.[2]

As companies were contemplating how to implement the EEOC guidelines, a controversy involving one of the country's highest-ranking female executives and one of its largest corporations erupted, focusing attention on the other problems that could develop when sexual expression—or rumors of it—entered the office. The case of Mary Cunningham, William Agee, and Bendix exposed how workplace sexuality undercut a woman's standing and highlighted the new problem of consensual sexual relationships among colleagues. Consensual relationships, of course, were old news, and in the past, companies had resisted getting involved, despite the prodding of 1950s management experts, who urged them to develop a policy. In large part business's attitude reflected the fact that the women were "'only secretaries' and could be replaced like disposable parts" whenever a relationship created discord. Now, however, women were in management and their numbers there were growing quickly, having doubled from 1970 to 1978; by 1980 they accounted for 26 percent of managers. The number of women entering MBA programs also had mushroomed, and in 1980 women occupied more than 20 percent of the seats in Harvard's prestigious program. Coupled with the changes brought by the sexual revolution, sex in the office among valued managerial employees was a real possibility, and employers faced the challenge of respecting their privacy while ensuring that a romance, sexual liaison, or even marriage did not destroy morale or interfere with productivity. As a management consultant noted in 1982, "It's even more difficult for companies to deal with sexual attraction than sexual harassment because there are no clear guidelines or sanctions."[3]

These ambiguities were evident in the Cunningham controversy, which began when Agee, Bendix's chairman, called an employees meeting to discuss current corporate activities. Agee prided himself on his openness, and such meetings were not unusual. This one, however, was different. In what the press called "highly unusual remarks," Agee discredited rumors of a romantic link between himself and Cunningham, twenty-nine. Agee had hired Cunningham, an "attractive blonde," as his executive assistant straight out of Harvard Business School fifteen months before, and he had quickly promoted her into a vice president position. Most recently, Agee had named her vice president of strategic planning, choosing her over men who had years of experience with the company. These promotions led to accusations of (sexual) favoritism, which prompted Agee's comments. As the forty-two-year-old recently divorced father of three said, "I know there have been a lot of questions. For once and for all, I want to slow down the rumor mill. Her rapid promotions are totally justified. It is true that we are very close friends, and she's a very close friend of my family. But that has nothing to do with the way that I and others in this company evaluate performance." Agee's remarks took only a minute in a twenty-minute presentation, but they fanned the gossip flames, and his relationship with Cunningham immediately made national headlines (especially because he had not *specifically* denied a romantic relationship). Within a few days, Cunningham announced that she had been "rendered ineffective" by the "false innuendoes and excessive attention" and asked the Bendix board for a temporary leave of absence. She also made clear she would not resign because to do so would set a "dangerous precedent" and make it easier for others to use "malicious gossip" to force out female executives. The board rejected her request and gave her a vote of confidence, but the national press coverage continued; ten days later she resigned.[4]

It was possible to view Agee's remarks as a positive step for female executives—as a journalist noted, he had "held up to the light of day" the "old shibboleth that when women get anything it's because of a sexual tradeoff"—but in openly discussing their relationship, he breached the public-private divide and diverted attention away from Cunningham's qualifications. Agee was the youngest corporate chairman of a Fortune 500 company. Promoting young talent was part of his leadership style, and he had appointed a twenty-eight-year-old man as corporate treasurer the year before without any trouble. Cunningham fit into this precocious paradigm: Harvard's dean once told the women's student association, "If there's a woman in America who can become chief executive officer of a Fortune 500 company anytime in the next ten years—on ability—it's Mary." Promoting a woman was also in keeping with Agee's principles; he was a cochairman of the National Business Council for the Equal Rights Amendment. What kept Mary from following in the footsteps of Agee or Bendix's treasurer, it seemed, was her gender and her attractiveness, which enabled her detractors to sexualize her and Agee's mentor-protégée relationship.[5]

As the Bendix situation played itself out, numerous commentators used Cunningham's plight to discuss how a successful woman's career could be derailed by sexual rumors, especially because many people assumed something sexual would be going on between an ambitious woman and the men who could help her. A "man's private life is his private life," one argued, but it was impossible for a woman to keep her personal and professional existence separate, regardless of her age or appearance. A forty-year-old woman complained that she still had to quash gossip, while the triumphs of unattractive women were dismissed as "winning ugly," the result of their having plenty of time to focus on their careers. Sexist executives, some articles predicted, would use Cunningham's story as an excuse not to support women: "If I promote Miss Smith, people will accuse me of partying her up, so I'd better think twice about this." Others remarked that professional women had to choose between their sexual or romantic desires and their ambitions, or pointed out that personal relationships played a role in virtually all promotions. If people were "really concerned about unfair advancement," the feminist Gloria Steinem stated, "they should look at all the sons-in-law of the world running companies." They were the ones who had really "slept their way to the top."[6]

Commentators also linked Cunningham's case to the issue of sexual harassment. Numerous studies, *Mademoiselle* magazine reported, showed the sexual harassment of women to be a much bigger problem than women using sex to advance. The author of a piece written shortly before the EEOC's final guidelines were issued wondered whether the innuendos that squeezed Cunningham out could be a form of sexual harassment under the hostile environment clause; cases in which an employer's fear of gossip kept him from promoting a woman were clear-cut examples of sex discrimination. Certainly Mary Cunningham saw her situation this way. She ultimately described what happened to her as "a case of sexual harassment, pure and simple. They couldn't fault my performance, so they went after my sex." Accusing a woman of sleeping her way to the top was "the ultimate weapon," said Cunningham, who received letters from thousands of women who also had to leave their jobs because rumors had destroyed their credibility. Cunningham landed on her feet, receiving more than seventy-five job offers, but her public support diminished in 1982, when she and Agee announced that they were getting married. According to both, their romantic and sexual relationship began well after Cunningham's resignation, but many found their denials unconvincing. One female executive doubted that they "magically got together" after Cunningham left Bendix and resented her for the "ugly notoriety" the marriage brought on every woman in a high position. Reviewers offered similar critiques of Cunningham's 1984 autobiography. One, for example, found unbelievable her assertion that she never looked at Agee "as a man" because he was her boss.[7]

If Cunningham's autobiography did little to clear up the question of when their relationship began, it made perfectly apparent that Cunningham had paid virtually no attention to how things looked during her time at Bendix. The popular author Gail Sheehy had made this point in a series on Cunningham. When rumors started about her second promotion, the joke around the office was that it just went to show "what it takes to get a good Catholic girl into bed." At that point, Cunningham was faced with a choice: "Censure herself or refuse to cater to appearances." She chose the latter, and also refused to cut off her long blond hair or pin it up. Cunningham offered her interpretation of her behavior in her book, presenting herself as too naïve to realize that people would think she and Agee were involved. As a result, she never gave a second thought to checking into a hotel with him or spending late nights at the office alone with him.[8]

Such behavior was almost willfully naïve. By the time Cunningham joined Bendix, there were plenty of advice books for professional women warning them about potentially compromising situations. One of the most popular, Betty Harragan's *Games Mother Never Taught You*, devoted a chapter to sex in which she unequivocally declared that any romantic or sexual liaison at work hurt an ambitious woman. Nevertheless, sex was in the office, and a professional woman would need to know how to handle it. In Harragan's analysis, women's historic subordination had allowed men to use sexual conquest to create alliances with or establish their superiority over other men, making women nothing more than pawns in men's game: "The rules never envisioned women as independent, decisive movemakers, so the scoring system rewards only males. *Women can't win this game.*" Any woman who consciously or accidentally entered it, Harragan warned, would get tagged with the designation "fair game."[9]

Harragan further described corporate America's sexual culture, including its masculine ideals, and it looked the same as ever. She began by noting that professional women challenged the very manner in which work was performed. Just as businessmen in the nineteenth century had feared that the presence of women would turn their offices into genteel parlors, so men in the 1970s worried that women would destroy the sports-and-sex lexicon of the boardroom. How, for example, could men talk about "scoring" when it meant not only to close a profitable deal but also "to 'lay' a desirable, reluctant woman"? Harragan also explained the role of office gossip in men's sex "game." It *required* "boasting, bragging, and bombast," so when a woman found herself the victim of untrue rumors, there was nothing she could do but take it in her stride. Given men's propensity to sexualize women—Harragan once heard a man dismiss an accomplished woman's presentation with a crass, "I don't remember what she said, but she sure has great tits"—she urged readers to adopt a "business uniform style" to convey authority. This self-presentation, however, would not necessarily stop men's attentions, and here Harragan retreated to the position that advice givers first staked out in the late nineteenth century. A woman needed to find a way to tactfully block men's passes and could never cast any "disparaging allusions on a male associate's attractiveness, desirability, or sexual competence." In terms of companies' attitudes toward adultery, Harragan contrasted their public disapproval with their private acceptance. A company's top executives would portray any man who was caught in a scandal as acting on his own, and they would expect him to do whatever was needed to restore the company's image. In reality, however, executives encouraged affairs, since it reconfirmed men's power by reducing women to "quarry," and it allowed men at the top to discern which men down the ladder had executive potential; once they reached the top, they earned the prize of high-priced call girls.[10]

Despite Harragan's and others' warnings, women did get involved in romances and affairs, and from management's perspective, this was a problem. Early research provided evidence for what journals like *Modern Office Procedures* had been saying since the 1950s: these relationships usually lowered morale and compromised productivity. The first major study, Robert Quinn's "Coping with Cupid," was published in 1977 and showed that such relationships were common; 62 percent of his participants knew of at least one such relationship. In 74 percent of the cases, the male was in a higher-level position; 48 percent involved a man's secretary. On occasion, a workplace romance could increase a participant's productivity, but the effect on other workers was never beneficial, even if it only stimulated gossip. The press covered the study, but, as Quinn noted, knowing that relationships caused problems was easier than developing a policy to address them. Management generally concluded that it was impossible to "legislate morality," but even as Quinn's study made the rounds, the problem was becoming more complicated. Relationships were now occurring between professional colleagues who worked as partners on projects and even traveled together on business. When something went awry, the solution was much more complicated than automatically dismissing the subordinate woman. (Nearly all of the studies on workplace relationships focused on heterosexual couples, but one from 1984 suggested that lesbians involved in office affairs experienced fewer negative consequences than heterosexual women because their relationships were usually with coworkers, not superiors.)[11]

Consensual romantic and sexual relationships between executives— not to mention more ordinary interactions—could be quite complex interplays of gender and desire, of power and fear. Some men liked the presence of female colleagues, which had increased the sexual energy and temptations of the workplace. Others, however, found "the assertive new breed of businesswoman" intimidating and saw them not as "sex objects but rather as competitors for promotions and titles." In some cases, a man's attraction for his coworkers proved distracting to his work; as one admitted, "It's tough for me to look at someone and not think, 'Boy, she's pretty.' I find myself spending a little too much time looking at them and not listening to what they're saying." As for the women, according to the head of human resources at Chase Manhattan Bank, they sometimes gave "explicit sexual cues" and then cried foul when men picked them up. This was especially true of women in their early thirties, who had concentrated on their careers and awakened one morning to find a few wrinkles. They wanted "to impress men sexually, not so much because they want to be treated sexually but because they want to feel like attractive females again."[12]

In 1983 Eliza G. C. Collins, in a piece on love affairs between executives for the *Harvard Business Review*, urged companies to take a hard line; such relationships represented a "conflict of interest" and the less essential employee would have to go. Brief, consensual affairs were bound to happen and posed only a "minor problem." Relationships involving real feeling, however, constituted a danger even in cases in which both participants were unmarried. As coworkers learned of the relationship, they would become jealous and fearful about their places in the organization. Managers, Collins believed, needed to be impersonal in order for a company to thrive. To this end, upper management needed to intervene as soon as it learned of the relationship, despite the "unwritten rule" that they should stay out of their subordinates' private lives. Management should persuade the couple that either both or the less essential member of the couple would have to go. Since, in general, women were still in lesser positions than men, this advice most often meant the woman. Collins acknowledged that this was sexist, and she urged management to help the ousted partner find a new job, as well as to continue to promote women into high positions.[13]

Collins matter-of-factly assumed that something sexual would happen when men and women worked together as colleagues, reflecting dramatic changes in Americans' values. Not quite twenty years before, *Modern Office Procedures* had vehemently denied Helen Gurley Brown's similar assertion. Now, Collins believed, casual encounters were ordinary and

Eliza Collins's 1983 piece in the *Harvard Business Review* generated a lot of press, including an article, "Love in the Executive Suite," which appeared in the *Washington Post* accompanied by this illustration. Reprinted with permission of CoulterIndustries.com.

insignificant; both male and female executives would "soon tire of a romp" and gladly forget it. Collins's examples included relationships involving married managers, and, although adulterous affairs created more disruption, she withheld all moral judgment. Married men's "conventional" wives, Collins believed, simply could no longer meet their needs.[14]

Collins's assessment reflected changes that had begun in the late 1960s, when some marital experts reevaluated extramarital sexual interactions. Their opinions, they argued, merely reflected behavior that was already occurring; as one psychologist described it in 1969, "The pleasantness of a short-term relationship within the bonds of mutual care seems to be accepted in our culture today, to a certain degree," and "typical" affairs often began in the workplace. A number of psychologists believed there were "healthy reasons" for such liaisons, and therefore adultery should not necessarily lead to guilty feelings or result in social condemnation. Sexual variety, for example, was a healthy motivation, and a happily married man could enjoy "mild or heavy petting with other females at office parties" without endangering his marriage. In the context of the sexual revolution, experts easily distinguished between the man who slept with another woman after "'one too many' at the office party" and a man who actually looked for an encounter. Other acceptable reasons included social inducements. A "normally monogamous" businessman would "think nothing of resorting to prostitutes . . . at business parties." Similarly, for "males socialized to a concept of success in the business world," affairs in middle age might even be thought of as "natural" for their life conditions. Even as their wives aged and lost some of their desirability, a man found that his attractiveness to other women increased the more he prospered. In these cases, adultery was not deviant but a natural outcome of the social structure. A poll taken in the middle of the Elizabeth Ray scandal in 1975 suggests just how expected infidelity was: 55 percent agreed with the statement that "many businessmen" had affairs with their staff. By the time of the Cunningham-Agee mess, scholars, management experts, and the popular media all agreed: work was a sexy place. Some emphasized the new possibility of egalitarian marriages rooted in shared professional experiences, while others worried about the "threat to the ideal of the monogamous conjugal family."[15]

Once again, the press treated stay-at-home wives to stories about the dangers workingwomen posed to their marriages. In 1972, for example, the *Chicago Tribune* published an interview with an attractive college graduate who worked as an executive secretary. All men were on the make, she declared, but single women were sexually "aggressive" as well, and many preferred to date married men because they provided the opportunity for "fun—without the involvement." Young women seemed to have adopted Helen Gurley Brown's new outlook, but the informant offered these men's wives decades-old advice: "If housewives knew what their competition is downtown . . . [they] wouldn't get up in the morning and serve [their husbands] breakfast looking like a witch." By the late 1970s articles had shifted to focusing on wives' concern about their husband's female associates, and advice guides regularly told women executives it was their responsibility to calm wives' worries. But being betrayed by a husband who cheated with a woman from his office was not the only possible source of pain. Wives also could feel deceived when they learned their husbands were forcing their attentions on employees. The wife of a corporate president accused of sexual harassment wrote a letter to a feminist activist but refused to sign her name because she felt "highly insulted by my husband's actions, just as much as the woman who feels humiliated by the sexual harassment."[16]

If wives had more to worry about, secretaries had their own axe to grind, as management began to take sex in the office seriously now that it involved women who were not "just secretaries." In 1981, for example, a reporter for the *Wall Street Journal* declared that there was more sexual tension in the office now that women were "not clerical helpers but professional colleagues, women who share the men's background and interests and are likely to be bright, energetic and independent." Clerical workers responded with resentment at the implication that they were not "bright." Office workers, one noted, were hardworking and underpaid. They had more pressing concerns than office romance. Another addressed her remarks to new career women who did not know how to handle sexual advances; she encouraged them to talk to those "professional" women who had abundant experience in this area: secretaries.[17]

The new focus on workplace liaisons exposed the politics of class as well as of gender in the office. This was especially apparent in Collins's piece in the *Harvard Business Review*, in which she drove a stake through the heart of the "marrying the boss" fantasy. In the past, Collins noted, men saw office affairs "as play," since the differences in the men's and women's social status ruled out marriage. Collins made the crass nature of these encounters clear in her discussion of how women managers now sometimes got iced out of office networks when they were having affairs. This exclusion made them feel dirty, and sometimes they "believed what others implied: that they were no better than the secretarial meat of the corporate-caveman era." An affair could turn an executive back into "just a woman," but in Collins's opinion, "genuine love" was more likely now that the office included women whose social status matched men's. This assertion effectively realigned the office. As we have seen, women office workers always paid close attention to the social class implications of their behaviors, and, as the office became more diverse in terms of class and ethnicity, secretaries and women in high-level clerical jobs drew attention to the ways their positions differed from those below. Even with this awareness, the office divide still centered on gender. Now that women occupied professional jobs, however, social class became the great division, as reflected in the degree of education and refinement required in one's job.[18]

Collins took a hard line against workplace relationships, but some personnel experts challenged the impersonal, bureaucratic ideal. In this view, management's refusal to acknowledge human emotions or sexual attraction caused problems. Employees who had these feelings felt guilty and sneaked around. And that, according to personnel consultant Kaleel Jamison, was what made sexuality so troublesome. Talking openly about relationships would clear the air and make management's expectations clear. Some organizations went even farther. The head of human relations at Penn Mutual Life Insurance, for example, let his employees "know that expressing emotions is okay." This change, adherents believed, could defuse desire's destructive spark. "When the air of the office is more conducive to the expression of natural emotions, when it no longer is strange and unusual for co-workers to exchange affections, the disruptive qualities of sexual attraction in the office will be lessened." Not surprisingly, advocates of emotion often echoed the sentiments that Helen Gurley Brown had articulated in the 1960s: attraction and desire could actually enhance productivity. This issue had come up during the Cunningham-Agee imbroglio in articles exploring the changing sexual culture of the office. One female executive described working closely with a colleague as "not a whole lot different from making love. When you see someone's mind unfold and you learn how it works and that you are able to trigger the best from that mind, it becomes a very sexy experience." Mary Cunningham also made the case for the compatibility of love and business: "People who work together come to know each other in a way that is far more meaningful by most standards than meeting in a singles bar." In her opinion, it was a "medieval notion that as soon as two people start sleeping together, one or both suddenly lose their judgment."[19]

Was sexual electricity invigorating or enervating? No two observers could agree, though everyone concurred that it was a "tricky" situation. By 1986 it was no longer novel for women and men to work together as colleagues, which made conditions for on-the-job romance "close to optimal." Yet in terms of policies, there had not been much change since Quinn's 1977 study. According to one report, 94 percent of companies still had no formal policies on office relationships, although they were becoming more aware of the need for communication and more open to discussion of personal issues. And, partly in response to pressure from feminists, companies had begun to change their nepotism policies, allowing married couples to continue to work for the company under certain conditions. Already by 1979, for example, companies like Bank of

America and IBM allowed married couples to work in the same department unless it endangered security or involved a direct supervisory role.[20]

In trying to explain why companies had such a difficult time figuring out how to respond to this new reality, the notion of "modernity" is key. In addition to the challenge of reconciling desire and the impersonal bureaucratic ideal, businesses also had to figure out their beliefs about both sexuality and gender. To put the issue simply, they needed to decide whether they held modern or traditional views. In the opinion of Ira L. Reiss, a sociologist writing in 1981, Americans' response to the Cunningham-Agee crisis indicated that they had not fully adopted modern ideology, which he described as emphasizing gender equality and deemphasizing gender difference. The modern outlook also accepted sexual desire and, most importantly, saw it as a strong, but manageable, emotion. The traditional position held to customary gender roles and a sexual double standard, in which men were driven by lust and women by love; desire was an extremely powerful emotion and should be treated with a degree of fear. In Reiss's assessment, those who assumed that Cunningham had "slept her way to the top" were reflecting the traditional position. In this appraisal, the power of desire was too much. Agee could not resist the beautiful blonde who was constantly by his side, and this attraction necessarily clouded his judgment. Friendship, by contrast, was an emotion not nearly as strong, which explained why traditionalists worried much less about the role of personal relationships between men in the awarding of promotions or contracts, especially since men were thought to be more naturally suited to business. Modernists, by contrast, emphasized Cunningham's talents and asserted that men and women could be platonic friends.[21]

NARRATIVES OF RACE, CLASS, AND GENDER AND WOMEN'S NEW AMBITIONS

Americans had another opportunity to think about these issues in the fall of 1991, after President George H. W. Bush nominated Clarence Thomas, an African American conservative, to the Supreme Court. Confirmation hearings began on September 10 and included impassioned speeches against the nominee by leaders of women's and civil rights groups. On September 27 the Senate Judiciary Committee split 7–7 on the confirmation and subsequently voted to send the nomination to the Senate floor without endorsement. On October 6, two days before the full Senate was scheduled to vote, an unknown source leaked information to the press about Anita Hill, a young attorney who had worked for Thomas for two years in the early 1980s, first at the Department of Education and then at the Equal Employment Opportunity Commission when Thomas became chairman. Hill had provided the Judiciary Committee with an affidavit alleging that Thomas had repeatedly asked her out on dates and, when she declined because she believed "having a social relationship with a person who was supervising my work would be ill-advised," began using work-related meetings to talk about pornographic films "depicting individuals with large penises, or large breasts involved in various sex acts." Other times he commented on what she was "wearing in terms of whether it made [her] more or less sexually attractive" and spoke of "the pleasures he had given to women with oral sex."[22]

When Americans learned that the Judiciary Committee had investigated but chosen not to reveal Hill's allegations during its hearings, there was a widespread call for additional sessions to examine Thomas's behavior. On October 11 the committee reconvened for three days of questioning of Thomas, Hill, and various witnesses for each side, a televised spectacle watched by millions of Americans. Senators and commentators alike immediately declared these hearings a crucial turning point in the history of gender, sexuality, and the workplace. "In America's workplaces," went a typical assessment, "men and women reintroduced themselves with a suspicion that their relationship had changed forever."[23]

That a reintroduction was possible suggests how little had changed in the sixteen years since feminists first named "sexual harassment." Republican senators' questioning of Hill and her supporters and the comments of Thomas's character witnesses merely rehashed century-old interpretations of women's treachery and instability. Those who believed that Hill was lying offered a laundry list of possible motivations, including, as one senator noted, "vindictiveness, a martyr-type complex, desire to be a hero, write a book, spurned woman or scorned woman in regards to romantic [sic], and then the issue of whether or not she has any fantasy or [is] out of touch with reality." If this moment was in fact when the country as a whole learned about sexual harassment—especially about the vast divide between men's and women's perception of and reaction to harassing behaviors—it is also possible that the hearings simply confirmed what many already thought about workingwomen.[24]

Immediately after Hill's allegations went public, Thomas's supporters began to offer variations of the stereotypical image of the woman scorned, a charge that soon took on an added psychological dimension. The Hill-Thomas hearings were the archetype of the so-called "nuts and sluts" defense, in which the accuser either made the whole thing up or was too promiscuous for her word to be trusted. The opening gambit came from Phyllis Berry, who had worked with Hill and Thomas at the EEOC. She told the press that Hill's allegations were a result of her "disappointment and frustration that Mr. Thomas did not show any sexual interest in her." Run-of-the-mill vengeance was quickly replaced with a more exotic explanation—erotomania—a rare delusional disorder. Jonathan H. Segal, a psychiatric expert on the condition, commented to the press, "Most patients treated for erotomania are young, single women whose scenario concerns an older male, often a boss," hurriedly adding, "but that is also the most common relationship involved in cases of sexual harassment." According to Thomas's supporters, Hill was so obsessed with Thomas that she fantasized their sexual conversations, and they discussed this theory with a psychiatrist, Park Dietz, who specialized in false allegations of sexual misconduct. Dietz came to Washington at his own expense and briefed several Republican senators. He also told the press, "I know it is entirely possible for someone to be coherent, competent, intelligent and attractive and have normal social relations while also holding an absolutely false belief about someone's harassment of them."[25]

In suggesting that Hill had fantasized Thomas's come-ons, Republican senators were merely adopting psychological views that had been around in some form with regard to sexuality in the workplace since at least the 1930s and embracing the distrust of women long codified in rape law. Erotomania was really not so different from the fantasies and daydreams psychiatrists ascribed to office women in the 1930s discussed in Chapter 3. And although feminists in the 1970s had succeeded in changing the adjudication of rape cases, abolishing culturally embedded suspicions of a woman's veracity was not so easy. Way back in the seventeenth century, the legal scholar Matthew Hale had asserted an accusation of rape was "easily" made and virtually impossible for an innocent man to defend against. In the twentieth century, similar concerns informed the recommendation by the evidence expert John Henry Wigmore that every rape complainant should be examined by a psychiatrist to determine whether she had fantasized the attack. In alleging that Thomas had sexually harassed her, Hill had to contend with the generalized problem of credibility that haunted any woman who made a charge that a man had sexually harassed or assaulted her, but she also had to overcome cultural understandings of women's romantic ambitions.[26]

Thomas's success gave weight to the notion that it was Hill, not Thomas, who was interested in a relationship and contradicted the stereotype of a harasser as a boorish office lech or an uneducated lout. A prominent economist, for example, dismissed Hill's assertion that she had turned down Thomas's social invitations as completely implausible: Thomas was "handsome, polished, brilliant, a man of the world. . . . Why would she say no?" Thomas would be "tempted" by the attractive young attorney, but, by this same gendered logic, he would have resisted. Thomas would know that becoming romantically or sexually involved with a subordinate would be a step down "a slippery slope" to trouble. And, of course, the popular understanding of a harasser was certainly not a prominent judge with a Yale law degree, which made the hearings an insult to Thomas's achievements. As one of his supporters remarked, "This process has treated Clarence Thomas like he is a foreman in a manufacturing plant."[27]

One witness in particular, John Doggett III, a Texas attorney who knew Thomas well and who had known Hill casually in Washington, provided ammunition for an attack on Hill as both delusional and sexually willing. According to Doggett, Hill had asked to speak to him in private at her going-away party. When they were alone, she allegedly chastised him about his behavior toward her. "I'm very disappointed in you. You really shouldn't lead women on . . . and then let them down." Doggett stated that he had never expressed any interest in Hill. In his opinion, her "fantasies about my sexual interest in her were an indication of the fact that she was having a problem with being rejected by men she was attracted to." Hill's statements about Thomas, he believed, were "yet another example of her ability to fabricate the idea that someone was interested in her when in fact no such interest existed."[28]

Senators opposed to Thomas's nomination gave Doggett a thorough grilling, but his testimony gave Thomas's supporters a way to discredit

Hill without blatantly calling her a liar. Senator Patrick Leahy of Vermont pooh-poohed Doggett's theory, asking, "Do you just feel that you have some kind of natural irresistibility?" Senator Howard Metzenbaum of Ohio asked about a woman who had contacted the committee accusing Doggett of harassing her when she was a teenaged clerk in his law firm. She alleged that he had once said, "Oh, you are making copies, that is sort of like reproduction isn't it?" which she interpreted as a sexual come-on, though Doggett denied the accusation. While Democrats attacked Doggett's recollections, Senator Arlen Specter of Pennsylvania, a Thomas supporter, used Doggett's testimony to spin his own theory that neither Hill nor Thomas was lying. "Perhaps they both think they are telling the truth, but in Professor Hill's case she thinks it is true but in fact it is not." Doggett concurred with this interpretation, and went on to offer more evidence that Thomas could not have behaved as Hill charged because he would not have risked endangering his career. "Quite frankly," Doggett declared, "Anita Hill is not worth that type of risk."[29]

Doggett acknowledged that he based his assessment on "intuition," not any psychological credentials, but the talk of fantasies and delusions and the involvement of psychiatrists and psychologists signaled a new development in the litigation of sexual harassment cases. Although the committee did not allow experts to testify at the hearings, several of the leading scholars on the psychology of women issued a statement that there was no evidence that Hill was delusional. Her description of what happened and how she responded, they argued, was characteristic of women's reactions as documented in the growing body of psychological research on sexual harassment.[30]

Today, members of the psychological profession are increasingly called upon to perform forensic mental health examinations of plaintiffs, and the adversarial nature of the legal system can make cases every bit as charged as the Senate hearings. Psychological assessments are used in a number of ways. Defense attorneys might seek to prove that a plaintiff's emotional state in some way precipitated the harassment—for example, by sending signals that sexual overtures would be "welcome." Expert opinion is also used to determine if a plaintiff is credible or if her or his reaction to the behavior was "reasonable," a determination that can be especially important in the assessment of damages. And, similar to the approach used by Republican senators in the Hill-Thomas hearings, defense attorneys have sought to identify a plaintiff's personality disorder to break out of the "he said, she said" impasse. Defense attorneys in these cases subpoena a wide variety of sources during the discovery process, such as high school records or files from divorce or custody cases, to gather evidence of a plaintiff's mental distress. Critics, meanwhile, charge that such digging amounts to an invasion of privacy and is merely cover for additional harassment.[31]

Already by the time of the Hill-Thomas hearings, psychologists had accumulated evidence that the majority of women who experienced harassment said nothing, but the issue of why Hill went with Thomas to the EEOC and kept in contact with him after she left Washington was repeatedly used to discredit her accusations. In the eight years between Hill's resignation from the EEOC and the hearings, Hill had seen Thomas twice in Oklahoma in work-related settings and had left eleven phone messages with his secretary, all of which, according to Hill, regarded professional matters. Senators supporting Thomas pressed Hill to explain her actions, and the subtext of their questioning was that a "lady" would never speak to a man who so insulted her. As Senator Alan Simpson of Wyoming asked: "If what you say this man said to you occurred . . . why in God's name did you ever speak to a man like that the rest of your life?" In his view, what she described was "so repugnant, so ugly, so obscene" that she presumably "would never have talked to him again." Here was the most recent incarnation of the long-standing advice given to working-women when faced with unwanted attentions: Quit. Now, however, women like Hill were professionals who had devoted a lot of time and money to their education and whose success depended on making and keeping professional contacts.[32]

Hill offered just this explanation. She testified that she "may have used poor judgment early on in my relationship with this issue," but she was aware "that telling at any point in my career could adversely affect my future career." It might be difficult for some to understand her decisions, but, as she told Simpson, continuing to work with Thomas "seemed the only reasonable choice." She wanted to work on civil rights issues, and she "did not want to let that kind of behavior control my choices." Ultimately, it did, and she began to look for another job when the harassing behavior escalated. When she found one as a law professor in Oklahoma, Thomas could no longer directly threaten her job, and at this point she "did not feel that it was necessary to cut off all ties . . . or to treat him in a hostile manner." A number of commentators and Hill's supporters offered the same rationale. Ellen Wells, one of Hill's witnesses, had stayed in touch with people who had insulted her "because you don't know who you may need later on." Indeed, according to Wells, it took "a great deal of strength and courage to *not* maintain some kind of a cordial relationship." Women's magazines and career seminars all told women "to network since we don't have the 'Old Boys Club.' Take up golf, ladies. Take up tennis. Learn to get out there so you can do these things to maintain these contacts. And so you don't burn your bridges."[33]

Republican senators, however, continued to suggest that no woman would have stayed in touch with a man such as Hill described, and if one did, she certainly could not play the injured maiden a decade later. Senator Specter presented Hill as a brazen careerist who was willing to overlook Thomas's foul verbiage because she "wanted to derive whatever advantage" she could from a professional relationship with him. In this view, which harkened back to ideas about gender and social class that had accompanied women when they first entered the white-collar workforce, an ambitious woman who put her desire for success above her demand to be treated respectfully was not entitled to protection from unwelcome advances. Such a woman did not need to be shielded from obscenities or illicit suggestions because her sensibilities could not be injured.[34]

The women who testified about Thomas's character continued in this vein, using the evidence of their personal experiences to challenge the veracity of Hill's assertions; since she had not responded to sexually harassing behavior the way they had, she could not be telling the truth. Patricia Cornwell Johnson described her harassment as "the most degrading and humiliating experience" of her career. She had confided in friends and family, and she had no further contact with the man after she left the job. Based on her personal and professional experience, Johnson determined, "I do not believe that a woman who has been victimized by the outrageously lewd, vile and vulgar behavior that has been described here would want to have, let alone maintain any kind of relationship with a man that victimized her." Janet Brown offered a similar assessment. She had been harassed, and "it was a demeaning, humiliating, sad and revolting experience. . . . Let me assure you that the last thing I would ever have done is follow the man who did this to a new job, call him on the phone or voluntarily share the same air space ever again." Nancy Altman also had been a victim of harassment and knew other women who had been, too. She argued that women "always shared the experience with a female co-worker they could trust," and that a woman's female coworkers would probably know if a woman was being harassed.[35]

J. C. Alvarez, who had worked at the EEOC with Thomas and Hill, also used her personal experience to conclude that Hill's behavior was inconsistent with the charges, and she added the element of race to her assessment. A woman who had "really been harassed" would put as much distance as possible between herself and her harasser and would never follow him to another job, "especially if you're a black female, Yale Law School graduate." In Alvarez's view, Hill did not need to curry Thomas's favor or stay in his good graces. "Let's face it," Alvarez told the committee, "out in the corporate sector, companies are fighting for women with those kind of credentials." With this statement, Alvarez implicitly raised the issue of relative power, an issue that might have resonated with many Americans. Hill was not a file clerk with limited skills and restricted opportunities or a single mother who could not risk losing her job. Hill was a young, single woman with an impressive résumé; unlike other women, she had options. Yet despite these qualifications, Hill was a black woman who faced the double burden of racism and sexism. As her supporter Ellen Wells testified, "Being a black woman, you know, you have to put up with a lot, and so you grit your teeth and you do it."[36]

In many ways, the question of how much a black woman should put up with was at the center of African Americans' response to the hearings, and views differed dramatically. African American women were deeply divided, and social class seems to have factored into this division. Those who believed Hill tended to resemble her in age, education, and professional experience. Other women who thought she had lied suggested that only an Ivy Leaguer could complain about a "little kidding around by her boss." A machine operator emphasized Hill's "highly paid position" and wondered why she had not been more assertive: "If anybody had done me like he did her . . . I would have told him where to go, and it wouldn't have taken me that many years to tell it." A dialysis technician stated, "When women burned their bras in the '60s, they gave up their rights to make claims such as this." For working-class women, equal pay and decent working conditions were matters of much more significance than verbal taunts, which were often downplayed as "men will be men." Yet despite disagreement about whether or not Hill was telling the truth, black women were in agreement with regard to how things would have turned out if Hill had been white. Thomas would not have been confirmed, and, as one woman put it, "I don't think [Hill] would have been raked through the coals like that. . . . They would have taken it easy on her." For many African American women, then, the hearings were more about race than about sexual harassment.[37]

The black community's response to Anita Hill and its increased support of Thomas after her allegations were made public highlights how dramatically race and class can affect a woman's experience of and response to sexual harassment. When Thomas referred to the hearings as a "high-tech lynching for uppity blacks," support for his nomination in the black community rose from 54 percent to almost 80 percent. (During the hearings, Senator Joseph Biden of Delaware tried to turn Thomas's appropriations of racial stereotypes to Hill's benefit. Building on Thomas's assertion that Hill's accusations played into the worst stereotypes of sexually voracious black men, Biden challenged Thomas's character witnesses to examine how the refusal to take Hill's charges seriously might reflect stereotypes about black women's veracity. This line of questioning, though, was quickly dropped.) In addition, many African Americans expressed anger that Hill broke the ranks of racial solidarity, especially given their belief that sexual harassment was a trivial issue compared with the problems facing black men. A columnist in the African American press, for example, commented on the hostility of black men, including professionals, to Hill. He had heard such comments as, "Personally, I don't believe the Black bitch," or "She probably been fantasizing 'bout his meat for the last 10 years." These men, the columnist argued, did not care whether Thomas was guilty; they "just saw a vindictive sister trying to discredit a fun-loving brother." Some black women saw their role as supporting black men, not bringing them down: "Black men have all of the problems. They are already under such great pressure and stress. It baffles me—it baffles my mother—why this black woman would do this."[38]

If attitudes regarding racial unity and masculinity made it difficult for many African Americans to take Hill's side, reactions among white women were similarly conflicted. Feminists spoke out loudly in support of Hill, but the majority of women did not, including many who had experienced harassment. Despite the lack of support for Hill, these women took the issue of sexual harassment seriously, but many also believed that a woman needed to learn how to handle such situations on her own and should not tolerate vulgar overtures. To some degree, then, women agreed with those senators who made the hearings about Hill's character, morals, and gumption. Many feminists had thought that making women's shared experiences visible, for example, by naming and breaking the silence surrounding sexual harassment, would lead to gender solidarity, but such was not the case. In many ways, it was still every woman for herself. And as Senator Specter pointed out, Hill had not done much to change this situation. If she really cared about women, he asked her, why hadn't she spoken out instead of leaving Thomas as chairman of the EEOC? The answer, in the opinion of one feminist, was that women were no longer "outsiders," but "insiders" who were pitted against each other for the few good jobs available to them in an economic downturn. The "best way [to] stop a revolution," she continued, "is by giving people something to lose."39

OUT WITH THE OLD, IN WITH THE (NOT-SO) NEW

Hill's testimony did not change a single vote on the committee, and two days later, the Senate confirmed Thomas, as had been expected before her allegations were made public. A commentator at the time portentously noted, "The seeds of fear and hope planted by Anita Hill's sexual harassment charges against Clarence Thomas will grow in America's offices for years to come," but twenty years later it is difficult to evaluate the harvest. Certainly the hearings serve as a touchstone, a moment in which the country's awareness of an issue suddenly changed, and it has remained in their consciousness ever since. Yet many Americans' understanding of sexual harassment and of its attendant controversies reflects perspectives and beliefs that were dominant decades before the hearings.40

In the short term, some notable gains for women could be traced back to the televised "he said, she said" clash. First, a little more than a month after the hearings, President Bush signed a civil rights bill that he had earlier threatened to veto; the legislation allowed plaintiffs in sexual harassment cases to collect both compensatory and punitive damages and to have their cases heard by a jury. Second, sexual harassment civil lawsuits almost doubled from 1991 to 1993. And finally, in the 1992 congressional elections an unprecedented number of women were elected, a victory commentators attributed in part to women voters' anger with male legislators, such as those on the Senate Judiciary Committee, who "just didn't get it." By this time, too, popular opinion had shifted away from Thomas to Hill.[41]

The U.S. Congress was one place that changed after the Hill-Thomas spectacle. The irony of senators who had exempted themselves from a wide array of employment laws, including Title VII, in effect adjudicating a sexual harassment case was not lost on observers. Newspapers interviewed unnamed congressional staffers, including one who commented, "Half the guys up there lamenting now what a serious charge this is had their hands on some underpaid female aide last week." Representative Pat Schroeder of Colorado, who had spoken out against harassment in Congress during the Wayne Hays scandal fifteen years before, noted, "The times they are a' changin' and the boys here don't get it on this issue. . . . They all think of themselves as potential victims, thinking, 'We need to stick together or all these women will come out and make allegations setting us up.' "[42]

In the time between Hays and Thomas, the U.S. Congress weathered a number of sex scandals, including some involving sex with or sexual harassment of employees. In 1983 the House Ethics Committee, the body to which a staff member would make a complaint of sexual harassment, investigated Congressmen Dan Crane of Illinois and Gerry Studds of Massachusetts regarding sexual relationships with underage House pages. In this case, the committee censured both men, a first for ethics breaches that involved sexual misconduct. In 1987 female aides and a female lobbyist accused California Representative Ernie Konnyu of sexual harassment; in one instance, Konnyu told a reporter that one of his aides was not "exactly heavily stacked." Konnyu lost his reelection bid the next year. In 1988 two female staffers charged Representative Jim Bates of California with making unwanted sexual advances. Bates denied the allegations but publicly apologized for flirting in ways that might have been inappropriate. The committee issued a letter of reproval, its mildest form of punishment, but for the first time a member of Congress had been disciplined for sexual harassment. The lightness of this sanction infuriated one of the women, who said she had endured Bates doing a "bump and grind" on her leg in full view of his staff.[43]

After Hill-Thomas, it did not take long before another scandal over sexual harassment rocked Congress. In 1992 the *Seattle Times* published a story in which six women, each of whom had at one time worked for Washington Senator Brock Adams, anonymously accused him of assaults ranging from drugging and raping to what might be called his signature moves, a friendly arm around a woman's shoulder that ended with his hand grabbing her breast or a hand up the skirt of any woman who chanced to be sitting next to him. Adams had been accused of sexual assault a few years before, and the article put a quick end to his reelection effort. The scandal came to a fitting conclusion when Washington voters elected Patty Murray to fill Adams's seat; "just a mom in tennis shoes," she had entered the Senate race well before the *Times'* story broke, motivated by the Hill-Thomas hearings. Shortly after her victory, she and four other female senators called for hearings on the sexual misconduct allegations involving Senator Bob Packwood of Oregon.[44]

When Bob Packwood characterized the Hill-Thomas hearings as a "defining moment" in modern politics, he had no idea how prophetic those words would be—for him. On November 22 the *Washington Post* reported that for the previous twenty-four years, from almost the moment he arrived in Washington, Packwood had made unwanted sexual advances to women who worked for him or with him. Ten women, including six who allowed their names to be published, told of being grabbed without warning and forcibly kissed or fondled. Packwood always stopped when the women made it clear his overtures were unwelcome, and none experienced any penalty for rejecting him, though a number began to look for new jobs and left when they could. One former aide said, "he couldn't seem to help himself," despite being repeatedly warned that his behavior would bring him "to a bad end. All your career's work on women's issues and on progressive issues is going to turn to dust."[45]

After a short-lived attempt to discredit the women, Packwood offered an apology, but it was too late; in the wake of Anita Hill and the strong showing of women in the recent elections, it was now, as one senator noted, "just a whole new environment." The Senate Ethics Committee quickly agreed to conduct a preliminary inquiry, the first of its kind, into the allegations. By early February, thirteen more women, six of whom

NOW activists began demonstrating for public hearings on the accusations of sexual harassment against Senator Bob Packwood shortly after the story broke in late 1992. This photo is from 1995, shortly before Packwood resigned. Reproduced with permission of the National Organization for Women.

agreed to have their names published, had come forward with similar stories of being grabbed and kissed "out of the blue." A year after the Senate inquiry began, the committee had interviewed 150 people and gone to court to get Packwood's diaries. Those diaries—like Ward Smith's lascivious letter to his son decades before—faithfully documented sexual encounters with an adolescent boy's glee—and lack of self-awareness. Packwood had "passionate relationships" with about seventy-five staff members and had "made love" to twenty-two others, including a woman with a lackluster sex life whom he slept with as part of his "Christian duty." If the cataloguing of sexual adventures was fairly juvenile, the diary's documentation of Packwood's efforts to sidestep campaign finance laws was fully mature. On September 6, 1995, the Senate Ethics Committee voted 6–0 to expel Packwood, the first time the Senate had taken such a step since the Civil War; Packwood resigned the next day. Earlier that year, members of Congress finally passed legislation that made them subject to the same labor laws that applied to the private sector.[46]

During the first half of the 1990s, sexual harassment was in the head-lines enough for everyone to have an opinion about it. Yet as divided as those opinions were, the majority of Americans acknowledged that sexual harassment was a real problem. An opinion poll taken the day the Anita Hill story broke showed that 56 percent of Americans thought that most or many women experienced such behavior at some point in their working lives. By the end of the hearings, the number rose to 77 percent, and after the Packwood exposé the next year, 83 percent of men and 88 percent of women thought harassment was a legitimate issue. Polling questions, though, do not allow for much nuance: what was behind these numbers?[47]

Helen Gurley Brown made her thoughts known, and she thought sexual harassment was both a real concern and an overblown issue. Brown's attitudes about sexuality and the workplace remained startlingly consistent with those she first articulated in the early 1960s. A few weeks after the Hill-Thomas hearings, Brown wrote an editorial for the *Wall Street Journal* entitled "At Work, Sexual Electricity Sparks Creativity." Though she began by asserting that she believed Hill's story and that it was "high time" women "blew the whistle" on this kind of behavior, it set off a frenzy of criticism, an angry and bewildered chorus of "She doesn't get it!" The outrage centered on Brown's discussion of Scuttle, the depantying game she had encountered in her first office job and described in *Sex and the Office*. Brown's boyish figure had rendered her "unscuttlable," much to her chagrin. Talk about sexual harassment, Brown proclaimed to the *Journal*'s readers, "I *know* about sexual harassment." The real time for women to "worry" about men's behavior, she believed, was when they didn't notice you.[48]

Wall Street Journal readers' condemnation of Brown's position came fast and furious. While pointing out that in 1940 women had no choice but to submit or quit, many readers also noted the difference between "natural sexual tension between men and women [that] can be a source of banter and wit, even in an office," and "assault" or sexual harassment. But Brown stuck by her statement, telling a reporter, "If a woman can't get a job, or if she can't get a promotion or she gets fired because she won't give her boss sex, or if she is made terribly uncomfortable by a sexual innuendo, that is sexual harassment . . . and she should sue and lodge a complaint." In the case of Scuttle, however, the women all "thought it was fun." The moral of the story, then, was that "we should lighten up and not make everything a federal offense." Of course, by 1991, the behavior

Brown described probably *was* a federal offense. And the law was not all that had changed: the roles of women in both the world of work and the ritual of courtship had evolved dramatically in the fifty years since Brown witnessed Scuttle and the thirty years since she first wrote about it. In the 1960s, however, Scuttle was so unremarkable that in the hundreds of reviews of *Sex and the Office*, it rarely rated even so much as a mention. By 1991 Brown's outlook and the story itself not only appalled many of the *Journal*'s readers—it was incomprehensible to them.[49]

The seventy-three-year-old Brown reentered the fray in 1995, when she voiced support for Senator Packwood, whom she respected for his support of abortion rights. Appearing on television's *Dateline*, Brown repeated the advice she had long given on how to handle a man's wandering hands. As she told the reporter, "I think you say, 'Willie, would you cut that out, you idiot? I'm crazy about you, but I don't like that so just please don't do it anymore.'" When the reporter suggested that Brown was "telling working women to put up and shut up with sexual harassment," Brown became angry. "I am not saying put up with sexual harassment. . . . I am simply saying before you think you're insulted because somebody tells you you look good in blue, could you stop being such a little ninny?" Brown also had no sympathy for the women who alleged that Packwood had forced his attentions on them years ago and were bringing it up now. "Did it kill them?" she queried. "Was it really the end of the world? I doubt it."[50]

Once again Brown's comments drew fire, but Brown also received letters of support from fans who shared her views. These people worried that efforts to stop harassment would also kill the erotically tinged camaraderie that gave a spark to heterosocial workplaces. A woman from Tennessee wrote that in her office, "we actually tell the men that we don't report sexual harassment—we grade it! Please don't take me wrong," she continued, "I do not tolerate true sexual harassment but we do 'cut-up' and try to make work a little more pleasant. After all, we do spend more time with coworkers than our own families so why not have fun?!" A fifty-five-year-old woman wrote, "If a man pinches my behind—or says something I don't like—I save his dignity and mine by simply telling him, quietly, that I do not like it. Funny how it doesn't happen again. Funny how we don't go to trial over it. Funny how we both go away feeling good about ourselves."[51]

Some letter writers saw sexual harassment as hostile to goals of sexual freedom and women's equality. A young African American woman from Michigan, who considered herself "a very confident, independent, sexually aware, hard-working, 90's woman," said she had "encountered sexual harassment at least ten to fifteen times a year." What she described as harassment, however, included welcome sexual overtures. As she said, "I do not always find it frustrating, sometimes I am very well complimented by it. If I do not approve of the person I simply stop him in his tracks." She did not believe in reporting these incidents; rather, she believed they "should be handled carefully with tact, by the individual who is being so called 'harassed.'" A seventy-three-year-old woman from California believed that "the whole subject is ridiculously exaggerated. The hypocrisy," as she saw it, was "that the very women doing all the complaining are those hard-core feminists who, unlike the rest of us, simply do not understand relationships between men and women. For all their bravado about being able to compete with men in the workplace, they have not yet learned how to handle themselves when a male co-worker 'gets out of line.'"[52]

Brown's vocal opinion on sexual harassment was one of the controversies that contributed to Hearst Corporation's efforts to force her out as editor of *Cosmopolitan*, and she stepped down in 1997 after thirty-two years at the helm. Her attitude toward sex in the office, however, has lived on. The surprise, here, is that Brown initially presented her giggling, wriggling career strategy as necessary for that specific moment. In the 1960s men occupied virtually all important positions, and Brown saw the power that accrued to sexually attractive women as a way of leveling the playing field. But if women could use sexuality to level the playing field in an unequal world, where would it figure in a society changed by the women's movement, one that mostly acknowledged women's business capabilities?[53]

At least some young women today see playing the "attractiveness card" as a strategic career move in a highly competitive business world. In 2001 the *Wall Street Journal* reported on young women who, in contrast to their mothers' generation, refused to deny their sexuality at work and were "less inhibited about using the personal tools at their disposal to get ahead professionally." As one woman explained, she and her friends had "come to peace with the idea" of getting "your foot in the door . . . because

you're pleasant to look at. . . . We all sort of leverage what we've got."
While some successful men had no problem with women's flirting,
others wanted to "call it out for what it is—psychological manipulation."
As one said, "Men's sex drive is their biggest source of vulnerability." For
a man to be around young attractive women, "It's like being an alcoholic
and seeing drinks all around him." It also, some men feared, made them
vulnerable to sexual harassment charges if they misread a woman's artifi-
cial flirtation and acted on it.[54]

Readers responded harshly to this article. Some were angry about the
double standard these women's behavior created and how it complicated
the issue of sexual harassment. An "average"-looking woman pointed out
the logical conclusion that could be reached: "If it's now OK for women to
use their feminine assets at work, is it OK too for men to show their
'innately masculine' side, such as sending tasteless jokes in the interoffice email, pinning up centerfold calendars, pinching women's derrieres,
and so on?" A Virginia man made the same point, "If I can't have 'elevator
eyes' without risking a sexual harassment complaint, then the professional ladies in my life shan't be allowed to flaunt their visual feminine
lures, either."[55]

Popular culture also portrayed at least some professional women as
willing to use their sexual desirability as a way to gain an advantage over
men. One of the first episodes of *Sex and the City* tackled the topic in a
conversation between Samantha, the sexually adventurous PR exec, and
Miranda, the relatively straitlaced attorney. When Samantha declared,
"Women have the right to use every means at their disposal to achieve
power," Miranda agreed, although she drew the line at sleeping one's way
to the top, which drew Samantha's ire. "Not if that's what it takes to
compete," she shot back. In 2004 Donald Trump's new TV series *The
Apprentice* addressed the issue. Only two women, Katrina and Amy, made
it to the final six players, and they found themselves on the same team in
a challenge at Trump's casino. After Katrina flirted with a vendor to secure
a better deal, Amy criticized this approach: "I think that Katrina has a
tendency to use sexuality as her prime negotiating tactic. When it wasn't
working for her at securing our deal, her strategy was just flirt a little
more. . . . You know what, turn off the sexual bullshit and let's talk business." Yet it turned out that even Amy, a player known for her professional know-how, was not averse to using such tactics in a pinch. As the

two women faced Trump in the Boardroom, their fate in his hands, he asked, "Do you believe in using womanly charm?" "Most definitely," Katrina replied, and Amy concurred. When Trump asked them whether such an approach was "unfair to men," Amy responded no, arguing that "every man . . . uses their charm in business."[56]

The issue of women's sexual power over men in the workplace—sometimes referred to as "sexual enticement"—has on occasion been presented as a corollary to "sexual harassment" that also needs to be stopped. A female blogger in Seattle, for example, saw no difference between a woman who tried to close a deal by subtly hinting to the client, "If you give me what I want, you may get laid," and a man telling his subordinate, "If you do it with me, you may get a promotion." Although a client could seemingly say "no" more easily than a subordinate, the blogger emphasized that both situations create an uneven playing field for competitors or coworkers. And according to one commentator, companies like to hire these "enticers" in sales positions, a strategy reminiscent of the 1950s "sex for sales" departments that the journalist Edward R. Murrow exposed.[57]

To compare a boss's influence over a subordinate to the power of an oblique promise of sex, one must believe that "men still filter their logic through their libido." In 2007 the HBO series *Entourage* devoted an episode to men's inability to think rationally in the presence of attractive women, prompting one of the characters to suggest that "hot looking women" should be barred from the workplace "because no man can say 'no' to them." This view is not limited to sitcoms or conventional wisdom. For more than a decade, evolutionary psychologists have criticized sexual harassment laws for disregarding reproductive instincts that compel men to "see the world through 'sexual glasses'" and to pursue women even when it is unclear whether such pursuit would be welcome. Evolutionary psychologists do not deny the linkage between power and sex but argue that feminists have it backward; "rather than men using sex to obtain power . . . they use power to obtain sex." In this view, sexual misunderstandings in the workplace are nothing more than the understandable, if regrettable, result of differing reproductive strategies hard-wired into men's and women's brains; as such, a juridical resolution is inappropriate. Moreover, this evolutionary perspective can be used to lend credibility to arguments that a businesswoman's sexual "enticement" of a prospective client is different from a salesman and a potential buyer bonding over beers and box scores. Rather, "enticement" is analogous to quid pro quo harassment in that both involve an abuse of power. Women have used their attractiveness to close a deal with sexually vulnerable men; men have used their position of authority to extort sex from economically vulnerable employees.[58]

Critics of "hostile environment" claims of sexual harassment use evolutionary psychology to support their position. The men's studies author Warren Farrell points out that many Americans now meet their lovers or spouses at work. In his view, the sexually charged interactions that precipitate these unions put men—but not women—at risk of being charged with sexual harassment. A man, culturally expected to take the initiative in courtship, tells a racy joke to a woman to gauge whether she is interested and endangers his career if it turns out she isn't; women's "indirect" flirtation, however, carries no danger. Other situations, according to Farrell, are similarly unfair to men. A woman who dresses provocatively at work—to catch a man or close a deal—escapes censure, while a man who hangs a pinup on his cubicle wall violates the law.[59]

Concerns about women's "enticement" return us to debates first raised in the 1860s, when women entered government offices during the Civil War. The issue of "sexual favoritism" also was on workers' minds back then, and worry about the unfair advantages of the boss's pet remained salient enough in 1980 that the EEOC included it as a subset of sexual harassment in its guidelines. In 2009 the issue of favoritism hit the news when late-night television host David Letterman admitted on the air, "I have had sex with women who work for me on this show," a revelation prompted by a blackmail attempt by the ex-boyfriend of one of the women. None of the women alleged that the relationship was anything but consensual, but as Letterman himself admitted, his behavior was "creepy." And given the power differential between the host and his subordinates, the issue of sexual harassment arose: could these women really have rejected him without losing their jobs? Yet the issue of favoritism got the most attention. Had the other women on his staff who had not caught his eye or their male coworkers suffered while Letterman's paramours prospered? And since the affairs seemed to have been common knowledge, did female employees get the message that the way to advance was via his bed?[60]

Nell Scovell, one of the few women ever to write for Letterman's show, provided fodder for these suppositions when she wrote a piece for *Vanity Fair* saying as much. "Without naming names or digging up decades-old dirt," Scovell addressed the "pertinent questions" based on her short stint on the show. "Did Dave hit on me? No. Did he pay me enough extra attention that it was noted by another writer? Yes. Was I aware of rumors that Dave was having sexual relations with female staffers? Yes. Did these female staffers have access to information and wield power disproportionate to their job titles? Yes. Did that create a hostile work environment? Yes. Did I believe these female staffers were benefiting professionally from their personal relationships? Yes. Did that me make me feel demeaned? Completely. Did I say anything at the time? Sadly, no."[61]

Scovell described a workplace overflowing with sexual intrigue and lacking a system of merit, but would the favoritism she identified violate Title VII? Ever since the EEOC issued its guidelines, the legal profession has debated whether and under what circumstances this phenomenon constitutes legally prohibited harassment. Early court decisions on the "paramour" question expressed divergent, mostly skeptical, views, and in 1990, the EEOC issued a statement establishing that favoritism based on the granting of sexual favors (regardless of whether those favors were given willingly or coerced) can create a hostile environment for male and female workers if it is "widespread" enough that a "message is implicitly conveyed that the managers view women as 'sexual playthings,'" thereby creating a demeaning atmosphere for women. An isolated instance of a supervisor involved in a consensual relationship favoring his or her lover, however, is not illegal. Such a situation is no different from a supervisor favoring a relative or friend, and though it may be unfair, it is not discrimination because both men and women are disadvantaged for reasons other than their gender.[62]

As of early 2011 the U.S. Supreme Court had yet to rule on a favoritism case, and it is uncertain whether the Court would uphold the EEOC's interpretation. In recent years, however, legal scholars have begun to question the EEOC's policy, especially the stipulation that the preferential treatment must be "widespread." Some courts have interpreted the requirement to mean that more than one supervisor must be engaging in sexual favoritism, a scenario that would leave an individual in

Scovell's situation with no legal options. But legal theorists have used studies on workplace romances (such as those discussed in the beginning of this chapter) to show that in some situations an isolated consensual affair between a supervisor and a subordinate can destroy all sense of fairness in a workplace and lead a reasonable woman to think a romance with her boss is the only way to advance. According to others, the "victims" of favoritism are hurt every bit as much as a victim of sexual harassment. As this brief discussion makes clear, the historical linkages between sexual coercion, sexual favoritism, and sexual enticement continue to this day. Sexual harassment law has in effect compartmentalized them as three distinct problems, yet in popular discourse the connections are still strong.[63]

Concerns about litigation over sexual harassment and sexual favoritism have led some companies to develop policies regarding consensual relationships in order to limit their liability. However, approximately 70 percent of American businesses still are without such a document, even as study after study has shown that approximately half of all workers have engaged in an office romance and that these liaisons can hurt morale. Forbidding workplace relationships has been likened to trying to "outlaw the weather," and the vast majority of companies now seem to turn a blind eye to consensual relations that do not involve a mixing of "passion and performance reviews"—that is, romances between supervisors and subordinates. Some companies forbid those relationships or require participants to sign a "love contract" to ward off later claims of sexual

In 1999, twenty years after *Cathy* raised awareness about the problem of sexual harassment, the cartoon proclaimed that policies to stop it had a chilling effect on consensual workplace romances. CATHY © Cathy Guisewite. Reprinted with permission of UNIVERSAL UCLICK. All rights reserved.

harassment and to ensure that management can preempt favoritism. While it is generally impossible for an employer to regulate employees' legal "off duty" conduct, policies that address a "conflict of interest"— such as when a supervisor and subordinate are romantically involved— are legal.[64]

The blind-eye policy includes extramarital affairs, and the issue of adulterous office romances has continued to garner attention. In the few states that still have "heart balm" torts, a spurned spouse can sue his or her partner's lover for alienation of affection; in 1997, for example, a North Carolina jury handed down a million-dollar award to a wife whose husband had left her for his secretary. Aggrieved wives and husbands also have continued to try to draw employers into their marital spats. In cases in which the "home wrecker" was a mate's work colleague, jilted spouses have sued the company for "negligent supervision," although as of June 2010, the courts had not recognized this action as applying to extramarital office romances.[65]

With almost 70 percent of married women with children under the age of eighteen working outside the home, the primary focus of discussions about infidelity is no longer on the vulnerable stay-at-home wife but on how workplace friendship can slowly slip into a full-blown love affair. In 2003 the marriage counselor Shirley Glass described the workplace as the "new danger zone" for marriages; of her patients who had been unfaithful, 46 percent of the women and 62 percent of the men had met their lover at work. The vast majority had not been deliberately seeking thrills but had unwittingly developed intimate feelings for coworkers whom they respected and trusted. It was women's infidelity, however, that was most eye-catching, and Glass and others directly tied the rising rate of such affairs to women's enhanced position in the labor force—an unintended outcome of married women's employment that Faith Baldwin had predicted in her Depression-era fiction.[66]

This chapter began with Lori Redfearn's 1979 request for a book on how to create a nonsexist business environment. She needed this information, she stated, because the principle of gender equality at work was still new. Almost twenty years before, Helen Gurley Brown had made a similarly temporal remark: most men still opposed women's rise up the ladder, but a strategic application of feminine charm could help a girl skirt their objections until things changed. But the passage of time has not relegated these issues to the past. As I have shown in this chapter, some employers still evaluate their employees according to their attractiveness or play favorites, and some employees still use their sex appeal for their own ends. The use of gender-neutral terms here is not accidental. Time has changed some things: women are now in positions of power; men, too, capitalize on their good looks; and heterosexuality is no longer the only *acknowledged* form of desire. That said, the continuation of gender stereotypes, such as the scheming or vindictive seductress, and of gender ideals that link masculinity to sexual prowess and femininity to being desirable, has ensured that the office's sexual culture remains, in many ways, the same. It is no surprise, then, that management still has not figured out how to handle sex and romance in the office.[67]

Conclusion

SEX AND THE OFFICE has changed since the last decades of the nineteenth century. Most notably, women who find themselves at the receiving end of an either-or proposition or in an environment too hostile to endure now have options. They do not have to pack up their things and go. Nevertheless, Americans' attitudes toward workplace sexuality have remained startlingly consistent from one generation to the next. The primary question Americans asked in the late nineteenth century is the one they still debate today: Who really needs protection from the predatory intentions of the opposite sex—women or men? Put differently, who really has the power: the woman who arouses desire or the man who wields authority? Other questions are also asked, but a close reading of coverage of the most (in)famous sexual harassment case—President Clinton, Monica Lewinsky, and was it harassment or something else?— exposes the persistence of the same old stereotypes and narratives.

The scandal began in May 1994, when Paula Jones filed a sexual harassment suit based on an incident that occurred in 1991, while Clinton was governor of Arkansas. Jones, a state clerk, alleged that Clinton had summoned her to his hotel room, where he dropped his pants and asked her to "kiss it." When she refused, he responded, "Well, I don't want to make you do anything you don't want to do," and she left. Jones's lawsuit led to more serious problems for the president when the judge allowed her attorneys to question Clinton about "sexual relations" with other government employees and to subpoena those they suspected of having been intimate with him. In January 1998 Monica Lewinsky, a former White House intern, filed an affidavit and the president gave a deposition; both denied any sexual involvement. When the press picked up the story a few days later, Clinton again denied having "sex with that woman." In March, as the Clinton-Lewinsky saga continued, another controversy erupted when Kathleen Willey, a former White House volunteer, went on 60 *Minutes* and accused Clinton of more workplace womanizing. During a private meeting in the Oval Office, she alleged, Clinton had kissed her, fondled her breast, and then placed her hand on his erect penis. Clinton denied this accusation. Jones ultimately settled her sexual harassment case out of court in November 1998. She received $850,000, and Clinton admitted no wrongdoing. Yet even as Jones's case was winding down, the president's troubles were ratcheting up. The independent prosecutor Kenneth Starr, who was investigating the Clintons' financial transactions, had determined in January to look into the president's relationship with Lewinsky. In August, Clinton confessed to a sexual relationship with Lewinsky, and in December the House of Representatives voted to impeach him for perjury and obstruction of justice. This process came to an end in February 1999, when the vote on each count in the U.S. Senate fell far short of the two-thirds majority required to remove the president from office.[1]

Clinton's troubles were more political than sexual, and as his supporters and detractors made their cases, their rhetoric spoke as much to cultural divisions between conservatives and liberals—especially feminists—as it did to the specifics of the president's involvement with Jones, Willey, and Lewinsky. Commentators often made their political points through the classic narrative regarding workingwomen and sexuality: were these women victims or vamps? Discussions of Lewinsky especially focused on this question, suggesting that many Americans still understood female sexuality in a bifurcated way—or at least that the press framed it that way. A Fox News poll conducted soon after the story broke asked whether the former intern, who was twenty-one at the time the events took place, was "an average girl taken advantage of" or "a young tramp looking for thrills." In response, 21 percent deemed her a victim, 54 percent a vamp. Meanwhile, a congresswoman anonymously told a reporter that she and other feminists were sticking by Clinton: we are "not falling on our swords for these types of women. We do not see Monica as some little naïf." Here was the gold digger as White House intern, complete with class-based allusions. Clinton supporters had dismissed Jones as "trailer trash," while comments about Lewinsky's hair, makeup, and fashion sense implied the same.[2]

As more details emerged about Lewinsky's previous relationships, even more Americans described her as an opportunist. Polls always showed that far more Americans believed she had gone after the president than that he had taken advantage of his position—even after he admitted to the affair—and the response reflected the most recent assessment of what a "modern" girl should know. As early as the 1930s office advice givers had retooled their guidance on how to interact with male employers and coworkers to take into account the relatively relaxed sexual atmosphere of the post–World War I era. Sexual standards had changed again by the early 1970s, especially for unmarried women. In this context, the majority of Americans assumed that Lewinsky knew what she was doing and was a modern young woman who understood men's desires. "I have had a lot of women tell me, 'Well, she is a kid,'" said a forty-nine-year-old woman from Massachusetts. "Well, I was married at 21, and I knew right from wrong. . . . No one can tell me that Monica Lewinsky didn't know what she was getting into."[3]

But did she? If she didn't, she would not have been the first young woman to flounder when she became sexually involved with an older, successful man, as we saw with the Jewish and Italian girls who worked in New York City in the 1930s discussed in Chapter 3, and this was the position her few sympathizers took. The columnist Richard Cohen described her as "possibly immature . . . needy," a woman who seemed to "lack cunning, basic survival instincts, not to mention wisdom." Any man could spot a "Monica" a mile away and knew she could be "manipulated, used, exploited." If such women "were fish, you would throw them back." "She's emotional, young, naïve," a forty-year-old mother argued. "Yes, she's aggressive and manipulative. But . . . I don't blame her at all. He was responsible for saying no." An older woman saw matters similarly: "I think she is a wide-eyed and impressionable woman," and "many young women could fall prey to Clinton, or other men with extraordinary clout."[4]

A female columnist ridiculed those who felt sorry for Lewinsky in language not so different from that of reformers seeking to abolish heart balm torts in the 1930s: "Just how old does a female have to be before she's acknowledged as an adult, rather than coddled with paternalistic excuses?" The columnist saw the affair as a natural—and fair—exchange: Lewinsky offered Clinton the "eternal allure of youth" that made men feel like they can "go out and kill animals or build nations," while he offered her "the ultimate aphrodisiac of unlimited power." This comment, while acknowledging female sexuality, nevertheless cast women's and men's sexual motivations in completely different terms. Women used sex to get something they wanted, while men *needed* sexual conquest as the essential fuel of manhood. This cultural belief did not necessarily excuse Clinton's adulterous transgression, but it did make it understandable—as it had countless times in the past for other men. These attitudes about young women's sexual aggressiveness and men's sexual essence might explain one poll's finding that 58 percent of Americans said that their view of Clinton's fitness for office would not be changed even if evidence surfaced that he had been sexually intimate with other young women while president.[5]

The comments of the columnist and others raised the venerable debate over women's and men's relative power—women's sexual influence versus men's social, economic, and political authority—a debate that historically has been tied to concepts of consent. Attitudes about women's ability to consent to sexual relations have changed dramatically as attitudes about female virtue and autonomy have changed. For example, female reformers in the nineteenth century operating under the idea of "passionlessness" believed that it was impossible for a chaste single woman to say "yes" and passed criminal seduction laws to protect them. By the twentieth century, however, changes in women's sexual behavior and fears regarding the sexual machinations of, especially, working-class women made many Americans think torts like the breach of promise to marry would be used as often to hurt men as to protect women. Around the same time, psychological theories of the unconscious and of personality disorders made it difficult for many to believe that a woman had truly said "no" in cases of rape or sexual assault. Feminists entered into this discussion in the early 1970s, when they argued that "no means no" and put forth explanations of rape and sexual harassment that redefined them as manifestations of men's power over women, not expressions of men's desires.

In March 1998 the feminist Gloria Steinem wrote an op-ed piece for the *New York Times* in which she supported Clinton because he had held to the principle that "no means no" and "yes means yes." If the accusations proved to be true, Clinton might "be a candidate for sex addiction therapy," but in Steinem's view he had done nothing to disqualify him from office. She distinguished Clinton's interactions with Jones and Willey from Thomas's with Hill and Packwood's with his legion by noting that Clinton accepted their "no" as an answer and never again pestered them with "clumsy" passes. Moreover, Jones and Willey did not directly work with Clinton and would not have to face him every day. With regard to Lewinsky, although the "power imbalance between them increased the index of suspicion," there was no evidence to suggest that she said anything but "yes." "Welcome sexual behavior," Steinem concluded, "is about as relevant to sexual harassment as borrowing a car is to stealing one." Most feminists and most Americans, she believed, "become concerned about sexual behavior when someone's will has been violated; that is, when 'no' hasn't been accepted as an answer."[6]

The published response to Steinem's piece was overwhelmingly critical, with many readers distressed by the way she glided over the issue of Clinton's—and more generally, men's—power. The *Times* published its own response, in which the newspaper's editorial board called Steinem's piece a "philosophical sell out." In legal terms Steinem might have been correct, but according to the editorial, her support of Clinton threatened to undo positive social changes. The *Times* doubted Steinem "meant to advocate a new kind of 'no harm, no foul' mentality in the workplace, but that is the dangerous implication of her analysis." A reader echoed this view: "There is something foul about an employer who can call in his employees one by one, make an advance and take his chances. Serial groping may not be harassment, but it is a workplace burden that no employee should have to put up with even once."[7]

Although many commentators assumed that feminists thought with one mind, the scholar Gwendolyn Mink penned an op-ed rebutting Steinem: "Feminism is supposed to be about taking seriously what women say about themselves. But here is a leading feminist rewriting another woman's experience—to protect a man." For Mink, power, not consent, was the real issue: "When power differences between the two people involved are extreme, consent counts for little. . . . Many women feel pressured to meet the sexual requests of their bosses—technically give their 'consent'—even though they may not welcome the requests or liaisons, may not solicit them and may also be offended by them." If even some feminists could not see the difference between welcomeness and consent, women were surely in trouble. "There would be precious little protection for women," Mink continued, "if all male bosses were entitled to one free hit."[8]

Mink focused on the distinction the Supreme Court had made in the *Meritor* decision, but Steinem also had moved far away from feminists' initial perspectives on sexual harassment. Even if Clinton had not run afoul of the law, he had, if Jones's and Willey's accusations were true, treated women whom he encountered in the workplace as sex objects first and workers second. His behavior seemed reminiscent of the old legal adage, there's "no harm in asking." In this regard, Steinem's essay could be read as reestablishing traditional gender roles of men pushing and women establishing boundaries. Certainly that was the way Georgette Mosbacher, a prominent Republican fund-raiser, saw it: "I thought that feminism was about making men responsible for their behavior. Now it becomes clear that, once again, it's the woman's responsibility to enforce morality. . . . The louts of the world must be breathing a sign of relief."[9]

The outrage over Steinem's assertion that "yes means yes" illustrates how polarized understandings of female sexuality still were at the end of the twentieth century and how such polarization made it difficult, if not impossible, to protect women from real sexual dangers and still grant them genuine autonomy, including the ability to make decisions that ultimately might not be in their best interest. The response to the Clinton-Lewinsky mess suggests that many Americans had a difficult time seeing sexual issues in colors other than black and white. Those who saw Lewinsky as a victim criticized Steinem for not interrogating the notion of consent. As a male psychoanalyst proclaimed, " 'Consenting' emotionally vulnerable 21-year-old interns" is an "oxymoronic concept." When Clinton admitted the affair a few months later, the journalist Andrew Sullivan made a similar argument. "What greater power differential could there be than that between a 22-year-old and the president of the United States, who also happened to be her employer," he wondered. "If that isn't an inherently exploitative relationship, then exploitative relationships simply don't exist."[10]

These comments painted Lewinsky—and other young or vulnerable women—as victims. Yet as we have seen, women in the past have often resisted this label and offers of protection, as the rector of Manhattan's St. Paul's Church found out in 1907, when he proposed opening a lunchroom to "save" stenographers from businessmen with evil designs. In an act of self-determination, office women responded that they had enough business sense and self-respect to defend their own honor. In Lewinsky's case, twenty-something "Third Wave" feminists argued for accepting her on her own terms, and she never described herself as a victim or suggested that Clinton's power had compelled her to do anything that she had not already wanted to do. Claiming Lewinsky as one of their own, Jennifer Baumgardner and Amelia Richards rejected paternalism for young women, whether from conservatives or feminists. "We want the right to be sexually active without the presumption that we were used or duped. We want the right to determine our own choices based on our own morality." For some women, male power was seductive, not coercive, and whatever feminists thought of that, if they held up Lewinsky "as a violated naïf," it meant that they did not believe "an adult woman can take responsibility for her own desires and actions." According to Baumgardner and Richards, then, feminists should support Lewinsky as a "young woman with a libido of her own." In the early twentieth century some young women asserted their right to be in public as workers and their ability to handle any problems that arose from that choice. By the end of the century, young women were accepted in the workforce, and their emphasis shifted to the issue of their sexual autonomy in the public world.[11]

In Lewinsky's case, talk of powerful men's appeal focused specifically on women's erotic desires, but this sentiment was not very far removed from the well-worn fantasy of marrying the boss, a staple of romance novels to this day. On first glance, series such as Harlequin's "At the Boss's Bidding" and Silhouette's "Loving the Boss" seem stuck in a time warp with their couplings between secretary (sometimes still a virgin in her twenties) and worldly boss. But in addition to showing powerful men's continued ability to inspire women's dreams and inflame their passions, these novels also can be read as reflecting the reality of both harassment and romance in the workplace. One popular author, who identifies as a feminist and who personally avoids boss-subordinate story lines because of the power differential, nevertheless suggests that the boss-as-hero in these novels reflects an ideal of manliness as responsible and respectful. The boss would never "come on" to a woman if she worked for him and "would worry if he came near the line." Far from living in the past, then, boss-secretary novels tackle real-life problems head on. The formulaic "misunderstanding" that must be resolved before the couple can be together reflects the complications that actually do develop when love and sex appear at work, and the hero's qualities are those a woman would desire in her mate or employer. However, in getting around the issue of harassment by having the woman pursue her boss, authors breathe life into the stereotype that women, not men, bring the personal and emotional into the office, perpetuating the view that female workers are women first, employees second.[12]

When we add the sexual desirability of powerful men to women's sexual power (whether real or imagined) over men, and the ability of those in power (including women, as the first popular film on sexual harassment, *Disclosure*, made sure all Americans knew) to extort sex, to the potential of a charge of sexual misconduct to ruin a boss or a coworker's life, we see that sex and power are intertwined in countless ways in the workplace. Despite the bureaucratic ideal of keeping the "irrational" feelings and behaviors associated with "private" life out of the rational "public" world, it is impossible, as this study has shown, to establish or enforce this boundary. And the ways it is regularly transgressed are endless. Comments about the Clintons' marriage during the Lewinsky imbroglio remind us that spouses and Americans more generally have long worried about the effects of workplace relationships on marriages. Sociologists have studied the ways in which men today use activities like "girl watching" at work to pump up their manhood in the eyes of other men—a practice that government supervisors had mastered by the late nineteenth century. The obligatory silver-framed photo of an attractive spouse and angelic children on an executive's desk is further evidence of the myriad ways in which sexuality permeates the office, in this case possibly discouraging gay or lesbian workers from revealing their sexual orientation in order to fit in. Some of the most visible manifestations of desire—consensual affairs—can also lead to trouble as coworkers worry about outright favoritism or even the subtle advantages of pillow talk. The boundary is blurred, too, when a woman reading an office romance or a man looking at one of the innumerable "sexy secretary" porn sites brings those ways of thinking about relationships to work. Not to be left out of the fun, college students can gain relevant job experience at "CEOs and Office Ho's" or "Secs and Execs" theme parties. (This might be their only chance at a wild office party: worries about sexual harassment and liability if a partygoer drives home drunk have led many businesses to abandon evening holiday parties with alcohol.) All of which is to say that sexuality, most particularly heterosexuality, permeates the office in reality and representation and always has.[13]

The movement against sexual harassment changed some aspects of this sexualized office and unintentionally deepened others. Most notably, it has been immensely effective in changing attitudes toward and reducing the actual number of quid pro quo situations. Yet "sexual harassment" has not in any way eliminated the victim-vamp stereotype or altered conceptions of female sexuality that make sexual expression in the workplace problematic for women; in fact, press coverage of prominent cases and representations of sexual harassment in popular media have, if anything, perpetuated notions of women as excessively prim or as vindictive and wildly avaricious. As a well-known strand of the cultural narrative goes, a woman now has the power to destroy a man's career via a charge of sexual harassment in addition to being able to use her sexual power to illegitimately advance. Here, then, is another way in which women are viewed as women first, workers, second.[14]

And in the past decade or so, a few feminists and legal scholars have made the argument that sexual harassment law has, if unintentionally, contributed to gender inequality. The feminist theorist Jane Gallop, for example, is critical of what she believes to be an antisex element in the movement that denies the range of women's desires, especially situations in which women occupy a subordinate position. She believes, too, that "moralistic right-wing forces" have co-opted the issue under the guise of protecting women in order to advance their understanding of women's appropriate place (in public and in sexual relationships). Sexual harassment jurisprudence has also been critiqued. According to the legal scholar Vicki Schultz, the courts' focus on sexual conduct has led management to "sanitize" the workplace, scrubbing away all signs of sexuality regardless of whether or not they hurt women's access to better jobs or equivalent opportunities. In addition, she believes that sexual harassment has taken attention away from other, more pressing types of sex discrimination, such as occupational segregation by gender. Gender harassment—that is, harassment aimed at enforcing norms of femininity and masculinity, such as when a supervisor taunts a low-performing salesman by asking whether he uses tampons—has also garnered attention in recent years, though courts have divided over whether it violates Title VII. The fact that Title VII does not outlaw discrimination based on sexual orientation further complicates the situation, and legal scholars have criticized this limitation. Legally and culturally, things are in flux. Even Catherine MacKinnon, who hopes that sexual harassment law will prove to be a foundational step in the development of an "equality-based sexual morality," recently remarked that it is unclear where the law will stand or what Americans will think about sexual harassment in twenty-five years.[15]

If history is anything to go on, it is quite possible that the issue will still be unsettled. As this study has shown, in terms of sexuality in the white-collar office, the way many Americans think about sex, gender, and power is surprisingly similar to what it was well over a century ago, despite vast changes in society and in the law. The naming of sexual harassment and the subsequent development of legal prohibitions altered the way Americans talked about unwelcome sex in the office and responded to it. Nevertheless, the continued controversy over sexual harassment, the eye rolling or head shaking that often arises when the subject is mentioned, reflects the fact that attitudes about gender, sexuality, and power at work remain, on a fundamental level, the same. Popular understandings of women as the emotional, even vindictive, sex and female sexuality as treacherous (often combined with racial and class-based myths), continue to affect how women in the workplace are treated and viewed by others. Even the issue of what to wear—how to be attractive and professional but not too sexy or too manly—still proves tricky for many women. In other words, a woman is rarely just a worker; she is a *woman* worker whose gender role often supercedes her identity and function as a worker. Meanwhile, work remains a core component of masculine accomplishment, an ideal compatible with, even enhanced by, sexual exploits. These continuities with the past make it possible for some Americans to see no difference between men's and women's use of sex and power; they tolerate or accept such actions as expressions of men's and women's natures. Until these attitudes toward gender, sex, and power change, sex in the office—whether wanted or unwelcome—will continue to be divisive, contested in some cases, accepted in others, and often frustrating the goal of gender equality.[16]

NOTES

INTRODUCTION

For more expansive notes, see http://history.sewanee.edu/facstaff/berebitsky/.

1. I use the term "white collar" to refer to women who worked in offices in a wide variety of clerical positions, from low-level clerks to private secretaries. Generic terms such as "women office workers" will be used when discussing situations that applied to these groups as a whole. When I use such specific terms as "stenographer," I am referring to the unique characteristics of that position. Though the term "white collar" refers to a wide range of occupations, this study focuses exclusively on the business, legal, or government office and the men and women who worked there.

2. "Typewriter's Memories," *Boston Daily Globe* (July 19, 1891), 23; Angel Kwolek-Folland, *Engendering Business: Men and Women in the Corporate Office, 1870–1930* (Baltimore: Johns Hopkins University Press, 1994), 4.

3. U.S. Department of Commerce, *Statistical Abstract of the United States, 1992,* 392–94. For more on Hill-Thomas, see Chapter 8.

4. Laura Evans, "Sexual Harassment: Women's Hidden Occupational Hazard," in Jane Roberts Chapman, ed., *The Victimization of Women* (Beverly Hills: Sage, 1978), 210; Augustus B. Cochran III, *Sexual Harassment and the Law: The Mechelle Vinson Case* (Lawrence: University Press of Kansas, 2004), 54, 173–77; Kimberlé Crenshaw, "Whose Story Is It, Anyway? Feminist and Antiracist Appropriations of Anita Hill," in Toni Morrison, ed., *Race-ing Justice, En-gendering Power* (New York: Pantheon, 1992), 408–12; Elizabeth Kolbert, "The Thomas Nomination: Sexual Harassment at Work Is Pervasive, Survey Suggests," *New York Times* (October 11, 1991).

Hill never made a legal claim of sexual harassment against Thomas. When Thomas's alleged behaviors took place, lower courts had not yet determined that a "hostile environment" violated Title VII. Therefore, had Hill made a claim of sexual harassment, it is unclear whether the courts would have seen it as such (Catharine A. MacKinnon, Afterword to Catharine A. MacKinnon and Reva B. Siegel, *Directions in Sexual Harassment Law* (New Haven: Yale University Press, 2004), 687–88).

5. "Typewriter's Memories"; Kolbert, "The Thomas Nomination." On the importance of historicizing sexuality and of language in shaping sexual experience, see Robert A. Nye, ed., Introduction to *Sexuality* (New York: Oxford University Press, 1999), 3–15. On the belief women would lie in rape cases, see Sharon Block, *Rape and Sexual Power in Early America* (Chapel Hill: University of North Carolina Press, 2006), 183–86.

6. Mary Bularzik, "Sexual Harassment at the Workplace: Historical Notes," *Radical America* 12 (1978), rpt. in James Green, ed., *Workers' Struggles, Past and Present: A "Radical America" Reader* (Philadelphia: Temple University Press, 1983), 117–36.

Recent work focusing on the history of sexual harassment (see http://history.sewanee.edu/facstaff/berebitsky/for a fuller discussion) includes Daniel E. Bender, " 'Too Much of Distasteful Masculinity': Historicizing Sexual Harassment in the Garment Sweatshop and Factory," *Journal of Women's History* 15 (2004): 91–116; Steve Meyer, "Workplace Predators: Sexuality and Harassment on the U.S. Automotive Shop Floor, 1930–1960," *Labor* 1 (2004): 77–93; Kimberly Jensen, "A Base Hospital Is Not a Coney Island Dance Hall," *Frontiers* 26 (2005): 206–35. On servants, see Sara McLean, "Confided to His Care or Protection: The Late Nineteenth-Century Crime of Workplace Sexual Harassment," *Columbia Journal of Gender and Law* 9 (1999): 47–50, and Faye E. Dudden, *Serving Women: Household Service in Nineteenth-Century America* (Middletown, CT: Wesleyan University Press, 1983), 213–19. On the different legal options enslaved women and white servants had, see Block, *Rape and Sexual Power*, chapter 2. On the rape of enslaved women, see Deborah Gray White, *Ar'n't I a Woman? Female Slaves in the Plantation South* (New York: Norton, 1985), 79–80; Elizabeth Fox-Genovese, *Within the Plantation Household* (Chapel Hill: University of North Carolina Press, 1988), 325–26; Darlene Clark Hine, *Hine Sight: Black Women and the Reconstruction of American History* (Brooklyn, NY: Carlson, 1994), 27–48.

Other scholarship includes Kerry Segrave, *The Sexual Harassment of Women in the Workplace, 1600–1993* (Jefferson, NC: McFarland, 1994); Christine Stansell, *City of Women: Sex and Class in New York, 1789–1860* (Urbana: University of Illinois Press, 1987), 20–37; Patricia Bell-Scott, " 'To Keep My Self-Respect': Dean Lucy Diggs Slowe's 1927 Memorandum on the Sexual Harassment of Black Women," *NWSA Journal* 9 (1997): 70–76; Patricia Cline Cohen, "Ministerial Misdeeds: The Onderdonk Trial and Sexual Harassment in the 1840s," *Journal of Women's History* 7 (1995): 34–57; Dorothy Sue Cobble,

Dishing It Out: Waitresses and Their Unions in the Twentieth Century (Champaign: University of Illinois Press, 1991), 44, 131, 201; Clara Bingham and Laura Leedy Gansler, *Class Action: The Story of Lois Jenson and the Landmark Case That Changed Sexual Harassment Law* (New York: Doubleday, 2002).

7. Max Weber, *From Max Weber: Essays in Sociology*, trans. and ed. Hans Heinrich Gerth and Bryan S. Turner (New York: Oxford University Press, 1946), 216.

8. Rosabeth Moss Kanter, *Men and Women of the Corporation* (1977; New York: Basic, 1993), 346, n. 29. For a summary of theorists who argue sexuality and work are incompatible, see Jeff Hearn and Wendy Parkin, *"Sex" at "Work": The Power and Paradox of Organisation Sexuality*, rev. ed. (New York: St. Martin's, 1995), 7–15. On sociologists' interest in the topic, see Jeff Hearn and Wendy Parkin, *Gender, Sexuality, and Violence in Organizations* (London: Sage, 2001), 162, n. 2.

9. Historically, many Americans have accepted that, given men's nature, even consensual sex might contain an element of violence (see, for example, Block, *Rape and Sexual Power*, chapter 3). The belief that employers noticed only beautiful employees can be seen in some of the romantic fiction and films of the 1920s, in which the professionally competent but plain and old-fashioned stenographer transforms herself into an alluring beauty and lands her boss (see, for example, Aaron David, "The Golden Calf," *Liberty: A Weekly for Everybody* (December 25, 1926), 48–52; *His Secretary* (MGM, 1925); and *Beautiful but Dumb* (Tiffany-Stahl Productions, 1928). The view that men would not harass an unattractive woman might have real-world consequences: one study suggests that juries are less likely to believe "unattractive" plaintiffs in sexual harassment cases; Wilbur A. Castellow et al., "Effects of Physical Attractiveness of the Plaintiff and Defendant in Sexual Harassment Judgments," *Journal of Social Behavior and Personality* 5 (1990): 547–62. More recently, the legal scholar Deborah L. Rhode has described the economic costs of Americans' "beauty bias" and made a case for "appearance discrimination"; *The Beauty Bias: The Injustice of Appearance in Life and Law* (New York: Oxford University Press, 2010).

10. Rosemary Pringle, "Bureaucracy, Rationality and Sexuality: The Case of Secretaries," in Jeff Hearn, et al., eds., *The Sexuality of Organization* (London: Sage, 1989), 164. On the development of the sexual double standard and women's responsibility to control men, see Richard Godbeer, *Sexual Revolution in Early America* (Baltimore: Johns Hopkins University Press, 2002), chapter 8; Rodney Hessinger, *Seduced, Abandoned, and Reborn: Visions of Youth in Middle-Class America, 1780–1950* (Philadelphia: University of Pennsylvania Press, 2005), chapter 1; Clare A. Lyons, *Sex Among the Rabble: An Intimate History of Gender and Power in the Age of Revolution, Philadelphia, 1730–1830* (Chapel Hill: University of North Carolina Press, 2006), 3–5, part III.

On the biological and/or psychological explanations dominating discussion today, see Christine L. Williams, Patti Giuffre, and Kirsten Dellinger, "Sexuality in the Workplace: Organizational Control, Sexual Harassment, and the Pursuit of Pleasure," *Annual Review of Sociology* 25 (1999): 73–93; Margaret A. Crouch,

Thinking About Sexual Harassment: A Guide for the Perplexed (New York: Oxford University Press, 2001), 10–15.

11. For how I arrived at these figures and the sources I used, see http://history.sewanee.edu/facstaff/berebitsky/. Although a wide gulf exists between a male clerk and an executive, I have grouped these men together because they shared a workspace and were united by the cultural idea of the male career path; see Clark Davis, *Company Men: White-Collar Life and Corporate Cultures in Los Angeles,* 1892–1941 (Baltimore: Johns Hopkins University Press, 2000), 10; E. Anthony Rotundo, *American Manhood: Transformations in Masculinity from the Revolution to the Modern Era* (New York: Basic, 1993), 248–51; Oliver Zunz, *Making America Corporate,* 1870–1920 (Chicago: University of Chicago Press, 1990); C. Wright Mills, *White Collar: The American Middle Classes* (1951; New York: Oxford University Press, 2002), xv, ix.

12. Alba Edwards, U.S. Department of Commerce, *Population: Comparative Occupation Statistics for the U.S.,* 1870–1940 (Washington, DC: Government Printing Office, 1943), 122–29; U.S. Department of Labor, "'Older' Women as Office Workers," Bulletin of the Women's Bureau, no. 248 (Washington, DC, 1953), 46–47; Rosalyn Baxandall, Linda Gordon, and Susan Reverby, eds., *America's Working Women: A Documentary History* (New York: Vintage, 1976), appendix; Mary C. King, "Black Women's Breakthrough into Clerical Work: An Occupational Tipping Model," *Journal of Economic Issues* 27 (1993): 1100; Stuart H. Garfinkle, "Occupations of Women and Black Workers, 1962–1974," *Monthly Labor Review* 98 (1975): 28.

13. "Sexual Harassment Lands Companies in Court," *Business Week* (October 1, 1979), 120–21. On the involvement of working-class women and women of color, see Carrie N. Baker, "Race, Class, and Sexual Harassment in the 1970s," *Feminist Studies* 30 (Spring 2004): 7–27.

14. This argument relies on Benedict Anderson, *Imagined Communities* (New York: Verso, 1983), esp. 5–7, 22–36.

15. National Secretaries Association, *Secretaries on the Spot* (Kansas City, MO: National Secretaries Association [International], 1961), 108, 148, 221.

16. On silences and the construction of sexuality, see Eve Kosofsky Sedgwick, *Tendencies* (Durham: Duke University Press, 1993), 23–51. On silence in organizations, see Hearn and Parkin, *Gender, Sexuality, and Violence,* 3.

17. Constance Balides, "Scenarios of Exposure in the Practice of Everyday Life," in Annette Kuhn and Jackie Stacey, eds., *Screen Histories: A Screen Reader* (New York: Oxford University Press, 1998), 68; Pringle, "Bureaucracy, Rationality and Sexuality," 158; see, for example, "A Woman Lawyer's Chances," *New York Sun* (October 30, 1911), 5. Women office workers occasionally disputed the cinematic and fictional view; see, for example, "The Typewriter Is All Right," *Browne's Phonographic Monthly-Weekly* (August 4, 1890), 454–55; Sharon Hartman Strom, "'We're No Kitty Foyles': Organizing Office Workers for the Congress of International Organizations, 1937–50," in Ruth Milkman, ed. *Women, Work, and Protest* (Boston: Routledge, 1985), 213–14.

18. Carrie N. Baker, "Sex, Power, and Politics: The Origins of Sexual Harassment Policy in the U.S." (Ph.D. diss., Emory University, 2001), 182.

19. Frank Luther Mott, *American Journalism: A History,* 1690–1960, 3rd ed. (New York: Macmillan, 1962), 442, 491, 523, 578; Joshua Gamson, "Normal Sins: Sex Scandal Narratives as Institutional Morality Tales," in Paul Apostolidis and Juliet A. Williams, eds., *Public Affairs: Politics in the Age of Sex Scandals* (Durham: Duke University Press, 2004), 39–68.

20. The office was, of course, sexualized even before women arrived; Ava Baron, "Masculinity, the Embodied Male Worker, and the Historian's Gaze," *International Labor and Working-Class History* 69 (Spring 2006): 154. On heterosexuality and male bonding, see Eve Kosofsky Sedgwick, *Between Men: English Literature and Male Homosocial Desire* (New York: Columbia University Press, 1985), 1–3, 49–51.

21. Michael Roper, " 'Seduction and Succession': Circuits of Homosocial Desire in Management," in David L. Collinson and Jeff Hearn, *Men as Managers, Managers as Men* (Thousand Oaks, CA: Sage, 1996), 210–26, examines how concealed desire can affect management decisions. Scholars have begun to unearth the experience of gay and lesbian office workers. In Chicago in the 1920s and 1930s, for example, gay men sometimes found jobs as clerks and stenographers; David K. Johnson, "The Kids of Fairytown," in Brett Beemyn, ed., *Creating a Place for Ourselves* (New York: Routledge, 1997), 108–9. A study of gay executives in the early 1970s showed that management did not mind having homosexual workers as long as they kept their sexual orientation to themselves; Richard Zoglin, "The Homosexual Executive," in Martin P. Levine, ed., *Gay Men: The Sociology of Male Homosexuality* (New York: Harper and Row, 1979), 68–77.

22. According to surveys of more than twenty-four hundred stenographers and secretaries in 1924–25, women would occasionally alert their employment agency or a newcomer about an aggressive man; Sharon Hartman Strom, *Beyond the Typewriter: Gender, Class, and the Origins of Modern American Office Work,* 1900–1930 (Urbana: University of Illinois Press, 1992), 373. Around 1920 Susan Porter Benson found examples of department store saleswomen using their company's newsletter to warn men against harassing workers; *Counter Cultures: Saleswomen, Managers, and Customers in American Department Stores,* 1890–1940 (Urbana: University of Illinois Press, 1986), 266. I have found more evidence, however, of workplace sexuality creating rifts between (especially older and younger) women than opportunities for gender solidarity. According to Meyer, "Workplace Predators," during World War II, female factory workers often believed women who received unwanted sexual advances had "asked for it" (85).

23. This analysis is based on Michel Foucault, *The History of Sexuality,* 3 vols., trans. Robert Hurley (New York: Vintage, 1990), 1: 42–49.

24. Ibid., 1: 45; Herbert Marcuse, *One-Dimensional Man* (Boston: Beacon, 1964), 74–75. For a feminist critique of Marcuse's lack of attention to gender differences, see Catharine A. MacKinnon, *Sexual Harassment of Working Women* (New Haven: Yale University Press, 1979), 21.

25. As late as the 1970s there was a widespread assumption that office work was middle-class, despite the mechanization of many office jobs; Ileen DeVault, *Sons and Daughters of Labor* (Ithaca, NY: Cornell University Press, 1990), ix; Stuart M. Blumin, *The Emergence of the Middle Class: Social Experience in the American City, 1760–1900* (Cambridge: Cambridge University Press, 1989); Edwards, *Population*, 179–80. In emphasizing values and behaviors, I am following the lead of Zunz, *Making America Corporate*, chapter 5, and Kwolek-Folland, *Engendering Business*, 10–14.

26. Margery W. Davies, *Woman's Place Is at the Typewriter: Office Work and Office Workers, 1870–1930* (Philadelphia: Temple University Press, 1982), 130; Strom, *Beyond the Typewriter*, chapter 7, esp. 346–47, 385–87; Zunz, *Making America Corporate*, 126–27; Roslyn Feldberg, "'Union Fever': Organizing Among Clerical Workers, 1900–1930," in Green, *Workers' Struggles*, 155–59.

27. Jurgen Kocka, *White Collar Workers in America, 1890–1940* (London: Sage, 1980), 96; Roger H. Nelson, "A Handbook of Selected Case Studies Involving Human Relations Problems of Office Workers" (D.Ed., Columbia, 1958), 83, 86; Vance Packard, *The Status Seekers* (New York: David McKay, 1959), 117.

28. National Archives, Washington, DC, Records of the House Committee on the Civil Service Pertaining to the Investigation of Civilian Employment in the Federal Government, 1942–46, General Correspondence, Record Group 233, box 16, folder 4–8, August 3, 1944, and November 5, 1945.

29. George Edmund Haynes, *The Negro at Work in New York City* (1912; New York: Arno, 1968), 71–72; King, "Black Women's Breakthrough," 1097–1100, 1105; Garfinkle, "Occupations of Women and Black Workers," 25–34. On segregation in the early twentieth century, see Kwolek-Folland, *Engendering Business*, 4–8, 155, 160. On the 1940s and 1950s, see George Davis and Glegg Watson, *Black Life in Corporate America: Swimming in the Mainstream* (New York: Anchor, 1982), chapter 2.

30. Gail Bederman, *Manliness and Civilization: A Cultural History of Gender and Race in the United States, 1880–1917* (Chicago: University of Chicago Press, 1995), 46–52.

31. Davis and Watson, *Black Life in Corporate America*, 114–18.

32. Baker, "Race, Class and Sexual Harassment," 10–15, quotation on 15. On sexual stereotypes, see Patricia Hill Collins, *Black Feminist Thought* (New York: Routledge, 1990), 81–85 and chapter 6.

33. Block, *Rape and Sexual Power*, 4.

CHAPTER ONE. DANGERS, DESIRES, AND SELF-DETERMINATION

1. "Has Left His Wife," *Boston Daily Globe* (July 29, 1904), 1.

2. "Mrs. Berry Not Alarmed," *Boston Daily Globe* (July 29, 1904), 12; "Has Not Eloped," *Boston Daily Globe* (July 30, 1904), 7.

3. "Suicide by Shooting," *Boston Daily Globe* (June 10, 1905), 1; "Was Ella Berry," *Boston Daily Globe* (September 16, 1905), 4. See also, "Girl Shot Herself as Her

Employer Did," *New York Times* (September 16, 1905), 18; "Scandal Killed Girl," *Washington Post* (September 16, 1905), 3.

4. Kathy Peiss, *Cheap Amusements: Working Women and Leisure in Turn-of-the Century New York* (Philadelphia: Temple University Press, 1986), 53–55, 109–14; "The Girl Who Comes to the City," *Harper's Bazar* 42 (March 1908): 277–78; Charlotte Wharton Ayers, "The 'Help Wanted' Sharks and Their Prey," *New York Times* (August 15, 1909), 5, 9.

5. Female office workers' class composition varied according to the city, the job's skill level, and the type of industry; Angel Kwolek-Folland, *Engendering Business: Men and Women in the Corporate Office, 1870–1930* (Baltimore: Johns Hopkins University Press, 1994), 31–32; Carole Srole, *Transcribing Class and Gender: Masculinity and Femininity in Nineteenth-Century Courts and Offices* (Ann Arbor: University of Michigan Press, 2009), 62, 66, 132, 177–79.

6. Cora Beamish, "In Defence of 'The Pretty Typewriter,'" *Phonographic World* (July 1890), 364.

7. "Deserted His Sick Wife," *New York Times* (May, 28, 1893), 1; "Alex and Alice," *Illustrated Buffalo Express* (May 28, 1893), 13; "Very Scandalous," *Buffalo Courier* (May 28, 1893), 6. For similar stories, see "A Lawyer's Two Wives," *Chicago Daily Tribune* (November 29, 1886), 2; "Eloped with the Pretty Typewriter," *Chicago Daily Tribune* (November 16, 1889), 1; "Infatuated with His Typewriter," *Chicago Daily Tribune* (October 16, 1890), 6.

8. "Alex and Alice"; "Very Scandalous."

9. "That Fortier Case," *Illustrated Buffalo Express* (June 4, 1893), 11; "May Be Withdrawn," *Buffalo Courier* (June 3, 1893), 6; "Fortier in Again," *Buffalo Courier* (June 7, 1893), 6; "Fugitive Fortier," *Buffalo Courier* (July 11, 1893), 6; "A Paymaster Disappears," *New York Times* (July 11, 1893), 2.

10. "Alex and Alice"; E. Anthony Rotundo, *American Manhood: Transformations in Masculinity from the Revolution to the Modern Era* (New York: Basic, 1993), 55; Andreas Huyssen, "Mass Culture as Woman: Modernism's Other," in *After the Great Divide: Modernism, Mass Culture, Postmodernism* (Bloomington: Indiana University Press, 1986), 52–55.

11. Fessenden N. Chase, *Women Stenographers* (Portland, ME: Southworth, 1910), 12–13; Glenda Riley, *Divorce: An American Tradition* (Lincoln: University of Nebraska Press, 1997), 124. On Victorian sexuality, see Steven Seidman, "The Power of Desire and the Danger of Pleasure: Victorian Sexuality Reconsidered," *Journal of Social History* 24 (Fall 1990): 48–49, and Karen Lystra, *Searching the Heart: Women, Men, and Romantic Love in Nineteenth-Century America* (New York: Oxford University Press, 1992), esp. 58–60.

12. Ellen Rothman, *Hands and Hearts: A History of Courtship in America* (New York: Basic, 1984), 255, 259; Elaine Tyler May, *Great Expectations: Marriage and Divorce in Post-Victorian America* (Chicago: University of Chicago Press, 1980), 49–51, 61, 78, 107, 113, 139–40.

13. "Home Is Menaced by Office Woman," *Los Angeles Times* (October 20, 1908), 11; "Girls All Like the Candy Kid," *Chicago Daily Tribune* (October, 14, 1908), 3.

14. Chase, *Women Stenographers*, 12–13; "Girls Not 'Love Pirates,'" *Washington Post* (October 22, 1908), 4.

15. "Girls Not 'Love Pirates'"; "The 'Love Pirate,'" *Washington Post* (October 23, 1908), 6; "Says Typists Are Neat," *Washington Post* (October 26, 1908), 7. On clerical workers as a new model for wives, see Lisa M. Fine, *The Souls of the Skyscraper: Female Clerical Workers in Chicago, 1870–1930* (Philadelphia: Temple University Press, 1990), 63–65.

16. Fine, *Souls of the Skyscraper*, 68–70; "'I Think It Must Be Love!' Lawyer's Office Romance," *Atlanta Constitution* (May 22, 1910), B2. Some stories can be read as cynically linking beauty, age, sexuality, and wealth: "Good Typewriting Won a Worthy Husband," *Browne's Phonographic Weekly* (January 13, 1890), 25; "Marries His Stenographer," *Washington Post* (May 5, 1903), 5.

17. Helen Stoddard, "Review of Age of Consent Legislation in Texas," *Arena* 14 (November 1895): 410; "Got $15 a Week to Look Pretty," *Daily Oklahoman* (June 21, 1908), 23; Chase, *Women Stenographers*, 14, 20–22; "How He Was Won Away," *Washington Post* (January 10, 1909), 15; "Petite Stenographer Rejects Millionaire," *Washington Post* (August 31, 1906), 3.

18. On women's entrance into the office, see Margery Davies, *Woman's Place Is at the Typewriter: 1870–1930* (Philadelphia: Temple University Press, 1984), chapter 5; Fine, *Souls of the Skyscraper*, chapter 4; Srole, *Transcribing Class and Gender*, 82–84, chapter 5.

19. Martha Ellsbeth, "For the Sake of the Office," *Typewriter and Phonographic World* (May 1902), 249–52.

20. S. E. Kiser, *Soul Sonnets of a Stenographer* (Boston: Forbes, 1903), originally published in *Saturday Evening Post*.

21. S. S. Packard, "The Pretty Typewriter," *Phonographic World* (March 1890), 201.

22. On reform efforts and civil and criminal seduction statutes in the United States, see Barbara Meil Hobson, *Uneasy Virtue: The Politics of Prostitution and the American Reform Tradition* (Chicago: University of Chicago Press, 1990), 66–76; Carroll Smith Rosenberg, *Disorderly Conduct: Visions of Gender in Victorian America* (New York: Oxford University Press, 1986), 109–28; Pamela Haag, *Consent: Sexual Rights and the Transformation of American Liberalism* (Ithaca, NY: Cornell University Press, 1999), chapters 1 and 2, 188–89, nn. 18–22.

23. Mary E. Odem, *Delinquent Daughters: Protecting and Policing Adolescent Female Sexuality in the United States, 1885–1920* (Chapel Hill: University of North Carolina Press, 1995), 2–3, chapters 1 and 3. By 1920 nearly all states had raised the age of consent to sixteen or eighteen (37).

24. On the sexual double standard in concerns about department store workers' immorality, see Val Marie Johnson, "'The Rest Can Go to the Devil': Macy's Workers Negotiate Gender, Sex, and Class in the Progressive Era," *Journal of Women's History* 19 (2007): 39, 46. Psychiatrists during this period dismissed patients' claims of sexual aggression and considered behaviors such as a boss slipping his hand up an employee's skirt as "normal heterosexuality." Women relied on the language of seduction to describe these events; Elizabeth Lunbeck,

The Psychiatric Persuasion: Knowledge, Gender, and Power in Modern America (Princeton: Princeton University Press, 1994), 212–26.

25. "If a Man Takes Liberties," *Woman's Home Companion* (March 1916), 10.

26. "A 'Frisco Girl," *Phonographic World* (July 1895), 265.

27. "Womanly Dignity," *Phonographic World* (June 1894), 313; Margaret E. Sangster, *Winsome Womanhood* (New York: Fleming H. Revell, 1900), 69–70.

28. Caroline A. Huling, *Letters of a Business Woman to Her Niece* (New York: R. F. Fenno, 1906), 81, 87–88, 92–93.

29. Ibid., 110, 98, 101, 111, 104.

30. Ruth Rosen, *The Lost Sisterhood: Prostitution in America, 1900–1918* (Johns Hopkins University Press, 1982), chapter 5, 38–46.

31. Alice Kessler-Harris, *Out to Work* (New York: Oxford University Press, 1982), 101–4, 180–91.

32. Ibid., 188–92; Rosen, *Lost Sisterhood*, 47–48.

33. "War on Girl Stenographer," *Washington Post* (December 4, 1904), 1.

34. Similarly, women's desire to solidify their place in public partially explains why women denied they "suffered from insults and indignities" on New York's subways in response to a 1909 plan to segregate subway cars; Clifton Hood, 722 *Miles* (Baltimore: Johns Hopkins University Press, 2004), 118–19.

35. Mary Christine Anderson, "Gender, Class, and Culture: Women Secretarial and Clerical Workers in the United States, 1925–55" (Ph.D. diss., Ohio State University, 1986), 386–87; Mary Bularzik, "Sexual Harassment at the Workplace: Historical Notes," *Radical America* 12 (1978), rpt. in James Green, ed., *Workers' Struggles, Past and Present* (Philadelphia: Temple University Press, 1983), 121, 132; Clara E. Laughlin, *The Work-a-Day Girl* (New York: Fleming H. Revell, 1913), 123–24.

36. Bularzik, "Sexual Harassment at the Workplace," 131–33.

37. Dorothy Richardson, *The Long Day: The Story of a New York Working Girl* (1905; Charlottesville: University Press of Virginia, 1990), 276; Robert A. Woods and Albert Kennedy, *Young Working Girls: A Summary of Evidence from Two Thousand Social Workers* (Boston: Houghton Mifflin, 1913), 27–28; Jane Addams, *A New Conscience and an Ancient Evil* (New York: Macmillan, 1912), 64, 213–15.

38. Joanne J. Meyerowitz, *Women Adrift: Independent Wage Earners in Chicago, 1880–1930* (Chicago: University of Chicago Press, 1988), 61; "Low Wages Do Not Drive Girls Astray," *New York Times* (June 22, 1913), S2, 10. Some department store workers refuted the charge that, as a group, they were immoral; Thomas Russell, *The Girl's Fight for a Living* (Chicago: M. A. Donohue, 1913), 161–66. For a scholarly assessment, see Johnson, " 'The Rest Can Go to the Devil,' " 34–35, 37.

39. Newspaper quotation from "Warning to Merchants Issued by the Committee," *Ladies Garment Worker* 3 (January 1912), 8. Other quotations from Nan Enstad, *Ladies of Labor, Girls of Adventure: Working Women, Popular Culture, and Labor Politics at the Turn of the Twentieth Century* (New York: Columbia University Press, 1999), 141–45. On working-class women dressing like ladies see

ibid., 22–30. Department store clerks were also concerned with presenting themselves in a middle-class mien; Johnson, " 'The Rest Can Go to the Devil,' " 39, 48.

40. "Len G. Broughton Repeats His Words," *Brooklyn Eagle* (January 30, 1900), 18; "Dr. Broughton Says That He Used the Word 'Many' in His Sermon," *Atlanta Constitution* (February 9, 1900), 5; "Dr. Broughton's Answer," *Atlanta Constitution* (February 18, 1900), 9.

41. "Len G. Broughton Repeats His Words"; "Typewriters and Clubs," *New York Times* (February 4, 1900), 22; "Miss Ware Denounces Dr. Broughton's Attack on Women Stenographers," *Atlanta Constitution* (February 9, 1900), 5; "Miss Ware's Statement to the Constitution," *Atlanta Constitution* (February 9, 1900), 5.

42. "Letters from the People," *Atlanta Constitution* (February 25, 1900), 18.

43. "Plans a Noonday Guild of Girl Stenographers," *New York Times* (January 12, 1907), 6; "Stenographers' Club Starts with 65 Girls," *New York Times* (January 17, 1907), 7.

44. "Stenographers' Club Starts with 65 Girls,"; "Business Women Protest," *New York Times*, (January 19, 1907), 6.

45. "Stenographers Resent Talk of 'Rescue Work,' " *New York Times* (January 20, 1907), SM2; "Women in Offices," *New York Times* (January 21, 1907), 8.

46. On these issues in the "white slavery" debate, see Haag, *Consent*, 66–67. Defenders of department store clerks also offered individualized and class-based explanations of why some women received insults; Johnson, " 'The Rest Can Go to the Devil,' " 35, 46.

47. Anderson, "Gender, Class, and Culture," 385–86; Lunbeck, *Psychiatric Persuasion*, 221–22. On safety at the cost of desire, see Judith Walkowitz, "Male Vice and Female Virtue," in Ann Snitow, Christine Stansell, and Sharon Thompson, eds., *Powers of Desire: The Politics of Sexuality* (New York: Monthly Review Press, 1983), 429–30, 432–33.

48. Karen M. Mason, "Feeling the Pinch: The Kalamazoo Corsetmakers' Strike of 1912," in Carol Groneman and Mary Beth Norton, eds., *"To Toil the Livelong Day": America's Women at Work, 1780–1980* (Ithaca, NY: Cornell University Press, 1987), 150–52, 157–58.

49. Julian T. Baird, Jr., "Ella Wheeler Wilcox," in Edward T. James, Janet Wilson James, and Paul S. Boyer, eds., *Notable American Women*, 3 vols. (Cambridge: Belknap Press of Harvard University Press, 1971), 3: 607–8.

50. Ella Wheeler Wilcox, "Liberties Men Take," in *Men, Women, and Emotions* (Chicago: W. B. Conkey, 1896), 106–7; Ella Wheeler Wilcox, "What Men Like and Dislike," in *Men, Women, and Emotions*, 78; Ella Wheeler Wilcox, "Women Help Men," in *Everyday Thoughts in Prose and Verse* (Chicago: W. B. Conkey, 1901), 71; Ella Wheeler Wilcox, "The Over-Gallant Man," in Chase, *Women Stenographers*, 11.

51. Beryl Satter, *Each Mind a Kingdom: American Women, Sexual Purity, and the New Thought Movement, 1875–1920* (Berkeley: University of California Press, 1999),

9–12; "Girl Stenographers and Their Employers," *Phonographic World* (February 1891), 184.

52. Satter, Introduction to *Each Mind a Kingdom;* Kathi Kern, *Mrs. Stanton's Bible* (Ithaca, NY: Cornell University Press, 2001), 60–63, 117, 147.

53. Wilcox, "Women Help Men."

54. Ferriss Clay Bailey, "'Preachers Without Pulpits': New Thought and the Rise of Therapeutic Self-Help in Progressive Era America" (Ph.D. diss., Vanderbilt University, 1999), 203–5; Ella Wheeler Wilcox, "My Belief," in *Men, Women, and Emotions,* 9. For more examples of Wilcox's views, see "Low-Salaries for Women" and "Flirting with Married Men," in *Everyday Thoughts,* and "Men or Women as Friends," "The Fallen Man and Woman," and "The Single Woman and the Married Man," in *Men, Women, and Emotions.*

55. Clifton S. Way, "To Employers of the Typewriter Girl," *Phonographic World* (September, 1890), 17; Douglas Graham, *Mildred McElroy: A Tale of Stenographic Life* (Philadelphia: Thomas MacTaggart, 1903), 39; Satter, *Each Mind a Kingdom,* 8, 14.

56. "A Woman's Worthy Work," *Browne's Phonographic Weekly* (January 20, 1889), 39–40.

57. "Liberty Perverted," *Browne's Phonographic Weekly* 15 (April 28, 1890), 259; Huling, *Letters of a Business Woman,* 60–61, 103.

58. "Proposals on Postal Cards," *Brooklyn Eagle* (October 20, 1893), 10; "Mr. Tyrer Asks for a Trial by Jury," *Brooklyn Eagle* (October 23, 1893), 1.

59. "Independence of Women," *Brooklyn Eagle* (October 23, 1893), 4.

60. On stalking laws, see Paul E. Mullen and Michele Pathe, "Stalking," *Crime and Justice* 29 (2002), 273–75.

61. "Miss Fisher Kept a Diary," *Boston Globe* (February 7, 1909), 11; "Her Diary Accuses Boston Officials," *New York Times* (February 8, 1909), 3. On problems associated with the growing informality of gender-integrated federal offices, see Cindy Sondik Aron, *Ladies and Gentlemen of the Civil Service: Middle-Class Workers in Victorian America* (New York: Oxford University Press, 1987), 171–78.

62. "Miss Fisher's Diary Jars Health Board," *Boston Post* (n.d.), rpt. in Chase, *Women Stenographers,* 7–9; Srole, *Transcribing Class and Gender,* 65–66, 132.

63. Michael Grossberg, *Governing the Hearth: Law and the Family in Nineteenth-Century America* (Chapel Hill: University of North Carolina Press, 1985), 33–51.

64. "Typist Awarded Half of Fortune," *Oklahoman* (March 11, 1911), 9.

65. "Gives Her $5,000 Heart Balm," *Washington Post* (December 19, 1911), 5; "Wooed His Typist in Blankest Verse," *New York Times* (December 15, 1911), 7; "Lawyer Says Girl Confessed Her Love," *New York Times* (December 16, 1911), 7. On the significance of where a newspaper placed a story, see Lisa Duggan, *Sapphic Slashers: Sex, Violence, and American Modernity* (Durham: Duke University Press, 2000), 32–40.

66. Calvert Magruder, "Mental and Emotional Disturbance in the Law of Torts," *Harvard Law Review* 49 (1936): 1055; Lisa R. Pruitt, "Her Own Good Name: Two

Centuries of Talk About Chastity," *Maryland Law Review* 63 (2004): 407, 410, 429–30, 440–41; Reva Siegel, Introduction to Catharine MacKinnon and Reva Siegel, eds., *Directions in Sexual Harassment Law* (New Haven: Yale University Press, 2004), 4–5. For a woman using the seduction tort to seek redress for actions now defined as quid pro quo sexual harassment, see Lea VanderVelde, "The Legal Ways of Seduction," *Stanford Law Review* 48 (1996): 894–97.

67. "Should Pretty Stenographers Be Caged?" *Atlanta Constitution* (October 31, 1915), B19; "Office Girls Oppose Cages," *Washington Post* (October 3, 1915), E8. At least a dozen newspapers across the country covered this story.

68. "Should Pretty Stenographers Be Caged?"

CHAPTER TWO. WHITE-COLLAR CASANOVAS

1. U.S. Congress, House of Representatives, *Report of the Select Committee of the House of Representatives, Investigating the Methods and Management and Practices of the Bureau of Pensions*, H. Rept. no. 1868, parts I and II, 52nd Cong., 1st sess., 1892, pp. xv, 326, 1051. See also Cindy Sondik Aron, *Ladies and Gentlemen of the Civil Service: Middle-Class Workers in Victorian America* (New York: Oxford University Press, 1987), 173–78.

2. Max Weber first noted the connection between the subordination of men at work and their domination of women; Max Weber, "Religious Rejections of the World and Their Directions," in *From Max Weber: Essays in Sociology*, trans. and ed. Hans Heinrich Gerth and Bryan S. Turner (New York: Oxford University Press, 1946), 344–47.

3. "In Uncle Sam's Service," *Washington Post* (November 10, 1889), 9; Aron, *Ladies and Gentlemen of the Civil Service*, 5, 33–39, chapter 5. On the gendered aspects of civil service reform, see Kevin P. Murphy, *Political Manhood: Red Bloods, Mollycoddles, and the Politics of Progressive Era Reform* (New York: Columbia University Press, 2008), 23–29.

4. Aron, *Ladies and Gentlemen of the Civil Service*, chapter 3, 70–78, 124–26.

5. U.S. Congress, House of Representatives, *Report of the Select Committee . . . to Investigate Certain Charges Against the Treasury Department*, H. Rept. no. 140, 38th Cong., 1st sess., 1864, 15, 154–55; L. C. Baker, *History of the United States Secret Service* (Philadelphia: L. C. Baker, 1867), 293, 296, 298.

6. U.S. House of Representatives, H. Rept. no. 140, 13–17; Baker, *History of the United States Secret Service*, 324, 314. For more on this investigation and concerns about sexual exploitation, see Aron, *Ladies and Gentlemen of the Civil Service*, 100–102, 166–69.

7. Judy Hilkey, *Character Is Capital: Success Manuals and Manhood in Gilded Age America* (Chapel Hill: University of North Carolina Press, 1997), 5, 8, 126–27, 148–51. On the importance of sexual self-control and middle-class manhood, see Anthony Rotundo, *American Manhood: Transformations in Masculinity from the Revolution to the Modern Era* (New York: Basic, 1993), 120–28, 231, and chapter 10; Rodney Hessinger, *Seduced, Abandoned, and Reborn: Visions of Youth*

in Middle-Class America, 1780–1950 (Philadelphia: University of Pennsylvania Press, 2005), chapter 5.

8. Timothy Gilfoyle, *City of Eros: New York City, Prostitution, and the Commercialization of Sex, 1790–1920* (New York: Norton, 1992), 92–116, 232–39.

9. Mrs. Frances Forrester Cougle, #1912, Records of the Appointments Division, Interior Department, RG 48, National Archives. For more on Cougle, see Aron, *Ladies and Gentlemen of the Civil Service*, 156–57, 164.

10. George Chauncey, *Gay New York: Gender, Urban Culture, and the Making of the Gay Male World, 1890–1940* (New York: Basic, 1994), 99–100, 111–27; Jonathan Ned Katz, *The Invention of Heterosexuality* (New York: Dutton, 1995), 10, chapter 2.
    For a discussion of other reformations of manhood around the turn-of-the-century, see http://history.sewanee.edu/facstaff/berebitsky/.

11. "Ring Off," *New York Sun* (n.d.), rpt. in Fessenden E. Chase, *Women Stenographers* (Portland, ME: Southworth, 1910), 7.

12. Hattie A. Shinn, "In Defense of 'The Pretty Typewriter,'" *Chicago Daily Tribune* (May 15, 1889), 8; Cora Beamish, "In Defence of 'The Pretty Typewriter,'" *Phonographic World* (July, 1890), 364.

13. On sexual humor and male bonding, see Peter Lyman, "The Fraternal Bond as a Joking Relationship: A Case Study of the Role of Sexist Jokes in Male Group Bonding," in Michael Kimmel ed., *Changing Men: New Directions in Research on Men and Masculinity* (Newbury Park, CA: Sage, 1987), 150–51, 158–60; Baird Jones, *Sexual Humor* (New York: Philosophical Library, 1987), chapter 7; David L. Collinson, *Managing the Shopfloor: Subjectivity, Masculinity, and Workplace Culture* (New York: W. de Gruyter, 1992), chapter 4; Gershon Legman, *Rationale of the Dirty Joke: An Analysis of Sexual Humor* (1968; rpt. New York: Simon and Schuster, 2006), 221, 236, 239.

14. "The Typewriter Girl," *Washington Post* (June 11, 1909), 6; on the fool and women's silence, see Legman, *Rationale of the Dirty Joke*, 113–14, 225–27.

15. "What Beautiful Hair You Have!" *St. Louis Republican* (March 10, 1895), rpt. in *The Phonographic World* (April 1895), 213. For a similar *true* story see "Typewriter Girl's Revenge," *Washington Post* (January 1, 1912), 7. Both of these stories can be read as a way that women responded to unwanted attentions. In both, the woman ends up out of a job.

16. On dictating proposals, see Lisa Fine, *The Souls of the Skyscraper: Female Clerical Workers in Chicago, 1870–1930* (Philadelphia: Temple University Press, 1990), 68.

17. I found about seventy-five cards that portray sexual interactions in the office, the majority of which were printed between 1907 and 1913. For more postcards and a fuller discussion of their history, see http://history.sewanee.edu/facstaff/berebitsky/.
    On surveillance see Michel Foucault, *Discipline and Punish: The Birth of the Prison*, trans. Alan Sheridan (New York: Vintage Books, 1979), 137–38, 214–23.

In *Male Sexuality Under Surveillance: The Office in American Literature* (Iowa City: University of Iowa Press, 2003), Graham Thompson explores how male sexuality finds expression in the surveillance systems established by the office's distinct geography. For the significance of the private office and secretary, see Kwolek-Folland, *Engendering Business*, 67, 116–19; Margery W. Davies, *Woman's Place Is at the Typewriter: Office Work and Office Workers, 1870–1930* (Philadelphia: Temple University Press, 1984), 152–53; Roland Marchand, *Advertising the American Dream: Making Way for Modernity, 1920–1940* (Berkeley: University of California Press, 1985), 238–48.

18. Kathy Peiss, *Cheap Amusements: Working Women and Leisure in Turn-of-the-Century New York* (Philadelphia: Temple University Press, 1986), 156–58; Fine, *Souls of the Skyscraper*, 73–74; Bob Adelman, Richard Merkin, and Art Spiegelman, eds., *Tijuana Bibles: Art and Wit in America's Forbidden Funnies, 1930s–1960s* (New York: Simon and Schuster, 1997), 4–10, 39.

19. "Smitty in an Office Idyll," ca. 1940s–1950s, available at http://tijuanabibles. org/cgi-bin/hazel.cgi?action=detail&item=TB057.

20. Judith Butler, *Gender Trouble: Feminism and the Subversion of Identity* (New York: Routledge, 1990), 25, 112, 140.

21. Kwolek-Folland, *Engendering Business*, 167–69; Mary Christine Anderson, "Gender, Class, and Culture: Women Secretarial and Clerical Workers in the United States, 1925–1955" (Ph.D. diss., Ohio State University, 1986), 29–31, 38–39; Mary Elizabeth Adams, "Women in the Modern Office: Female Clerical Workers, 1900–1930" (Ph.D. diss., University of California, Berkeley, 1989), 208–11; Caroline Huling, *Letters of a Businesswoman to Her Niece* (New York: R. F. Fenno, 1906), 57.

22. East Coast newspapers covered the story extensively, but papers in Los Angeles, Chicago, and Atlanta also followed the case. "Cook Girl Found; Shot to Death," *New York Times* (March 5, 1915), 1; "Scranton Woman Says She Is Wife of Virginius Mayo," *Hartford Courant* (March 11, 1915), 17; "Exonerates Mayo in Suicide Case," *New York Times* (March 6, 1915), 1; "Suit over Child Threatens Mayo," *New York Times* (March 12, 1915), 5; "Find Girl Shot Dead," *Washington Post* (March 5, 1915), 1.

23. "Cook Girl Shot Herself in Heart," *Hartford Courant* (March 5, 1915), 1; "Real Wife of Mayo, This Woman's Claim," *New York Times* (March 11, 1915), 1; "Mayo Was Liked by All the Girls," *Hartford Courant* (March 12, 1915), 17; "Mayo Suit Postponed," *New York Times* (March 28, 1915), S2; "Digging into Life of Virginius Mayo," *Hartford Courant* (March 14, 1915), 10; "May Settle With Mayo," *New York Times* (March 14, 1915), 6; "Call Dead Girl Made," *Washington Post* (March 6, 1915), 1; "Hamden Prosecutor's Hands Tied," *New York Times* (March 13, 1915), 7; "Mrs. Mayo Gets Decree," *New York Times* (June 12, 1915), 11; "Mayo-Wahlers Case Settled for $5,000," *Hartford Courant* (April 6, 1915), 22; "Mayo Fights Examination," *New York Times* (January 14, 1916), 20; "Jury Gives $100,000 to Mayo's Wife," *New York Times* (October 4, 1917), 23.

24. Michael McGeer, *A Fierce Discontent: The Rise and Fall of the Progressive Movement in America, 1870–1920* (New York: Free Press, 2003), chapter 5.

25. Ruth Rosen, *The Lost Sisterhood* (Baltimore: Johns Hopkins University Press, 1982), 42.

26. Louis Galambos, *The Public Image of Big Business in America, 1880–1940* (Baltimore: Johns Hopkins University Press, 1975), 80–82, 124–26; McGeer, *Fierce Discontent*, 152, 177–78; Howard B. Woolston, *Prostitution in the United States* (New York: Century, 1921), 1: 307.

27. Hilkey, *Character Is Capital*, 126–28; Karen Halttunen, *Confidence Men and Painted Women: A Study of Middle-Class Culture in America, 1830–1870* (New Haven: Yale University Press, 1982), xv, 198–207.

28. On the transition from character to personality, see Warren Susman, "Personality and the Making of Twentieth-Century Culture," in *Culture as History: The Transformation of American Society in the Twentieth Century* (New York: Pantheon, 1984), 271–85. Photo, *Hartford Courant* (March 22, 1915), 1; "Six Women Who Claim to Have Shared in the Life of Rich Virginius J. Mayo," *Washington Post* (March 13, 1915), 5; "Digging into Life"; "Mayo Was Liked by All the Girls"; "Suit over Child."

29. "Suit over Child"; "Mayo Was Liked by All the Girls." Mayo's behavior toward his office help reads like the beginnings of a narrative of a girl's descent into prostitution (Woolston, *Prostitution in the United States*, 1: 79).

30. "Virginius J. Mayo in Cell," *New York Times* (March 3, 1919), 13; "Mayo Gets One to Three Years in Jail," *Hartford Courant* (May 10, 1922), 1; "Virginius Mayo Guilty of Bigamy," *New York Times* (May 7, 1922), 1.

31. Anderson worked three stints in advertising primarily as a copywriter, 1900–1906, 1913–19, and 1920–22. In 1906 he moved to Cleveland to become head of a mail-order company. In 1907 he opened his own paint distribution company in Elyria, Ohio; Ray Lewis White, ed., *Sherwood Anderson's Memoirs: A Critical Edition* (Chapel Hill: University of North Carolina Press, 1969), xxxvi, n. 238.

  My discussion of Anderson builds on T. J. Jackson Lears's assessment in "Sherwood Anderson: Looking for the White Spot," in Richard Wightman Fox and T. J. Jackson Lears, eds., *The Power of Culture: Critical Essays in American History* (Chicago: University of Chicago Press, 1993), 13–37, especially 23, 28–29. Quotations from White, *Sherwood Anderson's Memoirs*, 386–90.

32. White, *Sherwood Anderson's Memoirs*, 263–64, 244, 387–88, 413–14, 231, 291–92.

33. Ibid., 264, 230–31, 241, 266, 388.

34. Ibid., 291, 413–15, 389, 550–51.

35. Page Smith, ed., *A Letter from My Father* (New York: William Morrow, 1976), 14, 464–65.

36. Ibid., 161, 295–99.

37. Ibid., 12–14, 471.

38. Ibid., 381, 393, 47.

39. Ibid., 60–61, 85, 122, 133, 116.

40. Ibid., 461–63; Chauncey, *Gay New York*, 195–96, 304–08, 327.

41. Smith, *Letter from My Father*, 78.

42. Ibid., 141, 143–45, 157, 205.

43. White, *Sherwood Anderson's Memoirs*, 389. For a discussion of sexual exchange among self-supporting women, see Joanne Meyerowitz, *Women Adrift: Independent Wage Earners in Chicago, 1880–1930* (Chicago: University of Chicago Press, 1988), 101–5. Some women assumed sex was a part of their job. A Vassar graduate who applied to the *New Yorker* in 1925 believed that it was expected in the magazine world; James Thurber, *The Years with Ross* (Boston: Little, Brown, 1957), chapter 9.

44. Smith, *Letter from My Father*, 235–36. In 1928 clerical workers suffered a greater disparity between workers and jobs than any other occupational group, with three to five applicants for every position; Grace L. Coyle, "Women in the Clerical Occupations," *Annals of the American Academy of Political and Social Science* 143 (May 1929): 187. On clerical unemployment during the Depression, see Sharon Hartman Strom, " 'We're No Kitty Foyles': Organizing Office Workers for the Congress of Industrial Organizations, 1937–50," in Ruth Milkman, ed., *Women, Work, and Protest: A Century of Labor History* (New York: Routledge, 1985), 209, and Davis, *Company Men*, chapter 8.

45. Smith, *Letter from My Father*, 242–50. For the *New York Times*' coverage, see "W. Ward Smith Held on Woman's Charge" (June 4, 1931), 5; "Accuses W. Ward Smith" (June 17, 1931), 12; "W. W. Smith Cleared of Woman's Charge" (June 21, 1931), 23.

46. Smith, *Letter from My Father*, 350–51. The dangers to women of fake want ads had long been a concern to reformers and police, and one of the early responsibilities of New York City policewomen was to investigate suspicious ads; "Girl Murder Leads Aldermen to Act," *New York Times* (March 30, 1910), 32; "He Hugged a Policewoman," *New York Times* (May 1, 1925), 11. Already by the 1910s, the film industry was beginning to get a reputation; "Attention and Punishment for Flirtatious Directors," *Variety* (March 13, 1914), quoted in *Taylorology* 41 (May 1996), available at http://www.public.asu.edu/~ialong/ Taylor41.txt (accessed May 17, 2009).

47. For other examples of sex as male bonding see Smith, *Letter from My Father*, 86, 93, 119.

48. Ibid., 401, 248, 316, 326, 375, 411, 436, 249, 333; Kevin White, *The First Sexual Revolution: The Emergence of Male Heterosexuality in Modern America* (New York: New York University Press, 1993), 116–20. In Philadelphia, for example, more than one-third of clerks in 1920 had immigrant parents; Jerome Bjelopera, *City of Clerks: Office and Sales Workers in Philadelphia, 1870–1920* (Urbana: University of Illinois Press, 2005), 21–22.

49. Smith, *Letter from My Father*, 270, 362, 159–60, 314–15.

50. Ibid., 161, 14, 464–65.

51. R. W. Connell, *Masculinities*, 2nd ed. (Berkeley: University of California Press, 2005), 76–81; Gillian Creese, *Contracting Masculinity: Gender, Class, and Race*

in a White-Collar Union, 1944–94 (Ontario: Oxford University Press, 1999), 26–27.

52. Davis, *Company Men*, 10, 148–49, 152–54, 158–64, 215–16.

53. "What Was Justice in This Case?" *Atlanta Constitution* (September 18, 1927), F3; Frank Dolan, "Girl's Slayer Moans Remorse," *New York Daily News* (February 28, 1926), 3; "Kills Ex-Fiancee and Shoots Himself," *New York Times* (February 27, 1926), 1; "Lover Who Killed Girl Is Dying of Bullet Wounds," *Brooklyn Daily Eagle* (February 27, 1926), 1; Elenore Kellogg, "Polite Slayer of Sweetheart Charms Court," *New York Daily News* (March 23, 1927), 2; Elenore Kellogg, "Kisses Daughter's Killer," *New York Daily News* (March 24, 1927), 7; Elenore Kellogg, "Mayer Gets Manslaughter" *New York Daily News* (March 25, 1927), 2; "Mayer Convicted of Manslaughter with Mercy Plea," *Brooklyn Daily Eagle* (March 25, 1927), 2.

   Some reports state that the couple was engaged; others say McIntyre repeatedly refused his proposal. Some reports say that McIntyre was twenty-five.

54. Jack O'Brien, "Girl's Slayer Planned Shooting a Week in Advance," *New York Daily News* (March 2, 1926), 6; Kellogg, "Mayer Gets Manslaughter"; "Mayer Convicted of Manslaughter with Mercy Plea"; "How Fate Stalked the Beauty with Too Much Talent," *Zanesville (Ohio) Times Signal* (April 4, 1926), 32. This last was a syndicated story that appeared in newspapers across the country.

   Manual workers' real wages rose 28 percent over the first three decades of the twentieth century, but those of clerical workers and minor executives showed no advance. The popularity of clerical occupations meant excess workers, which kept wages low, as did the predominance of women in the field; Coyle, "Women in the Clerical Occupations," 183, 186.

55. "What Was Justice"; Kellogg, "Polite Slayer"; "Angered Suitor Kills Fiancee, Shoots Self," *New York Daily News* (February 27, 1926), 2.

56. Jurgen Kocka, *White Collar Workers in America, 1890–1940* (Beverly Hills, CA: Sage, 1980), 184–85; George Weston, *The Horseshoe Nails* (New York: Dodd, Mead, 1927), 40; Davis, *Company Men*, 164–69, 214–15.

57. Florence Lasser, "Slogans in the Breeze," *Ledger* 2 (May 1936): 10–11, United Office and Professional Workers of America Records, WAG 190, box 1, Tamiment Library/Robert F. Wagner Labor Archives, New York University [hereafter WAG 190].

58. "White Collars and Brown Shirts," *Ledger* 1 (April 15, 1935): 9; Wm. E. Bohn, "White Collars and Red Blood," *Ledger* 1 (June 15, 1935): 1; "Top of the Morning to You—My Little Family!" *Ledger* 1 (August 15, 1935): 7; "We," *Ledger* 1 (March 1935): 5, all in WAG 190. On the family corporate model, see Kwolek-Folland, *Engendering Business*, chapter 5. On the muscular body and working-class men's identity, see Ava Baron, "Masculinity, the Embodied Male Worker, and the Historian's Gaze," *International Labor and Working Class History* 69 (Spring 2006): 147–49, 152–54.

59. Archie Green, "Boss, Workman, Wife: Sneaking-Home Tales," *Journal of American Folklore* 106 (Spring 1993): 157, 160, 163, 165–66.

Sneaking-home tales were not just allegories of workingmen's disempowerment; historians have documented cases in which factory supervisors demanded that the wives and daughters of workers submit to them sexually if they wanted their husbands or fathers to keep their jobs; Philip S. Foner, *Women and the American Labor Movement* (New York: Free Press, 1979), 421–23. I have not located any evidence that white-collar supervisors engaged in similar practices.

60. For a thorough and concise summary of developments in theorizing about masculinity, see Lisa Jean Moore, "Extracting Men from Semen: Masculinity in Scientific Representations of Sperm," *Social Text* 20 (2002), 94–96.

CHAPTER THREE. BETWIXT AND BETWEEN

1. Helen Woodward, *Through Many Windows* (New York: Harper, 1926), 54–55, 122, 364–65.

2. Margery W. Davies, *Woman's Place Is at the Typewriter: Office Work and Office Workers, 1870–1930* (Philadelphia: Temple University Press, 1982), appendix table 1, "Clerical Workers in the United States, by Sex, 1870–1930," n.p.; Nancy Cott, *The Grounding of Modern Feminism* (New Haven: Yale University Press, 1987), 131–32. Jobs included in the category of clerical occupations include bookkeepers, cashiers, accountants, office clerks, stenographers, and typists; Elyce J. Rotella, *From Home to Office: U.S. Women at Work, 1870–1930* (Ann Arbor: UMI Research Press, 1981), table AI, n.p.

3. Christina Simmons, "Modern Sexuality and the Myth of Victorian Repression" in Kathy Peiss and Christina Simmons, eds., *Passion and Power: Sexuality in History* (Philadelphia: Temple University Press, 1989), 160–70.

4. Woodward, *Through Many Windows*, 367–71. Woodward does not tell us what position the woman holds, although it seems clear that she is below the man in the organization; her office is described as a "little room," and she refers to him as "Mr. Roberts."

5. Sharon Hartman Strom, *Beyond the Typewriter: Gender, Class, and the Origins of Modern American Office Work, 1900–1930* (Urbana: University of Illinois Press, 1992), 251–53, chapter 6, 317–19; Ethel Erickson, "The Employment of Women in Offices," *Bulletin of the Women's Bureau*, no. 120 (Washington, DC: Government Printing Office, 1934), 1. Native-born women with foreign-born parents increasingly made up the ranks of stenographer-typists, which was the fastest growing job category; Lisa Fine, *The Souls of the Skyscraper* (Philadelphia: Temple University Press, 1990), 48–49, 171.

6. Elizabeth Gregg MacGibbon, *Manners in Business* (New York: Macmillan, 1936), 116–17, 122; "Business Etiquette," *Time* (January 20, 1936), 68–69.

7. John Chynoweth Burnham, "The New Psychology: From Narcissism to Social Control," in John Braeman et al., eds., *Change and Continuity in Twentieth-Century America: The 1920s* (Columbus: Ohio State University Press, 1968), 352–53, 367, 384; Stephen Leacock, "A Manual of the New Mentality," *Harper's* 148 (March 1924): 472–73, quoted in Donald S. Napoli, *Architects of Adjustment:*

The History of the Psychological Profession in the United States (Port Washington, NY: Kennikat, 1981), 42–43, 17–18, chapter 4; Warren I. Susman, *Culture as History* (New York: Pantheon, 1973), 195.

MacGibbon worked as an account executive with the advertising firm of Erwin, Wasey and Co., for five years; "Business Etiquette." In the 1920s Maule worked for the J. Walter Thompson ad agency. She was an active suffragist and a member of the radical feminist group Heterodoxy; Jennifer Scanlon, *Inarticulate Longings: The Ladies' Home Journal, Gender, and the Promises of Consumer Culture* (New York: Routledge, 1995), 187–89. She also was editor of *Independent Woman*, the journal of the National Federation of Business and Professional Women's Clubs; "Frances Maule, 88, Author and Editor," *New York Times* (June 29, 1966), 47. Parts of her books appeared in *McCall's, Independent Woman,* and the *Chicago Daily Tribune;* Doris Blake, "Keep Emotions on Tight Rein When at Office," *Chicago Daily Tribune* (May 19, 1935), C5.

8. Donald A. Laird, "Problems in Handling Women Workers," *Office Economist* 18 (1935): 4; Fine, *Souls of the Skyscraper,* 61; J. G. Morawski, "The Measurement of Masculinity and Femininity: Engendering Categorical Realities," *Journal of Personality* 53 (June 1985): 204–7. On woman as emotional, see also Anita M. Muhl, "Why Women Fail," in Morris Fishbein and William A. White, eds., *Why Men Fail* (New York: Century, 1928), 286–87; Lydia G. Giberson, "Dealing with Emotional Problems in the Office," in Harold B. Bergen et al., eds., *Attitudes and Emotional Problems of Office Employees* (New York: American Management Association, 1939), 27.

9. Christina Simmons, *Making Marriage Modern: Women's Sexuality from the Progressive Era to World War II* (New York: Oxford University Press, 2009), 211; Jane Gerhard, *Desiring Revolution: Second-Wave Feminism and the Rewriting of American Sexual Thought, 1920 to 1982* (New York: Columbia University Press, 2001), 21–23, 25, 28–29.

10. Morawski, "Measurement of Masculinity and Femininity," 208; Cott, *Grounding of Modern Feminism,* 155, 158.

11. Ernest Groves, "The Personality Results of the Wage Employment of Women Outside the Home and Their Social Consequences," *Annals of the American Academy of Political and Social Science* 143 (May 1929): 339–48, quoted in Cott, *Grounding of Modern Feminism,* 154.

12. Lois Scharf, *To Work and to Wed* (Westport, CT: Greenwood, 1980), 95–101. On the 1920s, see Alice Kessler-Harris, *Out to Work* (New York: Oxford University Press, 1982), 227–36.

13. "Women in Business: II," *Fortune* 12 (August 1935): 55. Employers used this view to justify low wages and limited advancement; Angel Kwolek-Folland, *Engendering Business: Men and Women in the Corporate Office, 1870–1930* (Baltimore: Johns Hopkins University Press, 1994), 58–69.

14. Emily Post, "Work at Hand and Not Projected Personality Important in Office," *Oklahoman* (June 6, 1937), 63; Donald A. Laird, *The Psychology of Supervising the Working Woman* (New York: McGraw-Hill, 1942), 144; Frances Maule, *She*

Strives to Conquer: Business Behavior, Opportunities, and Job Requirements for Women (New York: Funk and Wagnalls, 1937), 42, 51. Frances Maule, *Girl with a Pay Check* (New York: Harper, 1941), 242; Frances Maule and Louise Alteneder, *Student's Manual for Use with She Strives to Conquer* (New York, n.d.), 12–13; Gladys Torson, *Ask My Secretary* (New York: Greenberg, 1940), 155. Maule's *She Strives* was positively reviewed in a number of newspapers; "For Girls in Business," *New York Times* (October 21, 1934), 20; *Boston Transcript* (January 12, 1935), 3. See also Lena M. Phillips, " 'Sex Appeal' Out of the Business Life," *Washington Post* (March 11, 1928), SM10; Lillian G. Genn, "You Can't Vamp Your Way to Success," *Oklahoman* (April 29, 1928), 89; Mary E. McGill, *Into a Man's World: Talks with Business Girls* (Huntington, IN: Our Sunday Visitor, 1938), 57–58; Gulielma Fell Alsop and Mary Frances McBride, *She's Off to Work* (New York: Vanguard, 1941), 39, 161, 186; Helen Hoerle, *The Girl and Her Future* (New York: H. Smith and R. Haas, 1932), 4.

15. Maule, *Pay Check*, 234, 198, 200–201; Maule, *She Strives*, 155–57; Edith Johnson, "Has Sex Any Place in Today's Business?" *Oklahoman* (September 24, 1933), 42; Torson, *Ask My Secretary*, 151, 154; Hildegarde Dolson, "Man Across the Desk," *Mademoiselle* (May, 1940), 197. See also Doris Blake, "Doris Warns Business Girls Office Devotee Ends an Emotional Bankrupt," *Chicago Daily Tribune* (July 10, 1932), E6; Bess Wheeler Skelton, "Business Clothes," *The Gregg Writer* 29 (June 1927): 461; Catherine Oglesby, *Business Opportunities for Women* (New York: Harper, 1937), 49.

16. Maule, *She Strives*, 156.

17. Marie Carney, *The Secretary and Her Job* (Charlottesville, VA: Business Book House, 1939), 292; Johnson, "Has Sex Any Place?"; Maule, *Pay Check*, 237–38. Also see Helen McCormick Johnston, *A Day in the Office* (New York: Gregg, 1941) 2, 20–23; MacGibbon, *Manners in Business*, 118–19; "From Her That Hath," *Harper's* 153 (June 1926): 116.

18. Susman, *Culture as History*, 164–66, 195, 200; Dale Carnegie, *How to Win Friends and Influence People* (New York: Simon and Schuster, 1936), 32, 245–84.

19. MacGibbon, *Manners in Business*, 120–21.

20. Marilyn S. Quayle, *As Told by Business Girls: Problems in Personal Adjustment* (New York: Woman's Press, 1932), 81, 95–96, 107; Burnham, "New Psychology," 396–97.

21. MacGibbon, *Manners in Business*, 121–22; Maule, *She Strives*, 157–59.

22. Fishbein and White, *Why Men Fail*, 7–10; Smith Ely Jeliffe, "Sex Has Thrown a Bomb into Business," ibid., 71–73, 75–76, 82–83.

23. Jeliffe, "Sex Has Thrown a Bomb," 75, 83. Gladys Torson's *How to Be a Hero to Your Secretary: A Handbook for Bosses* (New York: Greenberg, 1941) is the exception to this literature. Torson straightforwardly tells men not to pursue their employees because the women are in an economically vulnerable position. She also is unusual in telling bosses to stop consensual relationships because they will hurt morale (chapter 7).

24. Loire Brophy, "Glamour Goes to Business," *Glamour* (April 1940), 36–37. See also Maule, *She Strives*, 89; Alsop and McBride, *She's Off to Work*, 38; Maule, *Pay Check*, 235; Genn, "You Can't Vamp"; Fanny E. Ray, "The Business Woman," *Independent Woman* 10 (October, 1926), n.p. On the 1920s and informal office attire, women's assertion of their individuality, and adding an element of sexuality at work, see Kwolek-Folland, *Engendering Business*, 175.

25. Edith Johnson, "There's Luck in Being a Plain Girl," *Oklahoman* (December 29, 1935), 46.

26. "From Her That Hath," 116; Edith Johnson, "Problems of Saturday's Child," *Oklahoman* (September 6, 1932), 6; Johnson, "Has Sex Any Place?" See also Maule, *Pay Check*, 237.

27. Strom, *Beyond the Typewriter*, 373–74; Mary Christine Anderson, "Gender, Class, and Culture: Women Secretarial and Clerical Workers in the United States, 1925–1935" (Ph.D. diss., Ohio State University, 1986), 78, 384–85; "Loses Alienation Action," *New York Times* (October 23, 1935), 44; "Lawyer's Wife Loses Suit," *New York Times* (June 6, 1922), 23.

28. I examined the 108 case histories of "Normal Single Women" in series III D, box 2, focusing on office workers. Women volunteered to participate because they had questions about sexuality or needed a gynecological exam. Each subject was interviewed for two and a half hours on her sexual history. 63N, folder 6; 81N, folder 7; 34N, folder 3; 83N, folder 7; 67N, folder 6, Carney Landis Papers, Kinsey Institute for Research in Sex, Gender, and Reproduction, Inc., Bloomington, IN [hereafter Landis Papers].

29. Strom, *Beyond the Typewriter*, 387, 395.

30. 7N, folder 1; 1N, folder 1; 22N, folder 2; 62N, folder 6, Landis Papers. The histories do not always specify how a woman met the men with whom she was involved, but at least four met a man at work.

31. 2N, folder 1, Landis Papers.

32. On Italians and dating, see Elizabeth Alice Clement, *Love for Sale: Courting, Treating, and Prostitution in New York City, 1900–1945* (Chapel Hill: University of North Carolina Press, 2006), 236–38.

33. 27N, folder 3, Landis Papers.

34. Beth Bailey, *From Front Porch to Back Seat: Courtship in Twentieth-Century America* (Baltimore: Johns Hopkins University Press, 1988), 20–28, 57–61; Clement, *Love for Sale*, 217–19, 224–27; 42N, folder 4, Landis Papers.

35. 52N, folder 5; 48N, folder 4, Landis Papers.

36. 52N, folder 5; 107N, folder 9, Landis Papers.

37. Clement, *Love for Sale*, 222–23.

38. *Do-News* (November 30, 1940), 4; *The Clothes Shop* (July 1941); "Scoop," *Our Office Echo* (December 1938); Hilda Mokover, "A Glimpse into Room 1006," *Do-News* (November 30, 1940), 5–6; "Pinaforial," *Creditorial* (n.d., circa June 1941), United Office and Professional Workers of America Records, WAG 190, box 222A, Boxed Newspaper Collection, Local 16, Tamiment

Library / Robert F. Wagner Labor Archives, New York University [hereafter UOPWA Records].

39. Kwolek-Folland, *Engendering Business*, 123–27; "Scoop," *Echo News* (March–April 1941); *Clothes Shop* (July 1941); "Scoop," *Echo News* (April 1939), box 222A, UOPWA Records.

40. Jeff Hearn and Wendy Parkin, *"Sex" at "Work": The Power and Paradox of Organisation Sexuality*, rev. ed. (New York: St. Martins, 1995), 123–26, 7–8, 12.

41. Torson, *Ask My Secretary*, 152–53.

42. 107N, folder 9, Landis Papers.

CHAPTER FOUR. GOLD DIGGERS, INNOCENTS, AND TEMPTED WIVES

1. Faith Baldwin, *Skyscraper* (1931; New York: Feminist Press, 2003 [originally serialized in *Cosmopolitan* (June—October 1931)]), 7, 70–71, 261; *Skyscraper Souls* (Metro-Goldwyn-Mayer, 1932). On the increase in sexualized representations of the office in the 1930s, see Van Rensselaer Halsey, Jr., "The Portrait of the Businessman in 20th Century American Fiction" (Ph.D. diss., University of Pennsylvania, 1956), 82–83. On the symbolism of the skyscraper during the Depression, see Merrill Schleier, *Skyscraper Cinema: Architecture and Gender in American Film* (Minneapolis: University of Minnesota Press, 2009), 60–61, 117.

2. On young women's reading preferences, see Ruth Shonle Cavan, *Business Girls: A Study of Their Interests and Problems* (Chicago: Religious Education Association, 1929), 4, 13, 36–37. On movie attendance, see Richard Busch, "American Movie Audiences of the 1930s," *International Labor and Working-Class History* 59 (Spring 2001): 107–9; Mary Ryan, "The Projection of a New Womanhood: The Movie Moderns in the 1920's," in Jean E. Friedman and William G. Shade, eds., *Our American Sisters: Women in American Life and Thought*, 2nd ed. (Boston: Allyn and Bacon, 1976), 372–75. On popular culture and its role in shaping interpretations of reality, see, for example, Regina Kunzel, "Pulp Fictions and Problem Girls: Reading and Rewriting Single Pregnancy in the Postwar United States," *American Historical Review* 100 (December 1995), 1470–73; Janice Radway, *Reading the Romance: Women, Patriarchy, and Popular Literature* (Chapel Hill: University of North Carolina Press, 1984); Ann Barr Snitow, "Mass Market Romance: Pornography for Women Is Different," in Kathy Peiss and Christina Simmons, eds., *Passion and Power: Sexuality in History* (Philadelphia: Temple University Press, 1989), 261–64.

3. Janet Staiger, *Bad Women: Regulating Sexuality in Early American Cinema* (Minneapolis: University of Minnesota Press, 1995), 148–52.

4. Joanne Meyerowitz, *Women Adrift: Independent Wage Earners in Chicago, 1880–1930* (Chicago: University of Chicago Press, 1988), 126–28. The Hays Code, as it was called, had come about because of growing criticism of the immorality of films in the 1920s. Catholics, who had been the most outspoken critics during the 1920s, began a new crusade against Hollywood in 1933. At the same time, social scientists were studying the links between bad behavior and immoral

films. Worried about possible federal censorship, studios agreed to cede enforcement of the code to a new Production Code Administration, headed by Joseph Breen.

There were at least thirty-four gold digger films between 1921 and 1930; (Ryan, "Projection of a New Womanhood," 376–77. Fiction and film featuring a gold digging or deceitful female office worker include Thomas Edgelow, "An Amateur Adventuress," *Young's Magazine* 36 (October 1918): 19–24, and the film version (Metro Pictures, 1919); *A Virtuous Vamp* (First National Exhibitors' Circuit, 1919); *Lonesome Ladies* (First National Pictures, 1927), and *Soft Living* (1928). In Anita Loos's novel *Gentlemen Prefer Blondes* (1925), the stenographer Lorelei Lee turns into a gold digger only after being nearly raped by her employer; (New York: Liveright, 1998), 31–33; the novel was adapted into a film (Paramount, 1928) and, much later, a musical for stage and then film. The comedy *Love, Honor and Oh, Baby!* (Universal Pictures, 1933) based on the popular Broadway play, *Oh, Promise Me!*, features a heroine who follows a similar trajectory from victim to sexual agent. A few films pit the loyal, virtuous secretary against a gold digger in a competition for their employer; see, for example, *Behind Office Doors* (RKO, Radio Pictures, 1931), *Fair Play* (William Steiner Productions, 1925), and *A Beggar in Purple* (Pathe Exchange, 1920).

5. Ryan, "Projection of a New Womanhood," 367, 372–77; Susan Ware, *Holding Their Own: American Women in the 1930s* (Boston: Twayne, 1982), 179; Lea Jacobs, *The Wages of Sin: Censorship and the Fallen Woman Film, 1928–1942* (Madison: University of Wisconsin Press, 1991), 5, 10–17; Sumiko Higashi, *Virgins, Vamps, and Flappers: The American Silent Movie Heroine* (Montreal: Eden Press Women's Publications, 1978), 107.

6. *Red-Headed Woman* (Metro-Goldwyn-Mayer, 1932), based on Katharine Brush's novel (New York: Farrar and Rinehart, 1931), 3; Jacobs, *Wages of Sin*, 18, 69, 81–83.

7. Margaret McFadden, "'Anything Goes': Gender and Knowledge in the Comic Popular Culture of the 1930s" (Ph.D. diss., Yale University, 1996), 86–87, 116–17.

8. *Baby Face* (Warner Brothers, 1933). My discussion of *Baby Face* is based and builds on the arguments put forth by Richard Maltby, "*Baby Face*, or How Joe Breen Made Barbara Stanwyck Atone for Causing the Wall Street Crash," *Screen* 27 (1986): 22–45, and Jacobs, *Wages of Sin*, 60, 68–84.

9. Michael Grossberg, *Governing the Hearth: Law and the Family in Nineteenth-Century America* (Chapel Hill: University of North Carolina Press, 1985), 52–63; M. B. W. Sinclair, "Seduction and the Myth of the Ideal Woman," *Law and Inequality* 5 (1987): 65–69; "Cinched," *Puck* (July 24, 1915), 11.

In addition to breach of promise and seduction, heart balm actions included alienation of affection and criminal conversation. In some states that enacted reform, concern about young women led legislators to keep the seduction statute; Sinclair, "Seduction and Myth," 91. In some states reform ran into roadblocks when rich and/or unmarried legislators worried that a vote for reform might seem self-serving; "Pepper and Salt," *Wall Street Journal* (May 27, 1935), 4.

10. Theodore E. Apstein, *The Parting of the Ways* (New York: Dodge, 1935), 17–27; Rebecca Tushnet, "Rules of Engagement," *Yale Law Journal* 107 (1998): 2589.

11. Jurist quoted in Apstein, *Parting of the Ways*, 18; Sinclair, "Seduction and Myth," 84; Tushnet, "Rules of Engagement," 2583–84. On the distrust of women, see Robert C. Brown, "Breach of Promise Suits," *University of Pennsylvania Law Review and American Law Register* 77 (1929): 491–96; Jane Larson, "Women Understand So Little, They Call My Good Nature 'Deceit': A Feminist Rethinking of Seduction," *Columbia Law Review* 93 (1993): 393–95.

12. Sinclair, "Seduction and Myth," 84–86, 90; Grossberg, *Governing the Hearth*, 55; Ariela R. Dubler, "Wifely Behavior: A Legal History of Acting Married," *Columbia Law Review* 100 (2000): 957–1021; Lisa Cardyn, "The Construction of Female Sexual Trauma in Turn-of-the-Century American Mental Medicine," in Mark Micale and Paul Lerner, eds., *Traumatic Pasts* (New York: Cambridge University Press, 2001), 197; Angus McLaren, *Sexual Blackmail: A Modern History* (Cambridge: Harvard University Press, 2002), 62–64, 102–3, 173–74, chapters 4 and 7; Delancey Knox, "The High Cost of Loving," *Forum* 61 (1919): 745.

13. *Indianapolis Times* (March 4, 1935), 6, as quoted in Sinclair, "Seduction and Myth," 92.

14. "Balm for Broken Heart," *Mansfield (OH) News* (February 19, 1913), 2; "$12,000 Award to Typist," *New York Times* (February 19, 1913), 7; "$12,000 Heart Balm," *Fitchburg (Mass.) Daily Sentinel* (February 24, 1913), n.p.; "Jilted Girl Wins $10,000," *New York Times* (May 14, 1927), 9.
    Defendants in sensationalized cases included Cornelius Vanderbilt Whitney, Enrico Caruso, and Frederic Gimbel of the department store Gimbels; Mary Coombs, "Agency and Partnership: A Study of Breach of Promise Plaintiffs," *Yale Journal of Law and Feminism* 2 (1989): 16. The former governor of Mississippi and a millionaire carpet manufacturer, who had served as president of the Bible-placing Gideons, found themselves on the receiving end of a suit filed by the woman who did their typing; "Woman Accuses Governor Russell," *New York Times* (February 7, 1922), 15; "Russell Acquitted of Woman's Charge," *New York Times* (December 22, 1922), 9; "Chicago Woman Sues Ex-Head of Gideons," *New York Times* (July 27, 1929), 8; "Girl's Suit Against Boggs Dismissed," *Washington Post* (August 6, 1929), 5. For a fuller discussion of press coverage of breach of promise suits, see http://history.sewanee.edu/facstaff/berebitsky/.

15. Coombs, "Agency and Partnership," 3, 17–18.

16. Ibid., 13–14.

17. Mary Beth Haralovich, "The Proletarian Woman's Film of the 1930s: Contending with Censorship and Entertainment," in Annette Kuhn and Jackie Stacey, eds., *Screen Histories: A Screen Reader* (New York: Oxford University Press, 1998), 82–95.

18. *Big Business Girl* (First National Pictures, 1931); Mordaunt Hall, "The Screen," *New York Times* (June 12, 1931), 29. For other exploitation films set in an office, see http://history.sewanee.edu/facstaff/berebitsky/.

19. *Female* (First National Pictures, 1933).

20. Dorothy Dix, "Women as Wage Earners," *The Typewriter and Phonographic World* 26 (July 1905): 6–7; Lisa Fine, *The Souls of the Skyscraper* (Philadelphia: Temple University Press, 1990), 64, 69, 140–45.

21. On the readership of "business girls," see Cavan, *Business Girls*, 4, 13, 36–37. By 1935 Baldwin had published a dozen romances featuring modern businesswomen, and many had undergone the same republication/adaptation process as *Skyscraper*, discussed at the start of the chapter. On Baldwin, see Harvey Breit, "Faith Baldwin Interviewed," *New York Times* (May 1, 1949), BR23, and Laura Hapke, Afterword to *Skyscraper*.

22. Baldwin, *Skyscraper*, 72. Baldwin also addressed how office work soured women's impression of young men in "The Office Wife," serialized in *Cosmopolitan* (October, November, December 1929, January, February, March 1930) and "Wife Versus Secretary," *Cosmopolitan* (May 1935). On wages, see Fine, *Souls of the Skyscraper*, 172.

23. Baldwin, *Skyscraper*, 62, 76, 171.

24. Maureen Honey, *Creating Rosie the Riveter: Class, Gender, and Propaganda During World War II* (Amherst: University of Massachusetts Press, 1984), 65–72.

25. Faith Baldwin, *Week-End Marriage* (New York: Triangle, 1944); Lois Scharf, *To Work and to Wed: Female Employment, Feminism, and the Great Depression* (Westport, CT: Greenwood, 1980), 26–28, 40–42, 46, 60–65, 104; "Man at the Fireside," *Harper's* (May 1933), 757, quoted in Alice Kessler Harris, *Out to Work* (New York: Oxford University Press, 1982), 250–57. Baldwin also addressed this issue in *Skyscraper* and in *Men Are Such Fools!* (New York: Farrar and Rinehart, 1936). Married women increased from 21 to 28 percent of all female workers during this decade and experienced the most discrimination in white-collar work.

26. "His Wife Was Wise's Typewriter," *Washington Post* (December 2, 1894), 1; "Wants Damages," *Syracuse Standard* (May 10, 1896), 1; "Divorced Husband's Balm Suit Names 2," *Washington Post* (July 27, 1928), 3. "Alienation of affection" stemmed from the English common law governing master-servant relations, in which a party could be held civilly liable for enticing a servant away from the master. This principle was extended to marriage based on the idea that a wife's body was her husband's property; Jeffrey Brian Greenstein, "Sex, Lies, and American Tort Law," *Georgetown Journal of Gender and the Law* 5 (2004): 732–33.

27. Baldwin, "Wife Versus Secretary," 187, 199–200.

28. Dorothy Dix, "Foolish Jealousy," *Boston Daily Globe* (March 11, 1918), 10; "Daytime Wives," *Atlanta Constitution* (July 6, 1924), B4; Dorothy Dix, "The Love Pirates," *Boston Daily Globe* (February 24, 1922), 20. Women who failed to meet the new ideal of sexual partner risked losing their husbands;

see Christina Simmons, "Companionate Marriage and the Lesbian Threat," *Frontiers* 4 (Autumn 1979): 57–58. Magazine fiction began to focus on a wife's shortcomings in the 1920s; Donald Makosky "The Portrayal of Women in Wide-Circulation Magazine Short Stories, 1905–55" (Ph.D. diss., University of Pennsylvania, 1966), 319; Angel Kwolek-Folland, *Engendering Business: Men and Women in the Corporate Office*, 1870–1930 (Baltimore: Johns Hopkins University Press, 1994), 66.

29. Doris Blake, "This Wife Fears the Bugaboo of the Office 'Love Pirate,'" *Chicago Daily Tribune* (September 18, 1926), 26.

30. Faith Baldwin, *White Collar Girl* (New York: Farrar and Rinehart, 1933), 49.

31. *The Office Wife* (Warner Brothers and Vitaphone), 1930; Mordaunt Hall, "The Screen," *New York Times* (September 27, 1930), 24; *Wife vs. Secretary* (Metro-Goldwyn-Mayer, 1936). For a discussion of the film versions of Baldwin's novels, see Schleier, *Skyscraper Cinema*, 98–111.

32. Patrick Johns-Heine and Hans H. Gerth, "Values in Mass Periodical Fiction, 1921–1940," *Public Opinion Quarterly* (Spring 1949), 107; George Gerbner, "The Social Role of the Confession Magazine," *Social Problems* 6 (Summer 1958): 31–38; Honey, *Creating Rosie the Riveter*, 148.

33. "Not the Marrying Kind," *True Story* (August 1934), 74, 41.

34. "I Mixed Love with Business," *True Confessions* (June 1927), 34.

35. Nancy Crosby, "Office Boyfriend," *Sweetheart Stories* (January 1939), 31–41; "Marrying Money," *True Romances* (December 1935) 14–18, 97–101.

36. Bernard Seaman, "An Interview with Angelica Balabanoff," *Ledger* 2 (March 1936): 12; Leonard Bright, "The Boss Is Always Right," *Ledger* 2 (March 1936): 11; Ethel Polk, "What Henrietta Ripperger Doesn't Know About Office Workers," *Ledger* 2 (April 1936): 6. On clerical unemployment, see Sharon Hartman Strom, "'We're No Kitty Foyles': Organizing Office Workers for the Congress of Industrial Organizations, 1937–50," in Ruth Milkman, ed., *Women, Work, and Protest: A Century of U.S. Women's Labor History* (New York: Routledge, 1985), 209–11.

37. Pearl Winik, "The Sad Story of Stylish Sedelle," *Ledger* 2 (February 1936): 12. Tess Slesinger, an author with leftist sympathies who supported striking office workers in the mid-1930s, similarly exposed the folly of pinning your hopes on the boss in the short story "The Mouse-Trap," published in 1935; see Laura Hapke, *Daughters of the Great Depression* (Athens: University of Georgia Press, 1995), 193–99.

38. Dorothy Thompson, "Is America a Paradise for Women?" *Pictorial Review* (June 1929), 60, quoted in Hapke, *Daughters of the Great Depression*, 206; Tania Modleski, *Loving with a Vengeance: Mass Produced Fantasies for Women* (New York: Routledge, 1984), 14–15.

CHAPTER FIVE. MORALS AND MORALE

1. Harrison R. Johnson, "Love-in-the-Office," *Modern Office Procedures* 4 (June 1959): 13–14, 16.

2. Sanford Jacoby, *Modern Manors: Welfare Capitalism Since the New Deal* (Princeton: Princeton University Press, 1997), 43–44, 246–47; Olivier Zunz, *Making America Corporate, 1870–1920* (Chicago: University of Chicago Press, 1990), 1–2 (the employment figure excludes agricultural workers); Stuart Ewen, *PR! A Social History of Spin* (New York: Basic, 1996), 292, 300–304, 353–56, 380, 400–401 (corporations began to employ P.R. firms around 1900 in response to muckrackers' and labor advocates' exposés).

3. Johnson, "Love-in-the-Office," 14.

4. Robert Ramspeck, "Civil Service Wonderland," *Colliers* (May 15, 1943), 26, 60.

5. Women wrote twenty-two of the twenty-five letters about favoritism in which the authors' gender was given. It is impossible to state definitely that the majority of those who complained about favoritism were older, but in those letters in which it is possible to gauge the age of the author, the vast majority were at least in their thirties, which made them older than most female clerical workers; by 1950 the average age had risen, yet more than half were still under thirty; U.S. Department of Labor, Women's Bureau, *"Older" Women as Office Workers*, bulletin no. 248 (Washington, DC, 1953), 48–52, 58.

6. Initials in text do not correspond with the correspondent's initials. All citations from National Archives, Washington, DC, Records of the House Committee on the Civil Service Pertaining to the Investigation of Civilian Employment in the Federal Government, 1942–46, RG 233. Box 15, folder 4–2–102, July 4, 1944, and July 6, 1944; box 8, folder 1–11–1-(8), October 8, no year. For similar complaints, all in RG 233, see box 19, folder 7–11–0, February 20, 1945; box 26, folder National Housing Agency, June 30, 1944; box 16, folder 4–8, February 12, 1943; box 7, folder 1–5–0, anonymous, February 2, 1943; box 11, folder 4–0–1, "Incidents Shedding Light on the Cause . . .," n.d.; box 16, folder 4–10, July 26, 1943; box 26, folder Office of Censorship, n.d.; box 20, folder 7–18–5–(11), April 5, 1942; box 15, folder 4–2–26, April 18, 1944; box 10, folder 3–6–18, February 6, 1943; box 11, folder 3–7–11, July 27, 1943, and August 16, 1943; box 11, folder 4–0–1, "A Tax Payer," October 27, 1942; box 21, folder 9–2–0, "One Who Knows," January 3, 1943; box 24, folder Federal Communications Commission, anonymous, April 3, 1943.

   Even before the war, federal workers complained that promotions went to girls with "looks, not brains"; "Government Girls Who Passed District Bar Exams Doubt Training Will Bring Success," *Washington Post* (February 27, 1941), 17. Because information regarding the correspondent's background is different in each letter, it is impossible to determine a pattern regarding which letters the committee took seriously and which they disregarded. It also is not always clear what, if any, action the committee took in investigating a complaint.

7. Beatrice Vincent, "How to Get Along with the Boss, *Washington Post* (August 12, 1951), S10; Women's Bureau, *"Older" Women*, 48–52, 58; Malvina Lindsay, "The Gentler Sex," *Washington Post* (February 9, 1946), 10; Adelaide Kerr, "Memo: Don't Yield to Those Tears," *Washington Post* (January 4, 1953), S3; RG 233, box 14, folder 4–5, February 24, 1943, March 29, 1943, June 2, 1943.

For complaints about young women, all in RG 233, see box 11, folder 4–0–4, November 20, 1942; box 18, folder 7–0–0, n.d.; box 15, folder 4–7, August 31, 1943; box 27, folder Region 1, October 21, 1942. On age discrimination, generational tensions, favoritism, and the role of popular culture in the 1910s and 1920s, see Sharon Hartman Strom, *Beyond the Typewriter* (Urbana: University of Illinois Press, 1992), 398–405.

8. In 1940 women accounted for 42 percent of the total number of government workers in the capital; by 1945 they were 59.7 percent of the total. These women's marital status and age is unknown, but the press implied that Washington's war workers were young and single; Margaret C. Rung, "Paternalism and Pink Collars: Gender and Federal Employee Relations, 1941–50," *Business History Review* 71 (Autumn 1997): 404, note 44, 406–10; "Young Women Urged to Avoid Meeting Little Known Men," *Washington Post* (October 9, 1944), 1; Jane Mersky Leder, *Thanks for the Memories: Love, Sex, and World War II* (Westport, CT: Praeger, 2006), 24–25. On the government girl's threatening independence, see Page Dougherty Delano, "Making Up for War: Sexuality and Citizenship in Wartime Culture," *Feminist Studies* 26 (Spring 2000): 45–46, 33.

9. Marilyn E. Hegarty, *Victory Girls, Khaki-Wackies, and Patriotutes: The Regulation of Female Sexuality During World War II* (New York: New York University Press, 2008), 125, 130–35.

10. Angel Kwolek-Folland, *Engendering Business: Men and Women in the Corporate Office, 1870–1930* (Baltimore: Johns Hopkins University Press, 1994), 143–58; Clark Davis, *Company Men: White-Collar Life and Corporate Cultures in Los Angeles, 1892–1941* (Baltimore: Johns Hopkins University Press, 2000), 179–84; RG 233, box 10, folder 3–4–0, March 18, 1943; "Mary Haworth's Mail," *Washington Post* (February 18, 1943), B2; "Mary Haworth's Mail," *Washington Post* (February 23, 1943), B3.

11. "Mary Haworth's Mail," *Washington Post* (February 15, 1943), B3.

12. "Mary Haworth's Mail," *Washington Post* (February 18, 1943), B2; "Mary Haworth's Mail," *Washington Post* (February 24, 1943), B2; "Mary Haworth's Mail," *Washington Post* (March 3, 1943), B3.

13. Martin Weil, "Ex-Post Columnist Mary Haworth, 80, Dies," *Washington Post* (November 2, 1981), B6; "Mary Haworth's Mail," *Washington Post* (August 25, 1943), 2B. Private industry introduced employee counselors around 1920 as part of welfare capitalism; Kwolek-Folland, *Engendering Business*, 138–39.

14. On the government's use of human relations and psychological counseling with civilian personnel during the war see Rung, "Paternalism and Pink Collars," 385–86, 390–93; "Mary Haworth's Mail," *Washington Post* (February 18, 1943); Elaine Tyler May, *Homeward Bound: American Families in the Cold War Era* (New York: Basic, 1980), 59–61.

15. Similar handwriting suggests one person might have written most of these letters. RG 233, box 11, folder 3–17–18.

16. RG 233, box 11, folder 3–17–18, April 6, 1943.

17. RG 233, box 11, folder 3–17–18, "Disgusted," n.d. "Disgusted" did not specify whether the woman was single or married. For a similar supervisor, see RG 233, box 24, folder Federal Communications Commission, "An Interested Observer," August 18, 1943. For another "immoral" office see RG 233, box 13, folder 4–3, November 19, 1942.

18. RG 233, box 16, folder 4–11, July 30, 1945; August 3, 1945; August 23, 1945.

19. RG 233, box 25, folder General Accounting Office, September 27, 1944; deposition, September 28, 1944; September 15, 1944; August 23, 1944; statement, n.d.

20. RG 233, box 20, folder 7–18–12–(23), June 24, 1943. The files do not provide enough information to assess how civil service personnel regulations, military rules, or military culture affected these situations.

21. RG 233, box 18, folder 7–4–0, February 26, 1943; December 31, 1942; Efficiency Rating Appeal, n.d.

22. Rung, "Paternalism and Pink Collars," 391–95, 398–404, 415. Evidence that Ramspeck investigators were attuned to psychology can be seen in their decision to investigate one man's charge that his supervisors were having affairs with female subordinates after an interview determined that he was "definitely not suffering from a persecution complex"; RG 233, box 20, folder 7–15–0, December 13, 1944. In another case, government psychiatrists determined that a woman who maintained that her supervisors belittled her work because she had spurned their advances was suffering from a "paranoic condition"; RG 233, box 20, folder 7–12–0–(4), November 2, 1942; October 26, 1942. The records do not generally indicate whether the specific supervisors or personnel heads I discuss had training in psychology or human relations, or whether these problems ever made their way to an agency's personnel office.

23. Rung, "Paternalism and Pink Collars," 399. On women's use of formulaic fiction to explain sexual harassment and single pregnancy, respectively, see Nan Enstad, *Ladies of Labor, Girls of Adventure* (New York: Columbia University Press, 1999), 142–45; Regina Kunzel, "Pulp Fictions and Problem Girls: Reading and Rewriting Single Pregnancy in the Postwar United States," *American Historical Review* 100 (December 1995), 1468, 1477–85.

24. "Mary Haworth's Mail," *Washington Post* (March 17, 1944), 7.

25. On the government and popular media see Kunzel, "Pulp Fictions and Problem Girls," 1466–67; Maureen Honey, *Creating Rosie the Riveter* (Amherst: University of Massachusetts Press, 1985), chapter 1.

26. David K. Johnson, *The Lavender Scare: The Cold War Persecution of Gays and Lesbians in the Federal Government* (Chicago: University of Chicago Press, 2004), 1–5, 12, 44–46, 148–51; Allan Bérubé, *Coming Out Under Fire* (New York: Penguin, 1990), 57–59, 61–64; *Before Stonewall* (New York: Before Stonewall, 1985). Although many letters to Ramspeck contained racist and anti-Semitic comments, I did not find comments about homosexuals.

27. Johnson, *Lavender Scare*, 153, 156.

28. Tyler May, *Homeward Bound*, chapter 4; Jane Sherron De Hart, "Containment at Home: Gender, Sexuality, and National Identity in Cold War America," in Peter J. Kuznick and James Gilbert, eds., *Rethinking Cold War Culture* (Washington, DC: Smithsonian Institution Press, 2001), 124–30; Miriam Reumann, *American Sexual Character: Sex, Gender, and National Identity in the Kinsey Reports* (Berkeley: University of California Press, 2005), chapter 1.

29. Alfred Kinsey, Wardell B. Pomeroy, and Clyde E. Martin, *Sexual Behavior in the Human Male* (Philadelphia: W. B. Saunders, 1948), 623, 585–87, 363–64. On the response to these statements, see James Gilbert, *Men in the Middle* (Chicago: University of Chicago Press, 2005), 85–86. On the "crisis" in masculinity, see Barbara Ehrenreich, *The Hearts of Men: American Dreams and the Flight from Commitment* (Garden City, NY: Anchor /Doubleday, 1983), 29–41; Gilbert, introduction to *Men in the Middle*; Reumann, *American Sexual Character*, chapter 2.

30. Frank S. Caprio, *Marital Infidelity* (New York: Citadel, 1953), 141, 57, and see also 34, 74–75; Edmund Bergler, *The Revolt of the Middle-Aged Man* (New York: A. A. Wyn, 1954), vi, 104, 118; "Middle-Aged Rake Called Mentally Ill," *Science Digest* 39 (April 1956): 26–27. About half the cases of husbands' and wives' adultery that Caprio examines have their origins in the office. Unfortunately, Bergler does not generally include information on where the adulterer met his lover. See also "Mary Haworth's Mail," *Washington Post* (September 10, 1953), 28, and "Mary Haworth's Mail," *Washington Post* (January 15, 1948), B7; Lynn Hurley, "Heart to Heart," *Chicago Daily Tribune* (April 28, 1957), E6; "Learns Hard Way: Other Woman Pays," *Chicago Daily Tribune* (June 30, 1958), B11; American Association of Marriage Counselors, *Marriage Counseling: A Casebook* (New York: American Association of Marriage Counselors Press, 1958), 164, 176, 189; John F. Cuber, *The Significant Americans: A Study of the Sexual Behavior of the Affluent* (New York: Appleton-Century, 1965), 37, 91, 146–51, 197.

31. Bergler, *Revolt of the Middle-Aged Man*, 7–9.

32. Louis P. Saxe and Noel B. Gerson, *Sex and the Mature Man* (New York: Gilbert, 1964), 20–21; Hyman Spotnitz, M.D., and Lucy Freeman, *The Wandering Husband* (New York: Tower, 1964), 116–17, 124.

33. William H. Whyte, Jr., "The Corporation and the Wife," *Fortune* 44 (November 1951): 109–11; William H. Whyte, Jr., "The Wives of Management," *Fortune* 44 (October 1951): 87, 208, 210; Tyler May, *Homeward Bound*, 101–2.

34. Spotnitz and Freeman, *Wandering Husband*, 116, 17; Bergler, *Revolt of the Middle-Aged Man*, 164–65, 122–23, 142–43; Caprio, *Marital Infidelity*, 196, 199–200.

35. Caprio, *Marital Infidelity*, 169–70.

36. Ibid., viii; J. P. Edwards, "Do Women Provoke Sex Attack?" *Cosmopolitan* (March 1960), 36–40; Estelle B. Freedman, " 'Uncontrolled Desires': The Response to the Sexual Psychopath, 1920–1960," *Journal of American History* 74 (June 1987): 101–2. Psychiatry redefined other problems with a social component into personal maladjustment; see Regina Kunzel, *Fallen Women, Problem Girls:*

Unmarried Mothers and the Professionalization of Social Work, 1890–1945 (New Haven: Yale University Press, 1993), chapter 6; Rickie Solinger, *Wake Up Little Susie: Single Pregnancy and Race Before Roe v. Wade* (New York: Routledge, 2000), chapter 3.

37. Caprio, *Marital Infidelity*, 15, 34; Max Lerner, "A Morals Case," *New York Post* (January 23, 1959), 38.

38. A. M. Sperber, *Murrow: His Life and Times* (New York: Freundlich, 1986), 546–48; "The Business of Vice," part 4, *New York Post* (February 25, 1959), 4; "The Business of Vice," part 1, *New York Post* (February 21, 1959), 4, 48.

39. Transcript in "The Business of Vice," 4: 25.

40. "Firms Deny Sex Sales," *New York Journal American* (January 22, 1959), 5; "Blast Murrow Show," *New York Journal American* (January 26, 1959), 7; Harry Benjamin and Robert E. L. Masters, *Prostitution and Morality* (New York: Julian, 1964), 344; Eve Merriam, "Sex as a Selling Aid," *Nation* (March 21, 1959), 240; "Reckless Smear," *New York Journal-American* (January 22, 1959), editorial page; George Sokolsky, "Quick Work in the Manner of Blackmail," *Lima (Ohio) News* (March 22, 1959), editorial page; Stan Opotowsky, "Business Firms Caught Deducting Call-girl 'Expenses' on Tax Returns," *New York Post* (February 22, 1959), 4.

41. Reumann, *American Sexual Character*, 70, 75–80, Mailer quotation on 65; Whyte, "The Wives of Management," 207; "Sin and Industry," *New York Post* (January 23, 1959), 39; Lerner, "Morals Case." On the relation between men's "softness" and larger political and social concerns, see Jessamyn Neuhaus, "The Importance of Being Orgasmic: Sexuality, Gender, and Marital Sex Manuals in the United States, 1920–1963," *Journal of the History of Sexuality* 9 (2000): 465–71. On the connections between American men's sexual virility and Cold War foreign policy, see Frank Costigliola, "'Unceasing Pressure for Penetration': Gender, Pathology, and Emotion in George Kennan's Formation of the Cold War," *Journal of American History* 83 (1997): 1309–39.

42. "Daily Close-Up: Irving Gitlin," *New York Post* (January 23, 1959), 30; Merriam, "Sex as a Selling Aid," 242.

43. On Riesman, see Gilbert, *Men in the Middle*, chapter 3.

44. "How to Create Good Will," *Time* (March 4, 1957), 93; "Woman, 31, Freed in Mann Act Case," *New York Times* (March 5, 1957), 32; Merriam, "Sex as a Selling Aid," 241–42; Eugene Spagnoli and Neal Patterson, "Wrote Orders for GE by Carload," *New York Daily News* (March 1, 1957), 3.

45. "How to Create Good Will"; Margaret Mead, *Male and Female* (New York: Mentor, 1955), 236, quoted in Reumann, *American Sexual Character*, 61.

46. Gayle Rubin, "The Traffic in Women: Note on the 'Political Economy' of Sex," rpt. in Joan Wallach Scott, *Feminism and History* (New York: Oxford University Press, 1996), 116–20; "The Business of Vice," part 2, *New York Post* (February 22, 1959), 18.

47. "The Business of Vice," 2: 18.

48. Cuber, *Significant Americans*, 5–7, 152, 154.

49. Ann Landers, "Hubby 'Entertains,'" *Indianapolis Star* (March 29, 1959), 4; Sara Harris, *They Sell Sex: The Call Girl and Big Business* (New York: Fawcett, 1960), 129–42. Spagnoli and Patterson, "Wrote Orders for GE"; Merriam, "Sex as a Selling Aid," 241.

50. This summary is based on "Connie Details Her Love Life with Slain Forrest Teel," *Indianapolis Star* (April 8, 1959), 2–3; "Connie Tells of Shooting," *Indianapolis Star* (April 11, 1959), 12–15, 25; "Connie Answers Final Questions," *Indianapolis Star* (April 14, 1959), 14; Suzanne Roberts, "He Said He'd Marry Me!" *True Story* 81 (August 1959): 18–20, 22, 24, 26, 28–30. On press coverage see "Trial Drawing Full Attention," *Indianapolis Star* (April 2, 1959), 11; Tom Faulconer, *In the Eyes of the Law* (Bloomington, IN: Authorhouse, 2006), 57, 83–84, 130; "Women Eat, Watch, and Weep," *Indianapolis Star* (April 8, 1959), 1.

51. Gary Alan Fine, "Scandal, Social Conditions, and the Creation of Public Attention: Fatty Arbuckle and the 'Problem of Hollywood,'" *Social Problems* 44 (August 1997): 297–98; Edward H. Frank, "Dying Teel Wouldn't Tell," *Indianapolis Star* (April 1, 1959) 1; Faulconer, *Eyes of the Law*, 114, 94, 159–60; "Connie Tells of Shooting," 13; Edward H. Frank, "Connie Tells of Killing," *Indianapolis Star* (April 11, 1959), 1; Jack V. Fox, "Woman Provoked Fatal Fight with Her Lover, Claim," *Sheboygan (Wisconsin) Press*, (March 31, 1959), 1.

52. Roberts, "He Said He'd Marry Me!" 36, 22, 29, 28, 19, 30.

53. Claudia Goldin, *Understanding the Gender Gap* (New York: Oxford University Press, 1990), 17–19. These percentages are for white women. The increase was especially dramatic for women ages thirty-five to forty-four. "Mary Haworth's Mail," *Washington Post* (May 3, 1959), F18; "Mary Haworth's Mail," *Washington Post* (May 29, 1959), C2. In *Sexual Behavior in the Human Female* (Philadelphia: W. B. Saunders, 1953), Kinsey et al. reported that by the age of forty, 26 percent of married women had committed adultery. No information on the origins of these affairs was provided (416).

54. Edward H. Frank, "Connie Guilty; Faces Prison," *Indianapolis Star* (April 16, 1959), 1; Edward H. Frank, "3 Who Oppose Capital Penalty Kept Off Jury," *Indianapolis Star* (March 17, 1959), 1; Faulconer, *Eyes of the Law*, 139–41; Ann Landers, "Erring Husband Faces 'Big Price,'" *Indianapolis Star* (March 23, 1959), 7.

55. On Teel's rise, see "He Said He'd Marry Me!" 22. On his lifestyle, see Faulconer, *Eyes of the Law*, 25, 39–40. On Cadillacs and the "pecking order" evident in the smallest details of the corporate office, see Vance Packard, *The Status Seekers* (New York: David McKay, 1959), chapter 8, 314–17; Helen Whitcomb and John Whitcomb, *Strictly for Secretaries*, rev. ed. (1957; New York: McGraw Hill, 1965), 51.

56. E. J. Kahn, Jr., *All in a Century: The First 100 Years of Eli Lilly and Company* (Indianapolis: Lilly, 1976), 12–13, 154, 165; Faulconer, *Eyes of the Law*, 25, 181.

57. Louis McLain, "Caution: Love at Work," *Washington Post* (August 30, 1959), AW4; "Claims Railroad Helped Break Up His Marriage, Demands $500,000,"

Sheboygan (Wisconsin) Press (June 24, 1959), 11; "Clears Railroad in Alienation of Affection Suit," *Mason City* (Iowa) *Globe-Gazette* (December 29, 1961), 2.

58. Frederick Dyer, *Executive's Guide to Handling People* (Englewood Cliffs, NJ: Prentice-Hall, 1958), 166–67. A textbook illustrates the HR approach's broad interpretation of work conditions. One case history involved a female factory worker who quit because her female supervisor told "vulgar stories" and passed around "dirty" pictures, which the employee found offensive. The personnel director sided with the employee, determining that all employees had "the right to expect that working conditions be reasonably agreeable." The discussion questions asked students, "How much responsibility should an employer assume regarding the 'questionable' conduct of employees within the plant? Outside the plant?" Florence Peterson, *Personnel Case Studies* (New York: Harper, 1955), 113–17, 309–16.

59. "Mary Haworth's Mail," *Washington Post* (May 20, 1958), B4.

60. "Mary Haworth's Mail," *Washington Post* (December 21, 1949), B4; "Mary Haworth's Mail," *Washington Post* (December 21, 1960), C22; "Mary Haworth's Mail," *Washington Post* (December 10, 1964), F6; Anson Campbell, *Kitty Unfoiled: An Informal Portrait of the American Secretary* (Pittsburgh: Reuter and Bragdon, 1952), 74–76; Norma Lee Browning, "Wanted: A Husband!" *Chicago Daily Tribune* (February 17, 1952), C4.

61. Harrison R. Johnson, Jr., "Let's Have a Controlled Christmas Party," *Modern Office Procedures* 3 (December 1958): 7; Johnson, "Love-in-the-Office," 16.

62. Merriam, "Sex as a Selling Aid," 242; Helen Gurley Brown, *Sex and the Single Girl* (New York: Bernard Geis, 1962), 30.

CHAPTER SIX. THE WHITE-COLLAR REVOLUTION

1. Helen Gurley Brown, *Sex and the Office* (New York: Bernard Geis, 1964), 183–88. For more on Brown, see Julie Berebitsky, "The Joy of Work: Helen Gurley Brown, Gender, and Sexuality in the White-Collar Office," *Journal of the History of Sexuality* 15 (January 2006): 89–127.

2. Jennifer Scanlon, *Bad Girls Go Everywhere: The Life of Helen Gurley Brown* (New York: Oxford University Press, 2009), 87. On Brown and the sexual revolution, see David Allyn, *Make Love, Not War: The Sexual Revolution, an Unfettered History* (New York: Routledge, 2001), chapter 1; Barbara Ehrenreich, Elizabeth Hess, and Gloria Jacobs, *Re-Making Love: The Feminization of Sex* (Garden City, NY: Doubleday, 1986), 56–63.

3. Scanlon, *Bad Girls Go Everywhere*, 6–56.

4. Arthur Berman, "Married Life Pleases Author," *New York Post* (June 15, 1962), 48, and Joan Didion, "Bosses Make Lousy Lovers," *Saturday Evening Post* (January 30, 1965), 36, box 21, Helen Gurley Brown Papers, Sophia Smith Collection, Smith College, Northampton, Massachusetts [hereafter HGB Papers]; Betty Bevan, "Office Sexpert," n.d., box 24, folder 8, HGB Papers; Helen Gurley Brown, *Sex and the Single Girl* (New York: Bernard Geis, 1962), 1; Helen Gurley Brown, *Having It All* (New York: Simon and Schuster, 1982), 10–11; Jesse

Kornbluth, "The Queen of the Mouseburgers," *New York* (September 27, 1982), 39–40; Brown, *Sex and the Office*, 7–9.

5. Elizabeth Gregg MacGibbon, *Manners in Business*, new ed. (New York: Macmillan, 1954), 133, 136, 138 (*Manners* had its ninth reprinting in 1969); Marylin C. Burke, *The Executive Secretary: Techniques for Success in the Secretarial Career* (New York: Doubleday, 1959), 23, 67, 158–59; Esther Becker and Richard L. Lawrence, *Success and Satisfaction in Your Office Job* (New York: Harper, 1954), 67–68.

6. Arthur Adler, *All Girl Office* (New York: Domino, 1965), back cover; Yvonne Keller, " 'Was It Right to Love Her Brother's Wife So Passionately?': Lesbian Pulp Novels and U.S. Lesbian Identity, 1950–1965," *American Quarterly* 57 (2005): 385–410. We also know that professional men read detective-story pulp magazines; Erin A. Smith, *Hard-Boiled: Working-Class Readers and Pulp Magazines* (Philadelphia: Temple University Press, 2000), part I.

7. Dean Hudson, *Office Party* (San Diego: Corinth, 1965); Lisa K. Speer, "Paperback Pornography: Mass Market Novels and Censorship in Post-War America," *Journal of American and Comparative Cultures* 24 (Fall–Winter 2001): 153–60; Kenneth C. Davis, *Two-Bit Culture: The Paperbacking of America* (Boston: Houghton Mifflin, 1984), 216–47.

    Novels following the traditional Cinderella plot include Gail Jordan, *Sins of a Private Secretary* (New York: Croydon, 1952); Joan Tucker, *Young Secretary* (New York: Venus, 1954); and Mark West, *Office Affair* (New York: Beacon, 1961). Novels showing work-related sexual encounters as important in a woman's acceptance of domesticity include Jerry Weil, *Office Wife* (New York: Lancer, 1956); Jack Hanley, *Very Private Secretary* (New York: Beacon, 1960); and Dirk Malloy, *Office Favorite* (New York: Midwood, 1966).

8. Smith, *Hard-Boiled*, 4–12, 165–66; Steve Meyer, "Workplace Predators: Sexuality and Harassment on the U.S. Automotive Shop Floor, 1930–1960," *Labor: Studies in Working-Class History* 1 (Spring 2004): 82; *Woman's World* (Twentieth Century–Fox, 1954). Pulps featuring an employer and his employee's wife include James Layne, *Lend Me Your Wife* (New York: Beacon, 1961); Max Collier, *The Payoff* (New York: Midwood-Tower, 1963); and Max Collier, *Group Sex* (New York: Midwood, 1968).

9. "Playboy's Office Playmate," *Playboy* (July 1955); "Playboy's Girl Friday," *Playboy* (September 1957), 39; Arv Miller, "The Perfect Secretary," *Playboy* (May 1956), 45–49; "Dear Playboy," *Playboy* (June 1954), 2. On *Playboy*'s office humor, see Elizabeth Fraterrigo, *Playboy and the Making of the Good Life in Modern America* (New York: Oxford University Press, 2009), 116–24.

10. Van Rensselaer Halsey, Jr., "The Portrait of the Businessman in 20th Century American Fiction" (Ph.D. diss., University of Pennsylvania, 1956), 115–17; Willard H. Temple, "The Available Male," *Saturday Evening Post* (January 2, 1954), 25; Donald Makosky, "The Portrayal of Women in Wide-Circulation Magazine Short Stories, 1905–1955" (Ph.D. diss., University of Pennsylvania, 1966), 321.

11. Judith Crist, "With the White Collar Girls," *Herald Tribune Book Review* (August 31, 1958), 6; Makosky, "Portrayal of Women," 32–37.

12. *The Apartment* (Mirisch, 1960).

13. Bosley Crowther, "Screen: Busy 'Apartment,'" *New York Times* (June 16, 1960), 37.

14. Sidney Porcelain, *Office Tramp* (New York: Midwood, 1962), 10, 25, 36; *The Best of Everything* (Twentieth Century–Fox, 1959).

15. Brown, *Sex and the Single Girl*, 5.

16. Brown, *Sex and the Office*, 112, 196–97; Neue Illustriertre Draft, box 36, folder 8, HGB Papers.

17. Brown, *Sex and the Office*, 3; Outline, Sex and the Office, box 22, folder 2, HGB Papers; "Helen Gurley Brown at Grossinger's," box 15, folder 6, 6, HGB Papers; Brown, *Sex and the Single Girl*, 93. For Brown's sexual experiences with bosses and coworkers, see Scanlon, *Bad Girls Go Everywhere*, 21–26.

18. Brown, *Sex and the Office*, 21; Sex and the Office Suggestions by DSG for HGB, box 22, folder 2, HGB Papers; Outline, Sex and the Office. On performing class, see Laurie Ouellette, "Inventing the Cosmo Girl: Class Identity and Girl-Style American Dreams," *Media Culture and Society* 21 (1999): 365–70.

19. "The Book I Wrote . . .," n.d., Speeches and Appearances, box 15, folder 5, HGB Papers; Robert L. Kirsch, "'Sex and Single Girl' Falls Short of Its Promising Title," *Los Angeles Times* (July 6, 1962), box 21, HGB Papers; Dorothy Jacobsen, "If Horatio Alger Were a Shapely Secretary," Sex and the Office Scrapbook, box 47, HGB Papers. See also "Meat Loaf, Anyone?" *Newsweek* (August 31, 1964), 53; Jean Martin, "Unhappily Ever After," *Nation* (January 11, 1965).

20. Beth Bailey, *From Front Porch to Back Seat: Courtship in Twentieth-Century America* (Baltimore: Johns Hopkins University Press, 1988), 21, 71–73.

21. Edwin Darby, "The Skirt Set's Horatio Alger?" *Chicago Daily News* (n.d.), Sex and the Office Scrapbook; *Business Week* quotation from Fraterrigo, *Playboy and the Making of the Good Life*, 124–25.

22. "Sex and the Office," *Modern Office Procedures* 10 (March 1965): 21–24.

23. "The Gurley Girl—A Myth?" *Modern Office Procedures* 10 (May 1965): 33.

24. Ibid.

25. Samuel Feinberg, "From Where I Sit," *Women's Wear Daily* (April 9, 1965), and Jack Kofoed, "Sex in Our Offices? That's a Big Laugh," *Miami Herald* (June 30, 1964), box 24, folder 8, HGB Papers; John F. Cubar, *The Significant Americans: A Study of the Sexual Behavior of the Affluent* (New York: Appleton-Century, 1965), 146, 37.

26. See Herbert Marcuse, *One-Dimensional Man: Studies in the Ideology of Advanced Industrial Society* (Boston: Beacon, 1964), 74; Michael Korda, *Male Chauvinism: How It Works* (New York: Random House, 1973), 107–15.

27. On Brown and homosexuality in the office, see Scanlon, *Bad Girls Go Everywhere*, 127–28. Theodore Caplow, et al., *Recent Social Trends in the U.S., 1960–1990* (Montreal: Carleton University Press, 1994), 123; Sex and the Office

Draft, box 22, folder 2, HGB Papers; Scanlon, *Bad Girls Go Everywhere*, 56, 77–78; Diana Lurie, "Living with Liberation," *New York* (August 31, 1970), 23.

28. Harold Mehling, "The Husband Hookers," *Saga* (April 1963), 45, and Brian O'Doherty, "What's a Uni-Sex?" *Diplomat* (June 1966), box 21, HGB Papers; Philip Wylie, "The Career Woman," *Playboy* (January 1963), quoted in Fraterrigo, *Playboy and the Making of the Good Life*, 125–28.

29. "*Playboy* Interview: Helen Gurley Brown," *Playboy* (April 1963), box 21, HGB Papers; Sex and the Office Draft, box 22, folder 4, HGB Papers. On postwar blaming of women for men's problems, see James Gilbert, *Men in the Middle* (Chicago: University of Chicago Press, 2005), chapter 4.

30. Brown, *Sex and the Office*, 121–25.

31. Letty Cottin to Mrs. David Brown (December 4, 1962), box 19, folder 7, HGB Papers; Bernard Geis to Mrs. Helen Brown (November 7, 1963), box 19, folder 8, HGB Papers; Brown to Berney dear (February 8, 1964), box 19, folder 2, HGB Papers.

32. Brown, *Sex and the Office*, 220–21.

33. Outline, Sex and the Office.

34. "When a Secretary Travels with a Boss . . .," Canadian Radio Scripts, box 16, folder 9, HGB Papers.

35. "The Phoniness of Women," box 22, folder 6, HGB Papers; Brown, *Sex and the Single Girl*, 60, 209; Brown, *Sex and the Office*, 194.

36. Brown, *Sex and the Single Girl*, 78–79. On 1950s courtship see Bailey, *From Front Porch to Back Seat*, 87–90; Elaine Tyler May, *Homeward Bound: American Families in the Cold War Era* (New York: Basic, 1988), chapter 5. Women's new willingness to say "yes" might have led men to approach women more often, since there was now a greater chance they would be willing partners; however, there is no evidence of this in any of Brown's writings, and Michael Korda's discussion of workplace sex in this period suggests men were wary of a sexually assertive woman; *Male Chauvinism*, 100–115.

37. "Dear Working Girl," Canadian Radio Scripts.

38. "Dear Girl Secretary," Canadian Radio Scripts; Brown, *Sex and the Single Girl*, 79.

39. Brown, *Sex and the Office*, 86–87, 93–94.

40. Ibid., 285–86; "Nixon vs. Kennedy," *Mad Men* (AMC, season 1, episode 12, 2007). Matt Weiner, the creator of *Mad Men*, recommended that the show's writers read Brown's books and view other popular-culture sources from the period; Amy Choszick, "The Women Behind 'Mad Men,'" *Wall Street Journal* (August 7, 2009), W1.

41. Helen Gurley Brown, *Having It All: Love, Success, Sex, Money Even if You're Starting with Nothing* (New York: Simon and Schuster, 1982), 49–50.

42. Ibid., 204; Charles E. Ginder, "Factor of Sex in Office Employment," *Office Executive* (February 1961), 11.

43. Karen Halttunen, *Confidence Men and Painted Women: A Study of Middle-Class Culture in America, 1830–1870* (New Haven: Yale University Press, 1986), epilogue; Barbara Ehrenreich, *Bright-Sided: How the Relentless Promotion of*

Positive Thinking Has Undermined America (New York: Metropolitan, 2009), 60–73. In the early 1970s Michael Korda assessed Brown's feminine strategy as an effective approach for a woman in business in the prefeminist 1960s; *Male Chauvinism*, 120, 135–39.

44. Sex and the Office Draft.

45. On scarcity, see Bailey, *From Front Porch to Back Seat*, 26–35. On panty raids, see Beth Bailey, *Sex in the Heartland* (Cambridge: Harvard University Press, 2002), 45–48, 82.

46. On the significance of "outing" workplace sexuality, see Berebitsky, "Joy of Work," 92–93.

47. Stephanie Harrington, "Two Faces of the Same Eve," *New York Times* (August 11, 1974); *Playboy* Interview; P.B. to H.G.B (April 27, 1964), box 16, folder 1, HGB Papers; Chris Welles, "Soaring Success of the Iron Butterfly," *Life* (November 19, 1965), 72; Korda, *Male Chauvinism*, 115. On encouraging wives and mothers to work, see *Sex and the Office*, chapter 17.

48. Dierdre Silverman, "Sexual Harassment: Working Women's Dilemma," *Quest* 3 (Winter 1976–77): 20.

CHAPTER SEVEN. DESIRE OR DISCRIMINATION?

1. Letty Cottin Pogrebin, *How to Make It in a Man's World* (New York: Doubleday, 1970), 178–81, 148.

2. Ibid., 127, 138–40, 166–67, 181–90.

3. On Pogrebin and feminism, see Mary Thom, *Inside Ms.: 25 Years of the Magazine and the Feminist Movement* (New York: Henry Holt, 1997), 5–9; Sarah Harriman, "Women's Legal Rights," *New York Times* (May 4, 1975); Letty Cottin Pogrebin, *Getting Yours: How to Make the System Work for the Working Woman* (New York: Avon, 1976), 90–99; on the first "speak-out," see Carrie N. Baker, *The Women's Movement Against Sexual Harassment* (New York: Cambridge University Press, 2008), 30–34; Letty Cottin Pogrebin, "Sex Harassment," *Ladies' Home Journal* (June 1977), 24, 28.

4. Letty Cottin Pogrebin, "Love on the Job," *Ladies' Home Journal* (March 1980), 10.

5. "Personal Business," *Business Week* (June 20, 1970), 107; Art Seidenbaum, "Where Are the Girls?" *Los Angeles Times* (April 25, 1972); Margie Albert, "Something New in the Women's Movement," *New York Times* (December 12, 1973). On protests against "dresses only" rules, see, for example, Marilyn Bender, "Pants-Ban Tempest at C.B.S.," *New York Times* (January 21, 1970). On the movement up to 1976, see Jean Tepperman, *Not Servants, Not Machines: Office Workers Speak Out* (Boston: Beacon, 1976); for a brief history of the movement, see Dorothy Sue Cobble, *The Other Women's Movement: Workplace Justice and Social Rights in Modern America* (Princeton: Princeton University Press, 2004), 211–15.

6. Tepperman, *Not Servants, Not Machines*, 88. On the numbers of employed women, see Alice Kessler-Harris, *Out to Work: A History of Wage-Earning Women in the United States* (New York: Oxford University Press, 1982), 301;

Stuart Garfinkle, "Occupations of Women and Black Workers, 1962–74," *Monthly Labor Review* 98 (November 1975): 25, 32; Ellen Carol DuBois and Lynn Dumenil, *Though Women's Eyes* (New York: Bedford/St. Martin's, 2005), 658.

On the histories of and differences between liberal feminism and radical or liberationist feminism, see Sara M. Evans, *Tidal Wave: How Women Changed America at Century's End* (New York: Free Press, 2003), chapter 2. In this chapter I use the generic terms "feminist" or "feminism" unless the strand is relevant to the discussion.

7. On being disdainful of equality, see Beth Anthony and Walter Russell, "Office Politics," *Women's Page* (n.d.), 1–5, in Rosalyn Baxandall: Women's Liberation Research Files (TAM 210), Tamiment Library, New York University [hereafter Baxandall Papers], box 6, folder 20.

On socialist feminism see Evans, *Tidal Wave*, 158–68. "A Straight Job," originally published in *Quick Silver Times* (Washington, DC, n.d.), in Baxandall Papers, box 1, folder 2; Anne Coe, "Woman as Secretary," *Womankind* 2 (November 1972), in Baxandall Papers, box 1, folder 14; Marilyn Salzman-Webb, "Woman as Secretary, Sexpot, Spender, Sow, Civic Actor, Sickie," in Michelle Hoffnung Garskof, ed., *Roles Women Play: Readings Toward Women's Liberation* (Belmont, CA: Wadsworth, 1971), 15; Kathi Roche, "The Secretary: Capitalism's House Nigger" (Pittsburgh: Know, n.d.), available at http://scriptorium.lib.duke.edu/wlm/sec/.

8. Lynn O'Connor Gardner, "Strategic View of the Labor Force," *Women's Page* (April 1972), 27; Pat Mialocq, "Rejects: The Back Office Girls," *Women's Page* (April 1971), 14, in Baxandall Papers, box 6, folder 20; Anthony and Russell, "Office Politics"; Roche, "Secretary."

9. Cobble, *Other Women's Movement*, 211–15. On the origins of Chicago's Women Employed and Boston's 9 to 5, see Evans, *Tidal Wave*, 85–89. Socialist feminists started Baltimore's Working Women, though their involvement was not long-lasting; Roberta Goldberg, *Organizing Women Office Workers: Dissatisfaction, Consciousness, and Action* (New York: Praeger, 1983).

10. Diehl quoted in Roslyn Feldberg, "'Union Fever': Organizing Among Clerical Workers, 1900–1930" in James Green, ed., *Workers' Struggles, Past and Present: A "Radical America" Reader* (Philadelphia: Temple University Press, 1983), 162; "Code of Ethics," *Secretary* (April 1959), 1; Clare H. Jennings, "Why Is a Secretary," *Secretary* (May 1959), 14; Beatrice P. Tuyt, "Goodwill," *Secretary* (March 1960), 14–15.

11. *Women Office Workers News* (January–February 1974), 2, 11. It is unclear when WOW started, but it had three hundred dues-paying members by the summer of 1976; *Women Office Workers Newsletter* (August–September 1976), 1. When the press asked the NSA about the office workers' movement, a spokeswoman declared that NSA's members were happy with their jobs—of course, those members represented less than 1 percent of clerical workers; Judy Klemesrud, "In Defense of the Secretary," *New York Times* (December 13, 1972); Judy

Klemesrud, "Secretary Image: A 'Tempest in a Typewriter'?" *New York Times* (March 7, 1972).

12. *Women Office Workers Newsletter* (November–December 1975), 2; "Pretty Faces Get Jobs, Say Pickets at Agency," *New York Post* (March 22, 1976); *Women Office Workers Newsletter* (April–May 1976), 3; Paula Bernstein, "WOW Protests Beauty-Before-Age Pattern in Job Market," *Daily News* (March 12, 1976).

13. *Women Office Workers Newsletter* (April–May 1976), 1–2; *Women Office Workers Newsletter* (Fall 1980), 2; *Women Office Workers Newsletter* (Fall 1981), 1. For additional examples of WOW's and other feminist organizations' protests, see http://history.sewanee.edu/facstaff/berebitsky/.

14. *Women Office Workers Newsletter* (November–December 1975), 4–5; *Women Office Workers Newsletter* (December 1979–January 1980), 4. For a fuller discussion of representations of office workers in advertisements, see http://history.sewanee.edu/facstaff/berebitsky/.

15. In 1977, six clerical organizations, including WOW, united to form the National Women's Employment Project (NWEP). In 1978 NWEP warned its members not to tackle sexual harassment since "problems of sexual harassment are too often portrayed as anti-male, not anti-boss"; Judith Ezekiel, *Feminism in the Heartland* (Columbus: Ohio State University Press, 2002), 199, 211–12. However, some groups, like WOW, disregarded this advice; Baker, *Women's Movement Against Sexual Harassment*, 42, 46, 88–89; Elizabeth Brenner, "Sexual Harassment: Hard to Define, Harder to Fight," *Chicago Tribune* (May 30, 1979), B1, 6. On liberal feminists' slow embrace of sexual harassment, see Susan Brownmiller, *In Our Time: Memoir of a Revolution* (New York: Delta, 1999), 284.

16. Madeline Belkin, "Drowning in the Steno Pool," in Deborah Babcox and Madeline Belkin, eds., *Liberation NOW! Writings for the Women's Liberation Movement* (New York: Dell, 1971), 80; Mary Thom, ed., *Letters to Ms., 1972–87* (New York: Henry Holt, 1987), 107.

17. Anthony and Russell, "Office Politics"; O'Connor, "Strategic View of the Labor Force"; "Sun Life Workers: A Protest," *Second Page* (February 1975), 1, in Baxandall Papers, box 6, folder 20.

18. Letter from J.R. to M.B.T. (July 25, 1973), in Gloria Steinem Papers, Smith College [hereafter Steinem Papers], box 55, folder 10; Wendy Martyna, *Everywoman* 30 (March 1972): 27. The ad appeared on June 30, 1971.

19. S.C. to Steinem (August 1, 1973), Steinem Papers, box 55, folder 10; Goldberg, *Organizing Women Office Workers*, 97–98. Not all members shared this woman's view and some considered harassment an important issue; ibid., 100, 106, 74–75. On the difficulties feminist clerical leaders faced, see Judith Sealander and Dorothy Smith, "The Rise and Fall of Feminist Organizations in the 1970s: Dayton as a Case Study," *Feminist Studies* 12 (Summer 1986): 331–32, 336.

20. Letter from Working Women United Institute, March 9, 1978, Steinem Papers, box 213, folder 9; Baker, *Women's Movement Against Sexual Harassment*, 27–28.

21. Baker, *Women's Movement Against Sexual Harassment*, 29–31; Lin Farley, *Sexual Shakedown* (New York: Warner, 1980), 32; Alliance Against Sexual Coercion, "Sexual Harassment and Coercion: Violence Against Women," *Aegis* (July–August 1978), 28–29.

22. Baker, *Women's Movement Against Sexual Harassment*, 15–17; Catharine A. MacKinnon, *Sexual Harassment of Working Women* (New Haven: Yale University Press, 1979), 9, 18–23.

23. Alliance Against Sexual Coercion, *Sexual Harassment at the Workplace* (Boston: Alliance Against Sexual Coercion, 1977), 2–3, 11. On the formation of WWU, AASC, and their differing analyses and approaches, see Baker, *Women's Movement Against Sexual Harassment*, 27–48, 94–100.

24. Presentation by Karen Sauvigné (n.d.), Women's Action Alliance Papers, Smith College [hereafter, WAA Papers], box 92, folder 34.

25. Farley, *Sexual Shakedown*, 33.

26. "Speak-Out on Sexual Harassment of Women at Work," Transcript, May 4, 1975, Karen Sauvigné Papers, available at "Women and Social Movements in the U.S., 1600–2000," AlexanderStreet.com.

27. "Sexual Harassment: The Working Woman's Dilemma," *Labor Pains* 1 (August, 1975), 4, 11, available at "Women and Social Movements in the U.S."

28. Ibid.; Baker, *Women's Movement Against Sexual Harassment*, 41–42; Freada Klein and Lynn Wehrli, "Sexual Coercion on the Job?" *Sister Courage* (October 1976), 6; Alliance Against Sexual Coercion, *Sexual Harassment at the Workplace*, 11.

29. "Three Male Views on Harassment," *Aegis* (Winter–Spring 1980), 52; "Sexual Harassment and Coercion," *Aegis* (July–August 1978), 29.

30. "Three Male Views," 52–59.

31. "How Do You Handle . . . Sex on the Job," *Redbook* (January 1976), 74–75.

32. Claire Safran, "What Men Do to Women on the Job," *Redbook* (November 1976), 149, 217–21.

33. See, for example, Constance Backhouse and Leah Cohen, *Sexual Harassment on the Job: How to Avoid the Working Woman's Nightmare* (Englewood Cliffs, NJ: Prentice-Hall, 1981), 151.

34. On changes in attitudes toward sexuality, see John D'Emilio and Estelle B. Freedman, *Intimate Matters: A History of Sexuality in America* (New York: Harper and Row, 1988), 327, 333–34.

35. Marion Clark and Rudy Maxa, "Closed Session Romance on the Hill," *Washington Post* (May 23, 1976).

36. Joshua Gamson, "Jessica Hahn, Media Whore: Sex Scandals and Female Publicity," *Critical Studies in Media Communication* 18 (June 2001): 162–64.

37. Rudy Maxa, "Paid Mainly to Provide Sex to Rep. Young, Ex-Aide Says," *Washington Post* (June 12, 1976); Myra MacPherson, "Occupational Sexism Found Alive, Rampant on Capitol Hill," *Washington Post* (August 1, 1976).

38. "Ray Waited Publisher's Nod," *Washington Post* (June 13, 1976); Clark and Maxa, "Closed Session Romance"; "What Liz Ray Has Wrought," *Time* (June 21, 1976), 21, 31.

39. "What Liz Ray Has Wrought"; John M. Crewdson, "Congressman's Ex-Aide Links Her Salary to Sex," *New York Times* (June 11, 1976); "Congress: Capsized by Scandal," *Economist* (June 26, 1976), 37.

40. "Indecent Exposure on Capitol Hill," *Time* (June 7, 1976), 12, 15; John M. Crewdson, "U.S. Studies Charge of Sex-for-Vote Bid," *New York Times* (June 12, 1976); Crewdson, "Congressman's Ex-Aide"; Tom Mathews, "Congressman's Lady," *Newsweek* (June 7, 1976), 26.

41. David S. Broder, "Hays' Abuse of Power," *Washington Post* (June 16, 1976); David Gelman and Lucy Howard, "Vice Squad," *Newsweek* (June 28, 1976), 79.

42. Caryl Rivers, "Where Women Are Credit Cards," *New York Times* (June 8, 1976).

43. MacPherson, "Occupational Sexism." Women held only 7 percent of the highest-paying Senate staff positions and 17 percent of the analogous House jobs.

44. Ibid.

45. Rudy Maxa and Marion Clark, "Investigators to Get Tapes," *Washington Post* (June 14, 1976); MacPherson, "Occupational Sexism."

46. Farley, *Sexual Shakedown*, 224–25, 255.

47. Ibid., 260, 124.

48. On early media coverage, see Baker, *Women's Movement Against Sexual Harassment*, 100–106.

49. "My Boss Wanted More Than a Secretary," *Good Housekeeping* (April 1978), 28, 32, 34, 36, 38; Susan B. Estrich, "Sex at Work," in Susan Sage Heinzelman and Zipporah Bashaw Wiseman, eds., *Representing Women: Law, Literature, and Feminism* (Durham: Duke University Press, 1994), 189.

50. "Jimmy Breslin, "Gloria Jabs at Job Sex," *New York Daily News* (October 23, 1977), 5, 25; "N.Y. Speakout: Women Describe Indignities They Face at Work," *Women's Agenda* 2 (December 1977): 9, in WAA Papers, box 208, folder 1; Ann Crittenden, "Women Tell of Sexual Harassment at Work," *New York Times* (October 25, 1977).

51. Jack Mabley, "European Prices Make Us Look Good," *Chicago Tribune* (August 26, 1975).

52. Abigail Van Buren, "Sexual Harassment Works Both Ways," *Rome News-Tribune* (September 3, 1980), 20.

53. Abigail Van Buren, "Both Sides Can Sing Sexual Overtures," *Los Angeles Times* (October 13, 1980), OC-A4.

54. "Executive Sweet," *Time* (October 8, 1979), 76, reporting on Barbara Gutek, et al., "Sexuality and the Workplace," *Basic and Applied Social Psychology* 1 (1980): 255–65.

55. Farley, *Sexual Shakedown*, 230–32, chapter 11; Backhouse and Cohen, *Sexual Harassment on the Job*, chapter 7.

56. MacKinnon, *Sexual Harassment of Working Women*, chapter 4; Baker, *Women's Movement Against Sexual Harassment*, 11–26, 49–58.

57. Baker, *Women's Movement Against Sexual Harassment*, 16–21; "A Steno Who Said 'No!'" *Newsweek* (April 30, 1979), 72; *Miller v. Bank of America*, 418 F. Supp. 233,

236 (N.D. Cal. 1976), quoted in Reva B. Siegel, Introduction to Catharine A. MacKinnon and Reva B. Siegel, eds., *Directions in Sexual Harassment Law* (New Haven: Yale University Press, 2004), 34, note 58.

58. Quotation from Jim Wright, "Now, Guidelines for That, Too," *Dallas Morning News* (May 4, 1976), quoted in Baker, *Women's Movement Against Sexual Harassment*, 24. For information on the case and press coverage, see ibid., 16, 18–19, 21–26.

59. Baker, *Women's Movement Against Sexual Harassment*, 19, 57–58, 111–26; James Norman, "Why They Go Beddie-Bye with the Boss," *New York Post* (July 31, 1979), 10.

60. Baker, *Women's Movement Against Sexual Harassment*, 116. Sexual harassment is a civil, not criminal charge. As in other cases charging unfair (discriminatory) employment practices, the employer (and in this case, not the individual harasser) is liable.

61. Fred Strebeigh, *Equal: Women Reshape American Law* (New York: Norton, 2009), 231–41.

62. MacKinnon, *Sexual Harassment of Working Women*, 44–48.

63. Ibid., 158–74.

64. Ibid., 17, 21; Strebeigh, *Equal*, 235–36.

65. Equal Employment Opportunity Commission, *Guidelines on Discrimination Because of Sex*, § 1604.11 (1980), reprinted in Laura Stern, *Sexual Harassment in America* (Westport, CT: Greenwood, 1999), 34; Baker, *Women's Movement Against Sexual Harassment*, 118–19.

66. Rhoda Koenig, "The Persons in the Office," *Harper's* (February 1976), 87–88, 90; Alice Bonner, "Winner of Sexual Bias Suit Hopes Case Will Help Others," *Washington Post* (April 22, 1976). One survey of managers found that 78 percent of women and 86 percent of men believed women used their attractiveness to their advantage; Eliza G. C. Collins and Timothy B. Blodgett, "Sexual Harassment: Some See It . . . Some Won't," *Harvard Business Review* (March–April 1981), 90.

67. Bill Raspberry, "Harassment—Is It Just Sexual?" *Chicago Tribune* (October 2, 1980); Baker, *Women's Movement Against Sexual Harassment*, 118–19. For MacKinnon on this issue, see *Sexual Harassment of Working Women*, 37–40.

68. Augustus B. Cochran III, *Sexual Harassment and the Law: The Mechelle Vinson Case* (Lawrence: University Press of Kansas, 2004), 55–59; Strebeigh, *Equal*, 271–74.

69. Strebeigh, *Equal*, 276–92.

70. "Girls' Employers Wolves, He Cries," *Chicago Daily Tribune* (January 12, 1907), 5; Louise F. Fitzgerald, "Who Says? Legal and Psychological Constructions of Women's Resistance to Harassment," in MacKinnon and Siegel, *Directions in Sexual Harassment Law*, 94, 97; Estrich, "Sex at Work," 200–207. The problems associated with allowing evidence of a woman's dress, speech, or sexual past into a trial led Congress to revise the Federal Rules of Evidence in 1994, effectively providing sexual harassment plaintiffs with a version of the "rape

shield" law; see Ellen E. Schultz and Junda Woo, "The Bedroom Ploy: Plaintiffs' Sex Lives Are Being Laid Bare in Harassment Cases," *Wall Street Journal* (September 19, 1994), A1.

71. Fitzgerald, "Who Says?" 95, 99–104; Katherine M. Franke, "What's Wrong with Sexual Harassment?" in MacKinnon and Siegel, *Directions in Sexual Harassment Law*, 174–75. For examples of commentators who believed women could control men, see Baker, *Women's Movement Against Sexual Harassment*, 134–45.

72. Robert Pear, "Sexual Harassment at Work Outlawed," *New York Times* (April 12, 1980); Art Buchwald, "Peace on Earth, Good Will Toward Zelda," *Los Angeles Times* (December 18, 1980); Linda Gordon, "The Politics of Sexual Harassment," *Radical America* (July–August, 1981), 8, 11–12; "N.Y. Speakout"; Walter Berns, "Terms of Endearment" *Harper's* (October 1980), 20. On feminists' assertion that they and sexual harassment litigation were not antisex, see Farley, *Sexual Shakedown*, 143; Backhouse and Cohen, *Sexual Harassment on the Job*, 149; Baker, *Women's Movement Against Sexual Harassment*, 146.

73. *Nine to Five* (Twentieth Century–Fox, 1980).

74. Vincent Canby, "Screen: 'Nine to Five,' Office Comedy," *New York Times* (December 19, 1980); Kevin Thomas, "Scoring Points in the '9 to 5' Game," *Los Angeles Times* (December 19, 1980).

75. Mary Haworth, "Saying No to a Married Boss," *Washington Post* (April 7, 1967).

76. Baker, *Women's Movement Against Sexual Harassment*, 6, 124, 131–34, 190–91; Cochran, *Sexual Harassment and the Law*, 197, 204–7.

CHAPTER EIGHT. TWO STEPS FORWARD, ONE STEP BACK

1. Lori Redfearn is a pseudonym. L.G. to Women's Action Alliance, April 2, 1979, and Jane Williamson to L.G., April 4, 1979, in Women's Action Alliance Papers, Smith College, box 263, folder 3.

2. Joanne S. Lublin, "Resisting Advances," *Wall Street Journal* (April 24, 1981), 1. A reader responded that a woman with a "come-hither look" could create a hostile environment for a man by distracting him, which could cost him his job; Letters to the Editor, *Wall Street Journal* (May 5, 1981), 31. On corporate training, see Carrie N. Baker, *The Women's Movement Against Sexual Harassment* (New York: Cambridge University Press, 2008), 132–33.

3. Susan Jacoby, "William and Mary," *New York Times* (October 19, 1980); Christine Doudaa, "Women at the Top," *New York Times* (November 30, 1980); U.S. Department of Labor, *Employment and Earnings* 44.4 (Washington, DC: U.S. Department of Labor, 1997), table A-17; Georgia Dullea, "The Issue of Office Romance," *New York Times* (May 17, 1982).

4. This paragraph is based on "Bendix Rumor Mill Runs at Capacity, Agee Finds," *Los Angeles Times* (September 26, 1980); Thomas C. Hayes, "Romance Is Disavowed in Bendix Promotion," *New York Times* (September 26, 1980); "Woman VP of Bendix Corp. on Leave Amid 'Gossip,'" *Los Angeles Times* (September 29, 1980); Judy Mann, "Woman's Promotion Grist for Rumor

Mill," *Washington Post* (October 1, 1980); Patricia O'Brien, "A Lesson a Woman in Business Must Learn," *Chicago Tribune* (October 3, 1980); Janet Key, "Firms with Girl Geniuses Face Double Bind," *Chicago Tribune* (October 5, 1980); Gail Sheehy, "The Mary Cunningham Story: Sex Rumors End Her 'Brilliant' Career at Bendix," *Chicago Tribune* (October 12, 1980); Gail Sheehy, "What Led Her to Success at Bendix Corporation?" *Chicago Tribune* (October 13, 1980). For Mary Cunningham's account, see *Power Play: What Really Happened at Bendix* (New York: Linden, 1984).

5. Hayes, "Romance Is Disavowed"; Sheehy, "Sex Rumors End"; Barbara Bry, "Bendix-Type Situations May Get Worse Before Better," *Los Angeles Times* (October 5, 1980); Key, "Firms with Girl Geniuses"; Mann, "Woman's Promotion."

6. O'Brien, "Lesson"; Bry, "Bendix-Type Situations"; Carol Kleiman, "Beauty Can Be Beastly When Scaling the Ladder," *Chicago Tribune* (November 11, 1985); Key, "Firms with Girl Geniuses"; Beverly Stephen, "Bendix Brouhaha Stirs Up Sex Issue," *Los Angeles Times* (October 23, 1980).

7. Judith Coburn, "Mary Cunningham: So Successful, She Had to Fail," *Mademoiselle* (January 1981), 24; Key, "Firms with Girl Geniuses"; Carol Kleiman, "Cunningham's Unhappy Legacy," *Chicago Tribune* (January 17, 1983); Cunningham, *Power Play*, 153, 234, 231; Gail Sheehy, "What's Next for Bendix Corp.'s Wonder Woman?" *Chicago Tribune* (October 16, 1980); Sandra Salmans, "Women in the Business World," *New York Times* (June 24, 1984).

8. Gail Sheehy, "The Fulfilling but Lonely Life of a Top Executive" *Chicago Tribune* (October 14, 1980); Cunningham, *Power Play*, 231.

9. Betty Lehan Harragan, *Games Mother Never Taught You: Corporate Games-Manship for Women* (New York: Warner, 1978), 348–51.

10. Ibid., 110–11, 352–62, 336–37, 346, 366–68, 374.

11. Robert Quinn, "Coping with Cupid: The Formation, Impact, and Management of Romantic Relationships in Organizations," *Administrative Science Quarterly* 22 (March 1977): 30–45; Robert E. Quinn and Noreen A. Judge, "The Office Romance: No Bliss for the Boss," *Management Review* 67 (July 1978): 45. Coverage included Beatryce Nivens, "The Office Romance: Should You or Shouldn't You?" *Essence* (February 1978), 16; Suzanne Adelson, "Business Sense in Office Affairs, *Los Angeles Times* (September 9, 1979); Nancy J. White, "Sex in the Office: It's Mostly Bad Business," *Ladies Home Journal* (October 1982), 104–6, 152, 154; Beth E. Schneider, "The Office Affair: Myth and Reality for Heterosexual and Lesbian Women Workers," *Sociological Perspectives* 27 (October, 1984): 443–64.

12. Marylin Bender, "The Changing Rules of Office Romance," *Esquire* (April 24, 1979), 46, 53–56; Jeanne Bosson Driscoll and Rosemary A. Bova, "The Sexual Side of Enterprise," *Management Review* (July 1980), 51–54; "Sexual Tension," *Wall Street Journal* (April 14, 1981), 1.

13. Eliza G. C. Collins, "Managers and Lovers," *Harvard Business Review* (September–October 1983), 149–52.

14. Ibid., 145.

15. Gerhard Neubeck, "Perspectives," in Gerhard Neubeck, ed., *Extramarital Relations* (New Jersey: Prentice-Hall, 1969), 3–5; O. Spurgeon English, M.D., "Values in Psychotherapy: The Affair," *Voices* 3 (Winter 1968): 9–14; Albert Ellis, "Healthy and Disturbed Reasons for Having Extramarital Relations," in Neubeck, *Extramarital Relations*, 154, 156; John F. Cuber, "Adultery: Reality Versus Stereotype," ibid., 191; Robert N. Whitehurst, "Extramarital Sex: Alienation or Extension of Normal Behavior," ibid., 134–37; Lin Farley, *Sexual Shakedown* (New York: Warner, 1980), 259; James A. Peterson, "The Office Wife," in Leonard Gross, ed., *Sexual Issues in Marriage: A Contemporary Perspective* (New York: Spectrum, 1975), 207–10; Lisa Kraymer, "Work: The Intimate Environment," *Alternative Lifestyles* 2 (February 1979): 11, 7–32.

16. Darrell Sifford, "If Housewives Knew What the Competition Is Downtown," *Chicago Tribune* (January 16, 1972); Bender, "Changing Rules"; Mary Bralove, "Career Women Decry Sexual Harassment by Bosses and Clients," *Wall Street Journal* (January 29, 1976), 1, 15. Sifford's article generated a lot of response, leading to a follow-up, Judy Neuman, "How Housewives Can Fight the Competition Downtown," *Chicago Tribune* (February 6, 1972). On the lives of corporate wives in the 1970s, see Rosabeth Moss Kanter, *Men and Women of the Corporation* (1977; New York: Basic, 1993), chapter 5.

17. "Sexual Tension," *Wall Street Journal* (April 14, 1981), 1; Letters to the Editor, *Wall Street Journal* (April 23, 1981), 27.

18. Collins, "Managers and Lovers," 143–44, 148.

19. Kaleel Jamison, "Managing Sexual Attraction in the Workplace," *Personnel Administrator* 28 (August 1983): 45–51; Geraldine Romano Spruell, "Love in the Office," *Training and Development Journal* (February 1985), 21–23; "Sexual Tension"; Cunningham, *Power Play*, 235.

20. Bender, "Changing Rules"; Michele Ingrassia, "The Office Romance: A Whole New State of Affairs," *Washington Post* (October 7, 1986); Ellen Graham, "My Lover, My Colleague," *Wall Street Journal* (March 24, 1986), 85.

21. Ira L. Reiss, "Some Observations on Ideology and Sexuality in America," *Journal of Marriage and the Family* 43 (May 1981): 279–81.

22. Neil A. Lewis, "Law Professor Accuses Thomas of Sexual Harassment in 1980's," *New York Times* (October 7, 1991); S. Hrg. 102–1084, Hearings on the Nomination of Judge Clarence Thomas to be Associate Justice of the Supreme Court of the United States, part 4 (October 11, 12, and 13, 1991), 27, 37–38, available at http://www.gpoaccess.gov/congress/senate/judiciary/scourt.html (accessed September 1, 2009), hereafter Thomas Hearings. About 30 percent of the homes with television watched Thomas's initial testimony, and countless more watched in their workplaces; "The Thomas Nomination; Hearing Captures Big TV Audience," *New York Times* (October 13, 1991).

23. Thomas Hearings, 4: 118; Nancy Gibbs, "Office Crimes," *Time* (October 21, 1991).

24. Thomas Hearings, 4: 299.

25. Ibid., 4: 356; Felicity Barringer, "The Thomas Nomination; Psychologists Try to Explain Why Thomas and Hill Offer Opposing Views," *New York Times* (October 14, 1991); Adam Clymer, "The Thomas Nomination; Parade of Witnesses Support Hill's Story, Thomas's Integrity," *New York Times* (October 14, 1991). Barry made this statement almost instantly after the story went public; Neil A. Lewis, "Law Professor Accuses Thomas of Sexual Harassment in 1980s," *New York Times* (October 7, 1991).

26. D. Kelly Weisberg, ed., *Applications of Feminist Legal Theory to Women's Lives* (Philadelphia: Temple University Press, 1996), 407–8, 417, note 40; Diane K. Shrier, *Sexual Harassment in the Workplace and Academia: Psychiatric Issues* (Washington, DC: American Psychiatric Publishing, 1996), 138–39.

27. Louise F. Fitzgerald, "Gender, Race, and the Politics of Supreme Court Appointments: Science v. Myth; The Failure of Reason in the Clarence Thomas Hearings," *Southern California Law Review* (March 1992), 1404–8; Alessandra Stanley, "Ideas and Trends," *New York Times* (November 10, 1991).

28. Thomas Hearings, 4: 97.

29. Ibid., 4: 576, 563, 570, 573.

30. Ibid., 4: 571; Fitzgerald, "Gender, Race, Politics," 1399–1400, 1407–9; Baker, *Women's Movement Against Sexual Harassment*, 158–60.

31. Liza H. Gold, *Sexual Harassment: Psychiatric Assessment in Employment Litigation* (Washington, DC: American Psychiatric Publishing, 2004), xvi–xvii; James J. McDonald, Jr., and Paul R. Lees-Haley, "Personality Disorders in the Workplace: How They May Contribute to Claims of Employment Law Violations," *Employee Relations Law Journal* 22 (Summer 1996): 75–76, 78–79.

32. Thomas Hearings, 4: 122, 128.

33. Ibid., 4: 39–40, 122–23, 83, 303, 312 (emphasis added).

34. Ibid., 4: 82; Tom Wicker, "In the Nation; Blaming Anita Hill," *New York Times* (October 10, 1991).

35. Thomas Hearings, 4: 587–88, 590.

36. Ibid., 4: 341, 303. My discussion is informed by Kimberlé Crenshaw, "Whose Story Is It, Anyway? Feminist and Antiracist Appropriations of Anita Hill," in Toni Morrison, ed., *Race-ing Justice, En-gendering Power* (New York: Pantheon, 1992), 402–40.

37. Beverly Grier, "Making Sense of Our Differences: African American Women on Anita Hill," in Geneva Smitherman, ed., *African America Women Speak Out on Anita Hill–Clarence Thomas* (Detroit: Wayne State University Press, 1995), 150–58, quotation on 157; Gwendolyn Etter-Lewis, "High-Tech Lynching on Capitol Hill: Oral Narratives from African American Women," ibid., 82–85, 97; Julianne Malveaux, "The Year of the Woman or the Woman of the Year: Was There Really an Anita Hill Effect?" ibid., 161–63, 166; Fareed Muwwakkil, "The People's Pulse," *Los Angeles Sentinel* (October 24, 1991), A6.

    Although it might seem logical that a professional woman could easily stand up to her harasser, researchers on sexual harassment have shown that this group is actually more likely not to say anything because jobs at that level are scarce; Fitzgerald, "Gender, Race, Politics," 1403.

38. Thomas Hearings, 4: 157, 425–26; Crenshaw, "Whose Story Is It, Anyway?" 416–17; Pamela Thomas, "Is the Black Community Sexist?" *Los Angeles Sentinel* (November 5, 1992), A7; James Strong, "The Black Sexist Chauvinist Pig," *New Pittsburgh Courier* (November 2, 1991), 4; Michel McQueen and Dorothy Gaiter, "Politics and Policy," *Wall Street Journal* (October 14, 1991), A14.

39. Elizabeth Kolbert, "The Thomas Nomination; Sexual Harassment at Work Is Pervasive, Survey Suggests," *New York Times* (October 11, 1991); Felicity Barringer, "Hill's Case Is Divisive to Women," *New York Times* (October 18, 1991); Thomas Hearings, 4: 134; Naomi Wolf, "Sex, Lies, and Silence; Feminism and Intimidation on the Job: Have the Hearings Liberated the Movement," *Washington Post* (October 13, 1991).

A little less than a year after the hearings, three national polls suggested that support had shifted to Hill, although their accuracy is disputed; Dianne Rucinski, "The Polls-Review: Rush to Judgment? Fast Reaction Polls in the Anita Hill-Clarence Thomas Controversy," *Public Opinion Quarterly* 57 (Winter 1993): 576, 585–86.

On feminists' support of Hill, see Marjorie Williams, "From Women, an Outpouring of Anger; Rhetoric Underscores Deep Divisions in How the Sexes View Harassment," *Washington Post* (October 9, 1991); Larry Witham, "Press Makes Thomas Case a Battle of Sexes," *Washington Times* (October 11, 1991), A7; Anna Quindlen, "Listen to Us," *New York Times* (October 9, 1991).

40. Cynthia Crossen, "Are You from Another Planet or What?" *Wall Street Journal* (October 18, 1991), B1.

41. Augustus B. Cochran III, *Sexual Harassment and the Law: The Mechelle Vinson Case* (Lawrence: University Press of Kansas, 2004), 173–77.

42. Wolf, "Sex, Lies, and Silence"; Maureen Dowd, "The Thomas Nomination: The Senate and Sexism; Panel's Handling of Harassment Allegation Renews Questions About an All-Male Club," *New York Times* (October 8, 1991).

43. Sandra Evans Teeley, "House Censures Crane and Studds," *Washington Post* (July 21, 1983); "Beaten Konnyu Gives Up Politics," *Sacramento Bee* (June 9, 1988); U.S. Congress, House, Committee on Standards of Official Conduct, "In the matter of Representative Jim Bates" (U.S. G.P.O. 1989), 6–8, 29, 49–50; Tom Kenworthy, "Rep. Bates Reproved for Misconduct," *Washington Post* (October 19, 1989); Rochelle Sharpe, "Capitol Hill's Worst Kept Secret," *Ms.* (January–February 1992), 28–31.

44. Susan Gilmore et al., "The Women's Stories," *Seattle Times* (March 1, 1992); Susan Gilmore et al., "8 More Women Accuse Adams," *Seattle Times* (March 1, 1992); Michael R. Fancher, "A Story That Had to Be Told," *Seattle Times* (March 1, 1992); Cynthia Tucker, "Stand Back, Fellas, We've Got Work to Do," *Seattle Times* (November 9, 1992); Barbara A. Serrano, "Sen. Murray Kicks Off Bid for Re-Election," *Seattle Times* (April 7, 1998).

45. Helen Dewar, "Senate's New Sensitivity," *Washington Post* (September 24, 1992); Florence Graves and Charles E. Shepard, "Packwood Accused of Sexual Advances," *Washington Post* (November 22, 1992).

46. Eric Pianin, "Senate Inquiry on Packwood Signals Sea Change in Attitude," *Washington Post* (December 7, 1992); Florence Graves and Charles E. Shepard, "List of Packwood Accusers Grows," *Washington Post* (February 7, 1993); Charles E. Shepard and Florence Graves, "Tracking the Packwood Probe," *Washington Post* (December 16, 1993); Evan Thomas and Thomas Rosenstiel, "Decline and Fall," *Newsweek* (September 18, 1995), 31–36; Kenneth J. Cooper, "House Sends Congressional Compliance Bill to Clinton," *Washington Post* (January 18, 1995).

47. "Sexual Harassment," *Time*/CNN Poll (October 10, 1991); "Sexual Harassment," Harris Poll (October 15, 1991); "Sexual Harassment," *Washington Post*/ABC News Poll (December 18, 1992).

48. Helen Gurley Brown, "At Work, Sexual Electricity Sparks Creativity," *Wall Street Journal* (October 29, 1991), A22.

49. "Sex and the Single 'Scuttler': Yucck," *Wall Street Journal* (November 6, 1991), A19; Lynn Povich, "You're Great, Helen, but You Went Too Far," *Wall Street Journal* (November 8, 1991), A15; Roger Simon, "Odd Ideas from the Original Cosmo Girl," *Los Angeles Times* (November 3, 1991); Deirdre Donahue, "Clarence Thomas' Questionable Decision," *USA Today* (November 8, 1991).

50. "Cosmo Girl" Transcript, *Dateline NBC* (August 30, 1995), 20–21.

51. Letters from R.B. and S.S. in box 16, folder 3, Helen Gurley Brown Papers, Sophia Smith Collection, Smith College [hereafter Brown Papers].

52. Letters from M.J.H., and G.S. in box 16, folder 3, Brown Papers.

53. *Cosmopolitan* first mentioned sexual harassment in 1977, and the message was not to let such behaviors derail one's momentum. It did not tackle the issue head-on until 1984, distinguishing between quid pro quo and more "ambiguous" situations in which a woman might "overreact"; Eliza G. C. Collins, "Handbook for the New Woman Executive," *Cosmopolitan* (June 1977), 204–5; Joan Iaconetti, "Sexual Harassment . . . or Is It?" *Cosmopolitan* (February 1984), 154, 157. On Hearst and Brown, see Jennifer Scanlon, *Bad Girls Go Everywhere: The Life of Helen Gurley Brown* (New York: Oxford University Press, 2009), 213–14, 218.

54. Ellen Joan Pollock, "Deportment Gap," *Wall Street Journal* (February 7, 2000), A1.

55. Letters to the Editor: "So Now We're Sex Kittens Again?" *Wall Street Journal* (February 18, 2000), A15.

56. "The Power of Female Sex," *Sex and the City* (HBO, season 1, episode 5, 1998); "Circus, Circus," *The Apprentice* (NBC, season 1, episode 12, 2004).

57. Alyssa Royse, "Quid Pro Blow: Sexual Enticement to Close the Deal" (August 29, 2009), http://www.seattle20.com/blog/?m=200908 (accessed January 1, 2010); Alyssa Royce, "Sexual Enticement in the Workplace, Round Two—Some Like It Hot" (September 1, 2009), http://www.seattle20.com/

blog/Sexual-Enticement-in-the-Workplace-Round-Two-Some-Like-It-Hot.
aspx (accessed January 1, 2010); also see William B. Irvine, "Beyond Sexual
Harassment," *Journal of Business Ethics* 28 (December 2000): 358.

58. Rosalie Osais, "A Working Woman's Weapons," *New York Times* (December 13,
1998); Alyssa Royce, "Sexual Enticement in the Workplace: It's a Chemistry
Thing" (September 7, 2009), http://www.seattle20.com/blog/Sexual-
Enticement-In-The-Workplace-It-s-a-Chemistry-Thing.aspx (accessed January
1, 2010); Kingsley R. Browne, "Sex, Power, and Dominance: The Evolutionary
Psychology of Sexual Harassment," *Managerial and Decision Economics* 27
(2006): 147–49, 151, 156; Cochran, *Sexual Harassment and the Law*, 180–81.
The evolutionary psychological approach is increasingly seen in mainstream
media; see Philip Weiss, "The Affairs of Men," *New York* (May 26, 2008), 22–25.

59. Warren Farrell, *The Myth of Male Power* (New York: Berkley, 1994), 289–92,
299–300, 307–8.

60. "Letterman: Will His Popularity Suffer?" *The Week* (October 16, 2009), 21.

61. Nell Scovell, "Letterman and Me," *Vanity Fair* (October 27, 2009), available
at http://www.vanityfair.com/hollywood/features/2009/10/david-
letterman-200910 (accessed January 4, 2010).

62. Jason Bent, "David Letterman, ESPN, and the Sexual Favoritism Mess,"
Workplace Prof Blog (October 28, 2009), http://lawprofessors.typepad.com/
laborprof_blog/2009/10/david-letterman-espn-and-the-sexual-favoritism-
mess.html (accessed November 10, 2009). For a summary of case law on
favoritism, see Jennifer Bercovici, "The Workplace Romance and Sexual
Favoritism: Creating a Dialogue Between Social Science and the Law of Sexual
Harassment," *Southern California Interdisciplinary Law Journal* 16 (2006):
183–214.

63. Bent, "David Letterman"; Bercovici, "Workplace Romance"; Irvine, "Beyond
Sexual Harassment," 358.

64. Glenn M. Gomes et al., "The Paramour's Advantage: Sexual Favoritism and
Permissibly Unfair Discrimination," *Employee Responsibilities and Rights Journal*
18 (2006): 75; Jocelyn Voo, "How to Handle an Office Romance," CNN.com
(2007), http://www.cnn.com/2007/LIVING/worklife/08/29/office.romance/
index.html (accessed January 6, 2010). On "love contracts" see Robin J. Samuel
and David R. Singer, "Sexual Favoritism: A Recent California Supreme Court
Ruling May Wake Up Employers," *Employee Relations Law Journal* 31 (Winter
2005): 9–10.

65. Carol Hymowitz and Joann S. Lublin, "Many Companies Look the Other Way
at Employee Affairs," *Wall Street Journal* (March 8, 2005), B1; Carol Hymowitz
and Ellen Joan Pollock, "Corporate Affairs: The One Clear Line in Interoffice
Romance Has Become Blurred," *Wall Street Journal* (February 4, 1998),
A1; Patrick Rogers, "Wages of Sin: A Jilted Wife Gets Even," *People Weekly*
(August 25, 1997), 103; Larry Miller, "Sex in the Office: Taboo or Not Taboo?"
Cosmopolitan (August, 1984), 207–9, 254; Joann S. Lublin and Carol Hymowitz,
"Scorned Spouses Can Wreak Havoc with Mates' Careers," *Wall Street Journal*

(June 14, 2005), B1; Vivia Chen, "Adulterous, But Professional," *Careerist* (June 17, 2010), http://thecareerist.typepad.com/thecareerist/2010/06/adulterous-but-professional.html (accessed May 26, 2011).

66. Sharon R. Cohany and Emy Sok, "Trends in Labor Force Participation of Married Mothers of Infants," *Monthly Labor Review* (February 2007), 9 (statistic from 2005); Shirley P. Glass, *Not "Just Friends": Protect Your Relationship from Infidelity and Heal the Trauma of Betrayal* (New York: Free Press, 2003), 26–32, 390, note 12.

67. In 2002, more than thirty-one thousand people responded to an *Elle*/MSNBC survey on all aspects of sex in the workplace. Thirty-four percent of women admitted to playing up their sexuality, while 20 percent of men did. Twenty-three percent of women said they deemphasized their sexuality, versus 19 percent of men; "Sex on the Job," http://www.stevequayle.com/News.alert/America_Over_The_Edge/Sex.on.job/020507.sex.on.the.job.html (accessed May 24, 2011). A 2007 study showed men using sex to gain status or resources more than women; John Tierney, "The Whys of Mating: 237 Reasons and Counting," *New York Times* (July 31, 2007).

CONCLUSION

1. Augustus B. Cochran III, *Sexual Harassment and the Law: The Mechelle Vinson Case* (Lawrence: University Press of Kansas, 2004), 178–80; John M. Broder, "White House Volunteer, on TV, Details Encounter with President," *New York Times* (March 16, 1998); The Clinton Impeachment, a Basic Chronology, http://academic.brooklyn.cuny.edu/history/johnson/clintontimeline.htm.

2. James Bennet, "Is the Ex-Intern Getting Hostility or Sympathy?" *New York Times* (January 31, 1998); Alessandra Stanley, "Workers See Easing of Sexual Tensions," *New York Times* (January 31, 1998).

3. *Newsweek* Poll (September 12, 1998); Ellen O'Brien, "Women Voice Wide Range of Opinion on Lewinsky," *Boston Globe* (September 17, 1998).

4. Richard Cohen, "Vanity Fair's Victim," *Washington Post* (June 11, 1998); O'Brien, "Women Voice Wide Range of Opinion."

5. Rosie DiManno, "Is Clinton Sex Scandal So Revolting?" *Toronto Star* (January 28, 1998), B1. Studies suggest that most Americans see sexual harassment through a "biological model," in which it is about a man's powerful sex drive, not his power; see Susan Halford and Pauline Leonard, *Gender, Power, and Organisations* (New York: Palgrave, 2001), 142–43.

6. Gloria Steinem, "Feminists and the Clinton Question," *New York Times* (March 22, 1998).

7. "Law in the Clinton Era," *New York Times* (March 24, 1998); Carol Sanger, "Are Feminists Right to Stand by Clinton? *New York Times* (March 25, 1998).

8. Ellen Goodman, "Why Are Feminists Taking Heat over the Lewinsky Matter?" *Boston Globe* (February 5, 1998); Gwendolyn Mink, "Misreading Sexual Harassment Law," *New York Times* (March 30, 1998). Not all feminists were Clinton fans—his support of welfare reform, for example, had alienated many

feminists like Mink—but they generally supported him, at least initially against Jones's allegations, which allowed critics to cast them as hypocrites who put politics over women; see, for example, Kathleen Parker, "Why P.C. Feminists Won't Back Up Bill's Floozies," *Cosmopolitan* (April 1998), 70; Jennifer Harper, "Clinton Gets Protection Behind Feminist Skirts," *Washington Times* (September 25, 1998). Similarly, when conservatives offered support for Lewinsky, liberals accused them of being political opportunists. Conservatives no longer lamented the excesses of sexual harassment law and its incursion into private issues; now they raved about protections for women from boorish men; Cathy Young, "The Scandal III; Harassment Hypocrites," *National Review* (November 9, 1998), 19; Katha Pollitt, "Free Willie," *Nation* (February 16, 1998), 9.

9. Georgette Mosbacher, "Defenders of Adultery," *New York Times* (March 25, 1998).

10. Stanley A. Renshon, "Not 'Consenting,'" *New York Times* (March 25, 1998); Andrew Sullivan, "Lewinsky's Ordeal: Young Woman Brutalized, Exploited and Now Abandoned by Everyone," *Toronto Star* (September 27, 1998), A13.

11. Amelia Richards and Jennifer Baumgardner, "In Defense of Monica," *Nation* (December 21, 1998), 6–7. Other young women were among Lewinsky's harshest critics; see, for example, Katie Roiphe, "Monica Lewinsky, Career Woman," *New York Times* (September 15, 1998).

12. Author correspondence with Alison Hart (aka Jennifer Greene), January 26, 28, and 30, 2004. Hart's assessment can be seen in Susan Meier's *Husband from 9 to 5*, in which a secretary's amnesia forces her boss to pretend that he's her husband. When she kisses him, he is both mortified and aroused: "A decent man didn't have sexual thoughts about . . . a woman he supervised. . . . It was inappropriate" (New York: Silhouette, 1999), 46. For a fuller discussion of contemporary office romance novels, see http://history.sewanee.edu/facstaff/berebitsky/.

13. *Disclosure* (Warner Brothers, 1994); Beth A. Quinn, "Sexual Harassment and Masculinity: The Power and Meaning of 'Girl Watching,'" *Gender and Society* 16 (June 2002): 392–95; James D. Woods, *The Corporate Closet: The Professional Lives of Gay Men in the Office* (New York: Free Press, 1993), xi–xviii; Janet Reitman, "Sex and Scandal at Duke," *Rolling Stone* (June 15, 2006), 76; Kelley Holland, "The Office Party, as a Tightrope Walk," *New York Times* (November 25, 2007).

14. On quid pro quo, see Candace Goforth, "Ending Sexual Harassment in Workplace Means Ongoing Employee Education," *Knight Ridder/Tribune Business News* (October 27, 2003); Cochran, *Sexual Harassment and the Law*, 170, 182–84. On excessive damages, see Wendy McElroy, "The Sad Evolution of Sexual Harassment," Fox News.com (October 27, 2004), http://www.foxnews.com/story/0,2933,136705,00.html (accessed October 27, 2004).

15. Jane Gallop with Lauren Berlant, "Loose Lips," in Lauren Berlant and Lisa Duggan, eds., *Our Monica, Ourselves* (New York: New York University Press, 2001), 246; Cochran, *Sexual Harassment and the Law*, 198–208; Vicki Schultz,

"The Sanitized Workplace," *Yale Law Journal* 112 (June 2003): 2067–70 (for a critique of Schultz, see Catherine A. MacKinnon, Afterword to Catherine A. MacKinnon and Reva Siegel, eds., *Directions in Sexual Harassment Law* [New Haven: Yale University Press, 2004], 696, note 22); Margaret Talbot, "Men Behaving Badly," *New York Times Magazine* (October 13, 2002); Jon D. Bible, "Disorder in the Courts: Proving Same-Sex Sex Discrimination in Title VII Cases Via 'Gender Stereotyping,'" *Employee Relations Law Journal* 31 (Spring 2006): 42–72; Jennifer L. Berdahl, "The Sexual Harassment of Uppity Women," *Journal of Applied Psychology* 92 (2007): 425–37; MacKinnon, Afterword, 693.

16. Two very recent news stories suggest how much the discourse remains the same. Women continue to receive the same advice regarding sex at work as they always have: in 2009 the corporate head-hunter Janice Reals Ellig stated that it was still "up to the woman to control a situation freighted with sex." She also warned women against consensual relationships, arguing that "men's reputations will not be tarnished for sex in the workplace," but the woman who is "tagged with the 'romance' label risks irrevocable career damage." According to Ellig, the situation had not changed because women still were not in real positions of power. Less than 10 percent held "corporate clout titles," around 13 percent were in corporate officer positions at Fortune 500 companies, and the percentage of women serving as CEOs of those companies was in the very low single digits. Looking across all industries, the percentage of women in management remained virtually unchanged between 2000 and 2007, and in all but three of the thirteen industry sectors, women were less than proportionately represented in management positions than in nonmanagement positions; Janice Reals Ellig, "Sex in the Workplace: Still a Challenge for the Corporate Woman," *WomensMedia* (March 24, 2009), http://www.womensmedia.com/work/77-sex-in-the-workplace-still-a-challenge-for-the-corporate-woman.html (accessed June 2, 2011); GAO, *Women in Management*, GAO-10-1064T (Washington, DC, September 28, 2010), 2–3. The issue of appropriate attire in the office was the subject of a recent lawsuit in New York City; Elizabeth Dwoskin, "Is This Woman Too Hot to Be a Banker?" *Village Voice* (June 1, 2010), http://www.villagevoice.com/2010-06-01/news/is-this-woman-too-hot-to-work-in-a-bank/1/ (accessed June 2, 2011).

INDEX

Biden, Joseph, 272
Big Business Girl (film), 126
Block, Sharon, 20
Blondie (comic strip), 71
Bogart, Nella, 166–67
Bookkeepers, Stenographers &
   Accountants Union, 89–92
Boston Daily Globe, 21–24
Brand, Alice, 25–26
Breach of Promise (tort), 40, 56–57,
   122–26, 290
Breslin, Jimmy, 235
Broder, David, 230
Broughton, Len, 43–45, 67
Brown, David, 179
Brown, Helen Gurley: connection
   between work and sexual freedom, 178,
   187–88; critics of, 189–92, 194;
   differences from other advice givers,
   179–80, 188–89, 206–7, 243;
   femininity as heterosexuality, 194–96;
   homosexuality, 193; the "Matinee,"
   195–96; offices as sexy, 177–78, 187;
   productivity and office romances, 176,
   190–91, 263; responding to unwanted
   sexual attentions, 196–205, 278–79;
   "Scuttle," 201, 204, 277–78; views on
   Hill-Thomas, 277; women's sexual
   agency, 192–93
Brown, Janet, 270
Bularzik, Mary, 5
Bundy v. Jackson (1981), 246
Burke, Marylin, 180
Bush, George H.W., 264, 273
Business, use of sex in, 79, 163–68
Business Week, 189, 208
Businessmen: adultery, 74–79, 159–63,
   169–71, 193, 261; in Atlanta, 44;
   attitude toward female executives,
   258–59; attitude toward working
   women, 84–85; character of, 41–43, 46,
   63–64, 75–78, 143, 164–66, 169–70,
   172–73, 183–85; cultural anxieties
   about, 189; importance of wives, 182;
   and male bonding, 60, 78, 81, 84;
   midlife crisis, 104, 160–61, 235;
   "organization man," 159; psychology
   and, 104–6; sexual access to women

workers, 70, 81, 185; sexual conquests
   of, 257–58; sexual practices of, 163–68;
   and status symbols, 72–74, 172–73; as
   uninterested in romance, 59; as
   victimizers, 34–51, 148

Caprio, Frank S., 162–63
Carnegie, Dale, 103–4, 180
Cathy (comic strip), 233, 285
Chicago & North Western Railway, 173
Chicago Tribune, 261
Clark, Spencer M., 62–63
Clinton, Bill, 287–94
Cohen, Richard, 289
Cohn-Stuntz, Elizabeth, 223
Cold War, 157–58, 165
Coleman, Dabney, 248
Collins, Eliza G.C., 259–60, 262
Confession magazines, 135–39
Consensual relations: policies, 114,
   252–54, 258–61, 284–85. *See also*
   Office romances
Cook, Lillian, 74
Coombs, Mary, 126
Corporate policies: on consensual
   relations, 114, 175, 258–61, 284–85; on
   sexual harassment, 253–54. *See also*
   Personnel management
Corporations, and public relations,
   75–76, 142, 164
Cosmopolitan, 117, 177–78, 205, 279
Cott, Nancy, 100
Cougle, Frances, 64–65
Crane, Dan, 274
Crenshaw, Kimberlé, 19
Crowd, The (film), 89, 185
Cunningham, Mary, 252–57, 264

Dateline (TV), 278
Dating culture, rise of, 111–12
Dear Abby, 236–38
Delorenzo, William, 57
Department store clerks, 43
Diehl, Elsie, 210
Dietz, Park, 266
Disclosure (film), 294
Divorce, 26–27, 40
Doggett, John, III, 267–68

Masculinity: character and, 63, 74, 76–78, 228; in Cold War, 158–59, 161, 165–66; and consumption, 26; and humor, 65–72; and lack of access to women, 88–93; and office work, 61; and relations between men, 13–14, 60, 78, 81, 84, 167–68; and sexual harassment, 223–25; and (sexual) self-control, 63; and workplace sexuality, 13–14, 78–80, 80–86

Maule, Frances, 99, 102–3, 105, 107, 129, 191

Mayer, Walter, 87–89, 93, 128

Mayo, Virginius J., 74–78, 93

McIntyre, Shirley, 87–89, 128

McLaren, Angus, 124

McNaboe, John, 124

Mead, Margaret, 167

Men: as salaried employees, 26; sexual nature of, 7, 36, 96, 191–92, 281, 290; as sexually vulnerable with women, 4, 29–33, 279–82; success manuals for, 76; as victims of sexual harassment, 236–38. *See also* Businessmen

Meritor Savings Bank v. Vinson (1986), 245–49, 292

Metzenbaum, Howard, 268

Middle-class status: and businessmen's attitude toward working-class female office workers, 84–85, 262; and effect on expressions of workplace sexuality, 16–17, 144, 188–89; and perception of businessmen as "gentlemen," 107–8; and symbols, 17, 172–73; and working-class women office workers, 56–58, 97–98, 119, 289

Milani, Emma, 57

Mills, C. Wright, 8

Mink, Gwendolyn, 291–92

Modern Office Procedures, 141, 175, 190–92, 258–59

Morgan, John, 173

Mosbacher, Georgette, 292

Ms., 195, 207, 218

Murray, Patty, 276

Murrow, Edward R., 163–68, 281

Nation, 165

National Association of Manufacturers, 164

National Office Managers Association, 108

National Organization for Women, 276

National Secretaries Association, 11, 211

New Thought, 49–51

New York City, 81–82, 108–15, 163–68

New York Daily News, 84, 238

New York Journal American, 164–65

New York Post, 165, 241

New York Sun, 1, 65–66

New York Times, 23, 44, 46–47, 207, 218, 229, 230, 291

Newsweek, 230

Nicholas, Connie, 169–73

Nicholson, Roberta West, 122–23

9 to 5 (film), 11, 248–49

Norton, Eleanor Holmes, 242

Nussbaum, Karen, 248

Office, the: dangers for women in, 34–48, 95; masculinity and, 77, 257–58, 261, 263; and meeting men, 183; as men's territory, 106; as middle-class space, 16–17, 43, 188–89; passionless ideal of, 6, 96, 98, 190–92, 263; physical space of and sexual opportunities, 10–12; and professional behavior, 101–2; and race, 18–19; social-class mixing, 55–56, 109–13; surveillance and, 15, 69–70; variety of sexual expression in, 4, 225. *See also* Office romances

Office, The (TV), 11

Office gossip, 114–15

Office parties, 145–50, 174–75, 182, 219, 239, 260–61, 295

Office Party, 181

Office romances, 27, 29, 32–33, 55–56, 108–15, 117–19, 135–39, 183, 293–95. *See also* Popular culture

Office Tramp, 186

Office Wife (film), 11, 134–35

Oklahoman, 102

Packard, Vance, 17

Packwood, Bob, 275–78, 291

Parton, Dolly, 248
Penn Mutual Life Insurance, 263
Personnel management: attitudes toward
    affairs, 173–75; consensual relations
    policies, 252–54, 258–61, 263–64; and
    emotions at work, 263; human
    relations theory, 140–52; sexual
    harassment policies, 253
Picard, Alfred L., 21–24
Playboy, 10, 177, 182, 194, 212, 241
Playgirl, 216
Playthings, 184
Pogrebin, Letty Cottin, 195, 206–8
Popular Culture: critique of office
    romance narratives, 138–39; lesbians
    and pulp novels, 180–81; narratives and
    describing unwanted sexual attentions,
    155–56; representations of male office
    workers, 89–93, 183–85; young women
    as audience, 117–19. *See also*
    Representations of the office
Post, Emily, 101
Press coverage of sex scandals, 13,
    25–26, 74–78, 87–88, 170–71,
    229–30
Pringle, Rosemary, 12
Prostitution, 39–40, 63, 76, 163–64,
    166–68, 261
Psychology and psychiatry: and adultery,
    160–63, 260; advice columnists and,
    147–48; and gender difference,
    99–100; and gender relations in the
    office, 101–2, 105–6, 144, 206, 208;
    Hill-Thomas hearings and, 266–68;
    rise of in 1920s, 96–99; and sexual
    harassment, 104–6, 155, 162–63, 235,
    249, 281–82, 290, 292
Public and private spheres, links between:
    and artificial boundaries, 294; and
    concept of privacy, 229–30; and
    executives' wives, 161, 176, 182; and
    expressions of power, 16; and gossip,
    115; and masculinity, 93; in
    relationships between employers and
    employees, 75, 77–78, 255. *See also*
    Adultery; Consensual relations; Office
    romances
Pulp Novels, 180–82

Quayle, Margaret, 104–5
Quest, 205
Quinn, Robert, 258, 263

Ramspeck, Robert, 142
Ray, Elizabeth, 227–33, 241, 261
Redbook, 225–27, 235
Red-Headed Woman (film), 118–20
Reformers: dangers of office work, 23;
    dangers to working women, 34–35;
    efforts to protect women workers,
    39–40; end of reform, 97; gold digger
    films, 119–20
Reiss, Ira L., 264
Rentzer, Hannah, 83–84
Representations of the office: in ads, 73,
    146, 214–16, 218; in confession
    magazines, 135–37; in fiction,
    128–38, 183; in film, 118–22, 126–28,
    134–35, 182–85, 248–49, 294; in
    general interest magazines, 33,
    182–83; in humor, 65–72, 212–13,
    233, 290; in men's magazines,
    182; on postcards, 70; in pulp novels,
    180–82; in romances, 70, 180–87,
    293–94; secretaries, 10–12; in
    stenography journals, 32–33; in
    Tijuana Bibles, 71–72; on TV, 202,
    216, 280–81
Richards, Amelia, 293
Riesman, David, 166
Rivers, Caryl, 230
Roosevelt, Teddy, 76

Saga, 194
San Francisco Examiner, 164
Saturday Evening Post, 10, 33,
    129, 182
Sauvigné, Karen, 221
Schroeder, Patricia, 9, 231, 274
Schultz, Vicki, 295–96
Science Digest, 160
Scovell, Nell, 283–84
"Scuttle," 202–4, 277–78
Seattle Times, 275
Secret, The (Byrne), 204
Secretaries on the Spot, (National
    Secretaries Association), 11

sexual power over men, 29–33, 290; sexually naïve, 82, 108–13; supplementing income, 82–83; as threat to marriages, 8, 24–29, 132–33, 146–47; using sexuality/attractiveness to advance, 188–89, 226, 252, 256, 264, 279–82; wages, 129. *See also* Representations of the office
Women Office Workers (New York City), 211–16
Women office workers' movement, 208–19, 222, 248

Women's Christian Temperance Union, 35
Women's Page, The, 217
Wood, Carmita, 219
Woodward, Helen, 95–97
Working-class men, 93, 181
Working-class women, 135
Working Women United, 220–23, 232, 236
Wylie, Philip, 194

Young, John, 229–30